Protecting the Last Frontier

Aerospace Law and Policy Series

VOLUME 25

Editors

Pablo Mendes de Leon, Professor of Air and Space Law, and Tanja Masson-Zwaan, Assistant Professor of Space Law, Leiden University, The Netherlands.

Introduction

The *Aerospace Law and Policy Series* critically examines the fundamental changes that international aviation and space activities have undergone since the last century, growing up as mature industries while freeing themselves from traditional regulatory constraints and displaying a variety of innovative applications that call for creative legal solutions.

Objective

The objective of the Series is to make a contribution to legal thinking on public international air and space law and policy, and their implementation at the regional and national levels, responsibility and liability of public bodies and service providers, competition law, insurance law, company law, and the complex relationship between EU law and public international law.

Readership

Aviation and space lawyers, academics, representatives of governments, international organizations, and companies involved in aviation and space activities.

The titles published in this series are listed at the end of this volume.

Protecting the Last Frontier

Space Mining and Environmental Sustainability

Gabrielle Leterre

Wolters Kluwer

Published by:
Kluwer Law International B.V.
PO Box 316
2400 AH Alphen aan den Rijn
The Netherlands
E-mail: lrs-sales@wolterskluwer.com
Website: www.wolterskluwer.com/en/solutions/kluwerlawinternational

Sold and distributed by:
Wolters Kluwer Legal & Regulatory U.S.
920 Links Avenue
Landisville, PA 17538
United States of America
E-mail: customer.service@wolterskluwer.com

ISBN 978-94-035-3317-9

e-Book: ISBN 978-94-035-3327-8
web-PDF: ISBN 978-94-035-3337-7

Table of Contents

List of Abbreviations

ABJL	American Business Law Journal
Adv. Space Res.	Advances in Space Research
AIAA	American Institute of Aeronautics and Astronautics
AJIL	The American Journal of International Law
Am. U. L. Rev.	American University Law Review
Ann. Air & Space. L.	Annals of Air and Space Law
Annu. Rev. Ecol. Evol. Syst.	Annual Review of Ecology and Systematics
APSCO	Asia-Pacific Space Cooperation Organization
ASAT	Anti-satellite Weapons
ASCFEA	American Space Commerce Free Enterprise Act
ASTEROIDS	American Space Technology for Exploring Resource Opportunities in Deep Space
Astron. Space Sci.	Frontiers in Astronomy and Space Sciences
ATS	Antarctic Treaty
B. C. Int'l & Comp. L. Rev.	Boston College International and Comparative Law Review
BELSPO	Belgian Science Policy Office
Br. Yearb. Int. Law	British Yearbook of International Law
Bus. Law Rev.	American Business Law Journal
CBD	Convention on Biological Diversity
CETEX	Committee on Contamination by Extraterrestrial Exploration
Colum. J. Envtl. L.	Columbia Journal of Environmental Law
COSPAR	Committee on Space Research
CSLCA	Commercial Space Launch Competitiveness Act
Denv. J. Intl'l L. & Pol'y	Denver Journal International Law & Policy
EIA	Environmental Impact Assessment

EMM	Emirates Mars Mission
ENMOD	Convention on the Prohibition of Military or Any Other Hostile Use of Environmental Modification Techniques
Environ. Impact Assess. Rev.	Environmental Impact Assessment Review
Environ	Environmental Law and Policy Journal
ESA	European Space Agency
ESRIC	European Space Resources Innovation Centre
FAA	(US) Federal Aviation Administration
FAI	Fédération Aéronautique Internationale
FCC	(US) Federal Communication Commission
GAOR	(UN) General Assembly Official Records
GEMET	General Multilingual Environmental Thesaurus
GEO	Geostationary Earth Orbit
Ger. Yearb. Int. Law	German Yearbook of International Law
Global Bus. L. Rev.	The Global Business Law Review
Hastings Int'l & Comp L Rev.	Hastings International and Comparative Law Review
Hastings Law J.	Hastings Law Journal
HSRGWG	Hague Space Resources Governance Working Group
IAA	International Academy of Astronautics
IADC	Inter-Agency Space Debris Coordination Committee
IAF	International Astronautical Federation
ICJ	International Court of Justice
ICW	International Whaling Commission
IISL	International Institute of Space Law
ILA	International Law Association
ILC	International Law Commission
ILM	International Legal Materials
Int. Community Law Rev.	International Community Law Review
Int. Environ. Agreem. Politics Law Econ.	International Environmental Agreements Politics, Law and Economics
Int. J. Astrobiology	International Journal of Astrobiology
Int. Lawyer	The International Lawyer
Int. Political Sci. Rev.	International Political Science Review
Ir. Stud. Int. Aff.	Irish Studies in International Affairs
ISC	International Council for Science
ISLE	Interdisciplinary Studies in Literature and Environment
ISO	International Organization for Standardization
ISPI	Italian Institute for International Political Studies
ISS	International Space Station
Issues Sci Technol	Issues in Science and Technology
ISU	International Scientific Unions

ITLOS	International Tribunal for the Law of the Sea
ITU	International Telecommunication Union
J. Air L. & Com.	Journal of Air Law and Commerce
J. Energy Nat. Resour. Law	Journal of Energy & Natural Resources Law
J. Environ. Law	Journal of Environmental Law
J. Environ. Psychol.	Journal of Environmental Psychology
J. Environ. Sustain.	Journal of Environmental Sustainability
J. Hum. Rts. & Env't.	Journal of Human Rights and the Environment
J. Int. Bioethique Ethique Sci.	Journal international de bioéthique et d'éthique des sciences
J. Space L.	Journal of Space Law
J. Space Saf. Eng.	Journal of Space Safety Engineering
J. Propuls. Power	Journal of Propulsion and Power
JAXA	Japan Aerospace Exploration Agency
Journal of Environmental Sustainability	Colorado Journal of International Environmental Law and Policy
JSRA	Japanese Space Resources Act
LCROSS	Lunar Crater Observation and Sensing Satellite
LEO	Low-Earth Orbit
LSA	Luxembourg Space Agency
LTS	Long-Term Sustainability
MARPOL	International Convention for the Prevention of Pollution from Ships
McGill Int'l J. Sust. Dev. L. & Pol'y	McGill International Journal of Sustainable Development Law and Policy
MEO	Medium-Earth Orbit
Mich. J. Int. Law	Michigan Journal of International Law
MURS	Cahier du Mouvement Universel de la Responsabilité Scientifique
NASA	(US) National Aeronautics and Space Administration
NASA	National Aeronautics and Space Administration
Nat. Sci. Soc.	Natures Sciences Sociétés
NEA	Near-Earth Asteroid
NEO	Near-Earth Orbit
NEPA	(US) National Environmental Policy Act
NGO	Nongovernmental Organizations
NPR	NASA Procedural Requirements
NPS	Nuclear Power Source
NSI	National Scientific Institutions
NYU J. Int'l L. & Pol	New York University Journal of International Law and Politics

OSC	(US) Office of Space Commerce
OSMA	NASA's Office of Safety and Mission Assurance
OSTP	(US) White House Office of Science and Technology Policy
PNAS	Proceedings of the National Academy of Sciences of the United States of America
Popul. Dev. Rev.	Population and Development Review
PP	Planetary Protection
PPIRB	(US) Planetary Protection Independent Review Board
PSRs	Moon's Permanently Shadowed Regions
QIL	Questions of International Law
Rev. Gen.	Revue générale de droit
Rev. Hist. CNRS	La revue pour l'histoire du CNRS
Rev. Eur. Comp. Int.	Review of European, Comparative & International Environmental Law
RIAA	Reports of International Arbitral Awards
RJE	Revue Juridique de l'Environnement
SAJELP	The South African Journal of Environmental Law and Policy
SCER	Supreme Court Economic Review
Sci. Total Environ	Science of the Total Environment
SDGs	Sustainable Development Goals
SDM	Space Debris Mitigation
SGAC	Space Generation Advisory Council
SOC	Society
SRL	(Lux.) Law of July 20, 2017, on the Exploration and Use of Space Resources
SSA	Space Situational Awareness
SSERVI	Solar System Exploration Research Virtual Institute
SWF	Secure World Foundation
TEC	(ESA) Directorate of Technology, Engineering and Quality
TRA	(UAE) Telecommunications Regulatory Authority
U. Mem. L. Rev.	University of Memphis Law Review
UAE	United Arab Emirates
UK	United Kingdom
UN	United Nations
UNCLOS	United Nations Convention on the Law of the Sea
UNCOPUOS LSC	United Nations Committee on the Peaceful Uses of Outer Space Legal Sub-Committee
UNCOPUOS STC	United Nations Committee on the Peaceful Uses of Outer Space Scientific and Technical Subcommittee

UNCOPUOS	United Nations Committee on the Peaceful Uses of Outer Space
UNEP	United Nations Environmental Programme
UNFCCC	United Nations Framework Convention on Climate Change
UNGA	United Nations General Assembly
Univ. Pa. J. Int.	University of Pennsylvania Journal of International Law
UNOOSA	United Nations Office for Outer Space Affairs
UNTS	United Nations Treaty Series
US/USA	United States of America
USC	United States Code
VCLT	Vienna Convention on the Law of Treaties
Wm. & Mary Envtl. L. & Pol'y Rev	William & Mary Environmental Law and Policy Review
WTO	World Trade Organization
Yale J. Int'l L.	Yale Journal of International Law
ZLW	German Journal of Air and Space Law

Foreword

How proud I am to be asked to introduce the first book of Gabrielle Leterre! From my perspective as a professor at the University of Luxembourg, her path leading to this publication may be labeled "from a talented student to a recognized researcher."

Gabrielle was one of the best students in the class of the Master in Space, Communication and Media Law at the University of Luxembourg, deeply interested in space and environmental law and always eager to learn more. After having successfully finished her studies in Luxembourg, she decided to continue the already started research in the form of doctoral studies.

Her main interest was the protection of environment connected with space activities. The subject could not be more topical: With large communication constellations, high frequency of space launches, upcoming space mining activities, and plans to create a permanent habitat on the Moon, the risk that space will be as polluted as we know it from the High Seas turned closer to the reality. If materialized, further space activities would be impeded if not made impossible by thousands of human-made objects, causing obstacles to services using space technology—telecommunication, Earth observation, broadband service, navigation. Gabrielle Leterre asked herself whether the instrument she knows the best—the law—can effectively help to stop the threatening pollution and offers tools which would prevent the continuing deterioration of the status quo.

The persuasive and structured manner in which Mrs. Leterre presented this situation convinced the Luxembourg National Research Fund to select her project for a full financing of her doctoral studies. This success led to an even more intense work for the new doctoral student—she searched in the literature, attended conferences, spoke with the specialists, and not only the lawyers. Already during her doctoral studies, she shared her knowledge with the students at the Faculty of Law, Economics and Finance in Luxembourg, was a welcome speaker on occasions in which the subject was discussed and finally successfully defended her doctoral thesis in 2023.

Based on her doctoral studies, the outcome of her efforts is a comprehensive picture of the potential and limits of law in shaping environmental protection related to space activities. It goes far beyond the original concern of first space navigators—the biological contamination, already regulated in the central source of international space law—the 1967 Outer Space Treaty. Starting therefrom, the book discusses the regulatory approaches to human-made space debris and their mitigation as well as the necessity to extend these discussions and consider how legal frameworks can help creating sustainable approaches of space mining. Very convincingly, the author demonstrates that the fact that space debris are covered only to a very limited extent by binding international law rules opens the floor for intensive but nonbinding regulations established by numerous regional and standard entities. The work ends with a discussion of the strengths and weaknesses of law in regulating societal phenomena such as space environment.

"From a talented student to a recognized researcher": If there had not been the deep interest and quickly increasing expertise in the subject and the perseverance of Gabrielle Leterre, this book could not represent such an extensive and deep study of the subject matter. Obviously, all this success is hers only, and it is my great pleasure to join in the most cordial congratulations and express my very best wishes for her future.

Prof. Dr. Mahulena Hofmann, CSc.
SES Chair in Space, SatCom and Media Law at the University of Luxembourg
Supervisor of the doctoral thesis

Preface

As space activities continue to develop and increase in number, so do environmental concerns in outer space. For decades now, humanity has continuously sent satellites into Earth orbits without caring for potential environmental consequences in outer space. Ultimately, these actions have raised issues regarding the sustainability of the activity (space debris proliferation, traffic management, light pollution etc.), issues which are now being addressed legally. Satellites were the first venture of humanity into space, and it is fair to admit we did not know better at the time. We do now. With the development of new types of space missions, such as space resource activities, it is safe to assume that new serious environmental problems will arise as well. Based on previous experience both on Earth and in outer space, it is logical, but also imperative, to question the environmental impact of these space resource activities and to consider legal solutions to promote and facilitate their long-term sustainability. Accordingly, this book assesses the applicability of existing rules and mechanisms promoting environmental protection and sustainability in outer space to the case of the exploitation of space resources. To that end, an array of mechanisms is considered, such as the framework of the UN Space Treaties, international environmental law, nonlegally binding instruments, such as the space debris mitigation guidelines and COSPAR's planetary protection policy, as well as national space legislations. Ultimately, this book aims at drafting the roadmap for the environmentally sustainable exploitation of space resources from a legal standpoint. It proposes a sustainability framework articulated around a set of standards and recommends the adoption of a mix of interdisciplinary approaches which balances an effective national approach with international guiding rules.

Acknowledgments

This book is a revised and updated version of my doctoral thesis, which I defended in March 2023 at the University of Luxembourg. As fellow PhDs will know, writing a doctoral thesis is a significant endeavor, characterized by numerous meaningful interactions. Throughout my tenure as a doctoral researcher at the University of Luxembourg, I had the privilege of crossing paths with individuals whose support, constructive criticism, and enriching presence significantly contributed to my both professional and personal growth. I extend my heartfelt gratitude to each of them for their invaluable contributions.

First and foremost, my profound gratitude goes to my PhD supervisor, Prof. Mahulena Hofmann. I am deeply indebted for her valuable advice, profound belief in my work, and engagement during this journey. I further extend my appreciation to the members of my supervisory committee, Prof. Matthew Happold and Prof. André Prüm, as well as my defense jury members, Prof. Lucien Rapp and Dr. Olga Stelmakh-Drescher, for their constructive feedback, expert advice, and engaging discussion during the defense.

Acknowledgment is also due to the Luxembourg National Research Fund for financially supporting my doctoral studies at the University of Luxembourg by awarding me the 2018 AFR PhD grant.

I cannot begin to express my gratitude to my family. These five years would not have been possible without their unwavering support, patience, and nurturing. Thank you for acting as my sounding board and listening to my space law-induced rants.

Finally, I would like to thank my friends and colleagues who followed my journey into space law. Your camaraderie has added significantly to my experience.

La protection de l'environnement n'est pas seulement indispensable pour notre avenir, elle représente la plus grande opportunité économique de notre époque.

—Bertrand Piccard

Introduction

In a world where humanity is intensifying efforts to mitigate the adverse effects of anthropogenic activities on Earth, we can observe these concerns progressively extending to areas beyond our terrestrial borders. More and more, we are witnessing rising awareness that, despite its vastness and distance, outer space is not without its limits, limits on which the long-term sustainability of space activities depends.

In practice, this generalized awareness translates into the development of a multiplicity of initiatives aiming to guide the space sector toward more sustainable practices. Most exemplary is the adoption by the United Nations, in 2019, of guidelines on the long-term sustainability of space activities; the adoption of the conclusions of the Council of the European Union on "the fair and sustainable use of space" is also noteworthy.[1] Overall, these initiatives try to rationalize efforts to funnel them toward a common goal: achieving space sustainability. Therefore, a question arises: why now? What has changed in our practice to explain such broad interest in the matter? A simple answer is the space sector.

Over the past 60 years, space activities have grown and evolved drastically. In the beginning, space is the exclusive domain of States and a matter of national prestige.[2] The venture is government-driven, with few States having space capabilities,[3] and

1. United Nations, Report of the Committee on the Peaceful Uses of Outer Space, UNGAOR, 74th Sess., Supp. No. 20, Annex II, UN Doc. A/74/20 (2019); European Union, Council Conclusions on Fair and Sustainable Use of Space, EU Council, 3949th Meeting, Annex, Doc. 9675/23 (2023).
2. Walter Peeters, *Evolution of the Space Economy: Government Space to Commercial Space and New Space*, 19 Astropolitics 206, 208–210 (2021) DOI: 10.1080/14777622.2021.1984001.
3. In the 1960s, only three States possess orbital launch capabilities: the Soviet Union, the United States of America and France, with the launch of *Asterix* in 1965. They are joined by Japan, China, and the United Kingdom in the 1970s. Some States, like Italy and Canada, proved capable to manufacture and operate a satellite in the 1960s but relied on the United States for the launch. As of mid-2022, only 16 space agencies, out of the 72 existing in the world, have the ability to carry out a space launch. Countries with Space Programs 2022, World Population Review (2022), available online; I-Shih Chang, *Overview of World Space Launches*, 16 Journal of Propulsion and Power 853 (2000); GTS Editorial, *Space Agencies Around the World*, Going to Space (2022), available online.

activities focus mainly on space research and development, with environmental concerns in outer space being limited to planetary protection issues.[4]

In the 1970s, the landscape shifts with private actors gradually entering the space market.[5] Space activities become about commercial uses of space technology, such as telecommunication and remote sensing applications.[6] The period is marked by the emergence of commercial telecom operators like Intelsat and SES Astra.[7] Space progressively leaves the exclusive domain of States, though they remain a driving force. The development of space activities and the democratization of knowledge cause another shift in the space economy, with private actors gradually becoming the leaders of the sector in the 21st century.[8] In the past, these activities were driven by political or social forces where they are now bound by market forces and financed privately.[9]

This "NewSpace" era we live in is characterized by the privatization and evolution of space activities. Private entities now possess space capabilities on par with States', both financially and technologically. In the last two decades, they have demonstrated their ability to, *inter alia*, launch objects and humans into space and to deploy mega constellations.[10] Private actors also act as a driving force by pushing commercial activities beyond the limits of Earth orbits. One such example is the case of space resource activities.

Also known as "space mining," space resource activities consist in extracting and exploiting *in situ* resources from celestial bodies for commercial purposes; it does not include scientific extraction and exploitation of these resources.[11] The primary goal is to exploit these natural resources to develop further our long-term presence in outer space, both technologically and humanly. On a secondary level, space resource activities are seen as an opportunity to import to Earth resources we sorely lack—sometimes because of terrestrial overexploitation—and will need.[12] Outer space possesses abundant quantities of iron and platinum group metal resources that are scarce or nonexistent on Earth.[13] Thus, space resource activities are thought out as a "second chance" for Earth, an opportunity to balance humanity's careless abuse of the environment in its industrial rush.

4. Report of the *Ad Hoc* Committee on the Peaceful Uses of Outer Space, UNGAOR, 14th Sess., at 76, UN Doc. A/4141 (1959); Peeters, *supra* note 2, 208–210.
5. Andrea Sommariva, *The Evolution of Space Economy: The Role of the Private Sector and the Challenges for Europe*, ISPI (2020), available online.
6. Peeters, *supra* note 2, 210–211.
7. *Id.*
8. *Id.*, 211–213; Sommariva, *supra* note 5.
9. Ken Davidian, *Definition of NewSpace*, 8 New Space 53, 53–54 (2020) DOI: 10.1089/space.2020.29027.kda. The year 2019 is representative of this shift. That year, commercial applications constituted two-thirds of the space economy turnover, with military and institutional orders only representing one-third of the total profit. Sommariva, *supra* note 5.
10. Top 3 Biggest Private Space Companies, Earth.com (2022), available online.
11. *See* Commercial Space Launch Competitiveness Act, 51 USC §51302 (US) [CSLCA]; Loi du 20 juillet 2017 sur l'exploration et l'utilisation des ressources de l'espace, Art. 3, Mémorial A No 674, 28 juillet 2017 (LU) [SRL].
12. Carol Dahl, Ben Gilbert & Ian Lange, *Mineral Scarcity on Earth: Are Asteroids the Answer*, 33 Miner Econ 29 (2020) DOI: 10.1007/s13563-020-00231-6.
13. Kevin MacWhorter, *Sustainable Mining: Incentivizing Asteroid Mining in the Name of Environmentalism*, 40 Wm. & Mary Envtl. L. & Pol'y Rev. 645, 652 (2016).

Beyond terrestrial concerns, space resource activities are a necessity when considering longer missions in outer space, especially ones that include sending out humans. Human presence in space requires meeting human basic needs: food, water, and breathable air, all of which are naturally absent in space. It would be unrealistic to believe that Earth could generate the ecological resources required to sustain humanity both on Earth and in space. Already, humanity's demands on Earth exceed what it can naturally regenerate.[14] This is why the discovery of water in outer space, in particular, has been a game changer.[15] Whereas, on Earth, water covers about 70% of the planet's surface, in space, it is a rarefied but still undeniably essential resource for life support.[16] It can be used to grow food and filtered to make drinkable water and breathable air.

In themselves, these resources have an incredibly high economic worth, as illustrated by the Japanese Aerospace Exploration Agency (JAXA)'s exploration of the asteroid Ryugu in 2018. The asteroid's economic worth was estimated at 82.7 billion dollars.[17] Nonetheless, to assess the true economic value of space resource activities, the value of the resources themselves is not sufficient. It is only the first step. It is also necessary to consider if there is a demand for them and to assess the costs and feasibility of their process and transportation.[18] Confining himself to the Near-Earth Asteroids (NEAs) population, Lewis draws numbers to estimate how many people could be sustained in space, in the long term, using these resources.[19] He concludes that: "the NEA population could support approximately 400 billion people at a generous level of affluence from now until the Sun enters the red giant phase several billion years from now."[20] Using NEA's resources, humanity could shield itself from radiation and hydroponically cultivated food and plants, and recreate nutrients and minerals necessary for our health.[21] Materially, we would be able to build habitat and make propellant using the Helium 3 naturally present in lunar regolith and other places.[22] These are ample possibilities: the expression "space resource activities" theoretically encompasses a wide range of activities that future practice will have to back up.

1 APPROACH OF THE BOOK

These new opportunities are not without consequences. The privatization and the resulting development of new space activities have not only changed how activities are

14. In 2022, Earth overshoot day, i.e., "the date when humanity's demand for ecological resources and services in a given year exceeds what Earth can regenerate in that year" fell on July 28. "Earth Overshoot Day," Overshoot Day, available online.
15. NASA, *Is There Ice on Other Planets?*, NASA Space Place, available online.
16. However, as emphasized by NASA on Twitter in May 2022, "71% of Earth's surface is water, but only 3.5 percent is drinkable freshwater!". @NASAEarth, *No Wonder It's Called the Blue Marble!*, Twitter (2022), available online.
17. A la conquête de l'espace, Chamber of Commerce Luxembourg (2019), available online.
18. John S. Lewis, Asteroid Mining 101: Wealth for the New Space Economy VIII (David Gump ed., 2015).
19. *Id.*
20. Lewis, *supra* note 17 at 101–102.
21. *Id.*, at 102–107.
22. *Id.*, at 109.

conducted in outer space but also given rise to unanticipated environmental issues. The most striking example is the space debris problem—i.e., the agglomeration of nonfunctional space objects—in, and the congestion of, low-Earth orbit (LEO). The rise of commercial activities in outer space has led to an intensification of satellite-based activities, most of which are focused on LEO. It means that the number of space objects launched into space, which has increased exponentially over the last 60 years, will continue to grow.[23] From an economic and social perspective, these developments are positive as great benefits can be derived from space activities. The problem is that States have initially failed to consider the impact of increased activities in LEO from an environmental perspective. Such a view would have reminded operators that Earth orbits are a limited natural resource and, as such, need to be managed rationally. The increased pace of satellite activities, in addition to the increased generation of debris, is pushing the capacity of LEO to sustain operations in the area. In other words, as the international community has grown acutely aware of it over the last decade, the long-term sustainability of space activities is threatened.[24]

From a legal standpoint, this awareness is reflected in the adoption of new nonlegally binding international instruments under the umbrella of the United Nations Committee on the Peaceful Uses of Outer Space (UNCOPUOS). We note, for instance, the adoption of a set of guidelines specifically dealing with the necessity to mitigate space debris in orbit in 2007.[25] Similarly, three years later, the Committee established a "Working Group on the Long-Term Sustainability of Outer Space Activities" under the Scientific and Technical Subcommittee (UNCOPUOS STC) to consider the broader topic of space sustainability. The outcome is the adoption, by 2019, of a set of 21 nonbinding guidelines.[26]

In practice, it is apparent that the question of the long-term sustainability of space activities—and *a fortiori* of the outer space environmental protection—is linked narrowly to the space debris problem. It is the main focus in the large majority of the literature relating to the protection of the outer space environment. A supplementary topic, as regards celestial bodies, is biological contamination.[27] Bringing live organisms to other planets has been a concern since the beginning of space activities, especially when it was still unknown whether there was life elsewhere in our solar system.

These different approaches have in common to focus on what we know of current problems. However, they might represent a too narrow perspective to ensure the

---

23. According to a study published by Euroconsult in 2021, it is expected that an average of 1,700 satellites will be launched per year by 2030. This represents a fourfold increase over the last decade. Saly Sadek, *New Satellite Market Forecast Anticipates 1,700 Satellites to Be Launched on Average per Year By 2030 as New Entrants and Incumbents Increase Their Investment in Space*, EUROCONSULT (2021), available online.
24. Unedited transcript, UNCOPUOS, 536th Meeting, at 23–26, UN Doc. COPUOS/T.536 (2005); Unedited transcript, UNCOPUOS, 593rd meeting, at 12, UN Doc. COPUOS/T.593 (2008); Gérard Brachet, *Protecting our space interests*, 10 ROOM, 2016.
25. Report of the Committee on the Peaceful Uses of Outer Space, UNGAOR, 62nd Sess., Supp. No. 20, at 117–118 and Annex, UN Doc. A/62/20 (2007) ["UNCOPUOS' SDM Guidelines"].
26. Report of the Committee on the Peaceful Uses of Outer Space, UNGAOR, 74th Sess., Supp. No. 20, at 163 and Annex II, UN Doc. A/74/20 (2019) ["LTS Guidelines"].
27. *See generally* COSPAR's policy on planetary protection *infra* in Chapter 3.

sustainability of activities in general and of space resource activities in particular: a more open understanding of sustainability is required. Because our knowledge of outer space remains limited, even more so when involving new space activities like space mining, uncertainty is a tempting excuse to avoid regulating activities from an environmental perspective. Still, it is eventually counterproductive when aiming for sustainability—a concept that relies on a careful balance between socio-economic development and the protection of the environment. Drawing from our experience on Earth, it is indubitable that exploiting natural resources in outer space will have an impact on the surrounding environment with a host of potential issues which go beyond the question of debris and the one of contamination, such as the risk of overexploitation.

If the reality of environmental concerns needs to be addressed from the beginning, it is because operating space resource missions without actively considering its environmental impact in outer space will only lead to outcomes similar to the one created by space debris. Admittedly, there seems to be a common understanding that space resource activities should be sustainable and that it involves considering their environmental impact on outer space.[28] While this is a welcome start, we need more than theoretical considerations. The problem of space debris began to be discussed in the late 1970s and early 1980s.[29] It, then, took the international community 15 years to acknowledge the issue as a priority matter in the UNCOPUOS, and almost as long to adopt formal mitigation guidelines.[30] Overall, about 30 years passed between the moment the international community realized there was a problem and the adoption of a formal solution. The question for new activities is whether we can shorten the lag period between the acknowledgment of problems and the implementation of solutions.

A logical path would be to anticipate the problem at the outset and act on it rather than wait for it to occur, especially if it takes another 30 years to solve it. As to the how, to quote Williamson, "[u]nless the space community, including its commercial segment, suddenly experiences a collective epiphany, there will eventually have to be guidelines, policies, sanctions or laws to protect the space environment."[31]

This book seeks to anticipate the inevitable framework that will need to be put in place and provides some insight as regards its main orientations in the field of space resource activities. In particular, it considers the necessity to create legal standards to support the environmental sustainability of such activities, despite their uncertain

28. *See, e.g.*, Mahulena Hofmann & Federico Bergamasco, *Space Resources Activities from the Perspective of Sustainability: Legal Aspects*, 3 GLOBAL SUSTAINABILITY (2020); 38 THE IAA COSMIC STUDY "PROTECTING THE ENVIRONMENT OF CELESTIAL BODIES," (Petra Rettberg, Mahulena Hofmann, & Mark Williamson eds., 2010); HSRGWG, *Building Blocks*, *in* BUILDING BLOCKS FOR THE DEVELOPMENT OF AN INTERNATIONAL FRAMEWORK FOR THE GOVERNANCE OF SPACE RESOURCES ACTIVITIES: A COMMENTARY 7 (Olavo de O. Bittencourt Neto et al. eds., 1 ed. 2020). Artemis Accords: Principles for Cooperation in the Civil Exploration and Use of the Moon, Mars, Comets, and Asteroids for Peaceful Purposes, section 10 (2020).
29. LOTTA VIIKARI, THE ENVIRONMENTAL ELEMENT IN SPACE LAW ASSESSING THE PRESENT AND CHARTING THE FUTURE 38 (2008).
30. UNCOPUOS' SDM Guidelines, *supra* note 25.
31. Mark Williamson, *Scope and Methodology*, 38 *in* THE IAA COSMIC STUDY ON PROTECTING THE ENVIRONMENT OF CELESTIAL BODIES 7 (Mahulena Hofmann, Petra Rettberg, & Mark Williamson eds., 2010).

environmental consequences. However, the creation of such legal standards presupposes that there do not already exist rules fulfilling this goal or that they exist but are ineffective in regulating environmental contingencies of space resource activities. Indeed, the purpose of this book is not to contribute to the unending multiplication of standards but, rather, to work, when possible, with existing instruments.

To that end, the book assesses the efficiency of space law in addressing environmental threats and reflects on the potential contribution international environmental law can offer. It further contemplates which normative approach would be the most appropriate to implement the framework. As such, it examines what kind of environmental problems may arise from space resource activities and which norms of international law might be applicable in addressing these threats within the framework of sustainability. It further considers domestic space legislations that directly address space resource activities or that are particularly relevant from an environmental perspective.

However, to strictly limit our analysis of international law to its formal sources would amount to ignoring a large part of international space law. Following a significant trend in scholarship about space law, it is important to not limit ourselves to sources outlined in the International Court of Justice (ICJ) Statute.[32] Jakhu et al., for instance, consider, *inter alia*, the value of soft law—i.e., nonlegally binding instruments—and resolutions adopted by the United Nations (UN). These same sources have been used extensively since the adoption of the last UN space treaty in 1979 to govern space activities. Thus, the book also takes into consideration the practice of States by reference to soft law written instruments from international organizations acting in the space sector, such as UNCOPUOS resolutions and the work of the Committee on Space Research (COSPAR).[33]

Use of treaty interpretation follows the customary rules of interpretation codified in Articles 31 to 33 of the Vienna Convention on the Law of Treaties (VCLT),[34] i.e., textual, teleological, or systematic interpretations. When necessary, recourse is made to the jurisprudence of international jurisdictions to substantiate the interpretation of a formal source of international law.[35]

2 DEFINITIONAL ISSUES

In order to avoid confusion, the usage of a number of terms should be clarified from the outset. "Sustainability" stands for, in the words of the ICJ, "[the] need to reconcile

32. Ram S. Jakhu, Steven Freeland & Kuan-Wei Chen, *The Sources of International Space Law: Revisited Space Law*, 67 ZLW 606, 607–608 (2018).
33. Accordingly, the book approaches the question of the sustainability of space resource activities from an environmental perspective on three levels: international, national, and, somewhat in between, international soft law instruments—i.e., international nonlegally binding instruments which States can voluntarily implement at the domestic level.
34. Vienna Convention on the Law of Treaties, *entered into force* Jan. 27, 1980, 1155 UNTS 331 ["VCLT"].
35. ICJ Statute, Art. 38§1, d.

economic development with protection of the environment."[36] Accordingly, "environmental sustainability" and "environmentally sustainable" refer to the environmental dimension of the concept, i.e., to the need to protect the environment. In the context of space resource activities, it is fundamental that space actors consider the impact of commercial exploitation of space resources on the outer space environment. Without carefully balancing the socio-economic benefits of commercial exploitation with the preservation of surrounding areas, they run the risks of compromising their and others' ability to peacefully explore and use outer space in the future. "Space actor" and "space operator" designate the entity authorized by the State to carry out space resource missions, regardless of their public or private nature.

Additionally, using the concept of "sustainability" requires further clarifying environmental terminology. Unfortunately, in the absence of a consensus, defining the "outer space environment" is less evident than it seems. Chapter 1 attempts to find elements of definition and gives it a better-delimited meaning. Broadly understood, "outer space environment" designates, in an initial definition, natural areas potentially affected by space resource activities on celestial bodies. "Environmental degradation" denotes a negative phenomenon resulting from human activities in space, which compromises the natural environment of celestial bodies and their surroundings. "Celestial bodies" refer to any natural object within the solar system from which space actors intend to commercially extract and exploit natural resources. In the current state of business, the term includes Earth's Moon, Mars and its Moons Phobos and Deimos, as well as NEAs and asteroids from the Main Belt situated between Mars and Jupiter.[37] Unless specified otherwise, "Moon" refers to Earth's sole natural satellite. "Space resources"[38] is used as an umbrella term for *in situ* abiotic resources originating from and located on celestial bodies. The term includes water but expressly excludes biological life. It applies indifferently to Lunar, Martian, and asteroid resources. "Renewable resources" designates natural resources that can be replenished to their original stock levels naturally on a human time scale. Conversely, "nonrenewable resources" are exhaustible natural resources that cannot be replenished after exploitation. For this reason, "space resources" should not be considered renewable resources. Although there is scientific evidence that NEAs can be replenished to their original level, full replenishment takes about 30 million years,[39] which is considerably beyond any human time scale.

In addition to the environmental terminology, there is a variety of legal terms used in this book, which stands to be clarified. "Soft law" designates norms that range from political or moral commitments to strictly legal ones but are not enforceable as such. For the most, soft laws used in this book find their origin in the recommendations, guidelines, and resolutions adopted by international organizations like the UNCOPUOS and COSPAR.

36. Gabčíkovo-Nagymaros Project (Hungary v. Slovakia) (Judgment), 1997 ICJ 7 (September 25).
37. SpaceResources.lu, Opportunities for Space Resources Utilization Future Markets & Value Chains (2018).
38. Gabrielle Leterre, *Providing a Legal Framework for Sustainable Space Mining Activities*, 38, 46 (University of Luxembourg, 2017).
39. Lewis, *supra* note 17 at 75, 91.

3 STRUCTURE

Four chapters divide the development of this book. After the introductory remarks, Chapter 1 presents elements of definition for the "outer space environment." It identifies potential environmental problems resulting from space resource activities and reflects on environmentalist ethical approaches to the discussion. Moreover, Chapter 1 contemplates the meaning of "space sustainability" and attempts to define a conceptual framework for sustainability that could be expanded to the exploitation of natural resources in outer space, thus, allowing to focus on the protection of the environment while keeping in mind the rationale for carrying out space resource activities.

Chapter 2 examines bodies of international law that have the potential to contribute to the sustainability of space resource activities, namely binding international space law and international environmental law. Additionally, Chapter 2 reflects on the juxtaposition of international space law with international environmental law and identifies potential gaps.

Chapter 3 concentrates on governance aspects. Since international treaties are not sufficient in themselves to deal with environmental issues, other instruments are investigated to substantiate existing international rules. It seeks solutions in other environmentally inclined international instruments developed specifically for space activities, namely so-called soft law space instruments.

Last, Chapter 4 considers national space legislations. In particular, it refers back to two environmentally advanced space legislations—Belgium's and Finland's—to create a baseline to which the four space resource national space legislations adopted so far can be confronted. It aims to evaluate the potential of mechanisms developed at the national level in ensuring the sustainability of space resource activities. Chapter 4 is followed by concluding remarks drawing up the contributions together.

4 THE WAY FORWARD

Clearly, covering all space resource activities from a legal standpoint would be a task too broad for one person and a single document. For this reason, this book limits itself to the legal study of space resource activities from a legal, environmental, and sustainable perspective. It, therefore, leaves aside a variety of legal questions that arise from the activity itself—such as issues relating to liability for environmental damage, the permissibility of space resource appropriation, or enforcement mechanisms and dispute settlement solutions. It is further limited by the number of uncertainties that linger over, *inter alia*, our small knowledge of the outer space environment, the methods of extraction that will be used on celestial bodies, and, more generally, how space mining will occur in practice. As we increase our knowledge, new legal issues will most likely arise and need to be addressed. Within these limitations, the work intends to lay the groundwork for the environmental sustainability of future space activities.

More broadly, it raises the issue of addressing legal issues regarding other NewSpace activities—i.e., new activities emerging from the recent commercialization of outer space by private operators—like space tourism or future human settlements in space. Most reflective of the NewSpace area is the recent separate trips to space of billionaires Richard Branson and Jeff Bezos aboard private rockets they helped fund on July 11 and July 20, 2021. Although NewSpace activities are likely to contribute to the sustainable economic development of space activities, it remains that the discussion is predominantly focused on only one-half of this development, i.e., its economic potential! Still, it will not be possible to shy away much longer from the fact that as varieties of activities develop in space, so will environmental issues.

CHAPTER 1

Uncertain Definitions, Real Issues

Chapter 1 aims to define a "conceptual sustainability framework" which will guide the legal discussion on the long-term sustainability of space resource activities throughout the work. For this purpose, the concept of sustainability is approached from the perspective of its environmental dimension—i.e., from the need to consider the limits of the outer space environment as a host for space activities. In this sense, the sustainability of space resource activities is intrinsically linked to the idea of the environmental protection of outer space. Thus, it is necessary to identify from the outset what makes up the "outer space environment" which needs to be protected and to assert the meaning of sustainability in outer space.

The present chapter is divided into two sections. Section 1 considers elements of definition for the "outer space environment" and identifies and analyzes concepts relevant to the object and purpose of the discussion. This includes potential environmental problems resulting from space resource activities as well as environmental ethical approaches to the discussion. Section 2 seeks to narrow the meaning of the term "sustainability" in order to identify practical steps toward its achievement in the context of space resource activities. To that end, section 2 first ponders the definition of "space sustainability" before referring to the broader concept of sustainable development.

1 WHAT IS THE "OUTER SPACE ENVIRONMENT"?

What is the "outer space environment"? Simple question, yet not so simple answer. As strange as it might seem, there is no established consensus on the definition of the terms "outer space environment," "outer space" or "environment."[1] None of the five

1. Qizhi He, *The problem of definition and delimitation of outer space*, 10 J. SPACE L. 157, 157 (1982); LOTTA VIIKARI, THE ENVIRONMENTAL ELEMENT IN SPACE LAW ASSESSING THE PRESENT AND CHARTING THE FUTURE 9–10 (2008).

Space Law Treaties[2] adopted by the United Nations General Assembly between 1967 and 1979 ("UN Space Treaties") offers an answer and, to use Romano's words, "'environment' is like 'time', a term everyone seems to understand but no one is able to define."[3]

The immediate problem such confusion poses is that it makes it difficult to develop a scientific discussion, without the minimum clarity derived from identifying terms and concepts relevant to the object and purpose of the discussion. The definition of the "outer space environment" influences the scope of a research about the protection of the said environment. In the absence of an already established one, it is still necessary to consider what needs to be protected from environmental damage, what should be excluded, and in both cases, why and to which extent. For instance, it would make no sense to include the "marine environment" in the scope of the protection of the "outer space environment": there is, as far as we know, no live marine organism in outer space. Conversely, it seems quite impossible not to include the protection—at least to some extent—of exploited surfaces of celestial bodies when discussing environmental protection in the context of space resource activities.

It is true that, so far, the lack of definition has not impeded space activities, a fact acknowledged by several States.[4] Humans have been going and sending objects into space for over half a century without needing one. A realistic conclusion could be that the effort to define "environment" is no more than a scholarly exercise.

Yet, the absence of a definition is not solely intellectually confusing; it is legally problematic when one considers that treaties in general—and treaties relevant to space activities in particular—carefully provide definitions of their legal concepts.[5] From a legal perspective, defining notions is not solely conceptually appropriate; it has a direct impact on the scope of the legal instruments, their enforcement, and the competence they provide.[6] While a term such as "damage" is understandable, when enforcing liability it may be useful to know already what types of damage are covered. Direct and/or indirect? To persons and/or objects? Physical and/or moral? Similarly, when discussing applicable rules for the environmental protection of outer space, it is most required, and probably necessary, to know what is included in the notion: celestial bodies? or only Moons and Planets? What about the "void" between them? Protecting something without knowing what type of reality it refers to may prove difficult.

2. The five "UN Space Treaties" are: the Outer Space Treaty and the Moon Agreement *supra*, as well as the "Return and Rescue Agreement," the "Liability Convention" and the "Registration Convention" *infra* Chapter 2.
3. Cesare Romano, The peaceful settlement of international environmental disputes: a pragmatic approach 15 (2000). Romano alludes here to Augustine's well-known reflection on time: "What then is time? If no one asks me, I know what it is. If I wish to explain it to him who asks, I do not know." St. Augustine, Confessions IX, 14.
4. Historical summary on the consideration of the question on the definition and delimitation of outer space. Report of the Secretariat, UNCOPUOS, 59th Sess., UN Doc. A/AC.105/769/Add.1(2020).
5. For instance, Article I of Liability Convention's only purpose is to define the terms used in it, like "damage," "space object" or "launching state." Convention on International Liability for Damage Caused by Space Objects, *entered into force* Oct. 9, 1973, Art. I, 961 UNTS 187.
6. Philippe Sands & Jacqueline Peel, Principles of international environmental law 13–14 (3rd ed. ed. 2012).

1.1 Key Notions

In the absence of a consensus on the scope of the expression "outer space environment," a first step toward clarification is to consider separately the notions of "outer space" and "environment," for which an already rich literature exists. The following subsections attempt to define each notion and eventually bring them together to offer a logical and fitting definition of the "outer space environment" in light of future space resource activities.

1.1.1 "Outer Space"

Simply put, outer space is the area above the airspace, beyond the atmosphere, which surrounds Earth.[7] This raises the question of establishing limits: where does outer space start exactly? Alternatively, where does the airspace end? These questions are not new: scientists and technical experts have tried to answer them since the beginning of space activities. A promising idea was to look for a shift in the composition of Earth's atmosphere to define clear boundaries. Unfortunately, studies showed that the shift is "gradual and continuous";[8] consequently, there is no precise physical criterion for the delimitation between airspace and outer space.

Although the "lack of a definition and delimitation of outer space ha[s] not hindered space exploration,"[9] it is a source of potentially arduous legal and political issues since airspace and outer space are governed by vastly different and distinct legal regimes.[10] The legal regime governing the airspace—air law—is greatly similar to the legal regime of the subjacent surfaces: the airspace above the national territory and territorial sea of a State is subjected to its "complete and exclusive sovereignty," whereas it is freely accessible above international areas, like the high seas.[11] By contrast, space law establishes outer space as an area that is beyond national appropriation, including by claims of sovereignty.[12] In other words, the area above the national territory of a State, beyond its airspace, is freely accessible to other States.[13] Accordingly, it is possible to freely fly over the national territory of a State from outer space, but restrictions apply when the overflight takes place within said State's airspace.

Without a clear delimitation between airspace and outer space, a question stands: how far up can a State extend its sovereignty? This issue has given rise to a series of endless, if intermittent, discussions within the international community. Already in

7. VIIKARI, *supra* note 1 at 1; He, *supra* note 1 at 157.
8. Lubos Perek, *Scientific Criteria for the Delimitation of Outer Space*, 5 J. SPACE L. 111, 122 (1977).
9. UNCOPUOS, Historical summary on the consideration of the question on the definition and delimitation of outer space, *supra* note 4.
10. For a brief overview of the main differences between the two legal regimes, *see* Paul Stephen Dempsey & Maria Manoli, *Suborbital Flights and the Delimitation of Air Space Vis-à-Vis Outer Space: Functionalism, Spatialism and State Sovereignty*, XLII ANN. AIR & SPACE L. 209, 218 (2017).
11. Convention on International Civil Aviation, *entered into force* Apr. 4, 1947, Arts. 1 and 2, 15 UNTS 295.
12. Outer Space Treaty, Art. II.
13. *Id.*, Art. I.

1959, States asked the recently established ad hoc UN Committee on the Peaceful Uses of Outer Space (ad hoc UNCOPUOS) to determine where outer space begins.[14] This ad hoc Committee is tasked by the UN General Assembly with considering "the activities and resources of the United Nations, the specialized agencies and other international bodies relating to the peaceful uses of outer space," "organizational arrangements to facilitate international cooperation in this field within the framework of the United Nations" and "legal problems which may arise in the carrying out of programmes to explore outer space."[15] It became a permanent body of the United Nations in 1959,[16] with the addition of two subcommittees in 1961: the Scientific and Technical Sub-Committee (UNCOPUOS STC) and the Legal Sub-Committee (UNCOPUOS LSC).[17] In 1959, the Committee decides in its initial answer that the subject of the delimitation of outer space is not a "priority consideration" and that "such an agreement now, based on current knowledge and experience, would be premature."[18] However, the question of the delimitation of outer space is formally put on the agenda in 1967.[19]

Despite States having broached the topic regularly over the last 60 years, the issue has yet to be met with consensus.[20] This is in part due to the international community disagreeing over which approach should be taken to deal with the matter at hand. While there are still some who consider that there is no need for a definition/delimitation of outer space since the lack of it has not impeded the development of space activities, the great majority is split over two predominant approaches: the functional approach and the spatial approach.[21] The former approach focuses on the nature of activity conducted or the nature of the vehicle used, whereas the latter requires the establishment of a

14. Report of the ad hoc Committee on the Peaceful Uses of Outer Space, UNGA, §67, UN Doc. A/4141 (1959).
15. GA Res. 1348(XIII), UNGAOR, 13th Sess., UN Doc. A/RES/1348(XIII). Citations respect the original spelling in the quoted text without further indication, even if the chosen English spelling is different from the standard adopted in this work.
16. GA Res. 1472(XIV), UNGAOR, 14th Sess., UN Doc. A/RES/1472(XIV).
17. The UNCOPUOS STC works on questions related to the scientific and technical aspects of space activities, such as space weather, global navigation satellite systems, near-Earth objects, disaster management support and the long-term sustainability of outer space activities. The LSC meets every year to discuss legal questions related to the status and application of the five UN Space Treaties, the definition and delimitation of outer space, national space legislation, space debris mitigation, international mechanisms for cooperation and to negotiate international agreements relating to outer space within the United Nations. On the role and evolution of the Legal Subcommittee *see* Sergio Marchisio, *The Evolutionary Stages of the Legal Subcommittee of the United Nations Committee on the Peaceful Uses of Outer Space*, 31 J. Space L. 219 (2005).
18. 1959 Report of the *ad hoc* UNCOPUOS, *supra* note 14, §§24, 28.
19. Report of the Committee on the Peaceful Uses of Outer Space, UNGAOR, 22nd Sess., Annex III, UN Doc. A/6804. Add. 1 (1967). For a historical summary of the views exchanged in COPUOS by States regarding the question of the delimitation and definition of outer space, *see* UNCOPUOS, Historical summary on the consideration of the question on the definition and delimitation of outer space, *supra* note 4.
20. For a historical summary of the views exchanged in the UNCOPUOS by States regarding the question of the delimitation and definition of outer space, *see* UNCOPUOS, Historical summary on the consideration of the question on the definition and delimitation of outer space, *supra* note 4.
21. *Id.*

geographical boundary line between airspace and outer space.[22] The functional approach rests upon the idea that outer space begins where space activities begin.[23] It relies on the technological capabilities and designs of the vehicle, its purpose or destination, to determine the nature of the activity and, by extent, the applicable legal regime.[24] This interpretation has merits, especially in the absence of a technical criterion to distinguish the atmosphere from outer space:[25] an aircraft will fall under the regime of air law, whereas a spacecraft will call for the application of space law. However, as highlighted by Dempsey and Manoli,[26] the functional approach may reach its limits with the development of "space" technologies and activities. Taking the case of the American National Aeronautics and Space Administration (NASA) Space Shuttle, for instance, raises the question of the nature of an activity carried out using an "aerospace" vehicle. The shuttle used two rockets to support its launch and ascent in order to overcome Earth's gravitational pull, but, then, the orbiter was shaped much like an airplane and it landed like a glider on Earth.[27] If we were to apply the functional approach strictly here, it would mean that the vehicle was simultaneously subjected to two different legal regimes depending on the phase of the mission: space law during the launch and air law when landing. Similarly, private suborbital flights will likely be capable of going over a 100 km altitude, yet they would not be reaching orbital velocity.[28] What, then, is the legal nature of such vehicles? What legal regime should be applicable? Does the applicable legal regime change during the activity?

In that sense, the spatial approach offers a greater guarantee: there is one line delaminating both areas above which space law would theoretically apply and under which air law would be the principle. The difficulty here lies in the lack of scientific findings to define such a line with precision. As noted earlier, there is no drastic change in the composition of the atmosphere that would justify a strict line to be drawn.[29] The most prominent proposal for such delimitation is the altitude-based limit suggested by Hungarian physicist von Kárman, located between 100 and 110 km above sea level. It is supposedly the "general area where the atmosphere is so thin that aircraft wings cannot generate sufficient lift for flight, while a spacecraft cannot orbit because the atmospheric drag is excessive."[30] However, while the Kárman line is broadly referred to,[31] the international community has yet to agree to use it formally as a delimitation for

22. He, *supra* note 1 at 162; Bin Cheng, *The Legal Status of Outer Space and Relevant Issues: Delimitation of Outer Space and Definition of Peaceful Use*, 11 J. SPACE L. 89, 93 (1983).
23. Gbenga Oduntan, *The Never Ending Dispute: Legal Theories on the Spatial Demarcation Boundary Plane Between Airspace and Outer Space.*, 1 HERTFORDSHIRE LAW JOURNAL 64, 69 (2003).
24. Dempsey and Manoli, *supra* note 10 at 219.
25. Perek, *supra* note 8 at 122.
26. Dempsey and Manoli, *supra* note 10.
27. NASA, *The Aeronautics of the Space Shuttle* (2017) available online.
28. The altitude of 100 km above sea level, give or take 10 km, was suggested by von Kárman as a theoretical limit between the fields of aeronautics and astronautics. *See e.g.* Dempsey and Manoli, *supra* note 10 at 226–227.
29. Perek, *supra* note 8.
30. Dempsey and Manoli, *supra* note 10 at 230.
31. For instance, the Karman line was used as a boundary for the Ansari X-Prize and discussed in an undated official document published on the website of the Astronautics Records Commission of the Fédération Aéronautique Internationale, which certifies world records for aeronautics and

outer space. This could be so because "the determination of the appropriate line raises policy problems that have not yet been resolved amongst States,"[32] such as the question of where the sovereignty of States ends.

Ultimately, the issue of the delimitation and definition of outer space might be less stringent than it appears. Once again, space activities are not affected by the lack of consensus among States. Representatives have stressed on several occasions during UNCOPUOS meetings that the absence of a definition does not affect, in practice, the development of space activities, nor the accession to the five UN Space Treaties.[33] Furthermore, it might even be less of an issue when discussing space activities from an environmental perspective. In Matte's radical terms: "the artificial separation of air space and outer space is totally irrelevant."[34] This clear-cut statement emphasizes the fact that environmental damage does not stop at a border, be it between States or between airspace and outer space. Space activities by nature affect both environments since space objects are launched from Earth's ground and go through the airspace before they reach outer space. Hence, the potential for environmental harm is not limited to outer space, wherever it may begin.

1.1.2 "Environment"

Defining the concept of "environment" is an even more daunting task than trying to delimitate outer space. In a way, the definition problem is opposite between the two notions. Whereas "outer space" does not have a definition, "environment" appears to have a multitude. Etymologically, the word comes from the Old French word "environ," meaning which surrounds, encompasses.[35] This suggests that the notion of "environment" exists in relation to a central object: the environment being what surrounds and encompasses said object.[36] Consequently, it is not surprising to find that "environment" is polysemous since it bears a relative reference point. The word takes on different meanings depending on the perspective adopted, be it philosophical, biological, cultural, or legal.[37] For instance, a philosopher will consider the environment as the differentiation between man and nature, whereas, for a biologist, it relates

astronautics. *See* S. Sanz Fernández de Córdoba, *100km Altitude Boundary for Astronautics*, FAI (n.d.), available online; Nadia Drake, *Where, Exactly, Is the Edge of Space? It Depends on Who You Ask*, NATIONAL GEOGRAPHIC (2018), available online.

32. *See* Cheng quoting Prof. Almond *in* Cheng, *supra* note 22 at 93.
33. For example, UNCOPUOS, Historical summary on the consideration of the question on the definition and delimitation of outer space, *supra* note 4, §6(a), (c), (d) and (g).
34. Nicolas M. Matte, *Environmental Implications and Responsibilities in the Use of Outer Space*, 14 ANN. AIR & SPACE L. 419, 421 (1989).
35. Environ, THE CONCISE OXFORD DICTIONARY OF ENGLISH ETYMOLOGY (T. F. Hoad ed., 2003).
36. Marcel Jollivet & Alain Pavé, *L'environnement: un champ de recherche en formation*, 1 NATURES SCIENCES SOCIÉTÉS 6, 7 (1993) DOI: 10.1051/nss/19930101006.
37. For an analysis of the different meanings given to the term "environment" depending on the perspective adopted, *see* ROMANO, *supra* note 3.

to the relationship between living organisms and their milieu.[38] Similarly, most dictionaries do not offer a single definition but rather a range of notions.[39]

This polysemy of the word "environment" also exists in the legal field, including, surprisingly enough, within environmental law itself.[40] A possible explanation could be that legal instruments generally use dictionaries as a starting point.[41] Looking at "environmental" conventions, guidelines, declarations and others, there appear to be two predominant approaches: those who define the term within the instrument—giving it a "special meaning"[42]—and those who prefer to set aside the issue and give no definition. Both approaches have their interests.

Giving meaning to key concepts can be critical to determinate the scope of a legal instrument. It will be particularly necessary in cases where instruments aim to produce enforceable rules.[43] A well-known example, in the field of environmental protection, of failure to provide a definition entailing uncertainty about the rule itself is the 1946 *International Whaling Convention*.[44] Despite the existence of an appendix listing 12 species, it led to conflicting views regarding the International Whaling Commission (ICW)'s jurisdiction over dolphins.[45] Some States Parties believed that the ICW's mandate was limited to catches of the "Great Whales" species, whereas others considered that small cetaceans, like dolphins, were also included.[46]

Such a mistake was not made in the *Convention on the International Liability for Damage Caused by Space Objects* ("Liability Convention")[47] which defines in its Article 1 paragraph (a) the notion of "damage"; without it, it would have been impossible to know what type of damage the Convention covers.[48] However, the Liability Convention is both a model and an exception: environmental instruments do not all define the

38. For an analysis of the different meanings given to the term "environment" depending on the perspective adopted, *see id.*
39. The word "environment" refers to, *inter alia*, "the aggregate of surrounding things, conditions, or influences" or to "chemical and biological factors and social factors likely to have a direct or indirect, immediate or long-term effect on living beings and human activities." Paul Robert, Alain Rey & Josette Rey-Debove, *Environnement*, LE PETIT ROBERT: DICTIONNAIRE ALPHABÉTIQUE ET ANALOGIQUE DE LA LANGUE FRANÇAISE (2015); Environment, COLLINS ENGLISH DICTIONARY; ROMANO, *supra* note 3 at 16.
40. In this case, "environmental law" refers to the corpus of rules and legal instruments relating to environmental matters.
41. SANDS AND PEEL, *supra* note 6 at 13.
42. VCLT, Art. 31§4.
43. SANDS AND PEEL, *supra* note 6 at 13–14.
44. International Convention for the Regulation of Whaling, *entered into force* Nov. 18, 1948, 161 UNTS 72.
45. International Whaling Commission, *Small cetaceans: dolphins and porpoises* (n.d.), available online; SANDS AND PEEL, *supra* note 6 at 13–14.
46. *Id.*, Small cetaceans.
47. Liability Convention, *supra.*
48. Under the Liability Convention, "damage" means "loss of life, personal injury or other impairment of health; or loss of or damage to property of States or of persons, natural or juridical, or property of international intergovernmental organizations." Although the Convention provides an extensive definition, there are still questions regarding whether "indirect" or "consequential" damage is included in its scope. *See* Carl Q. Christol, *International Liability for Damage Caused by Space Objects*, 74 THE AMERICAN JOURNAL OF INTERNATIONAL LAW 346, 360 (1980) DOI: 10.2307/2201505; Elena Carpanelli & Brendan Cohen, *Interpreting "Damage Caused by Space Objects" under the 1972 Liability Convention*, 56 *in* IISL PROCEEDINGS 29 (2013).

notion they refer to in general, and the one of "environment" in particular. The most spectacular omission of a definition of a term essential to an international law instrument precisely happens in the *Treaty on Principles Governing the Activities of States in the Exploration and Use of Outer Space, Including the Moon and Other Celestial Bodies*[49] ("Outer Space Treaty"), which includes no definition of "outer space." This is what justifies the long and, so far, unsolved discussion about what "outer space" is that we have analyzed. The lack of a generally accepted definition and the multitude of interpretations of any definition even within the same field of study force lawmakers to create one when one is needed. Still, this is never a final decision. Many elements come into play before a definition may be adopted. Each word would have to be chosen carefully—in addition to being generally accepted by Parties when the discussion pertains to multilateral instruments—to fit the purpose of the instrument. Other limits lie in the purpose itself. For instance, in the case of outer space, some of our limits in the discussion about a consensual definition include a lack of knowledge of the stars and the constant evolution of space technologies and capabilities.[50] If a definition of "outer space" were to be adopted, it would have to be able to withstand these evolutions at the risk of legal instruments becoming obsolete.

An answer to this problem has been to consider the adoption of a broad definition by piecing together all common elements found in various legal instruments. The idea was proposed by the Working Group of Experts on Liability and Compensation for Environmental Damage arising from Military Activities established by the United Nations Environmental Programme (UNEP). The Working Group argues in its 1996 Report that the concept of the environment should "be broadly construed" because "a narrow and exclusionary construction should only be taken if a broad approach would lead to absurd or unreasonable results."[51] Following this recommendation means to reach a definition of "environment" under international law that is sufficiently general.[52] The Working Group first stresses "the absence of a commonly agreed definition in international law of [the concepts of environment and environmental damage], although they are referred to in international environmental agreements."[53] It further observes that "the term "environment" includes abiotic and biotic components, including air, water, soil, flora, fauna and the ecosystem formed by their interaction" and that "[t]here is also authority in international environmental agreements for the proposition that "environment" also includes cultural heritage, features of the landscape and environmental amenity."[54] Eventually, the efforts of the Working

49. Treaty on Principles Governing the Activities of States in the Exploration and Use of Outer Space, including the Moon and Other Celestial Bodies, *entered into force* October 10, 1967, 610 UNTS 205 ["Outer Space Treaty"].
50. Sylvie Durrieu & Ross F. Nelson, *Earth Observation from Space—The Issue of Environmental Sustainability*, 29 SPACE POLICY 238 (2013) DOI: 10.1016/j.spacepol.2013.07.003; Space Security Index, *Condition and Knowledge of the Space Environment* (n.d.), available online.
51. UNEP, *Report of the Working Group of Experts on Liability and Compensation for Environmental Damage Arising from Military Activities*, 27 ENVIRONMENTAL POLICY & LAW 134, 43 (1996).
52. ROMANO, *supra* note 3 at 23–24.
53. UNEP, *supra* note 50 at 41.
54. *Id.*, at 42.

Group remained indecisive, as it could not "conclude that the international community has taken a clear and consistent direction on definitional aspects."[55]

More accurately, when referring to the "environment," the international community leans toward a sectorial approach to the notion.[56] Consequently, there are almost as many concepts of the "environment" as there are environmental instruments; international law abounds with various examples. For instance, the Declaration of the 1972 *United Nations Stockholm Conference on the Human Environment* ("Stockholm Declaration"),[57] while not providing a definition for the word "environment," refers, in Principle 2, to Earth resources as including "the air, water, land, flora and fauna and [...] natural ecosystems." The preamble also makes a clear distinction between "natural and man-made" environments.[58] The 1982 *World Charter for Nature* does not define the notion either but lists principles that are applicable to all life forms, habitats, all areas of Earth, ecosystems and organisms, and land, marine, and atmospheric resources.[59] In the 1991 *Convention on Environmental Impact Assessment in a Transboundary Context* ("Espoo Convention"), "environment" includes "landscape and historical monuments" in addition to "flora, fauna, soil, air, water";[60] the *Convention on the Prohibition of Military or Any Other Hostile Use of Environmental Modification Techniques* ("ENMOD") extends its environment to "outer space," while the *Protocol on Environmental Protection to the Antarctic Treaty* considers potential "adverse effects" on, *inter alia*, "areas of biological, scientific, historic, aesthetic or wilderness significance."[61] This cornucopia of heterogeneous references offers no solid ground for a definition of "environment" that could be used as a universal interpretation of the notion of "outer space environment," as there is neither a generally accepted definition of the word nor a specific definition adopted in space law instruments. At the same time, it shows that the lack of a universal (legal) definition of the term "environment" or, more precisely, "outer space environment" is not a dead end; it is still possible to operate within more contextual definitions, even if the "broad definition" of the environment is impossible to reach. If anything, the above analysis can help develop a methodology to identify what constitutes the "outer space environment," at least for the purpose of this book. Namely, the meaning given to the expression must be fitted to the purpose of the research.

55. *Id.*, at 41.
56. ROMANO, *supra* note 3 at 21–22.
57. United Nations Conference on the Human Environment, UNGA, 27th Sess., UN Doc. A/RES/2994 (1972) ["Stockholm Declaration"].
58. *Id.*
59. World Charter for Nature, UNGAOR, 37th Sess., 1 §§2–4, UN Doc. A/RES/37/7 (1982).
60. Convention on Environmental Impact Assessment in a Transboundary Context, *entered into force* Sept. 10, 1997, Art. 1 §vii, 1989 UNTS 309.
61. Article II states that "'environmental modification techniques' refers to any technique for changing—through the deliberate manipulation of natural processes—the dynamics, composition or structure of the Earth, including its biota, lithosphere, hydrosphere and atmosphere, or of *outer space*" [italics added]. Convention on the Prohibition of Military or Any Other Hostile Use of Environmental Modification Techniques, *entered into force* Oct. 5, 1978, Art. II, 1108 UNTS 151 ["ENMOD"]; Protocol on Environmental Protection to the Antarctic Treaty, *entered into force* Jan. 14, 1998, Art. 3 §(b)(vi), 2941 UNTS 3.

1.2 Identification of Key Concepts

This book aims at drafting the roadmap for the sustainable utilization of space resources from a legal standpoint. This scope does not neglect—and, in reality, does integrate—the many scientific uncertainties with which this utilization is associated. Accordingly, any definition of the "outer space environment" needs to promote this goal, even if it may be regarded as lacking generality or applicability in other contexts, including other contexts within space law. This requires returning to the two key elements pertaining to sustainability defined in the introduction of this book: economic development (1) and environmental protection (2). Rather than providing a general definition, it is crucial to identify what the outer space environment would need to be protected from (2) within the context of space resource activities (1). This, in turn, calls for a little environmentalist thinking and being aware of the difference between anthropocentric and ecocentric approaches. They do not always appreciate similar situations in the same manner despite sharing the same goal of protecting the environment; the former focuses on humans and their interests, whereas the latter considers that the environment has an intrinsic value that is worthy of protection, independent of human interests. In other words, *what the outer space environment would need to be protected from* can be understood in significantly different ways.

1.2.1 Environmental Issues Related to Space Resource Activities

Space exploration—and by extension, space utilization—is a polluting industry during all phases of the mission, from its design to the disposal of a space object, on Earth as well as in outer space.[62] The first environmental impact that can be mentioned is the "traditional" one which results from the use of raw materials, their transport as well as the transport of the final product, i.e., a space object. In addition, space objects are often using toxic substances, notably for propellants.[63] Then comes the time for launching the space object into outer space, which creates noise pollution and produces a "ground-cloud" made of, *inter alia*, exhaust gas, cooling water, and dust.[64] Although the resulting pollution on the terrestrial ground and in the air constitutes no danger, in the future, the increase of space activities—especially in the context of NewSpace activities—might have a greater effect. Indeed, the area surrounding launching sites would be repeatedly polluted in a short period, thus, not allowing the

62. As the UNESCO Working Group on "Ethics of Outer Space" noted, "space technology represent[s] a factor of damage to the circumterrestrial, terrestrial and planetary environments." THE ETHICS OF SPACE POLICY, 7 (2000). In 2012, ESA launched its Clean Space Initiative and has been looking since at how it can reduce the environmental impact, on Earth and in outer space, throughout the life cycle of its activities. ESA, *How much do space activities pollute?* (2018) available online.
63. *Id.*
64. For an evaluation of the environmental effect of space activities, *see, e.g.*, Qizhi He, *Environmental Impact of Space Activities and Measures for International Protection*, 16 J. SPACE L. 117, 119 (1988); VIIKARI, *supra* note 1 at 29–30.

pollution to dissipate naturally.[65] Qizhi notes in particular that the atmosphere is the most affected by the launching stage of the mission due to the existence of "only very rarefied natural gas"; it makes it "difficult to mix up and dilute even a small amount of released exhaust gases and substances which could stay for a long time and spread horizontally over a large area."[66] The release of these gases certainly contributes to the deterioration of the ozone layer, which, as we know, diminishes the protection from ultraviolet radiation.[67] Incidentally, this human-made pollution adds itself to the one naturally occurring in the atmosphere with the entry of meteoroid materials.[68]

Still, the greater extent of the pollution caused by space activities occurs in outer space after the launching phase. This is why we focus in this book on the "forward contamination" that is likely to result in outer space from the utilization of space resources.[69] "Forward contamination," in opposition to "backward contamination," relates to the contamination of outer space due to human activities there. It revolves around the idea that humans may contaminate outer space by bringing with them terrestrial material and, in particular, live organisms. "Backward contamination," on the other hand, is caused by bringing back extraterrestrial material on Earth. However, since space resource activities have not yet started, and since it is equally too soon to know exactly which technologies will be used in practice to extract and process minerals *in situ*, current environmental issues will be used as a basis for the study.

1.2.1.a Space Debris

Currently, the most prominent environmental problem connected to space activities is space debris. "Space debris" is the general term used for human-made objects orbiting Earth or reentering its atmosphere, and which are no longer functional. There are some variations in the terminology; NASA, for instance, uses the term "orbital debris" instead of "space debris,"[70] but both expressions refer to the same environmental problem. NASA's "orbital debris" is defined as "any human-made object in orbit about the Earth that no longer serves a useful function."[71] Such debris includes "nonfunctional spacecraft, abandoned launch vehicle stages, mission-related debris, and fragmentation debris." In comparison, the UNCOPUOS and the Inter-Agency Space Debris Coordination Committee (IADC) use a more general definition: "space debris" encompasses "all [hu]man-made objects, including fragments and elements thereof, in Earth orbit or re-entering the atmosphere, that are non-functional."[72] In both cases, the definition refers to three common elements: (1) a human-made object, (2) in Earth

65. He, *supra* note 63 at 118–119.
66. *Id.*, at 119–120.
67. Tereza Pultarova-Senior, *Air pollution from reentering megaconstellation satellites could cause ozone hole 2.0*, SPACE.COM (n.d.) available online.
68. *Id.*
69. *See* S. Gorove, *Pollution and Outer Space: A Legal Analysis and Appraisal*, 5 N.Y.U. J. INT'L L. & POL. 53, 54–57 (1972).
70. Mark Garcia, *Space Debris and Human Spacecraft*, NASA (2021) available online.
71. *Id.*
72. *Id;* UNCOPUOS' SDM Guidelines.

orbit, (3) that is nonfunctional. Points 1 and 3 are easily applicable to space mining scenarios; it is not difficult to imagine that the mining activity will require human-made objects and that these objects will become nonfunctional in the future. Point 2, however, shows that when dealing with environmental problems caused by space debris, the international community is solely focused on Earth and its close surroundings, i.e., its orbits. This is an important difference when we consider space resource activities since *in situ* extraction operations are not planned to take place in Near-Earth Orbit (NEO). On the contrary, the current efforts are set toward using resources from Near-Earth Asteroids (NEAs), the Moon, Mars, and asteroids from the belt situated between Mars and Jupiter: the "Main Belt."[73] Therefore, the question is whether the circumstances making space debris an environmental issue around Earth would also create troubles when around other celestial bodies.

In her study of the history of space debris, Hall sorts them into three categories based on their origin.[74] In her view,[75] space debris may originate from mission-related operations, accidents, or intentional creation.[76] The most common mission-related space debris happens during on-orbit breakup and originates, *inter alia*, from the exhaust of solid fuels that are released.[77] Space activities are also known to be ultra-hazardous; thus, it is not surprising that, sometimes, accidents happen. One such example is the accident that happened in 2008 to American Astronaut Heidemarie Stefanyshyn-Piper.[78] While working outside the International Space Station (ISS), her tool bag slipped out away and stayed in orbit for eight months before it burnt up while reentering Earth's atmosphere. More typically, accidental debris generally originates from explosions or collisions. The first confirmed damage to an operational spacecraft due to a collision with a space debris was recorded in June 1983, during the US Space Shuttle Challenger "windshield incident."[79] It was first thought that the windshield had been hit by a micrometeorite but further studies showed the debris that had hit the shuttle was human-made.[80] The debris responsible for the impact turned out to be a tiny 0.2 mm paint chip that created a 0.4 mm-diameter pit in the windshield, rendering it unusable.[81] Lastly, space debris can originate from intentional acts, such as anti-satellite weapon (ASAT) tests or the willful crash of probes on celestial bodies. As Williamson recalls, "between 1970 and 1972, a total of five Saturn V third stages, each weighing about 11 tonnes, were purposely crashed onto the lunar surface to provide 'thumper' impulses for previously placed seismometers."[82] These successive crashes

73. Ian Christensen et al., *New Policies Needed to Advance Space Mining*, 35 Issues in Science and Technology 26, 27 (2019).
74. Loretta Hall, *The History of Space Debris*, *in* Roadmap to the Stars, 2 (2014), available online.
75. Viikari, for instance, proposes another categorization "explosions (intentional or accidental), collisions, or degradation of spacecraft." Viikari, *supra* note 1 at 31–44.
76. Hall, *supra* note 73 at 2.
77. *Id.*
78. James Sturcke, *Astronaut Loses Tools During Spacewalk*, The Guardian, Nov. 19, 2008.
79. Thomas O'Toole, *Man-Made Junk Jams Space*, Washington Post, Mar. 29, 1985.
80. *Id.*
81. Viikari, *supra* note 1 at 39; Hall, *supra* note 73 at 3.
82. Mark Williamson, *Lunar Exploration and Development—A Sustainable Model*, 57 Acta Astronautica 161, 163 (2005) DOI: 10.1016/j.actaastro.2005.02.002.

aimed at allowing lunar geologists to "draw conclusions regarding the Moon's interior."[83] Another, more recent, example is the experiment conducted by NASA, in 2009, with the Lunar Crater Observation and Sensing Satellite (LCROSS). LCROSS was designed to operate in two stages: first, it would crash into the Moon's Cabeus crater in order to create a cloud of lunar dust, and second, a spacecraft would fly through the cloud to analyze its content.[84]

Thus, to the question of whether space debris can occur outside of Earth orbit, the answer is a loud "yes!" Already, the Moon is "contaminated"—by opposition to a lunar pristine environment—by debris from previous missions. More specifically, there are metallic debris leftovers from spacecraft and launch vehicles that crashed on the Moon and created (unnatural) craters.[85] It has even been suggested that the situation might be direr for the Moon and for Mars than it is currently for Earth.[86] The rationale for such an assessment is rooted in the fact that space resource activities will not be limited to the ground; it is likely that satellites will be placed in lunar orbit—or any used celestial body's orbit—to control operations on the ground.[87] It means that these orbits will become more crowded, which is not without reminding us how NEOs have become congested. A key difference, however, is the nature of the atmosphere surrounding other celestial bodies, such as the Moon or Mars: they do not have an appreciable atmosphere that would allow for debris to burn on their way to the lunar and Martian surface; they will simply crash and create more debris.[88] In the absence of a "graveyard orbit" analogous to the one around the Earth, space resource activities thus create the need to rethink some of the space debris mitigation techniques used to clean Earth orbit.

1.2.1.b Biological, Chemical, and Radiological Contamination

Another source of concern for the outer space environment is biological, chemical, and radiological contamination. Aside from space debris, exobiological issues are certainly the most studied as well as the oldest. In its report to the General Assembly in 1959, the ad hoc UNCOPUOS notes that "scientific studies indicate that certain activities related to lunar and planetary impacts might result in biological, chemical and radiation contamination" which could "jeopardize[e] subsequent physical and chemical studies and endange[r] possible living organisms."[89]

83. *Id.*
84. Abigail Tabor, *What Is LCROSS, the Lunar Crater Observation and Sensing Satellite?*, NASA (2019), available online.
85. Mark Williamson, *Planetary Spacecraft Debris: The Case for Protecting the Space Environment*, 42 445, 447 (2000) DOI: 10.1016/s0094-5765(00)00109-0.
86. *See* Williamson, *supra* note 84; Mark Williamson, *Scope and Methodology*, 38 *in* The IAA Cosmic Study on Protecting the Environment of Celestial Bodies 7 (Mahulena Hofmann, Petra Rettberg, & Mark Williamson eds., 2010); Luboš Perek, *Outer Space As Natural Resource*, *in* The Settlement of Disputes on the New Natural Resources 217 (René-Jean Dupuy ed., 1983).
87. For instance, in *ispace 2040 Vision Movie,* the startup envisages "the Moon supporting construction, energy, steel procurement, communications, transportation, agriculture, medicine, and tourism..." ispace Inc., *ispace 2040 Vision Movie*, YouTube (13.12.2017), available online.
88. Williamson, *supra* note 84 at 447.
89. 1959 Report of the *ad hoc* UNCOPUOS, *supra* note 14, §76.

In practice, some amount of contamination on celestial bodies is expected during and after having conducted space activities; it is simply unavoidable.[90] This contamination principally originates from terrestrial material used on landers and gas released from rocket exhaust and astronaut life support systems.[91] Human presence in space also adds to the contamination by spreading organic material.[92] For instance, the Apollo 14 mission recorded, in 1971, the presence of "descent engine exhaust, Lunar Module depressurization, spacesuit materials and exhaust and leakage, human and food waste products and two golf balls" on the Moon.[93] Although the golf balls could have been avoided, the other contaminating materials could not. Thus, when discussing the protection of the environmental impact of space activities in the outer space environment, it is important to keep in mind that some contamination is unavoidable and that the real question is to which extent it is acceptable.

In general, the focus is rather narrowed to biological contamination of outer space because of scientists' search for extraterrestrial life, which can result in non-biological contamination being somewhat overlooked.[94] Mars, for instance, already is contaminated with small amounts of radioactive leftover materials.[95] Admittedly, the impact on research from the foreign material on the Martian surface is relatively limited since all contaminated sites are known.[96] As such, when conducting activities near these sites, it is possible to distinguish between radioactive leftovers and natural Martian substances. Furthermore, it can be observed that—due to the lack of a tenuous atmosphere on the Moon, Mars, and asteroids—gases released during missions are quickly dissipated by the solar winds through photoionization.[97]

However, with the development of NewSpace activities in general and space resource enterprises in particular, this could change rather quickly. Clearly, part of the reason why contamination is being disregarded is that it is short-lived. Yet, this shortness of time is intrinsically linked to the recurrence of space activities.[98] Though the lack of atmosphere contributes to the dissipation of gases, it is also the key factor in their large spreading. Studies show that gases will spread over a distance of "hundreds of kilometers."[99] Consequently, even if the mining sites were to be remote from one another, there would still be a risk of overlaps. These overlaps in addition to recurrent—or even permanent—activities could lead to a permanent modification of

90. Michael B. Duke, Wendell W. Mendell & Paul W. Keaton, Report of The Lunar Base Working Group 9 (1984).
91. Richard R. Vondrak, *Lunar Base Activities and the Lunar Environment, in* Lunar Bases and Space Activities of the 21st Century 337, 340 (Wendell W. Mendell et al. eds., 1992); A. Debus, *Estimation and assessment of Mars contamination*, 35 Advances in Space Research 1648, 1650 (2005) DOI: 10.1016/j.asr.2005.04.084.
92. D.P. Glavin et al., *Biological Contamination Studies of Lunar Landing Sites: Implications for Future Planetary Protection and Life Detection on the Moon and Mars*, 3 International Journal of Astrobiology 265, 265–266 (2004) DOI: 10.1017/s1473550404001958.
93. *Id.*, at 266.
94. Williamson, *supra* note 81 at 163.
95. Debus, *supra* note 90 at 1651.
96. *Id.*
97. Vondrak, *supra* note 90 at 341.
98. Williamson, *supra* note 81 at 164.
99. Vondrak, *supra* note 90 at 341.

the lunar, or Martian, atmosphere.[100] The continuous release of chemicals, or gases naturally trapped in extraterrestrial minerals, would not allow the solar winds to do their work and "clean" the environment.[101]

Moreover, it is necessary to consider the nature of the power sources spacecraft and satellites will use in the context of space mining operations. Although it is still unknown whether methods to extract and process space resources will involve the use of nuclear materials, it can already be noted that both American missions to Mars launched in 2020—Perseverance and Curiosity—rely on nuclear power sources, using plutonium dioxide to allow for a longer mission.[102] It is not farfetched to imagine similar sources being used for mining activities on Mars or asteroids from the Main Belt due to their distance from Earth. It means that the seriousness of the threat of nuclear explosions also needs to be considered.[103] Mining activities will certainly increase satellite operations in lunar and Martian orbits and, with it, the risks of collision events. A nuclear explosion resulting from a collision between a nuclear-powered space object and another object in space—including debris—could spread radioactive materials over thousands of kilometers and create an electromagnetic field that would break all electronic communications.[104]

1.2.1.c Overexploitation of Space Resources

As with any natural resource, overexploitation is a cause for issues. Earth is full of overexploitation examples for both limited and renewable resources: overfishing, deforestation, fossil fuels, and metal, to name a few.[105] In outer space, the situation is no different.

Although outer space is infinite, it would be delusional to think its resources are as well. There is simply a definite number of resources in an infinite space. Even this theoretically infinite (outer) space is not practically so. Although there is no known natural limit to the extent of outer space, there is certainly a human one, and human activities—such as space resource activities—can only spread as far as humans are capable of. This limited character of resources available in space is already being acknowledged legally in the case of radio frequencies. The International Telecommunication Union (ITU) Convention states in its Article 44 paragraph 2 that "radio frequencies and any associated orbits, including the geostationary-satellite orbit, are *limited natural resources*" (emphasis added).[106] Accordingly, the provision calls for their "rationa[l], efficien[t], and economi[c]" use.

100. Williamson, *supra* note 81 at 164.
101. For an explanation on the effects of solar winds on the lunar surface, *see* Serm Murmson, *Does the Moon Have Solar Wind Storms?*, SCIENCING (2017), available online.
102. NASA, *Electrical Power*, MARS NASA SCIENCE, available online. Meghan Bartels, *Why NASA's Mars rover Perseverance Will Use Nuclear Power to Keep Itself Warm*, SPACE.COM (2020), available online.
103. VIIKARI, *supra* note 1 at 47-48.
104. *Id.*, at 48-49.
105. ESA, *13. Exploitation of Natural Resources* (2008), available online.
106. Although the provision was amended to include the term "rationally" in addition to "efficiently and economically" in 1998 during the Plenipotentiary Conference, the Constitution was already extending the expression "natural resource" to radiofrequencies and GEO since the 1973

However, it would be too simple, and quite a thin justification for their regulation, to stop ourselves at only stating celestial bodies' resources are limited. Rather, a distinction must be drawn between the types of celestial bodies that are targeted for space resource exploitation and processing. Among the ocean of scientific uncertainty that reigns in the domain of space studies, there exist some known facts: the Moon is Earth's only natural satellite, there is only one "planet Mars" in our solar system, and there are plenty of asteroids out there, such as from NEAs and the Main Belt. Consequently, while the Moon and Mars' resources can be quantified and qualified, it is not so easy for asteroids.[107] Therefore, the Moon and Mars appear more susceptible to risks of overexploitation, while their resources are more limited in quantity.

For instance, it was suggested that in order to obtain 1 kg of Helium 3—a material particularly sought by space actors for its use as propellant—250 tons of lunar regolith would have to be collected and processed.[108] Thus, lest a total prohibition of the exploitation of space resources should be promoted, it does raise the question of the extent to which exploitation of space resources should be allowed.

Pushed to the extreme, overexploitation could lead to the exploitation "out of existence" of celestial bodies. Celestial bodies contain materials that are, for some, extremely scarce on Earth—like Helium 3—or scarce in space, like water. These materials are considered essential for the development of a long-term presence in space.[109] Then, it would be logical for space actors to want to extract a maximum of the sought material for optimal benefice, to the point where nothing of the celestial body would be left behind. This problem is generally referred to in relation to the appropriability of space resources since full exploitation of a celestial body can be regarded as equivalent to its appropriation.[110] However, there is more to it since it can be argued that the loss of an entire celestial body amounts to an environmental degradation of outer space.

Realistically, such cases are more likely to occur with asteroids rather than with the Moon or Mars. It is hardly fathomable that the international community would accept otherwise, especially considering, *inter alia*, the Moon-Earth system.[111] Nonetheless, the question remains whether exploiting asteroids out of existence is acceptable from an environmental perspective.

Plenipotentiary Conference. Constitution of the International Telecommunication Union, *entered into force* July 1, 1994, Art. 44§2, 1825 UNTS 330.

107. According to Lewis, in 2014, there were about 980 NEAs and "well over" 100,000 catalogued asteroids in the Main Belt. JOHN S. LEWIS, ASTEROID MINING 101: WEALTH FOR THE NEW SPACE ECONOMY 75, 91 (David Gump ed., 2015).
108. Williamson, *supra* note 81 at 163.
109. LEWIS, *supra* note 106 at 99.
110. Steven Freeland, *Common Heritage, Not Common Law: How International Law Will Regulate Proposals to Exploit Space Resources*, 35 QIL, 23 (2017); Gabrielle Leterre, *Providing a Legal Framework for Sustainable Space Mining Activities*, 32–35 (2017).
111. Earth and the Moon are dependent of each other. Among other benefits, the Moon helps protecting Earth from being hit by meteorites and keeps it on a stable orbit. Jonathan O'Callaghan, *What Would Happen If We Blew up the Moon?*, SPACE ANSWERS (2013), available online.

1.2.2 *Ethical Approaches to (Outer Space) Environmental Protection*

Without drifting into the intricacies of the ethics of space exploration—i.e., what we should and should not do in space—[112] considering ethical approaches to environmental protection is fundamental when asserting that outer space is an "environment."[113] At this stage, we already accept that outer space is an "environment" rather than a "mere phenomenon" and that it is worthy of protection.[114] The question remains though of the extent to which it "deserves" to be protected. This is where ethics—and more precisely environmental ethics—come into play. These ethical approaches originate in the terrestrial environment; they have been subsequently extended to outer space.[115] Various versions exist, but two are particularly prominent, with the others gradually moving toward one or the other: anthropocentrism and ecocentrism. The former focuses on humans and their interests, whereas the latter considers that the environment has an intrinsic value that is worthy of protection in itself, independent of human interests. Depending on the ethical approach through which a situation is viewed, the response is likely to vary.

1.2.2.a Anthropocentrism

For the anthropocentric environmentalist, the natural environment has no intrinsic value;[116] rather, its value is measured by the extent to which it can answer human

112. Mark Williamson, *Space Ethics and Protection of the Space Environment*, 19 Space Policy 47, 48 (2003) DOI: 10.1016/s0265-9646(02)00064-4. According to Arnould, space ethics can be described as the "duty [...] to question ourselves about the raison d'être for our activities, [about] why do we today, like yesterday and hopefully tomorrow, send rockets, satellites, men and women into outer space, and then [...] about the consequences of these activities. The direct [positive and negative] consequences on the environments that these men, women or objects encounter; the consequences for us, earthlings, who do not go to space but enjoy [it]." Jacques Arnould *"On a besoin d'aller dans l'espace pour mieux vivre sur Terre"*, Podcast de l'Aviation (2021). For a brief history of space ethics, *see* Jacques Arnould, Icarus' Second Chance: The Basis and Perspectives of Space Ethics 2 (2011). Space ethics covers several areas of space exploration and use. For instance, the UNESCO/COMEST's Working Group on "Ethics of Outer Space" chose to focus on "the presence of man in space and manned flights, the development of science and space technology, the use of space technologies, protection of the environment and protection of public freedoms and cultural identities." The Ethics of Space Policy, *supra* note 61 at 6.
113. J. D. Rummel, M. S. Race & G. Horneck, *Ethical Considerations for Planetary Protection in Space Exploration: A Workshop*, 12 Astrobiology 1017, 1019 (2012); Saara Reiman, *Is Space an Environment?*, 25 Space Policy 81, 84 (2009) DOI: 10.1016/j.spacepol.2009.03.005.
114. The question of whether outer space is considered an environment or not is fundamental when discussing the environmental protection of outer space. As Reiman explains, "the concept of environment is a term loaded with implications and background assumptions." To accept that outer space is an "environment" rather than only a phenomenon implies in itself ethical considerations. Reiman, *supra* note 112 at 81; Federico Bergamasco, *Space Mining and The Protection of Extra-Terrestrial Environment in The Light of Article IX of The Outer Space Treaty*, 60 *in* IISL Proceedings 1, 1 (2017).
115. Bergamasco, *supra* note 113 at 1; Rummel, Race, and Horneck, *supra* note 112 at 1019.
116. Walter E. Block & J. H. Huebert, *Space Environmentalism, Property Rights, and the Law*, 37 U. MEM. L. REV. 281, 283 (2007).

needs.[117] Admittedly, environmental protection and anthropocentrism could appear contradictory, as if the ethical approach was directly opposing human interests to nature's preservation. However, as explained above, "environment" does not automatically refer to the "natural environment," and, by extension, environmental protection is not limited to protecting nature per se. Rather, the anthropocentric environmentalist believes in the protection of the natural environment to the extent that it is necessary to safeguard human interests. The Stockholm Declaration—seen by some as "the mother of all environmental declarations"[118]—is a good example of instruments aiming to protect the environment and, yet, conforming to an anthropocentric approach.[119]

On Earth, this desire to protect the environment is justifiable by the terrestrial environment being practically a close system.[120] Simply put, it means that disregarding the environment hurts us in the end. Earth is filled with examples where our lack of concern for the environment has come back biting us. An example of a chain reaction is the increasing extinction of bumblebees.[121] Bumblebees are the most important pollinators on Earth; they contribute to the spreading of pollen and fertilizing wild flora as well as crucial agricultural crops like tomatoes.[122] Their decline in numbers is the result of climate change and global warming, which, as we know, is caused by human activities.[123] More generally, studies show that only focusing on human interests without taking into account the environment—such as cases of overexploitation of natural resources—leads to, *inter alia*, "declines in economic growth."[124] Thus, there is a rationale, even when adopting an anthropocentric approach, to protect the terrestrial environment.

But, what about outer space? Contrary to Earth, outer space is considered mostly lifeless.[125] There is no ecosystem that humans are dependent on that would justify protecting the environment. Thus, it is unlikely that outer space would benefit from the same status in the eyes of anthropocentrists.[126] Roberts, for instance, remarks that due to their inhospitable nature, most celestial bodies "serve no purpose except in their

117. Viikari, *supra* note 1 at 15.
118. Romano, *supra* note 3 at 21.
119. The Declaration focuses heavily on human interests, referring to the *human* or *man-made* environment throughout its text. Paragraph 1 of the preamble, in particular, states that "[b]oth aspects of man's environment, the natural and the man-made, are essential to his well-being and to the enjoyment of basic human rights the right to life itself"; thus, making the natural environment an element of the human environment. Stockholm Declaration, *supra* note 57.
120. Bergamasco, *supra* note 113 at 1.
121. Douglas Main, *Bumblebees Are Going Extinct in a Time of 'Climate Chaos,'* Animals (2020) available online.
122. *Id.*
123. Peter Soroye, Tim Newbold & Jeremy Kerr, *Climate Change Contributes to Widespread Declines among Bumble Bees Across Continents*, 367 Science 685 (2020) DOI: 10.1126/science.aax8591; IPCC, *Climate Change 2014: Synthesis Report. Contribution of Working Groups I, II and III to the Fifth Assessment Report of the Intergovernmental Panel on Climate Change*, 32 2 (2014).
124. Adam Lampert, *Over-Exploitation of Natural Resources Is Followed by Inevitable Declines in Economic Growth and Discount Rate*, 10 Nature Communications 1419 (2019) DOI: 10.1038/s41467-019-09246-2.
125. Bergamasco, *supra* note 113 at 2.
126. Reiman, *supra* note 112 at 82.

relationship to human activity."[127] Nonetheless, he assures that is no reason to allow unlimited exploitation of these celestial bodies, only that the imitation should be considered from a "human-centered perspective."[128] He also goes a step further by suggesting moving polluting industries into space, thus, sparing Earth from their negative effects.[129] This textbook case of anthropocentrism leads to a very limited protection of the outer space environment.

Yet, when confronted with existing situations, anthropocentrism is not as lenient as it sounds initially. After all, turning outer space in our messy backyard is not particularly conclusive of space activities. The problem caused by space debris is a good illustration: if not controlled eventually, it will hinder space activities. Without taking care of reducing space debris in Earth orbit—and once activities start in other celestial bodies' orbits—the risks of collision will increase to dangerous levels.[130] For this reason, States have made sure to adopt policies and guidelines that aim at reducing space debris, thus limiting the pollution of the outer space environment.[131] Similarly, since the beginning of space activities, States have concerned themselves with planetary protection—i.e., limiting the contamination of visited celestial bodies—in order to preserve their environment for future scientific research.[132] It is also possible to imagine that, for the same reason, the exploitation of space resources will not be carried out without limits. When approaching these limitations from a human-centered perspective, as suggested by Robert,[133] it becomes apparent that in order for space resource activities to be sustainable, space actors cannot allow themselves to be shortsighted.[134] As previously indicated, space resources are limited and nonrenewable. Without a rational management of the exploitation, space actors run the risk of overexploiting and losing their long-term investment. It follows that anthropocentrism—while not primarily concerned with the environment—does offer solutions to existing environmental problems in outer space.

It could even be argued that anthropocentrism goes further than commercial and scientific values when considering ethically acceptable activities in outer space.[135] In addition to balancing environmental protection and human interests, one must also consider various human interests among themselves. How does the protection of cultural

127. Lawrence D. Roberts, *Ensuring the Best of All Possible Worlds: Environmental Regulation of the Solar System*, 6 N.Y.U. ENVTL. L. J. 126, 148 (1997).
128. *Id.*
129. *Id.* For an extreme anthropocentric view of outer space, *see* Block and Huebert, *supra* note 115. In their opinion, outer space should be, *inter alia*, treated as the "ultimate waste dump," notably for toxic materials with which we struggle to eliminate. *Id.*, 296–297.
130. Dietrich Rex, *Will Space Run out of Space? The Orbital Debris Problem and Its Mitigation*, 14 SPACE POLICY 95 (1998) DOI: 10.1016/s0265-9646(98)00004-6.
131. *See*, for instance, UNCOPUOS SDM Guidelines.
132. To that end, the ISCU established COSPAR in 1958, an international group of experts entrusted with defining a planetary protection policy. This "Planetary Protection Policy" is regularly updated by the Committee and has been implemented by, *inter alia*, the American National Aeronautics and Space Administration (NASA), the European Space Agency (ESA) and the Japan Aerospace Exploration Agency (JAXA). *See* COSPAR in Chapter 3 *infra*.
133. Roberts, *supra* note 126 at 148.
134. Bergamasco, *supra* note 113 at 2.
135. Reiman, *supra* note 112 at 83.

and historical sites fare against the economic interest in strip mining the Moon?[136] Could economic development justify the degradation of the Apollo missions' sites and artifacts like the footprints and trails taken by astronauts or the American flags they raised?[137] In a similar manner, Williamson highlights aesthetical and cultural concerns when asking to what degree mining craters on the Moon should be visible.[138] There is a possibility that craters from extensive mining activities on the near side of the Moon—the one visible from Earth—might be visible with the naked eye. Would that be acceptable? From an anthropocentric perspective, these questions could be considered when determining to which extent the Moon should be used. Thus, though anthropocentrism limits the scope of environmental issues considered directly linked to the environment per se, it also allows for a broader understanding of "environmental" issues.

1.2.2.b Ecocentrism

Ecocentrism is often presented as the opposite of anthropocentrism, for it supports the preservation of the environment, even at the expense of human material quality life.[139] For ecocentric environmentalists, the environment has an intrinsic value that is independent of human needs and worthy of protection.[140] There is beauty in nature's work, and it should be protected and preserved rather than be sacrificed at the altar of human fancy.

It could be argued that in outer space, ecocentrism—also called "astro-environmentalism"—[141] has developed in its purest form; the environment is not only valued beyond humans' interests but also regardless of the presence of living organisms since outer space is mostly lifeless.[142] Rolston argues that the outer space environment should be appreciated for its "exotic extreme."[143] Who is to say that Saturn's rings are paralleled somewhere else in the Universe? Just as humans should enjoy Earth's diversity, they should enjoy the solar system's. The outer space environment should also be respected for its aesthetic value, its "poetry."[144] Each celestial

136. *Id.*, III Holmes Rolston, *The Preservation of Natural Value in the Solar System*, *in* BEYOND SPACESHIP EARTH: ENVIRONMENTAL ETHICS AND THE SOLAR SYSTEM 140, 174–175 (1986).
137. Reiman, *supra* note 112 at 83. On the preservation of lunar historical sites, *see* OFFICE OF SCIENCE AND TECHNOLOGY POLICY, *Protecting & Preserving Apollo Program Lunar Landing Sites & Artifacts*, 8 (2018).
138. Williamson, *supra* note 81 at 164.
139. Vito De Lucia, *Beyond Anthropocentrism and Ecocentrism: A Biopolitical Reading of Environmental Law*, 8 J. HUM. RTS. & ENV'T. 181, 191 (2017); Suzanne C. Gagnon Thompson & Michelle A. Barton, *Ecocentric and Anthropocentric Attitudes Toward the Environment*, 14 JOURNAL OF ENVIRONMENTAL PSYCHOLOGY 149, 150 (1994) DOI: 10.4337/jhre.2017.02.01.
140. Gagnon Thompson and Barton, *supra* note 138 at 149; Williamson, *supra* note 111 at 42; Mark Williamson, *Protection of the Space Environment: The First Small Steps*, 34 ADVANCES IN SPACE RESEARCH 2338, 2340 (2004) DOI: 10.1016/j.asr.2003.01.034.
141. Astro-environmentalism finds its origins in the idea that humanity should learn from past (terrestrial) experiences and avoid repeating the same mistakes with regard to the environment. Ryder W. Miller, *Astroenvironmentalism: The Case for Space Exploration as An Environmental Issue*, 1 ELECTRONIC GREEN JOURNAL, 1 (2001) DOI: 10.5070/g311510439.
142. Bergamasco, *supra* note 113 at 2.
143. Rolston, *supra* note 135 at 170–182.
144. *Id.*, at 177.

body has its own inner beauty, be it its morphology, its geology, or energy.[145] For instance, Hartmann underlines that, on Mars, there are "volcanoes bigger than Everest and canyons a hundred times bigger than the Grand Canyon" in the United States of America.[146]

Consequently, the primary concern of astro-environmentalists is to preserve the outer space environment in its pristine state.[147] Such an approach would thus consider terraforming activities—that is, the process of planetary engineering modifying a celestial body's atmosphere and topography to create an Earth-like ecosystem—[148] unacceptable.[149] For instance, in order to terraform Mars, the first steps would involve thickening the atmosphere and raising the surface temperature to melt water, a necessity to create an Earth-like ecosystem.[150] Then, considering that the interest in terraforming other celestial bodies is to allow humans to live there, it is possible to imagine that the Martian environment would suffer drastic changes in its morphology and topology, Earth being a prime example of environmental changes caused by human civilization.

Yet, when considering the value of ecocentrism to protect the outer space environment, it is necessary to remember that terraforming is an extreme expression of environmental modifications—and, from an ecocentric standpoint, of environmental degradation. Similarly, pushed to its extreme, ecocentrism would not allow for any change in the environment; any type of contamination of the outer space environment would be rejected, human interests becoming subsidiary and conditioned to the maintaining of a pristine environment.[151] Such an extreme approach in outer space would not be sustainable unless the international community ceases space activities entirely since there is always some degree of unavoidable contamination when exploring celestial bodies.[152]

Thus, when considering ethical models for the protection of the outer space environment, it is necessary to confront them with the reality of space activities. Currently, space activities doubtlessly rely on an anthropocentric model, with elements of biocentrism—a form of ecocentrism focused on biological elements—showing. This conclusion is supported by the various "environmental" measures adopted by the international community to address environmental issues. Since the beginning of space activities, the international community has sought to protect the space environment from "harmful contamination" to preserve the integrity of the scientific exploration of

145. Rolston, *supra* note 135.
146. William K. Hartmann, *Space Exploration and Environmental Issues, in* BEYOND SPACESHIP EARTH: ENVIRONMENTAL ETHICS AND THE SOLAR SYSTEM 119, 130–131 (1986).
147. Bergamasco, *supra* note 113 at 2.
148. James S. J. Schwartz, *On the Moral Permissibility of Terraforming*, 18 ETHICS AND THE ENVIRONMENT 1, 1 (2013) DOI: 10.2979/ethicsenviro.18.2.1.
149. Miller, *supra* note 140 at 2.
150. Schwartz, *supra* note 147 at 6.
151. Bergamasco, *supra* note 113 at 2.
152. DUKE, MENDELL, AND KEATON, *supra* note 89 at 9.

outer space, including the search for indigenous life.[153] As a result, a committee was created in 1958: the Committee on Space Research (COSPAR).[154] It has since developed a "planetary protection policy" which is regularly updated to limit forward and backward contamination.[155] In a similar instance, the international community has adopted "space debris mitigation guidelines" to address the hindrance resulting from the increase of space debris in Earth orbit.[156]

Therefore, it is clear that both ecocentrism and anthropocentrism display environmental concerns and an interest in preserving the outer space environment; their distinction lies in the motives for their interests.[157] Neither ethical approach is superior; it is only a matter of how one perceives outer space's value. For some, its value is intrinsic, whereas for others, it lies in its infinite possibilities for humanity to unfold. Ecocentrism is particularly useful to overcome the diversity of—and sometimes contradictory—human interests, but it lacks an objective criterion to distinguish between legitimate and unacceptable space activities.[158] Anthropocentrism easily adapts to current human interests and needs. However, since we are not omniscient, only the most obvious problems are considered when trying to anticipate the needs of future generations.

Neither of the two ethical approaches stands out as being objectively *the* one to assist in the definition of the outer space environment and its protection. Although anthropocentrism is reflected in the practice of space actors, it has failed to anticipate the space debris problem and will most likely fail to anticipate environmental issues arising from space resource activities. Ecocentrism would be more conducive to avoiding unforeseen environmental problems, but in the absence of a complete scientific understanding of the space environment, it is particularly limiting.

In the end, despite an extensive analysis of various elements that would, prima facie, assist in articulating a comprehensive definition of the outer space environment, we are left with several questions and only the beginning of an answer: where does outer space begin? To what does the word "environment" refer? What consequences will space resource activities have on the outer space environment? Which ethical approach is more conducive to protecting the environment without impeding humanity's new venture into space? Under these circumstances, it is difficult to provide a definition of the outer space environment beyond "the area where space resource activities are carried out."

Although the consideration of the outer space environment is important when aiming for the long-term sustainability of space resource activities, it is only one-half of the equation. According to the ICJ, sustainability infers the "need to reconcile

153. Committee to Review the Planetary Protection Policy Development Processes et al., *Chapter 2. Historical Origins of Planetary Protection Policies*, *in* THE GOALS, RATIONALES, AND DEFINITION OF PLANETARY PROTECTION: INTERIM REPORT (2017).
154. *See infra* Chapter 3.
155. *See* Chapter 3, COPSAR on the organization's PP policy.
156. UNCOPUOS' SDM Guidelines.
157. Gagnon Thompson and Barton, *supra* note 138 at 149.
158. Bergamasco, *supra* note 113 at 2.

economic development with protection of the environment."[159] Thus, rather than framing the general problem of regulating the unknown environmental consequences of space resource activities in terms of where it will occur physically, I propose to analyze it through the lens of sustainability.

2 WHAT IS "SUSTAINABILITY" IN OUTER SPACE?

In its 1987 report *Our Common Future* ("Brundtland report"),[160] the UN World Commission on Environment and Development (WCED) refers to outer space as a "key to planetary management."[161] It calls attention to the utility of space systems in the pursuit of sustainable development on Earth, noting that Earth observation activities help increase knowledge about Earth's systems and contribute to scientific discoveries.[162] The Commission also underlines the value of the Geostationary Earth Orbit (GEO) for communications and weather satellites—it is "the most valuable part of the Earth's orbital space"—emphasizing its "scarce and limited" nature as a global resource.[163] The Brundtland report further includes a noteworthy reference to the "growing threat" of space debris to human activities in space,[164] a topic that has just started gathering interest at the national and international levels.[165]

Although the WCED only allocates a couple of pages to "space," it is not without importance. The Commission is often credited with having defined the concept of sustainable development at the international level.[166] Before its work, there was no authoritative definition, the concept having only been mentioned by a handful of scholars.[167] Therefore, the Brundtland report not only establishes the concept of sustainability but also connects it to outer space from the start.

This connection was emphasized on several occasions within the framework of the United Nations, notably during UNCOPUOS meetings.[168] More remarkably, the matter was mentioned, albeit briefly, by the UN General Assembly in the context of the adoption of Sustainable Development Goals (SDGs) in 2015, as part of the *2030 Agenda*

159. Gabčíkovo-Nagymaros Project (Hungary v. Slovakia) (Judgment), §140, 1997 ICJ 7 (September 25).
160. Report of the World Commission on Environment and Development: Our Common Future, Chapter 2, para. 1, *in* Report of the World Commission on Environment and Development, UNGAOR, 42nd Sess., Supp. 20, Annex, UN Doc. A/42/427 (1987) ["Brundtland report"].
161. World Commission on Environment and Development, *Report of the World Commission on Environment and Development: Our Common Future*, 186 (1987).
162. The WCED recalls how satellites helped confirm, in 1986, that a "hole" had formed in the ozone layer above Antarctica. *Id.*, at Chapter 10, paras. 58-60.
163. *Id.*, at Chapter 10, paras. 64-73.
164. *Id.*
165. Henry T. Scott, *Improving the Shield: Mitigating the Danger of Space Debris by Enforcing and Developing Already Existing Space Law Section II: Space Law: Part A: Leading Articles*, 34 Annals Air & Space L. 713, 723 (2009).
166. Oluf Langhelle, *Sustainable Development: Exploring the Ethics of Our Common Future*, 20 International Political Science Review 129, 131 (1999) DOI: 10.1177/0192512199202002.
167. *Id.*
168. *See, e.g.*, Unedited transcript, UNCOPUOS, 536th Meeting, COPUOS/T.536 (2005); Future role and activities of the Committee on the Peaceful Uses of Outer Space, UNCOPUOS, 50th Sess., UN Doc. A/AC.105/L.268 (2007).

for Sustainable Development.[169] They set out a series of objectives for all Member States to achieve by 2030.[170] In this regard, the body alluded to the utility of Earth observation and geolocation systems for the realization of societal goals on Earth.[171] This connection between terrestrial sustainability and outer space is further made apparent by the development, within the United Nation Office for Outer Space Affairs (UNOOSA), of an initiative that resulted, *inter alia*, in the publication of a joint study with the European GNSS Agency in 2018; it analyzes the contribution of space systems to each of the 17 SDGs.[172] Accordingly, space-based services and technologies support, *inter alia*, the forecasting of natural disasters, the optimization of crop productivity, the enablement of remote healthcare, high-speed internet, remote participation in democratic processes as well as search and rescue operations.[173]

Gradually, the growing awareness within the space community of the socio-economic benefits of space activities led to the question of the sustainability of space activities themselves.[174] This evolution of the common mindset is reflected in the notes of the 2007 UNCOPUOS Chairman about "the role and future activities" of the Committee. He remarks that:

> [the work done] during the last few years on space debris mitigation has demonstrated that a safe environment for space activities is no longer a given if one takes a long-term view. Not only is the space debris situation of concern to all, but the ever-larger number of actors in space, including the commercial actors, makes it imperative to agree on some kind of "rules of the road" to avoid interference, collisions and other mishaps that may hamper the use of outer space by all, particularly by the newcomers in space operations.[175]

In other words, the Chairman calls for the development of practical steps, or guidelines, which will help achieve sustainability in outer space. However, as noted by delegations to the UNCOPUOS in 2008, defining these rules is a "very complex and a

169. GA Res. 70/1, UNGAOR, 70th Sess., UN Doc. A/RES/70/1 (2005).
170. The Member States agreed on, *inter alia*, a set of 17 goals and 169 targets. The 17 SDGs are: no poverty; zero hunger; good health and well-being; quality education; equality; clean water and sanitation; affordable and clean energy; decent work and economic growth; industry, innovation and infrastructure; reduced inequalities; sustainable cities and communities; consumption and production; climate action; life below water; life on land; peace, justice and strong institutions; and partnerships for the goals.
171. Transforming our world: the 2030 Agenda for Sustainable Development, *supra* note 169, §76.
172. UNOOSA, European Global Navigation Satellite System and Copernicus: Supporting the Sustainable Development Goals (2018).
173. For a detailed overview of how space-based services and technologies may contribute to each of the SDGs, *see* Space4SDGs: How space can be used in support of the 2030 Agenda for Sustainable Development, UNOOSA (n.d.), available online.
174. For instance, former Chairman of the UNCOPUOS' STC Dr. Karl Doetsch notes that "in the future it will not be enough to restrict attention simply to space applications on Earth. It is clear that our future has a component in space, and it is this component that will increasingly capture the attention of future generations, not only because of the innate desire to explore, but more importantly, because of the significance that extraterrestrial resources will eventually play in life on Earth." UN Doc. COPUOS/T.536, *supra* note 168, §26.
175. Future role and activities of the Committee on the Peaceful Uses of Outer Space, *supra* note 168.

comprehensive task."[176] It requires delimiting the scope of the work, starting with the definition of "space sustainability."[177]

Although headways have been made since then—notably through the work of the UNCOPUOS Working Group on the Long-Term Sustainability of Outer Space Activities ("UNCOPUOS' LTS Working Group") established in 2010—the focus remains predominantly on achieving sustainability in LEO.[178] As a result, this targeted approach has led to space sustainability being associated with phrases such as "space situational awareness" and "space traffic management."[179] Admittedly, these mechanisms contribute to the sustainability of space systems in LEO. Yet, they are not sufficient to address the specific challenges raised by space resource activities. As an example of the shortcomings of such a restricted approach, one can consider that activities on the Moon will likely require the development of satellite constellations in lunar orbit, satellites which at some point will cease to be functional.[180] In LEO, one of the key measures developed to mitigate the generation of new space debris is deorbiting. It consists in moving nonfunctional objects to a lower orbit so that they may reenter the Earth's atmosphere and burn up. However, as underlined earlier, on the Moon, this measure is not sustainable: Earth's only natural satellite has no tangible atmosphere which would allow for space objects to burn up and disintegrate upon entry into the lunar atmosphere.[181] Accordingly, achieving "space sustainability" within the context of space resource activities will require adopting different practical measures than the ones already developed for LEO.

Another key difference is that measures adopted for activities in LEO were developed based on existing issues, such as the ones created by space debris. In the case of space resource activities, there is no issue to solve since activities have yet to start. One short-term—and shortsighted—solution would be to wait and see how activities—and related problems—develop. This is not the approach promoted in this work. A simple reference to the space debris issue in LEO shows that such an approach is not sustainable. Even now, with space debris measures in place, the outcome is not the "clean-up" of Earth orbits. There are no remediation measures, only mitigation ones that focus on avoiding the generation of new space debris. Another solution—the one proposed here—is to anticipate problems before they arise. To that end, we propose to anchor the long-term sustainability of space resource activities into existing legal concepts, starting with the definition of "space sustainability" before referring to the broader concept of sustainable development.[182]

176. Interventions of Chile and of the Russian Federation *in* UN Doc. COPUOS/T.536, *supra* note 168, pp. 13–15.
177. *Id.*, Interventions of Chile and of France.
178. Christopher J. Newman & Mark Williamson, *Space Sustainability: Reframing the Debate*, 46 Space Policy, Volume 46, pp. 30–37, 30, 31 (2018) DOI: 10.1016/j.spacepol.2018.03.001.
179. *Id.*
180. *Id.*, at 32.
181. *Id.*
182. Interventions of Chile *in* UN Doc. COPUOS/T.536, *supra* note 168.

2.1 Space Sustainability

> [T]he ability to maintain the conduct of space activities indefinitely into the future in a manner that realizes the objectives of equitable access to the benefits of the exploration and use of outer space for peaceful purposes, in order to meet the needs of the present generations while preserving the outer space environment for future generations.
>
> —UNCOPUOS' Long-Term Sustainability Guidelines[183]

The expression "space sustainability" finds several equivalents in literature, such as "usability of outer space" or "continuity" and "viability" of space activities.[184] They all refer to the same ambition: ensuring humankind's capacity to continue "us[ing] outer space for peaceful purposes and socio-economic benefit over the long-term."[185] Yet, an overview of the literature on the matter shows that the complexity of the notion does not lay in the plurality of synonyms for the same goal, but rather in the fact that space sustainability is a concept with several layers. Indeed, the expression takes a different meaning depending on the perspective adopted and the context in which it is analyzed.

In outer space, the concept of space sustainability first manifested regarding the "sustainability of the hardware."[186] At the beginning of the Space Age, the longevity of activities was not a priority; the scientific community is focused on accomplishing singular goals, such as launching a satellite into orbit.[187] It is a period of acclimatization, where the focus is on space discovery and technology development. Gradually, the experience gained led space scientists to develop more resistant space systems to allow for a longer observation of the outer space environment and its evolution over time: they make the hardware sustainable.[188] In turn, the reliability of hardware allows for the development of bigger space projects, spanned over longer periods of time. It is the beginning of space programs.

With this expansion of space activities comes new concerns regarding their sustainability, such as their financial, political, and environmental sustainability. From a financial standpoint, sustainability translates into the necessity to maintain the

---

183. Guidelines for the Long-term Sustainability of Outer Space Activities of the Committee on the Peaceful Uses of Outer Space *in* Report of the Committee on the Peaceful Uses of Outer Space, UNGAOR, 62nd Sess., at Annex II §5, UN Doc. A/74/20 (2019) ["2019 LTS Guidelines"].
184. *See, e.g.*, Rada Popova & Volker Schaus, *The Legal Framework for Space Debris Remediation as a Tool for Sustainability in Outer Space*, 5 Aerospace 55, 55 (2018); M. Palmroth et al., *Toward Sustainable Use of Space: Economic, Technological, and Legal Perspectives*, 57 Space Policy 101428, 101428 (2021); Annie Handmer & Steven Freeland, *The Use of Law to Address Space Debris Mitigation and Remediation: Looking Through a Science and Technology Lens*, 87 Journal of Air Law and Commerce 375, 385 (2022) DOI: 10.25172/jalc.87.3.2; Newman and Williamson, *supra* note 177 at 31.
185. Ray A. Williamson, *Assuring the Sustainability of Space Activities*, 28 Space Policy 154, 155 (2012) DOI: 10.1016/j.spacepol.2012.06.010.
186. Newman and Williamson, *supra* note 177 at 31.
187. *Id.*
188. *Id.*

financial ability to execute a space program within a realistic budget over time.[189] For governmental activities, financial sustainability is further intrinsically linked to the project's political sustainability. Governmental space programs are often fully financed by public funds, which means that their liberation generally requires the approval of a political entity.[190] Moreover, they are also often scheduled to be executed over a period that spans longer than the duration of political mandates. Accordingly, space programs must be developed in a way that allows them to withstand political shifts, as a lack of political approval could result in the abandonment of the project.[191] To that end, they must, for instance, promote the long-term interests of the sponsoring States to maintain both public and political support.[192] The importance of financial and political sustainability is illustrated by the case of the American Apollo space program. It was cut short in 1972, with the last three missions being canceled because of, *inter alia*, a lack of political support. In particular, the financial strain of the Vietnam War resulted in budgetary cuts which made maintaining the space program unsustainable.[193] Until then, the program had been able to withstand three American presidencies.[194]

Another approach to sustainability—and the one of interest here—is environmental sustainability. With the increase in space activities, this approach has become the subject of many discussions. It focuses on the environmental impact of (space) activities and calls attention to the necessity to "maintain the natural capital" unimpaired for as long as the activity needs to be sustained.[195] It emphasizes responsible behavior toward the environment, by looking at the use of renewable and nonrenewable resources and avoiding wasting and polluting practices.[196] In outer space, ensuring environmental sustainability means acknowledging the limits of the outer space environment as a host for activities and acting accordingly. In this sense, the adoption of space debris mitigation measures contributes to the environmental sustainability of NEOs.

However, as previously indicated, these measures are not sufficient to address sustainability concerns resulting from space resource activities on celestial bodies. They do not provide, for instance, an indication of how to rationally manage the utilization of *in situ* resources. Accordingly, discussing "space sustainability" requires

189. *Id;* Luis Carrio et al., *Understanding Sustainability in the Human Exploration Campaign, in* 2022 IEEE Aerospace Conference (AERO) 1, 8 (2022) DOI: 10.1109/aero53065.2022.9843579.
190. Newman and Williamson, *supra* note 177 at 31.
191. David A. Broniatowski & Annalisa L. Weigel, *The political sustainability of space exploration*, 24 Space Policy 148, 148 (2008) DOI: 10.1016/j.spacepol.2008.06.004.
192. *Id.*
193. *See generally* Monika Gisler & Didier Sornette, *Exuberant Innovations: The Apollo Program*, 46 Soc 55 (2009) DOI: 10.1007/s12115-008-9163-8.
194. The Apollo program lasted over a decade and was executed under three different presidencies: Kennedy's, Johnson's and Nixon's. Amy Shira Teitel, *How JFK, LBJ and Nixon All Put Their Stamp on the Apollo 11 Moon Landing*, HISTORY (2019), available online.
195. Robert Goodland, *The Concept of Environmental Sustainability*, 26 Annual Review of Ecology and Systematics 1, 10 (1995) DOI: 10.1146/annurev.es.26.110195.000245; John Morelli, *Environmental Sustainability: A Definition for Environmental Professionals*, 1 Journal of Environmental Sustainability Article 2, 1 (2013).
196. Goodland, *supra* note 194 at 10.

not only adopting a specific approach to the matter but also considering the specific context to which it is applied. As Aganaba-Jeanty puts it:

> [d]epending on the forum for discussion [...] the concept of space sustainability is also used interchangeably with the following: (1) space security, which entails access to space and freedom from threats; (2) space stability addressing space situational awareness; (3) space safety, which is protection from all unreasonable levels of risk (primarily protection of humans or human activities); and (4) responsible uses of space.[197]

Because the meaning of "space sustainability" operates on a large spectrum of interpretations, based on the perspective adopted and the context, it acts as an umbrella term which covers a wide range of topics.[198]

As a result, some authors opt not to define the concept, focusing instead on its finality—i.e., ensuring the long-term continuity of the activity—or highlighting the absence of an authoritative definition.[199] Others explicitly define their approach to the matter or rely on the definition adopted, in 2018, by the UNCOPUOS' LTS Working Group in the preamble of their *Guidelines for the Long-Term Sustainability of Outer Space Activities*[200] ("LTS Guidelines").[201] It states that space sustainability is:

> the ability to maintain the conduct of space activities indefinitely into the future in a manner that realizes the objectives of equitable access to the benefits of the exploration and use of outer space for peaceful purposes, in order to meet the needs of the present generations while preserving the outer space environment for future generations.[202]

---

197. Timiebi Aganaba-Jeanty, *Space Sustainability and the Freedom of Outer Space*, 14 Astropolitics 1, 11 (2016).
198. *See, e.g.*, the list of topics identified by the UNCOPUOS' LTS Working Group in 2011. Terms of reference and methods of work of the Working Group on the Long-Term Sustainability of Outer Space Activities of the Scientific and Technical Subcommittee *in* UNGAOR, Report of the Committee on the Peaceful Uses of Outer Space, UNGA, 54th Sess., Annex II, UN Doc. A/66/20 (2011).
199. For examples of academic work discussing space sustainability without defining the concept, *see, e.g.*, Kevin MacWhorter, *Sustainable Mining: Incentivizing Asteroid Mining in the Name of Environmentalism*, 40 Wm. & Mary Envtl. L. & Pol'y Rev. 645 (2016); Larry F. Martinez, *Legal Regime Sustainability in Outer Space: Theory and Practice*, 2 Global Sustainability e26 (2019) DOI: 10.1017/sus.2019.21; Mahulena Hofmann & Federico Bergamasco, *Space Resources Activities from the Perspective of Sustainability: Legal Aspects*, 3 Global Sustainability (2020) DOI: 10.1017/sus.2019.27. The lack of authoritative definition has been underlined, for instance, by Viikari, *supra* note 1 at 143; Anthi Koskina & Konstantina Angelopoulou, *Space Sustainability in the Context of Global Space Governance*, 2 Athena 29, 31 (2022); Rong Du, *China's Approach to Space Sustainability: Legal and Policy Analysis*, 42 Space Policy 8, 8 (2017) DOI: 10.1016/j.spacepol.2017.10.005.
200. 2019 LTS Guidelines, *supra* note 183.
201. "space sustainability is understood to be [...]" Peter Martinez, *Space Sustainability*, *in* Handbook of Space Security: Policies, Applications and Programs 257 (Kai-Uwe Schrogl et al. eds., 2015); "space sustainability is explored as [...]" Aganaba-Jeanty, *supra* note 196; "[t]his study understands the concept of space sustainability as defined by the working group on the long-term space sustainability of outer space activitie [...]" Aurélie Trur, *Governance Aspects of Space Sustainability: The Role of Epistemic Actors as Enablers of Progress*, 180 Acta Astronautica 451, 451 (2021) DOI: 10.1016/j.actaastro.2020.10.012.
202. 2019 LTS Guidelines, *supra* note 183, §5.

Such a definition reflects a consensus among UNCOPUOS' Member States, granting it some authority.[203] Furthermore, the definition has the benefit of being comprehensive; it encompasses a wide range of activities. Yet, the price to pay for inclusiveness is a lack of guidance on how to achieve space sustainability. In practice, the definition is part of a broader instrument—the LTS Guidelines—which aims to guide States into implementing sustainable practices. However, as will be discussed in Chapter 3, it remains that these Guidelines are rather limited in scope, as they focus foremost on space activities in NEO. As a consequence, referring to the definition of "space sustainability" provided by the UNCOPUOS' LTS Working Group means that we are left with only the vague guidance of a broad text.

Still, several elements of the Working Group's definition echo the one adopted by the WCED, in 1987, regarding the concept of sustainable development. Therefore, in the absence of an authoritative legal interpretation of the concept addressing the sustainability of space resource activities from an environmental approach, it may be possible to find answers in the broader concept of sustainable development under international law.

2.2 Sustainable Development

> Sustainable development is development that meets the needs of the present without compromising the ability of future generations to meet their own needs.
>
> —Brundtland report

The concept of sustainable development has been debated in legal circles since the UN Conference on the Human Environment held in Stockholm, Sweden, from June 5 to 16, 1972. Since then, numerous scholars have contributed to the growing literature on the subject.[204] Although it offers rich material, this advantage is paid for by an extreme diversity of points of view regarding its nature and content.[205] In fact, the only consensus to date among scholars appears to be on the lack of common agreement regarding the definition of "sustainable development."[206]

203. The UNCOPUOS adopted the 21 LTS Guidelines and the preamble—which defines space sustainability—during its 62nd session. Report of the Committee on the Peaceful Uses of Outer Space, UNGAOR, 62nd Sess., §163, UN Doc. A/74/20 (2019).

204. *See, e.g.*, SUSTAINABLE DEVELOPMENT IN INTERNATIONAL AND NATIONAL LAW (Hans Christian Bugge & Christina Voigt eds., 2008); KLAUS BOSSELMANN, THE PRINCIPLE OF SUSTAINABILITY: TRANSFORMING LAW AND GOVERNANCE (2016); INTERNATIONAL LAW AND SUSTAINABLE DEVELOPMENT: PAST ACHIEVEMENTS AND FUTURE CHALLENGES (Alan E. Boyle & David Freestone eds., 2001).

205. Iliopoulos and Esteban observe, for instance, that "the notion of sustainability which is multi-dimensional and ambiguous in nature has brought to life a number of divergent discourses over time." Nikolaos Iliopoulos & Miguel Esteban, *Sustainable Space Exploration and Its Relevance to the Privatization of Space Ventures*, 167 ACTA ASTRONAUTICA 85, 86 (2020) DOI: 10.1016/j.actaastro.2019.09.037.

206. Koskina and Angelopoulou, *supra* note 198 at 31; Thomas Cheney et al., *Planetary Protection in the New Space Era: Science and Governance*, FRONT. ASTRON. SPACE SCI. 1, 7 (2020); Olaf

Yet, it would be a mistake to confuse diversity of opinions for lack of substance. On the contrary, the broadness of the concept is partially responsible for the "considerable consensus" which has developed regarding its core idea,[207] as evidenced by its incorporation in numerous international instruments.[208] Therefore, while no international consensus has yet been reached regarding the concept's content, it is possible to identify elements that are commonly accepted as part of sustainable development by referring, *inter alia*, to its evolution within international instruments and jurisprudence.

When the concept of "sustainable development" was first explicitly introduced at the international level, it was by the WCED, in 1987, with the adoption of the Brundtland report.[209] Established by a UN General Assembly resolution in 1983,[210] the Commission acts as an independent body "linked to but outside the control of governments and the UN system."[211] In order to "reflect world realities" and to "formulate an interdisciplinary, integrated approach,"[212] the Commission itself had to be as inclusive and diverse as possible. Careful attention is paid to including members with different competences, experiences, and cultural backgrounds. Among a total of 22 members, 21 nations are represented, including countries from the North and the South—i.e., developed and developing countries, and from East and West—i.e., from both blocs of

Steffen, *Explore to Exploit: A Data-Centred Approach to Space Mining Regulation*, 59 SPACE POLICY 1, 2 (2022) DOI: 10.3389/fspas.2020.589817.

207. The Brundtland report, which is often cited as a reference for defining the concept, touches on this aspect, noting that "[i]nterpretations will vary, but must share certain general features and must flow from a consensus on the basic concept of sustainable development and on a broad strategic framework for achieving it." Brundtland report, *supra* note 160, Chapter 1, §2. Also *see* Herman E. Daly, *Sustainable Development: From Concept and Theory to Operational Principles*, 16 POPULATION AND DEVELOPMENT REVIEW 25 (1990) DOI: 10.2307/2808061.

208. The core ideas of sustainable development have been introduced in, *inter alia*, Agreement on the Conservation of Nature and Natural Resources, July 9, Art. 1, §1, 1985, 15 Environmental Policy & L. 64 (not yet in force) "sustainable development"; United Nations Framework Convention on Climate Change, *entered into force* Mar. 21, 1994, Arts. 2 and 3, §4, 1771 UNTS 107 ["UNFCCC"] "sustainable manner" and "sustainable development"; United Nations Convention on the Law of the Sea, *entered into force* Nov. 16, 1994, Arts. 61 and 119, 1833 UNTS 3 ["UNCLOS"] "sustainable yield." More generally, *see* Carlos Alberto Ruggerio, *Sustainability and Sustainable Development: A Review of Principles and Definitions*, 786 SCIENCE OF THE TOTAL ENVIRONMENT 1, 1 (2021) DOI: 10.1016/j.scitotenv.2021.147481.

209. Brundtland report, *supra* note 160. Although the Brundtland report is the first explicit international instrument to use the expression, several authors argue that the concept can be traced back further than the 20th century. Techera et al. remark that, in Europe, variations of the concept of sustainable development can be observed as early as the 14th century. ROUTLEDGE HANDBOOK OF INTERNATIONAL ENVIRONMENTAL LAW, 38–39 (Erika J. Techera et al. eds., 2nd ed. 2021). Going back further, Bosselmann suggests that "the underlying idea [of sustainable development] is probably as old as humanity's struggle with the forces of nature." 1 ENVIRONMENTAL LAW FOR A SUSTAINABLE SOCIETY, 97 (Klaus Bosselmann & David P Grinlinton eds., 2nd ed. 2013). Likewise, Vice President Weeramantry observes, in a Separate Opinion in *Gabčíkovo-Nagymaros*, that "[t]he concept of reconciling the needs of development with the protection of the environment [i.e., sustainable development] is thus not new. Millennia ago, these concerns were noted, and their twin demands well reconciled in a manner so meaningful as to carry a message to our age." Separate Opinion of Vice President Weeramantry *in* Gabčíkovo-Nagymaros, *supra* note 159, §98.

210. GA Res. 38/161, UNGA, 38th Sess., UN Doc. A/RES/38/161 (1983).

211. Brundtland report, *supra* note 160, From One Earth to One World, §9.

212. *Id.*, Foreword.

the Cold War.[213] Appointed members are a mix of scientists, politicians, economists, and ecologists.[214] To ensure broader participation, the WCED also conducted public hearings and invited various entities to provide their input.[215] Ultimately, the aim is to bring to the work of the Commission "a variety of values and attitude, perceptions of the problems they were to discuss, and expectations."[216]

In practice, the Commission was asked to work on two main themes: (1) development, as it was noted that it is still not uniform between countries and (2) environment, as a result of the increased awareness regarding the limited nature of natural resources.[217] It is not the first time that these two topics are brought together within the framework of the United Nations. As early as 1972, the Stockholm Declaration calls for the reconciliation of "any conflicts" between the two.[218] This conciliatory approach is confirmed a decade later with the adoption of the *World Charter for Nature* by the UN General Assembly in 1983.[219] This nonlegally binding document calls, *inter alia*, for the management of resources to "achieve and maintain optimum sustainable productivity," affirming that "living resources shall not be utilized in excess of their natural capacity for regeneration."[220] It further supports that:

> [i]n formulating long-term plans for economic development, population growth and the improvement of standards of living, due account shall be taken of the long-term capacity of natural systems to ensure the subsistence and settlement of the populations concerned, recognizing that this capacity may be enhanced through science and technology.[221]

Here, the preservation of the environment is seen "as a prerequisite for the use of natural resources and development planning."[222]

The Charter provides many elements that are common with the ones promoted by the WCED. This is the case with the idea of environmental integration. However, the Commission's approach to sustainability is sensibly broader. As Bosselmann explains

213. Hans Christian Bugge, *1987–2007: "Our Common Future" Revisited*, *in* SUSTAINABLE DEVELOPMENT IN INTERNATIONAL AND NATIONAL LAW 2, 4 (Hans Christian Bugge & Christina Voigt eds., 2008).
214. Brundtland report, *supra* note 160, Foreword. Also *see* Annex I for a list and description of the background of each WCED member.
215. *See* the end of the Brundtland report which provides a list of many of the "thousands of individuals, institutes, and organizations the world over" which have provided the Commission with their input. *Id.*, at 352–374. Also *see* Bugge, *supra* note 212 at 5.
216. *Id.*, Bugge.
217. Brundtland report, *supra* note 160, Foreword; BOSSELMANN, *supra* note 203 at 31.
218. For instance, Principle 14 of the Stockholm Declaration provides that "[r]ational planning constitutes an essential tool for reconciling any conflict between the needs of development and the need to protect and improve the environment." The reconciliation approach adopted in the *Stockholm Declaration* is particularly noteworthy when compared to the one defended by the Club of Rome the same year. In *Limits to Growth*, the latter argues that development and environment are "on a collision course." Thus, where the former advocates for the reconciliation of the two elements, the Club of Rome sees them as opposite value. DONELLA H. MEADOWS ET AL., THE LIMITS TO GROWTH: A REPORT FOR THE CLUB OF ROME'S PROJECT ON THE PREDICAMENT OF MANKIND (2. ed. 1974).
219. GA Res. 37/7, UNGAOR, 37th Sess., UN Doc. A/RES/37/7 (1982).
220. *Id.*, at 4 and 10§a.
221. *Id.*, at 8.
222. BOSSELMANN, *supra* note 203 at 26.

it,[223] originally, the concept of "sustainability" referred to "ecological sustainability," meaning "the preservation of the substance or integrity of ecological systems."[224] Thus, it is understandable that when initially discussing the terms of reference for the WCED, some members of the UN General Assembly argued in favor of limiting the scope solely to "environmental issues."[225] However, in Brundtland's opinion, such constraints would have been "a grave mistake" since "[t]he environment does not exist as a sphere separate from human actions, ambitions, and needs."[226] "Environment" and "development" are seen here as two "inseparable" elements which are "inexorably linked."[227]

This is the reason why the concept of "sustainable development" is quite broader than—and to an extent distinct from—the original concept of "sustainability."[228] Sustainable development is seen as a multidimensional concept, which is based on three equally important pillars: social, economic, and environmental.[229] Thus, it would be tempting to consider that (ecological) sustainability only amounts to one-third of the concept, i.e., the environmental pillar. Yet, as Bosselmann underlines, "[t]here is only ecological sustainable development or no sustainable development at all."[230] Indeed, it is impossible to establish "sustainable" practices in the long term without taking into account the impact of human activities on the environment. In this sense, we agree with Bosselmann's affirmation that "[s]ustainable development needs to be understood as an application of the principle of sustainability, not the other way round."[231]

It does not mean that the broader concept of sustainable development should be abandoned for the exclusive benefit of the notion of sustainability when promoting environmental protection. First, the concept explicitly balances the anthropocentric notion of development and the ecological sense of environmental protection. Therefore, in the context of space activities—a predominantly anthropocentric domain—the concept seems more relevant to the work than ecological sustainability. Second, it is important to keep in mind that sustainable development has been the subject of discussions for a half-century, thus amassing rich literature regarding its content, legal value, and implementation. These discussions, in addition to increased implementation efforts globally, make it a proven tool. It can also be noted that, though the matter is not yet settled among scholars, there is a tendency to consider that the concept of sustainable development has now replaced the much older concept of sustainability.[232]

It is true that the richness of the discussions around the notion of sustainable development is often reduced to a single sentence of the Brundtland report, the one which defines sustainable development as:

---

223. For a comprehensive analysis of the distinction between the concepts of "sustainability" and the "sustainable development," *see generally* BOSSELMANN, *supra* note 203.
224. *Id.*, at 25.
225. Brundtland report, *supra* note 160, Foreword.
226. *Id.*
227. *Id.*, Foreword and Chapter 1, §40.
228. BOSSELMANN, *supra* note 203 at 23.
229. Hugh Wilkins, *The Integration of the Pillars of Sustainable Development: A Work in Progress*, 4 MCGILL INT'L J. SUST. DEV. L. & POL'Y 163 (2008).
230. BOSSELMANN, *supra* note 203 at 21.
231. *Id.*, at 10.
232. *Id.*, at 23.

> the development that meets the needs of the present without compromising the ability of future generations to meet their own needs.[233]

This isolated sentence is often quoted by the literature as defining the entire concept.[234] This simplification amounts to neglecting the reality of the work of the WCED, which actually devotes an entire paragraph to expanding on its meaning. Specifically, the Commission affirms that the concept of sustainable development "contains within it two key concepts:

- the concept of 'needs', in particular the essential needs of the world's poor, to which overriding priority should be given; and
- the idea of limitations imposed by the state of technology and social organization on the environment's ability to meet present and future needs."[235]

Starting with the notion of "needs," it can be observed that it is a central concern of the WCED and a recurring theme in the Brundtland report. It is closely linked to the concept of development since, in the words of the Commission, "the satisfaction of human needs and aspirations" is "the major objective of development."[236] Although the Commission's definition of sustainable development emphasizes the needs of "the world's poor"—i.e., of developing countries—[237] a careful reading of the report shows that its interest goes beyond purely economic needs. Indeed, "[p]erceived needs are socially and culturally determined";[238] they include, *inter alia*, food, water supply, sanitation, shelter, health care, and employment.[239] Already, this conception goes further than a simply "economic" definition. A note from Katappo, included in the report, also makes it clear that the list is neither limited to these needs nor limiting. It asserts that "[people's] basic needs include the right to preserve their cultural identity, and their right not to be alienated from their own society, and their own community."[240] Ultimately, the Commission affirms that "sustainability requires views of human needs and well-being that incorporate such non-economic variables as education and health enjoyed for their own sake, clean air and water, and the protection of natural beauty."[241] Therefore, the concept of "needs" adopted by the WCED encompasses both social and economic development.

The Commission goes even further by emphasizing the connection of such considerations with the question of the environment. It comes from the observation

233. Brundtland report, *supra* note 160, Chapter 2, §1.
234. Andrew Blowers & Pieter Glasbergen, *7 The search for sustainable development*, 1 *in* ENVIRONMENTAL POLICY IN AN INTERNATIONAL CONTEXT 163, 163 (Pieter Glasbergen & Andrew Blowers eds., 1995); Ruggerio, *supra* note 207 at 3.
235. The expression "world's poor" refers to "developing countries," which is understood in the report as "the UN grouping of developing-country market economies and the socialist countries of Asia." Brundtland report, *supra* note 160, Foreword and Chapter 2, §1.
236. *Id.*, Chapter 2, §4.
237. In this context, "developing countries" refers to "the UN grouping of developing-country market economies and the socialist countries of Asia." *Id.*, Foreword.
238. *Id.*, Chapter 2, §5.
239. *Id.*, Chapter 2, §§4, 43, 47.
240. *Id.*, Chapter 1, §10.
241. *Id.*, Chapter 2, §38.

that "[p]overty reduces people's capacity to use resources in a sustainable manner," thus "intensif[ying] pressure on the environment."[242] Accordingly, rather than promote a limit to economic growth, the Brundtland report advocates for the achievement of "full growth potential *in places where such needs are not being met*" [emphasis added].[243] Though the Commission does not deny economic growth elsewhere, it remains mindful of the danger that strong inequalities between societies pose to the environment.[244] In this sense, "[g]rowth has no set limits in terms of population or resource use beyond which lies ecological disaster."[245] Effectively:

> ultimate limits there are, and sustainability requires that long before these are reached, the world must ensure equitable access to the constrained resource and reorient technological efforts to relieve the pressure.[246]

With this in mind, the WCED makes suggestions on how to achieve a careful balance between growth and environmental protection to achieve sustainable development. It puts forward that the exploitation of renewable resources should be "within the limits of regeneration and natural growth."[247]

These considerations are per se easily applicable to space activities, but the Commission does not limit itself to the conceptualization of sustainable development. Ultimately, the concept of sustainable development, as outlined in the Brundtland report, aims to provide "a framework for the integration of environment policies and development strategies."[248] This leads, among other aspects, to articulate a recommendation regarding the exploitation of nonrenewable resources which are of particular interest in the context of space resource activities. The Commission argues that, though "their [non-renewable resources'] use reduces the stock available for future generations," "this does not mean that such resources should not be used."[249] Transposed to the conditions of space resource activities, this recommendation leads to affirming that the exploitation of space resources can be considered sustainable despite their availability in limited quantity. According to the Commission, to be sustainable:

> [their] rate of depletion should take into account the criticality of that resource, the availability of technologies for minimizing depletion, and the likelihood of substitutes being available. [...] [With minerals], the rate of depletion and the emphasis on recycling and economy of use should be calibrated to ensure that the resource does not run out before acceptable substitutes are available. Sustainable development requires that the rate of depletion of non-renewable resources should foreclose as few future options as possible.[250]

242. *Id.*, Chapter 2, §§4, 6 and 29; Bugge, *supra* note 212 at 7–8.
243. *Id.*, Brundtland report, Chapter 2, §6.
244. *Id.*, Chapter 2, §6.
245. *Id.*, Chapter 2, §10.
246. *Id.*
247. *Id.*, Chapter 2, §12.
248. *Id.*, Chapter 1, §40.
249. *Id.*, Chapter 2, §13.
250. *Id.*

The emphasis on "future options" points out the relationship between present and future generations, which is another key feature of the concept of sustainable development.[251] It is often reflected in the expression "long-term sustainability of." The *rationale* is that, even if we were not seeking to continue a given activity in the long term, it still has an environmental cost. As noted by the WCED:

> [m]any present efforts [...] draw too heavily, too quickly, on already overdrawn environmental resource accounts to be affordable far into the future without bankrupting those accounts. They may show profit on the balance sheets of our generation, but our children will inherit the losses. We borrow environmental capital from future generations with no intention or prospect of repaying.

As such, it is not sufficient to consider what can be achieved today; humankind further needs to be concerned with what it will do tomorrow. Although generations change, the environment remains. However, without careful management of natural resources, the environment does not have the time to regenerate. In other words, although the environment remains generation after generation, it may not remain the same. Incidentally, the Brundtland report does not only refer to the needs of future generations but their "own" needs. The subtlety is noteworthy as it acknowledges that, in the future, societies may have needs that differ from ours, hence, the necessity to "foreclose as few future options as possible."[252]

Eventually, the work of the Commission was received with both praise and criticism.[253] Specifically, the Brundtland report has been criticized by scholars for "diluting" the environmental question as well as for the vagueness of the concept it outlines.[254] Some consider that it has "obscured" the original meaning of sustainability; others consider that it has "no real substance," thus allowing for multiple—if not contradictory—interpretations.[255]

Nevertheless, the impact of the Brundtland report on the international scene is not negligible: it has played a major role in the growing environmental awareness at the international level, and its ramifications extend to the major landmark of the "Rio Declaration,"[256] which was "designed as the successor to the Stockholm Conference."[257] However, "legal and political developments as identified in the Brundtland

---

251. The expression "present generation," on the one hand, encompasses all the people living now, including newborns and elderly. In this context, they are part of the same "present" generation. "Future generations," on the other hand, refer to all the generations yet to be born. They "do not vote; they have no political or financial power; they cannot challenge our decisions." *Id.*, From One Earth to One World, §25.
252. *Id.*, Chapter 2, §13.
253. Brian R. Keeble, *The Brundtland Report: "Our Common Future,"* 4 MEDICINE AND WAR 17, 24 (1988) DOI: 10.1080/07488008808408783.
254. Bugge, *supra* note 212 at 19.
255. *Id;* BOSSELMANN, *supra* note 203 at 23.
256. Rio Declaration on Environment and Development *in* Report of the United Conference on Environment and Development, UNGAOR, Annex I, UN Doc. A/CONF.151/26/rev.1 (Vol. 1) (1992), endorsed by GA Res. 47/190, UNGAOR, 47th Sess., UN Doc. A/RES/47/190 (1992) ["Rio Declaration"].
257. Dinah Shelton, *Stockholm Declaration (1972) and Rio Declaration (1992)*, MAX PLANCK ENCYCLOPEDIAS OF INTERNATIONAL LAW 29 (2008).

report shifted the focus of the conference."[258] In the evolution of the UN General Assembly, which went within 20 years from addressing the topic of the "human environment" (Stockholm Declaration) to the one of "environment and development" (Rio Declaration), the Brundtland report has represented a major step forward.

Bugge's description of the Rio Conference is one of "high tensions, vigorous debates and extremely active participation from civil society, scientists, business leaders and many others."[259] The UN Conference brought together over 172 States, including 116 heads of States or government, and more than 2,400 nongovernmental organization (NGO) representatives.[260] Yet, despite high and diverse participation, as well as the achievement of global consensus on several topics, the event is still considered by most a "lost opportunity." Although it resulted in the elaboration of five texts,[261] including the Rio Declaration and *Agenda 21*, none resulted in the adoption of a legally binding document on "environment and development."[262] Nor do they provide a consensus on the definition of the concept of sustainable development. Still, the Rio Declaration and *Agenda 21* do provide "rules of the road" toward the achievement of sustainable development.

Notwithstanding its voluntary character, the Rio Declaration is an "important landmark" in interpreting the concept of sustainable development.[263] Composed of 27 "interlinked and [...] interdependent" principles, the document represents a carefully negotiated balance between a plurality of diverse interests.[264] From an ethical standpoint, the Rio Declaration explicitly adopts an anthropocentric approach to environmental protection. Principle 1 states that:

> *[h]uman beings are at the centre* of concerns for sustainable development. They are entitled to a healthy and productive life in harmony with nature [emphasis added].

Interestingly, in comparison to the Stockholm Declaration, Principle 1 seems to subtly move away from the environmental question per se, choosing instead to contextualize it in relation to economic development by reference to sustainable development.[265]

---

258. *Id.*
259. Bugge, *supra* note 212 at 19.
260. Klaus Bosselmann, *Sustainable Development Law, in* Routledge Handbook of International Environmental Law 30, 33 (Erika J. Techera et al. eds., 2020); Shelton, *supra* note 256 at 29.
261. Agenda 21 *in* Report of the United Conference on Environment and Development, UNGAOR, Annex II, UN Doc. A/CONF.151/26/rev.1 (Vol. 1) (1992); Non-legally Binding Authoritative Statement of Principles for a Global Consensus on the Management, Conservation and Sustainable Development of All Types of Forests *in id.*, Annex III; UNFCCC *supra* note 208; Convention on Biological Diversity, *entered into force* Dec. 29, 1993, 1760 UNTS 79 ["CBD"].
262. The two legally binding conventions—i.e., the UNFCCC and CDB—address respectively global climate change and the conservation of biological diversity. *Id.*
263. Luc Hens, *The Rio Declaration on Environment and Development*, II *in* Area Studies: Regional Sustainable Development: Africa 162, 162 (Emmanuel Kwesi Boon ed., 2002).
264. Rio Declaration on Environment and Development: application and implementation, ECOSOC, 5th Sess., at 15, UN Doc. E/CN.17/1997/8 (1997).
265. Principle 1 of the Stockholm Declaration provides, *inter alia*, that "[humanity] bears a *solemn responsibility to protect and improve the environment* for present and future generations" [emphasis added]. Stockholm Declaration, *supra* note 57.

It can also be observed that Principle 2 updates the text of the Stockholm Declaration's Principle 21 to reflect developmental concerns.[266] Principle 2 provides that:

> States have, *in accordance with the Charter of the United Nations and the principles of international law*, the sovereign right to exploit their own resources pursuant to their own environmental *and developmental* policies, and the responsibility to ensure that activities within their jurisdiction or control do not cause damage to the environment of other States or of areas beyond the limits of national jurisdiction [emphasis added].[267]

The wording clearly affirms the necessity to anchor environmental and developmental questions in policies, therefore advocating a focus on adequate implementation. Moreover, Principle 2 grounds its statement in binding international law, and the reference to principles of international law allows for a dynamic interpretation of the provision, one able to reflect evolutions in international environmental law.

More generally, the Rio Declaration encompasses in a formal form all the elements of sustainable development outlined by the Brundtland Commission. For instance, Principle 3 of the Declaration recalls the necessity to balance environment and development for the benefit of both present and future generations when affirming a right to development.[268] In a similar manner, Principle 4 reaffirms the inherent link between environment and development, asserting that:

> [i]n order to achieve sustainable development, environmental protection shall constitute an integral part of the development process and cannot be considered in isolation from it.

This connection between environment and development is consistently reinforced throughout the instrument.[269]

In addition to formalizing the findings of the WCED, the Rio Declaration identifies and formulates rules—"principles"—aimed at guiding States into their pursuit of sustainable development, most of them now forming part of international environmental law. Among them are, for instance, the precautionary approach as well as a general obligation for States to undertake an environmental impact assessment (EIA);[270] both are discussed in detail *infra* in Chapter 2. The instrument also repeatedly calls for international cooperation, as it would, *inter alia*, improve the exchange of useful scientific and technological knowledge for achieving sustainable development.[271] Last,

266. Jeffrey D. Kovar, *A Short Guide to the Rio Declaration United Nations Conference on Environment and Development (UNCED*, 4 Colo. J. Int'l Envtl. L. & Pol'y 119, 125 (1993).
267. The emphasis reflects the amendments of the Rio Declaration to the original formulation of Principle 21 of the Stockholm Declaration. *See* Stockholm Declaration, *supra* note 57, Principle 1.
268. It provides "[t]he right to development must be fulfilled so as to *equitably meet developmental and environmental needs* of *present and future generations*" [emphasis added]. Rio Declaration, *supra* note 256, Principle 3.
269. For example, *id.*, Principles 7 and 8; Shelton, *supra* note 256 at 35.
270. Rio Declaration, *supra* note 256, Principles 15 and 17.
271. *Id.*, Principle 9. More generally, the Rio Declaration refers to international cooperation in its preamble as well as in Principles 5, 7, 12, 13, 14, 24 and 27.

the Rio Declaration encourages the adoption, at the national level, of adapted environmental legislation to implement the results of the Conference.[272]

Therefore, the Rio Declaration provides an elaborated road toward sustainability, one which has been agreed upon by over 175 States, including both developed and developing countries. The price for consensus, however, is a Declaration with broadly phrased principles recognizing the necessity for the language of the principles to allow for different degrees of implementation. Although the Rio Declaration is a nonlegally binding instrument, this strategic use of language mirrors the approach of international treaties: imprecision in the terms or in the statement of general obligations is characteristic of instruments negotiated by several States, as we will *see infra*.

This is where *Agenda 21* comes into play.[273] This instrument is the second outcome of the 1992 Rio Conference. It identifies "programme areas and specific action" to operationalize the concept of sustainable development.[274] In particular, *Agenda 21* addresses "the pressing problems of [the time] and also aims at preparing the world for the challenges of the next century."[275] It can further be noted that the instrument "reflects a global consensus and political commitment at the highest level on development and environment cooperation."[276]

In substance, *Agenda 21* is divided into a preamble and four umbrella sections covering a total of 39 chapters,[277] each identifying diverse "programme areas."[278] These programs are structured around four elements: (1) basis for action, (2) objectives, (3) activities, and (4) means of implementation. They focus, *inter alia*, on "management-related activities," "financing and costs evaluation" as well as "data and information" collection. Altogether, *Agenda 21* formulates some 3,500 recommendations for action in a variety of areas, such as deforestation, climate change, ocean protection, and desertification. Although some of these recommendations are incidentally relevant to sustainable mining,[279] it must be underlined that *Agenda 21* does not directly discuss the activity.

This changed in 2012, when Heads of State and Government as well as high-level representatives met in Rio de Janeiro once more for the UN Conference on Sustainable

272. *Id.*, Principle 11; Kovar, *supra* note 265 at 132.
273. Agenda 21, *supra* n. 261.
274. *Id.*, at 6. Also *see*, *e.g.*, Chapter 8 which concerns the integration of the environment and development in decision-making.
275. *Id.*, §1.3.
276. *Id.*
277. The four umbrella sections are: (1) social and economic development, (2) conservation and management of resources, (3) strengthening the role of major groups, and (4) means of implementation.
278. For instance, Chapter 8 focuses on "[i]ntegrating environment and development in decision-making" and contains four program areas: (a) integrating environment and development at the policy, planning and management levels; (b) providing an effective legal and regulatory framework; (c) making effective use of economic instruments and market and other incentives; and (d) establishing systems for integrated environmental and economic accounting. *Id.*, §8.1.
279. Elizabeth Bastida, *Integrating Sustainability into Mining Law: The Experience of Some Latin American Countries*, 51 *in* International Law and Sustainable Development: Principles and Practice 575, 581 (2004). For instance, paragraph 12.12 advises governments to "[u]ndertake and update existing inventories of natural resources, such as [...] minerals" when working on "the issue of desertification and drought." Agenda 21, *supra* n. 261, §12.12.

Development, also known as "Rio + 20." The outcome of the Conference is a document entitled "The future we want" ("Rio + 20 Statement"), which was later endorsed by the UN General Assembly in Resolution 66/228.[280] In addition to reaffirming "all the principles of the Rio Declaration" as well as "past action plans,"[281] the Rio + 20 Statement emphasizes a commitment to, *inter alia*, "address remaining gaps in the implementation of the outcomes of the major summits on sustainable development," identifying "mining" as part of the "thematic areas and cross-sectoral issues."[282] Specifically, it acknowledges that—in the interest of sustainable development—"mining activities should maximize social and economic benefits, as well as effectively address negative environmental and social impacts."[283] To that end, governments and businesses should develop "strong and effective legal and regulatory frameworks, policies and practices" which, *inter alia*, "reduce [...] environmental impacts" of mining.[284] In the 20 years which separate the two Rio Conferences, sustainable mining has become a topic of general interest.

2.3 Developing a Sustainability Conceptual Framework

Despite the existence of several instruments aiming to conceptualize and operationalize sustainable development, we find ourselves circling back to a core issue of the concept: its practical implementation. How does one create, or assess the existence of, "strong and effective legal and regulatory frameworks"? What are the constitutive elements? Or, in Cordonier Segger's words, "[w]hat is the international law on sustainable development?"[285] Scholars have tried their hand at answering this question for years and come to different conclusions.[286] In the absence of an international or scholarly consensus on the subject, it is only possible to identify similarities between proposals. In 2002, the International Law Association (ILA) adopted the *New Delhi Declaration of Principles of International Law Relating to Sustainable Development*[287] ("New Delhi Declaration") which recognizes seven "instrumental" principles: (1) the duty of States to ensure sustainable use of natural resources, (2) the principle of equity and the eradication of poverty, (3) the principle of common but differentiated responsibilities, (4) the precautionary approach, (5) public participation and access to information and justice, (6) the principle of good governance, and (7) the principle of

280. GA Res. 66/228, UNGAOR, 66th Sess., UN Doc. A/RES/66/288 (2012) ["Rio + 20"].
281. *Id.*, §§15–16. "Past action plans" refers, *inter alia*, to *Agenda 21*, the Plan of Implementation of the World Summit on Sustainable Development and the Johannesburg Declaration on Sustainable Development. Report of the World Summit on Sustainable Development, UNGAOR, at Resolutions 1, 2 and Annex, UN Doc. A/CONF.199/20 (2002).
282. *Id.*, §§104, 227–228.
283. *Id.*, §227.
284. *Id.*, §§227–228.
285. Marie-Claire Cordonier Segger, *Sustainable Development in International Law, in* SUSTAINABLE DEVELOPMENT IN INTERNATIONAL AND NATIONAL LAW 86, 181 (Hans Christian Bugge & Christina Voigt eds., 2008).
286. ILA, Resolution 3/2002 on sustainable development, at Annex (2002). Also *see, e.g.*, Bugge, *supra* note 212 at 20.
287. *Id.*, ILA, Resolution 3/2002.

integration and interrelationship, particularly in regard to the three dimensions of sustainable development. Other scholars shorten the list. Bugge, for instance, identifies four "core elements" based on the work of the WCED: (1) social equity and justice, (2) integration of environmental considerations, (3) an "absolute" prohibition to destroy the environment and natural resources, and (4) a long-term view in decision-making.[288]

In the absence of an international or scholarly consensus on the question, it is not possible to affirm that there is one "right list." It is nonetheless possible to identify similarities between proposals. Sands observes that "four recurring elements appear to comprise the legal elements of the concept of 'sustainable development'":[289]

(1) the *principle of inter-generational equity*, which requires to preserve resources for future generations;
(2) the *principle of sustainable use*, which relates to the "rational" or "prudent" use of resources;
(3) the *principle of intra-generational use*, or of equitable use, of natural resources between the present generation;
(4) the *principle of environmental integration*, which requires environmental considerations to be considered when developing social and economic policies.

Sands' list has merits, though it provides more of a direction toward achieving sustainable development than a clear path. While these principles can be used in the context of this work to compare existing standards to their overall aim, they need to be adapted to the context of space activities and mining activities.

For this reason, we choose to have recourse to the less known but highly relevant *Berlin II Guidelines for Mining and Sustainable Development* ("Berlin II Guidelines").[290] There is, it is true, a measure of mystery surrounding the document. There is little information in the literature regarding the implementation of the instrument. The text itself, though published by the United Nations, is difficult to access online. Nonetheless, reference to multiple sources leaves no doubt as regards the content of both the original (Berlin I) and revised (Berlin II) Guidelines as well as their origin.[291]

The Guidelines were first adopted by a body of international mining experts, as an outcome of the 1991 International Roundtable on Mining and the Environment

288. Bugge, *supra* note 212 at 20.
289. Philippe Sands, Principles of International Environmental Law 253 (2nd ed. 2003).
290. The text of the Berlin II Guidelines is reproduced in Annex I. United Nations, Berlin II: Guidelines for mining and sustainable development (2002), available online ["Berlin II Guidelines"].
291. *See, e.g.*, *id.*; Thomas Wälde, *Environmental Policies Towards Mining in Developing Countries*, 10 Journal of Energy & Natural Resources Law 327, 355–357 (1992) DOI: 10.1080/02646811.1992.11432933; Paul G. W. Henderson, *Fiscal Incentives for Environmental Protection: The Way Forward*, 2 The South African Journal of Environmental Law and Policy 151, 168 (1995); Tracy-Lynn Field, State Governance of Mining, Development and Sustainability 245 (2019).

organized by the United Nations and the German Foundation for International Development.[292] The purpose of the roundtable was to discuss sustainable mineral development.[293] The original text of the Berlin Guidelines was revised in 1999, following a second roundtable, thus, giving place to the *Berlin II* Guidelines.[294] This revised version adds a 15th principle that recognizes the "importance of socio-economic impact assessments and social planning in mining operations."[295] The instrument is not legally binding upon States—or the mining industry—and the implementation of the Berlin II Guidelines is entirely voluntary. However, it has the immense merit of providing guidelines outlining a "workable framework for sustainability in mining."[296] Although they do not provide a blueprint for sustainable *space* resource mining, they do offer a workable model and relevant criteria to frame our analysis.

The balance struck in the Berlin II Guidelines between socio-economic development and environmental protection is noteworthy. On the one hand, it calls for "[g]overnments, mining companies and the mineral industries" to recognize *ad minima* "environmental management as a high priority."[297] On the other, it explicitly states that environmental regulations should not create "unnecessary barriers to trade and investment."[298] It is noteworthy because the idea that environmental regulations could create barriers echoes concerns from the space mining industry. They are often seen as a burden, both technically and financially. Ultimately, the link between development and environment—and the essence of sustainable development—can be inferred from Guideline 15. It calls for governments and industries to:

> [e]ncourage long-term mining investment by having clear environmental standards with stable and predictable environmental criteria and procedures.

Thus, Guideline 15 clearly pushes for the mining industry to adopt a long-term view in its operations. It is not dissimilar to the difference between a sprint and a marathon: if you want to last the distance, you must pace yourself. Short-term investments in the use of natural resources lead to maximizing profits—i.e., mining as much as possible in a short period—which is unsustainable. In the words of the WCED, "[these practices] draw too heavily, too quickly, on already overdrawn environmental resource accounts to be affordable far into the future without bankrupting those accounts."[299] The lesson has obviously been learned by the group at the origin of the Berlin Guidelines.

Ultimately, drawing from Sands' list of principles as well as from the model provided by the Berlin II Guidelines, we retain that to be environmentally sustainable, space resource activities need to be governed by a framework that includes, *inter alia*:

292. Berlin II Guidelines, *supra* note 290, at 1.
293. Georges W. Pring, *International Law and Mineral Resources*, *in* MINING, ENVIRONMENT AND DEVELOPMENT: A SERIES OF PAPERS PREPARED FOR THE UNITED NATIONS CONFERENCE ON TRADE AND DEVELOPMENT, 39.
294. FIELD, *supra* note 290 at 245.
295. Berlin II Guidelines, *supra* note 290, at 4.
296. Bastida, *supra* note 278.
297. Wälde, *supra* note 290 at 355.
298. Berlin II Guidelines, *supra* note 290, Guideline 11.
299. Brundtland report, *supra* note 160, From One Earth to One World, §25.

(1) Environmental integration.
(2) The rational management of natural resources.
(3) Inter-generational equity.[300]
(4) A licensing regime to integrate environmental management systems.[301]
(5) Monitoring and auditing of the activity.[302]
(6) An environmental impact assessment.[303]
(7) Preventive and mitigative measures.[304]
(8) Best environmental practices.[305]

Additionally, the framework should encourage parties to adopt reciprocal agreements to reduce the environmental impact of space resource activities (Table 1.1).[306] It could, for instance, allow for one operator to mine space resources and sell part of it to another rather than opening two mines.

Table 1.1 Sustainability Framework for Space Resource Activities

Aim	Action	Rationale
Environmental integration in policies	Incorporate rules on the protection of the outer space environment	Sustainability requires balancing socio-economic development and environmental protection. Hence, the necessity to include rules regarding the protection of the extraterrestrial environment in the framework governing the activity.
	Adopt a licensing process integrating environmental management processes	Licensing can be used to ensure that nongovernmental activities comply with environmental standards set by the authorizing State.
	Require mandatory EIA	EIA requirements compel space actors to consider their environmental impact on outer space when designing the activity. It further provides authorities with relevant data to make an informed decision on whether to authorize the activity.
	Monitor and audit activities	Ensure the continuous compliance of space operators with (environmental) obligations.

300. Although the principle of intra-generational equity is an essential element of sustainable development, it relates to the relationship between the social and economic dimensions of the concept; it would thus be more relevant, *inter alia*, to the topic of the sharing of space benefits among nations than to the environmental protection of outer space. Ruggerio, *supra* note 207 at 1.
301. Berlin II Guidelines, *supra* note 290, Guideline 1.
302. *Id.*
303. *Id.*
304. *Id.*
305. *Id.*, Guideline 6.
306. *Id.*, Guideline 14.

Aim	Action	Rationale
Rational management of natural resources	Manage space resources rationally	This is necessary to avoid overexploitation of space resources.
	Encourage reciprocal agreements to reduce pollution	Celestial bodies offer a variety of resources. It is possible that a mining site will have several resources, not all of which will be needed by the mining entity. Reciprocal agreements would allow other interested entities to negotiate the extraction of these resources by the already operating entity, rather than to extract them from a different mining site. It would maximize the use of existing mining sites and reduce their number on a celestial body.
Inter-generational equity	Integrate a long-term perspective in mission design	Policies should be designed in such a way as to promote long-term activities, notably by emphasizing the need for sustainability.
	Adopt best environmental practices	Best practices continuously evolve, as time increases our knowledge of the outer space environment and our capacity to develop new "environmentally sound technologies."
	Develop preventive and mitigative measures	Mitigative and preventive measures reduce the risks of unnecessary pollution and, as such, contribute to the long-term continuity of activities.

3 CONCLUSION

Words have a meaning, and their meaning, in turn, holds power in the legal field. It is the difference between a legal instrument applying or not, between having rules or anarchy. But what do we do when there are rules and no legal consensus on their meaning? We interpret.

The concept of sustainable development relies on a balance between socio-economic development and environmental protection. As the book considers the sustainability of space resource exploitation from an environmental perspective, defining the object of the protection—i.e., the "outer space environment"—is critical. In the absence of a consensus on the definition, the logical step was to look at the component of the expression separately. Yet, despite being used in all five of the UN Space Treaties, there is no agreement on the delimitation of "outer space." However, as it has been noted, the absence of a definition has not impacted the governance of activities carried out in outer space. Thus, it can be inferred that the outer space environment can be protected without being precisely defined. A further study of the polysemy of the word "environment" showed that, in the context of regulations, what matters is to know exactly what the purpose of the rule is. In the present context, the aim is to prevent the harmful impact of space resource activities on the outer space environment.

As activities have yet to begin, the threats to the environment had to be inferred by drawing parallels between existing terrestrial and potential extraterrestrial environmental threats. Chapter 1 identified three issues. First, space resource activities will likely require the use of satellites in lunar orbit to control operations on the ground. They will also require material on the ground for, *inter alia*, the extraction and processing of *in situ* resources. The use of space objects naturally raises the question of their disposal and runs the risk of creating new debris around exploited celestial bodies. Another issue is the (over) contamination of celestial bodies due to the use of chemical or radiological materials, as well as possible biological contamination through the transfer of organisms or human settlements. Although some contamination is unavoidable due to the nature of space activities, long-term activities may result in unacceptable levels of contamination. Lastly, as with natural resources on Earth, there is a risk for overexploitation, where minerals are exploited without consideration for the depletion rate. Therefore, the definition of the "outer space environment" which is to be protected must allow for rules to mitigate those risks.

However, mitigating risks raises ethical considerations, namely to which extent the environment is to be protected. From an ecocentric approach—the purest form of astro-environmentalism, there arguably is—no contamination would be allowed. It would ensure the outer space environment remains in a pristine state but mark the end of space activities. This is not acceptable from a sustainability perspective, as it would erase the socio-economic component of the concept of sustainable development. On the opposite side of the environmentalism spectrum is anthropocentrism. The latter approach also encourages environmental protection but only to the extent it is in humankind's interests; this is more in line with the concept of sustainability which requires balancing environmental protection with development. Ideally, the environmental approach adopted for space resource activities would be somewhere toward the middle of the spectrum, though having regard to the anthropocentric nature of space activities, it may lean more toward its own end of the spectrum. Ultimately, neither attempts at defining key notions nor ethical considerations allow for a working definition of the "outer space environment," beyond "the area where space resource activities are carried out."

This called for a change of perspective by looking at the research question through the length of sustainability rather than based on what must be protected. A review of the concept showed that space sustainability relied on two elements: longevity of the activity and integration of the environmental elements when designing space activities. Although progress has been made in the development of sustainability measures in the last two decades—such as the adoption of SDM guidelines as well as the LTS Guidelines—it is apparent that efforts are concentrated on achieving sustainability in LEO and GEO. As a result, these instruments are difficult to adopt as a model for space resource activities.

Therefore, the last recourse was to go back to the basis of space sustainability, that is, the broader concept of sustainable development. Although the concept is criticized for its vagueness, it has the merit of having been implemented in and adapted

to a variety of domains, including the mining sector. In this context, the Berlin II Guidelines provide a workable framework to analyze environmental standards within international law and space law and confront them to the requirements of sustainability in the mining industry.
Accordingly, the model provided by the Berlin II Guidelines is used to consider standards relevant to the sustainability of space resource activities on three levels of sources of law:

(1) "traditional" sources of international law, as listed in Article 38 paragraph 1 of the ICJ Statute;
(2) international "soft" law instruments developed in the field of space activities; and
(3) national space legislations, relevant to space resource activities and/or to the environmental protection of outer space.

Chapter 2

International Law

In 1957, humankind successfully launched for the first time an artificial satellite into orbit, thus, showing promise in its capacity to conquer the "last frontier." In a context where the international community is struggling to control the arms race between the two Cold War superpowers on Earth, ensuring the peaceful exploration and use of outer space becomes a priority.[1]

To that end, the UN General Assembly established, in 1958, an ad hoc Committee—the UNCOPUOS—and tasked it with, *inter alia*, "study[ing] and report-[ing] on the legal problems which may arise from the exploration and use of outer space." Securing the peaceful use of outer space is to be achieved by defining international rules which will govern space activities.[2] Accordingly, UNCOPUOS' Member States must work together "[to develop] international law pertaining to the further elaboration of basic legal principles governing [their] [space] activities" and "co-operate in the further development of law for outer space."[3] The outcome is the adoption by the UN General Assembly, between 1967 and 1979, of no less than five space treaties.

At the time of the drafting of the last space treaty, the technology necessary to support space activities related to resource exploitation had yet to develop. As a result, the legal discussion on the exploitation of outer space natural resources could not be anchored into reality. More broadly, all five treaties were adopted prior to the formulation of the sustainable development concept by the WCED Commission,[4] thus, raising the question of their capacity to promote environmental sustainability in outer space, which was initially neither a concept nor a concern as regards these treaties.

1. Leonard C. Meeker, *The First Decade of Law in Space*, 3 Int Lawyer 193, 194–195 (1969); Report of the Legal Sub-Committee on the work of its 1st session (May 28–June 20, 1962), UNCOPUOS, 5th Sess., at 8–9, UN Doc. A/AC.105/6 (1962) ["1962 UNCOPUOS LSC Report"].
2. GA Res. 1721 (XVI), UNGA, 16th Sess., at section A, UN Doc. A/RES/1721 (1961); *Id.*, at 194.
3. GA Res. 1802 (XVII), UNGA, 17th Sess., UN Doc. A/RES/1802 (1962).
4. *See* Chapter 1 *supra*.

These essential considerations will guide our reflection in Chapter 2: it first considers the efficiency of these binding space law instruments in addressing environmental threats raised by space resource activities, before addressing the question of other bodies of international law susceptible of complementing the environmental regime for the protection of outer in the UN Space Treaties. Specifically, section 2 considers the contribution of international environmental law to the environmental sustainability of space resource activities.

1 INTERNATIONAL SPACE LAW

The first significant step in the elaboration of international legal principles governing space activities was achieved in 1963, with the adoption by the UN General Assembly of the *Declaration of Legal Principles Governing the Activities of States in the Exploration and Use of Outer Space*[5] ("1963 Legal Principles"). It outlines nine fundamental principles of space law, including the freedom of exploration and use of outer space and the prohibition for States to appropriate (part of) the area.[6]

Although the instrument is not legally binding upon States, it would be a mistake to dismiss it as inconsequential. As previously mentioned, soon after the adoption of the Legal Principles, the UNCOPUOS succeeded in negotiating five general multilateral treaties, which incorporate and develop concepts included in the 1963 instrument.

The first binding space law instrument adopted is the 1967 Outer Space Treaty;[7] it lays down guiding principles for human space activities in outer space.[8] Often considered the "Magna Carta" of international space law,[9] the treaty is a crucial reference instrument for the conduct and regulation of all space activities.[10]

The second space treaty adopted within the UN framework is the 1968 *Agreement on the Rescue of Astronauts, the Return of Astronauts, and the Return of Objects Launched into Outer Space*,[11] which defines the rights and obligations of States regarding the rescue of persons in outer space.

The third instrument, the 1972 *Convention on International Liability for Damage Caused by Space Objects*,[12] further develops the rules of liability set in the 1967 Outer Space Treaty.

5. GA Res. 18/1962, UNGA, 18th Sess., UN Doc. A/RES/18/1962 (1963) [1963 Legal Principles].
6. *Id.*
7. Treaty on Principles Governing the Activities of States in the Exploration and Use of Outer Space, including the Moon and Other Celestial Bodies, *entered into force* Oct. 10, 1967, 610 UNTS 205 ["Outer Space Treaty"].
8. Paul G Dembling & Daniel M Arons, *The Evolution of the Outer Space Treaty*, 33 J.A.L.C. 419, 432 (1967).
9. Qizhi He, *The Outer Space Treaty in Perspective*, 25 J. Space L. 93, 93 (1997).
10. Frans von der Dunk, *International Space Law*, *in* Handbook of space law 29, 59–60 (2017).
11. Agreement on the Rescue of Astronauts, the Return of Astronauts, and the Return of Objects Launched into Outer Space, *entered into force* Dec. 3, 1968, 672 UNTS 119 ["Return and Rescue Agreement"].
12. Convention on International Liability for Damage Caused by Space Objects, *entered into force* Oct. 9, 1973, 961 UNTS 187 ["Liability Convention"].

The fourth, and second to last, multilateral space law instrument elaborated is the 1976 *Convention on Registration of Objects Launched into Outer Space*;[13] it imposes upon States a duty to, *inter alia*, inform the UN about launched objects.

Lastly, the fifth UN space treaty adopted by States is the 1979 *Agreement Governing the Activities of States on the Moon and Other Celestial Bodies* ("Moon Agreement").[14] Twelve years after the adoption of the 1967 Outer Space Treaty, the Moon Agreement constitutes the first and only binding instrument to date to explicitly address space resources activities. Perhaps more importantly, it is also the second and last binding international agreement to directly confront the issue of the protection of the outer space environment.

The Outer Space Treaty and the Moon Agreement are the only internationally binding space law instruments directly addressing the issue of governing space activities and, *a fortiori*, their environmental impact on outer space, including the Moon and other celestial bodies. This is why, having regard to the scope of this research, this section only considers the first and last UN Space Treaties.

Before going into the details of these two instruments, some preliminary remarks are necessary. First, it must be underscored that, with over a hundred States Parties to date,[15] the Outer Space Treaty benefits from widespread acceptance among both spacefaring and non-spacefaring nations. For this reason, several commentators consider the rights and obligations outlined in the instrument as declaratory of customary international law,[16] which would render them applicable to all States, regardless of their adherence to the instrument.[17]

Second, notwithstanding its incorporation of the 1963 Legal Principles, the adoption of the Outer Space Treaty allowed States to expand on the rules governing human activities in space. In particular, the drafting of the 1967 treaty made it possible to address issues that, in 1963, had been deliberately left out and postponed,[18] as was the case of outer space environmental protection.

Third, despite its low rate of ratification by States—only 18 to date—[19] the 1979 Moon Agreement remains a multilateral binding instrument adopted by the UN General

13. Convention on Registration of Objects Launched into Outer Space, *entered into force* Sept. 15, 1976, 1023 UNTS 15 ["Registration Convention"].
14. Agreement Governing the Activities of States on the Moon and Other Celestial Bodies, *entered into force* July 11, 1984, 1363 UNTS 3 ["Moon Agreement"].
15. As of January 2022, 112 States Parties have ratified the Outer Space Treaty. Status of International Agreements relating to activities in outer space as of Jan. 1, 2022, UNCOPUOS LSC, 61st Sess., at 10, UN Doc. A/AC.105/C.2/2022/CRP.10 (2022) ["2022 Status of the UN Space Treaties"].
16. *See, e.g.*, Ram S. Jakhu & Steven Freeland, *The Relationship Between the Outer Space Treaty and Customary International Law*, *in* IISL Proceedings (2016); Valentina Vecchio, *Customary International Law in the Outer Space Treaty: Space Law as Laboratory for the Evolution of Public International Law*, 66 ZLW 491 (2017).
17. On the formation and effects of customary international law, *see, e.g.*, Pierre-Marie Dupuy & Yann Kerbrat, Droit international public (12 ed. 2014).
18. 1962 UNCOPUOS LSC Report, *supra* note 1, at 8–9.
19. In comparison, the Outer Space Treaty has been ratified by 112 States as of January 2022. 2022 Status of the UN Space Treaties, *supra* note 15, at 10.

Assembly by consensus that is particularly relevant for this research:[20] it aims at establishing a comprehensive legal regime for the exploitation of natural resources present in celestial bodies.[21] Last but not least, from an environmental standpoint, the Moon Agreement is undoubtedly the most advanced out of all five UN Space Treaties.[22]

Accordingly, the present section analyzes the two selected space treaties within the conceptual sustainability framework, elaborated in the previous chapter.[23] For this purpose, we must accept the principle of a retroactive reading of the two instruments since both the Brundtland report and the Berlin II Guidelines—on which the framework is based—were drafted after the adoption of the last UN space treaty in 1979. This is of little consequence since our aim is to deal with the question of sustainability in a coherent and rigorous fashion and not to resort to a purported history. In practice, the present section is divided into two parts: first, it provides a general overview of space law principles contributing to the sustainability of space (resource) activities before focusing on the two treaties' environmental regimes.

1.1 Overview of the Sustainability Factor

From the outset, it must be underscored that the fundamental principles of the Outer Space Treaty were incorporated into the Moon Agreement, which is in line with the affirmed purpose of the latter instrument to "define and develop the provisions of [the previous UN Space Treaties] in relation to the moon and other celestial bodies, having regard to further progress in the exploration and use of outer space."[24] For this reason, this subsection considers the two treaties simultaneously.

Reference to the literature shows that there is a common agreement among legal scholars that several established space law principles echo constitutive elements of sustainable development.[25] Specifically, both Gupta and Viikari consider that the principles of "province of all mankind,"[26] "equitable use,"[27] "benefit of all countries,"[28] "common heritage of mankind,"[29] "non-appropriation"[30] and "due regard"[31] are

20. General Assembly official records, 34th session: 89th plenary meeting, Wednesday, 5 December 1979, New York, UNGAOR, 34th Sess., at 1622, UN Doc. A/34/PV.39 (1979).
21. Moon Agreement, preamble, and Art. 11§5.
22. Lotta Viikari, The environmental element in space law assessing the present and charting the future 62 (2008).
23. *See* Chapter 1 *supra*.
24. Moon Agreement, preamble.
25. Vishakha Gupta, *Critique of the International Law on Protection of the Outer Space Environment*, 14 Astropolitics 20, 32 (2016) DOI: 10.1080/14777622.2016.1148462; Viikari, *supra* note 22 at 145.
26. Outer Space Treaty, Art. I, and Moon Agreement, Art. 4§1.
27. Moon Agreement, Art. 7.
28. Outer Space Treaty, Art. I, and Moon Agreement, Art. 4§1.
29. Moon Agreement, Art. 11§1. For a comparison of the concepts of "province of all mankind," "for the benefit and interests of all countries," and "common heritage of mankind," *see* 2 Georges T. Hacket, Space debris and the Corpus Iuris Spatialis 75–86 (1994).
30. Outer Space Treaty, Art. II, and Moon Agreement, Art. 11§2.
31. Outer Space Treaty, Art. IX, and Moon Agreement, Art. 4§1.

expressions of the concept of sustainable development.[32] They all relate—sometimes in an intertwined manner—to the principles of intra- and inter-generational equity, which are core expressions of sustainable development.

Incidentally, the Moon Agreement is in a unique position compared to the earlier Outer Space Treaty. Indeed, though the 1979 Moon Agreement was adopted prior to the 1987 Brundtland report—and the articulation of the sustainable development concept—it was also drafted after the adoption, by the UN General Assembly, of the 1972 Stockholm Declaration.[33] Although the Declaration does not name sustainable development as such, its 26 principles capture several facets of the concept.[34] We note, in particular, that the Moon Agreement's preamble[35] as well as Principles 1 and 2 all refer to the need to improve and safeguard the environment for the benefit of "present and future generations," an expression which embodies a core principle of sustainable development: inter-generational equity. Consequently, the inclusion of this expression in the Moon Agreement is particularly noteworthy.

Furthermore, Article 4 paragraph 1 provides that States Parties shall pay "due regard" to, *inter alia*, "the interests of present and future generations." A similar obligation already existed under the 1967 Outer Space Treaty, but it only referred to the "corresponding interests" of other States rather than to future generations.[36] Therefore, between 1967 and 1979, something motivated the international community to expand on the due regard obligation to include future interests. A plausible explanation for this evolution of the text could be that it is due to the adoption of the 1972 Stockholm Declaration, which has been called the "mother of all environmental declarations"[37] and had a considerable influence.

As a matter of fact, principles of the Moon Agreement other than the implied connection through the concern for future generations mirror the content of the Stockholm Declaration. Article 11 paragraph 7 of the treaty, for instance, emphasizes the necessity to implement the rational use of natural resources. In comparison, Principles 5 and 14 of the 1972 Declaration call for the guarding of "non-renewable resources [...] against the danger of their future exhaustion" and emphasize that "rational planning" is an "essential tool for reconciling [development] and [environmental protection]." Therefore, there seems to exist a correlation between the adoption of the Stockholm Declaration and the evolution of space law principles under the Moon.

32. Gupta, *supra* note 25 at 32; VIIKARI, *supra* note 22 at 145.
33. United Nations Conference on the Human Environment, UNGA, 27th Sess., UN Doc. A/RES/2994 (1972) ["Stockholm Declaration"].
34. THE OXFORD HANDBOOK OF INTERNATIONAL ENVIRONMENTAL LAW, 49 (Daniel Bodansky, Jutta Brunnée, & Ellen Hey eds., 2007).
35. Stockholm Declaration, preamble, §6.
36. A similar obligation to the one encompassed in Article IX of the Outer Space Treaty was inserted in Article 2 of the Moon Agreement. Accordingly, the latter instrument includes two different due regard obligations: the first is similar in scope to Article IX, whereas the second applies to both present and future generations. Outer Space Treaty, Art. IX; Moon Agreement, Arts. 2 and 4§1.
37. CESARE ROMANO, THE PEACEFUL SETTLEMENT OF INTERNATIONAL ENVIRONMENTAL DISPUTES: A PRAGMATIC APPROACH 21 (2000).

Lastly, Articles VI of the Outer Space Treaty and 14 of the Moon Agreement contain elements that can be used in the context of the protection of the outer space environment. Both provisions establish the States Parties' obligation to authorize and supervise the space activities of nongovernmental entities. Although the two instruments leave the implementation of the obligation to the discretion of the Parties, it can be observed that, in practice, States tend to include in domestic space legislation an authorization process.[38] These legislations often condition the delivery of authorization to conduct a space activity to the respect of some environmental standards, such as the adoption of space debris mitigation measures.[39] They further provide for a supervising mechanism by requiring, for instance, that operators report annually on their activity.[40] In this sense, the international obligation to authorize and supervise nongovernmental activities incentivizes States to adopt a domestic licensing regime, one which can be used to integrate environmental management systems, which is a key element of the conceptual sustainability framework outlined in Chapter 1.

Therefore, both the Outer Space Treaty and the Moon Agreement encompass principles of international space law that can be leveraged to promote sustainability in outer space. They include elements of inter-generational equity and provide an obligation to authorize and supervise activities which are often implemented through the enactment of a domestic licensing process. Nonetheless, in order to properly assess the efficiency of binding international space law to promote the environmental sustainability of space (resource) activities, it is necessary to first consider the environmental regimes developed in the UN Space Treaties.

1.2 Environmental Regime[41]

Out of the five UN Space Treaties, two provisions directly consider the potential environmental impact of space activities: Article IX of the Outer Space Treaty and Article 7 of the Moon Agreement. These constitute real innovations: the 1963 Legal Principles on which the Outer Space Treaty is based did not address environmental matters. The addition shows how the Outer Space Treaty has been an opportunity to address new issues in space, and not just a way to make the 1963 principles binding.

---

38. Frans von der Dunk et al., *Scoping National Space Law: The True Meaning of "National Activities in Outer Space" of Article VI of the Outer Space Treaty*, IISL PROCEEDINGS 227 (2020). Also *see, e.g.*, Loi N° 2008-518 du 3 juin 2008 relative aux opérations spatiales, No. 2008-518 (2008) (FR) ["French Space Act"]; Loi du 20 juillet 2017 sur l'exploration et l'utilisation des ressources de l'espace, Mémorial A No 674, 28 juillet 2017 (LU) ["SRL"]; Law of Sept. 17, 2005 on the Activities of Launching, Flight Operation or Guidance of Space Objects, consolidated text as revised by the Law of 1 December 2013, Art. 8, B.O.J. of Jan. 15, 2014 (2014) (BE) ["Belgian Space Act"].
39. *Id.*, French Space Act, Art. 5; Act on Space Activities, Arts. 5 and 10, 63/2018 (2018) (FI) ["Finnish Space Act"].
40. *See, e.g.*, *id.*, Finnish Space Act, Art. 14.
41. This subsection is based on the previous published work of the author. *See* Gabrielle Leterre, *Space Mining and Environmental Protection: Recycling International Agreements into New Legal Practices*, 62 *in* IISL PROCEEDINGS 83 (2020).

1.2.1 Article IX of the Outer Space Treaty

> [...] States Parties to the Treaty shall pursue studies of outer space, including the moon and other celestial bodies, and conduct exploration of them so as to avoid their harmful contamination and also adverse changes in the environment of the Earth resulting from the introduction of extraterrestrial matter and, where necessary, shall adopt appropriate measures for this purpose. [...]
>
> —Article IX of the Outer Space Treaty

Article IX of the Outer Space Treaty encompasses the only provision in the treaty directly addressing environmental matters in outer space. In comparison with Paragraph 6 of the 1963 Legal Principles, which inspired Article IX, the environmental provision is a clear novelty. The idea to address concerns about the contamination of outer space originally came from the United States.[42] It was then formally included, as a stand-alone provision, in the US draft proposal for the treaty.[43] The proposed provision stated that:

> States shall pursue studies and, as appropriate, take steps to avoid harmful contamination of the celestial bodies and adverse changes in the environment of the Earth resulting from the return of extraterrestrial matter.[44]

However, it was the Soviet draft proposal that suggested including the environmental provision to the content of Paragraph 6 of the Legal Principles, i.e., between the principle of due regard and the consultation mechanism for cases of harmful interference.[45] It read:

> States Parties to the Treaty shall conduct research on celestial bodies in such a manner as to avoid their harmful contamination.[46]

The Soviet proposal was more limited and more loosely worded, and, more importantly, did not make the protection of the environment the object of a specific article but an item among others.

The outcome is a compromise between the two proposals, with the second sentence of Article IX of the Outer Space Treaty reading as follows:

42. Letter dated June 16, 19676 from the Permanent Representatives of the United States of America addressed to the Chairman of the Committee on the Peaceful Uses of Outer Space, *in* Draft Treaty Governing the Exploration of the Moon and Other Celestial Bodies, UNCOPUOS, UN Doc. A/AC.105/32 (1966).
43. *Id.*
44. Draft Treaty Governing the Exploration of the Moon and Other Celestial Bodies, UNCOPUOS, Art. 10, UN Doc. A/AC.105/32 (1966) ["US Proposal"].
45. Draft Treaty on Principles Governing the Activities of States in the Exploration and Use of Outer Space, the Moon and Other Celestial Bodies, *in* Letter dated July 11, 1966 addressed to the Chairman of the Legal Sub-Committee by the representative of the USSR, UNCOPUOS LSC, UN Doc. A/AC.105/C.2/L.13 (1966) ["USSR Proposal"].
46. USSR Proposal, Art. VIII.

> States Parties to the Treaty shall pursue studies of outer space, including the moon and other celestial bodies, and conduct exploration of them so as to avoid their harmful contamination and also adverse changes in the environment of the Earth resulting from the introduction of extraterrestrial matter and, where necessary, shall adopt appropriate measures for this purpose.

The environmental regime of Article IX of the Outer Space Treaty, therefore, addresses two distinct issues: (1) "forward contamination," i.e., the contamination of the outer space environment caused by human activities[47] and (2) "backward contamination"[48] which is the contamination of the Earth from the introduction of extraterrestrial material. In the case of forward contamination, the one of interest here, the provision further requires States to adopt "appropriate" measures. Accordingly, the environmental regime of the treaty includes the substantial elements put forward by the United States.

However, rather than operating as a stand-alone provision in the Outer Space Treaty as it had been suggested by the United States, the environmental regime is confined to a single sentence cramped in between other general principles of space law, as was proposed by the Soviet Union. Specifically, similarly to Paragraph 6 of the Legal Principles, Article IX of the Outer Space Treaty requires States Parties to, *inter alia*, show due regard to each other's interests when carrying out space activities, to avoid both forward and backward contamination and to prevent "harmful interference" from occurring with other States' activities. In cases where such "harmful interference" would manifest, it provides the possibility for the affected party or for the party responsible for the interference to request consultations. Thus, weighting the importance of this sentence is particularly decisive.

It is tempting to see that this second sentence of Article IX only reflects the marginal importance of environmental concerns, considering there is no distinct provision in the Outer Space Treaty solely dealing specifically with outer space environmental protection.[49] Yet, this choice must not be perceived as a disinterest of the international community in protecting the outer space environment. To give Article IX sentence 2 its full weight, it is necessary to contextualize the provision in its drafting period.[50] Japan, for instance, suggested that the provision be "expanded and elaborated" so as to provide a more detailed regulation to protect outer space from contamination.[51] The suggestion was rejected; the space community did not want to establish "too rigid procedures" that might impede future space activities, considering

47. Sergio Marchisio, *Article IX*, I *in* Cologne Commentary on Space Law 169, 176–177 (Stephan Hobe, Bernhard Schmidt-Tedd, & Kai-Uwe Schrogl eds., 2009).
48. *Id.*; Francis Lyall, *Planetary Protection from a Legal Perspective—General Issues*, 38 *in* The IAA Cosmic Study on Protecting the Environment of Celestial Bodies 55, 58 (Mahulena Hofmann, Petra Rettberg, & Mark Williamson eds., 2010).
49. Federico Bergamasco, *Space Mining and The Protection of Extra-Terrestrial Environment in The Light of Article IX of The Outer Space Treaty*, 60 *in* IISL Proceedings 1, 3 (2017).
50. The *travaux préparatoires* can be used as a supplementary means of interpretation. VCLT, Art. 32.
51. *See* Japan's statement, *in* LSC Summary Records, UNGAOR, 5th Sess., at 7, UN Document. A/AC.105/C.2/SR.58 (1966); Howard A Baker, *Protection of The Outer Space Environment: History and Analysis of Article IX of The Outer Space Treaty*, 12 Ann. Air & Space. L. 143, 161 (1987).

that knowledge about the outer space environment "was still meagre" at the time and "required scientific study."[52] Rather than a mere dismissal, it was also noted that a group of experts was working on the question—the Consultative Group on the Potentially Harmful Effects of Space Experiments.[53] Established by COSPAR, this group had the task to "examine any possible effects of space experiments on other scientific activities and observations."[54]

Eventually, the fact that environmental matters in the Outer Space Treaty are restricted to a single sentence had less to do with a disinterest of the space community in the protection of the outer space environment and more with a lack of knowledge about what this protection would take.[55] This position was also elaborated in the context of the quick evolution of space capabilities. It did not diminish the understanding that Article IX was to be aptly described as "a provision, which is designed to protect outer space and celestial bodies from contamination and pollution and to protect the legitimate programs of states from undue interference."[56]

In practice, the environmental regime regarding forward contamination of the outer space environment requires States Parties to avoid conducting activities that would cause its "harmful contamination." It is worthy of note that such an expression is far narrower than in the case of backward contamination: the protection of the Earth environment is seemingly wider than the one of outer space and also more precise with regard to its substance.[57] It applies to "adverse changes" in the Earth's environment, notably through the introduction of extraterrestrial matter.[58] The use of "harmful," however, suggests that not all types of contamination are prohibited.[59]

This is consistent with the purpose of the treaty which is for humans to explore and use outer space.[60] Once again, any activity in space is bound to cause some form of contamination.[61] For instance, the Moon's environment was temporally contaminated by rocket exhaust during the Apollo missions.[62] Similarly, it is foreseen that mining activities will cause, *inter alia*, gas contamination.[63] Therefore, if all types of contamination were prohibited, it would be simply impossible to carry out space activities.

---

52. *See* US' Statement, *in* LSC Summary Records, UN GAOR, 5th Sess., at 7, UN Document. A/AC.105/C.2/SR.68 (1966) ["1966 US' Statement"].
53. *Id.*
54. Baker, *supra* note 51 at n. 13.
55. 1966 US' Statement, *supra* note 52.
56. Speech by Dr. Kurt Waldheim before the 13th Annual Meeting of the American Astronautical Society, Texas (1967), *in* Dembling and Arons, *supra* note 8 at 440.
57. Bergamasco, *supra* note 49 at 4.
58. Outer Space Treaty, Art. IX.
59. Bergamasco, *supra* note 49 at 4.
60. In accordance with article 31§1 VCLT, a treaty must be interpreted "in light of its object and purpose."
61. Carl Q. Christol, *Protection of Space from Environmental Harms*, 4 ANNALS AIR & SPACE L. 433 (1979); Richard R. Vondrak, *Lunar Base Activities and the Lunar Environment*, *in* LUNAR BASES AND SPACE ACTIVITIES OF THE 21ST CENTURY 337, 340–341 (Wendell W. Mendell et al. eds., 1992).
62. Vondrak, *supra* note 61 at 340–341.
63. *Id.*

It also follows that the degree of contamination of the outer space environment varies from one activity to another; the type and the duration of the activity foreseen are criteria that influence the degree of contamination.[64] This explains why States Parties are only required to adopt "appropriate measures" when it is "necessary" since they are better placed to determine how their activity will impact the environment. This being said, it remains that Article IX of the Outer Space Treaty imposes upon the States Parties a positive obligation to prevent "harmful contamination," as demonstrated by the use of the term "shall."[65] Consequently, the treaty does impose environmental obligations upon the Parties: an absolute passive obligation to avoid harmful contamination of the outer space environment and a conditional active obligation to adopt "measures" when necessary.

Having established the existence of such obligations, the question is now when does the active obligation come into play? The simple answer would be when there is a risk of "harmful contamination." Without "harmful contamination" of the outer space environment, indeed, there is no obligation to adopt protective measures pursuant to Article IX. Thus, it becomes apparent that the enforcement of the provision is dependent on the meaning of "harmful contamination."[66] Yet, the Outer Space Treaty provides no definition for this cornerstone concept. Consequently, in the absence of an explicit definition, the expression thus requires to be clarified and interpreted in accordance with the customary rules of treaty interpretation enshrined in the VCLT.

The first step is to adopt the textual interpretation of the expression.[67] The term "contamination" can be understood as the modification of the environment by the introduction of or exposure to undesirable elements.[68] Such interpretation of Article IX of the Outer Space Treaty is supported, as we will *see infra*, by the wording of Article 7 paragraph 1 of the Moon Agreement which refers to "harmful contamination through the introduction of extra-environmental matter." As the Moon Agreement intended to, *inter alia*, "define and develop"[69] the provisions of the 1967 Treaty and was adopted by consensus, it can legitimately be used to interpret Article IX.[70]

Now referring to the historical context, a recognized supplementary means of interpretation to confirm a given interpretation of a provision,[71] we do see that in its 1959 report, the then ad hoc UNCOPUOS considered that it would be necessary to reach "appropriate agreements to minimize the adverse effects of possible biological, radiological, and chemical contamination."[72] We retrieve the same elements to define

64. *Id.*
65. Treaties can be interpreted "in accordance with the ordinary meaning to be given to the terms of the treaty in their context." VCLT, Art. 31§1.
66. Bergamasco, *supra* note 49 at 4.
67. VCLT, Art. 31§1.
68. ILA, Draft International Instrument on the Protection of the Environment from Damage Caused by Space Debris, ILA Conference, Buenos Aires (1994); Gupta, *supra* note 25 at 35.
69. Moon Agreement, preamble.
70. VCLT, Art. 31§3(a).
71. *Id.*, Art. 32.
72. Report of the *Ad Hoc* Committee on the Peaceful Uses of Outer Space, UNGAOR, 14th Sess., at 76, UN Doc. A/4141 (1959).

contamination by the introduction of, or exposure to, undesirable elements. If not in the treaty itself, but at least through the rules of interpretation, the meaning of the term "contamination" appears to be clearly established.

Yet, the price for clarity here might be restriction: should such an interpretation be retained, it would exclude other forms of environmental modifications that were not anticipated in 1967 and 1979.[73] This would even be the case of what is currently considered one of the most pressing issues as regards the contamination of outer space: space debris. Satellites from the 1970s and 1980s that are no longer of use remain in orbit around the Earth, thus increasing the risk of collision with on-orbit functional satellites.[74] It might also leave aside some harmful consequences resulting from the extraction of space resources. Indeed, it has also been suggested that this restrictive interpretation of the term "contamination" would exclude modifications of celestial bodies' landscape resulting from space resource activities, like a change in typology.[75] It may not even encompass environmental issues resulting from over-exploiting space resources.

Ultimately, accepting such a restriction would be consistent neither with the purpose of the Outer Space Treaty—which is to allow States Parties to carry out space activities—nor with the rest of Article IX which calls for the consideration of other States' interests. Hence, the necessity to consider both a systematic and a teleological interpretation, which requires respectively interpretation of a treaty in accordance with its textual context and its purpose and object.[76] These two methods are primary forms of interpretation, just like textual interpretation; one does not trump the other.[77] Then, "harmful contamination" could be interpreted as encompassing polluting practices, like space debris generation. In the end, it is therefore not possible to strictly delineate the elements that determine the exact nature of the "contamination" triggering the active obligation, under the Outer Space Treaty, to take environmental protection measures.

However, if we are unable to define precisely what contamination is about without leaving aside the very scope of the treaties, maybe we can find a greater degree of clarity by dealing with the issue of "harmfulness"; not all forms of contamination are prohibited under the space treaties. Therefore, it is necessary to determine—or at least define a method to establish—the threshold of "harmfulness" required for the environmental regime to apply.

But no more than it defines "contamination," the Outer Space Treaty defines a threshold of harmfulness for the outer space environment's contamination. Indeed, what level of contamination is too much? The qualificative "harmful" implies a form of

73. Bergamasco, *supra* note 49 at 3.; Gordon Chung, *Emergence of Environmental Protection Clauses in Outer Space Treaty: A Lesson from the Rio Principles*, *in* A Fresh View on the Outer Space Treaty 1 (Annette Froehlich ed., 2018).
74. Dietrich Rex, *Will Space Run Out of Space? The Orbital Debris Problem and Its Mitigation*, 14 Space Policy 95 (1998).; Viikari, *supra* note 22 at 31–45.
75. Bergamasco, *supra* note 49 at 4.
76. VCLT, Art. 31§1.
77. *Id.*

contamination that is perceived as negative.[78] But it is more than likely that the State Party causing the contamination will not see it that way.

This raises another question: to whom the contamination must be harmful?[79] Is it to a State Party that is prevented from conducting its own space activities due to the environmental modification of celestial bodies? Or is it to the environment itself? Once again, no answer is given in the treaties, though the anthropocentric interpretation is more likely to be chosen by the spacefaring nations, whereas developing countries may favor a more ecocentric perspective.[80]

It is thus apparent that the terminology used in the Outer Space Treaty suffers from a critical lack of precision. This, in its turn, severely undermines the enforcement of environmental measures actually included in the treaty.[81] The regime is based on the principle that measures must be adopted by the States Parties to avoid a certain degree of harm to be caused to the environment of celestial bodies.[82] However, in the absence of an agreement between said Parties, or a settled practice,[83] on what is harmful to the environment of celestial bodies and on the degree of harm that can be tolerated, it is difficult to apply this regime in practice.[84] Ultimately, the lack of agreement leaves the environmental regime of Article IX without an objective criterion to define its applicability.

This, in turn, gives rise to a second issue undermining the outer space environmental regime, namely the large degree of discretion granted to States Parties in the fulfillment of their legal obligations.[85] The Outer Space Treaty provides in its Article IX sentence 2 that "where necessary, [States Parties] shall adopt appropriate measures."

As previously noted, it is apparent from the term "shall" that the treaty imposes upon the States Parties a positive obligation in addition to the requirement of avoiding harmful contamination of the environment.[86] However, the obligation of the relevant State—that is, the one carrying out the space activity—to take measures is dampened by the addition of the terms "necessary" and "appropriate" in the provision.[87] Such conditional phrasing of the obligation leaves indefinite the circumstances in which measures would be necessary or appropriate.[88]

As a result, the States Parties to the Outer Space Treaty are left with wide latitude to determine when they should adopt protection measures.[89] First, the treaty gives no

78. Steven Freeland, *Article 7 of the Moon Agreement*, II *in* COLOGNE COMMENTARY ON SPACE LAW 372, 375 (Stephan Hobe, Bernhard Schmidt-Tedd, & Kai-Uwe Schrogl eds., 2013).
79. Gupta, *supra* note 25 at 26.
80. *Id.*
81. Bergamasco, *supra* note 49 at 4.
82. Outer Space Treaty, Art. IX sentence 2 and Moon Agreement, Art. 7§1.
83. Pursuant to Article 31 paragraph 3(b) of the VCLT, subsequent practice in the application of a treaty can be used to establish the meaning of a provision.
84. Freeland, *supra* note 78 at 372.; Michael C. Mineiro, *FY-1C and USA-193 ASAT Intercepts: An Assessment of Legal Obligations under Article IX of the Outer Space Treaty*, 34 J. SPACE L. 321 (2008).
85. Freeland, *supra* note 78 at 372.
86. Sergio Marchisio, *supra* note 47 at 177; Freeland, *supra* note 78 at 374.
87. Lyall, *supra* note 48 at 58.
88. *Id.*
89. VIIKARI, *supra* note 22 at 60; Mineiro, *supra* note 84 at 340.

indication as to the form they should take;[90] second, it is not possible from the wording of Article IX to determine whether the obligation arises when measures are necessary for the protection of the outer space environment per se or only when the relevant State deems so.[91] It can only be suspected that spacefaring nations will likely find the latter more favorable to their cause.[92]

Eventually, despite a host of obligations that are per se useful and significant when considering the legal issue of the environment in outer space, on its own, the Outer Space Treaty's environmental regime *stricto sensu* is not enough to efficiently protect the outer space environment. The flaws of the treaty are even more evident as regards space resource activities since there are not yet rules specifically adapted to this type of activity in outer space. This is partially because space treaties are the result of compromises between spacefaring and non-spacefaring nations, developed and developing countries,[93] all having individual interests to protect. Since the principle at UNCOPUOS is the adoption of international instruments by consensus, reaching an agreement between all the parties requires to adopt not too precise provisions so as to allow for some flexibility.[94] Another reason is that leaving the treaty open for interpretation ensures its perennity. As noted above, a broader interpretation of "contamination" could encompass harmful environmental practices such as space debris generation and the overexploitation of space resources. Therefore, the question is to know whether this situation is the *terminus ad quem* of the protection of the outer space environment or if other considerations have to be noted which may play in favor of a more substantial interpretation of environmental protection of outer space.

At least part of the answer is to be found if we underline that our analysis of the environmental mechanism is, so far, solely focused on the single environmental provision in the Outer Space Treaty which creates obligations regarding the protection of the outer space environment. It is entirely contained in the second sentence of Article IX. However, it is important to consider the provision within the greater context of Article IX at large. This may be the key to a more effective protection regime.

More precisely, attention should be paid to another cornerstone provision of Article IX: it carries the obligation for States Parties to show "due regard to the corresponding interests of all other States Parties." It has already been noted that due regard contributes to sustainability. The principle implies that a State Party shall not undertake activities that would threaten the exercise of the freedoms of exploration and use of outer space for peaceful purposes by other States.[95]

Moreover, Article IX of the Outer Space Treaty further requires States Parties to avoid causing "harmful interference" with other activities and lays down a procedural

90. *Id;* Sergio Marchisio, *supra* note 47 at 177.
91. Freeland, *supra* note 78 at 374.
92. Gupta, *supra* note 25 at 26.
93. Stephan Hobe, *Historical Background*, I *in* COLOGNE COMMENTARY ON SPACE LAW 105, 106–107 (Stephan Hobe, Kai-Uwe Schrogl, & Bernhard Schmidt-Tedd eds., Carl Heymanns Verlag ed. 2009).
94. P.J. Blount, *Renovating Space: The Future of International Space Law*, 40 DENV. J. INTL'L L. & POL'Y 515, 527 (2011).
95. Sergio Marchisio, *supra* note 47 at 175.

requirement for consultations between the planning and affected parties.[96] In this context, the obligation to avoid contaminating the environment of celestial bodies by conducting space activities could be envisaged as a sub-obligation to not cause harmful interference; hence, the contamination caused would only be "harmful"—as per sentence 2—to the extent that it would disrupt other States' activities, such as scientific research for instance.[97]

Such interpretation of the expression "harmful contamination" is a typically "anthropocentric" approach to environmental protection: it makes human interests the rationale for intervention rather than the degradation of the environment.[98] By the same token, anthropocentrism engages inter-human mutual obligations.[99] This is particularly important when one considers that associating harmful contamination with harmful interference opens the door to invoking the consultation mechanism established under Article IX of the Outer Space Treaty.[100] This provision states that:

> A State Party to the Treaty which has reason to believe that an activity or experiment planned by another State Party in outer space, including the moon and other celestial bodies, would cause potentially harmful interference with activities in the peaceful exploration and use of outer space, including the moon and other celestial bodies, may request consultation concerning the activity or experiment.

Accordingly, a State could legally request consultations with another State to discuss potential harm. However, the State would have to prove that the environmental damage is affecting its own activity since arguing that the environment is being contaminated would not be sufficient ground for the mechanism to be triggered.[101] It would still provide consistent protection for the environment. It is even more robust when one considers that the mechanism allows for the possibility to request consultation even before the damage has occurred since it applies to "planned" activities and experiments.[102] Consultations could thus be used to discuss future activities whose effects on the environment are yet unclear.[103] Space resource activities are undoubtedly one of these potentially harmful activities.[104]

Nonetheless, the mechanism of consultation is no foolproof guarantee. It must be underlined that it seems to have never been used by States in practice.[105] Should it be evoked in a dispute between States, while it could be used for the betterment of the outer space environment, the legal obligation to enter consultations does not amount to an obligation to reach an agreement between the parties involved.[106] Even if it were to be found that the planned activity is damaging to the environment—thus impeding

96. Outer Space Treaty, Art. IX sentences 1 and 3.
97. Leslie I. Tennen, *Towards a New Regime for Exploitation of Outer Space Mineral Resources*, 88 NEB. L. REV. 794, 817 (2009); Sergio Marchisio, *supra* note 47 at 177.
98. Baker, *supra* note 51 at 167.
99. Bergamasco, *supra* note 49 at 2.
100. VIIKARI, *supra* note 22 at 60–61.; Baker, *supra* note 51 at 169.
101. *Id.*
102. Sergio Marchisio, *supra* note 47 at 180.
103. VIIKARI, *supra* note 22 at 60.
104. Vondrak, *supra* note 61 at 340–341.
105. Mineiro, *supra* note 84 at 340.
106. VIIKARI, *supra* note 22 at 61.

another State's activity—the mechanism would not permit to force to an end the contentious activity; consultations do not open a veto right.[107] They must, however, be genuine and conducted in good faith.[108] It is not a simple formality.

In spite of such limitations, this interpretation of Article IX has merits since it not only helps contextualize the abstract environmental regime of the Outer Space Treaty which legally binds future space mining actors but also offers a potential platform between States to discuss environmental issues.

1.2.2 Article 7 of the Moon Agreement

> In exploring and using the moon, States Parties shall take measures to prevent the disruption of the existing balance of its environment, whether by introducing adverse changes in that environment, by its harmful contamination through the introduction of extra-environmental matter or otherwise. States Parties shall also take measures to avoid harmfully affecting the environment of the earth through the introduction of extraterrestrial matter or otherwise.
>
> —Article 7, paragraph 1 of the Moon Agreement

Out of the five space treaties, the Moon Agreement is undeniably the most advanced from an environmental standpoint,[109] even though it has been ratified by considerably fewer States than the Outer Space Treaty[110]—none of which are major spacefaring nations—and its acceptance is controversial.[111]

Though it has little to offer as regards territorial application, it is nonetheless relevant when addressing the issue of the protection of the outer space environment in general, and for space resource activities in particular. Contrary to the Outer Space Treaty, the Moon Agreement presents the advantage of explicitly applying to space resource exploitation activities, its purpose being the establishment of a comprehensive legal regime to "govern the exploitation of the natural resources of the Moon [and other celestial bodies]."[112] The applicability of the environmental regime set in the Agreement to space resource activities is further made evident by the phrasing "in exploring and using the Moon" at the beginning of Article 7 paragraph 1—the provision hosting the instrument's environmental regime—and the fact that the Agreement only

107. *Id.*
108. Lake Lanoux (France/ Spain) (1957) 12 RIAA 281, pp. 15–16 ["Lake Lanoux Arbitration Award"].
109. Viikari, *supra* note 22 at 62.
110. The Outer Space Treaty has been ratified by 112 States, whereas the Moon Agreement only has 18 States Parties. 2022 Status of the UN Space Treaties, *supra* note 15, at 10.
111. Stephan Hobe, Peter Stubbe & Fabio Tronchetti, *Historical Background and Context*, II *in* Cologne Commentary on Space Law 336, 336 (Stephan Hobe, Bernhard Schmidt-Tedd, & Kai-Uwe Schrogl eds., Carl Heymanns Verlag ed. 2013).
112. Moon Agreement, preamble, and Art. 11§5.

applies to the Moon and "other celestial bodies within the solar system."[113] Consequently, the Moon Agreement only includes in its scope areas where space resources can be extracted.

In essence, the Moon Agreement "define[s] and develop[s]"[114] the provisions of the Outer Space Treaty.[115] With regard to the environmental regime specifically, in 1967, the duty to adopt measures to protect the outer space environment from harm was dependent on the risk of "harmful contamination."[116] Under Article 7 paragraph 1 of the Moon Agreement, there is a paradigm shift with the introduction of the concept of the existence of an "environmental balance" on celestial bodies.[117] States Parties to the Moon Agreement must thus "prevent the disruption" of this balance. Such disruption can come into being by the introduction of "adverse changes" in the environment of the celestial body, by its "harmful contamination through the introduction of extra-environmental matter," or "otherwise."[118] These specifications bring more understanding to the meaning of the provision than they did to the Outer Space Treaty.[119] Furthermore, the addition of "or otherwise" at the end of the first sentence of paragraph 1 plays the role of a catch-all phrase which allows for future possibilities, ones that might not have been foreseen at the time of the drafting.[120]

With regard to the States Parties' obligations, where they were only required to "avoid" harmful contamination under the 1967 Treaty, they must now "prevent" it. Hence, States Parties to the Moon Agreement are required to take an active role in the protection of the outer space environment. Lastly, the 1979 Agreement establishes new information duties. States Parties must inform the UN Secretary-General of the preventive measures they have adopted and, as soon as possible, of the placement on celestial bodies of radioactive materials.[121] Finally, States Parties are requested to inform other States Parties and the UN Secretary-General of the discovery of areas of celestial bodies "having special scientific interest" so that they can potentially be declared "international scientific preserves," thus beneficiating from a special protection regime.[122]

However, despite an expansion of the environmental mechanism compared to the Outer Space Treaty, we retrieve similar definitional issues: where the former failed to define the expression "harmful contamination," the Moon Agreement remains silent regarding the expression "disruption of the existing balance" and "adverse changes.[123] As a result, it is equally unlikely that a State Party will recognize that its activity has

113. *Id.*, Art. 1§1.
114. *Id.*, preamble.
115. Sergio Marchisio, *supra* note 47 at 29.; Freeland, *supra* note 78.
116. Outer Space Treaty, Art. IX.
117. Jean-François Mayence, *Article IX of the Outer Space Treaty and the Concept of Planetary Protection: Toward a Space Environment Law?*, 53 *in* IISL PROCEEDINGS, 3 (2010).
118. Moon Agreement, Art. 7§1.
119. Bergamasco, *supra* note 49 at 4.
120. Qizhi He, *Environmental Impact of Space Activities and Measures for International Protection*, 16 J. SPACE L. 117, 123 (1988).
121. Moon Agreement, Art. 7§2.
122. *Id.*, Art. 2§3.
123. Freeland, *supra* note 78 at 375.

adverse effects on the outer space environment when it would give rise to a legal obligation to prevent it.[124]

Ultimately, we retrieve the same problems as we did with the Outer Space Treaty: the regime is based on the principle that measures must be adopted by the States Parties to prevent a certain degree of harm from being caused to the environment of celestial bodies.[125]

However, it can be noted that these issues were partially remedied in the Moon Agreement.[126] Article 7 does not openly allow its States Parties to discretionarily decide when measures are necessary: neither the term "necessary" nor "appropriate" are present in the provision.[127] Another improvement is the obligation for the Parties, in paragraph 2 of Article 7, to inform the UN Secretary-General of the measures adopted.[128]

Nonetheless, on both accounts, such improvements are limited. First, just as is the case with the Outer Space Treaty, the form the measures of environmental protection should take remains undisclosed.[129] Second, the obligation to inform the UN Secretary-General seems to fall short as it fails to provide any procedural requirements to pair with the information duty;[130] there is no indication regarding when the UN Secretary-General should be informed—prior to or during the activity—and how detailed the information needs to be. States Parties are once more given latitude in the application of their international obligation, particularly so since there is no sanction mechanism established in case a State fails to inform the UN Secretary-General.[131]

Therefore, though the Moon Agreement partially fills the lacunae of the Outer Space Treaty's environmental regime, it comes with its own legal shortcomings, the most significant of them being that—contrary to the Outer Space Treaty—none of the major spacefaring nations have ratified it. Ultimately, this means that the loose environmental regime of Article IX is the one that is more likely to be applied in practice, and the only real limits to States' actions reside in the mandatory compliance with their international obligations under the Outer Space Treaty to be fulfilled in good faith.[132]

1.3 Conclusion

At this early stage of the development of space resource activities, the question of their environmental sustainability is inseparable from the question of how to regulate space activities at large. Space mining will certainly pose, in the near future, specific harmful environmental challenges.

124. Moon Agreement, Art. 7§1.
125. Outer Space Treaty, Art. IX sentence 2 and Moon Agreement, Art. 7§1.
126. He, *supra* note 120 at 123.
127. *See* Moon Agreement, Art. 7§1 and Outer Space Treaty, Art. IX sentence 2.
128. Viikari, *supra* note 22 at 64.
129. Freeland, *supra* note 78 at 374.
130. Viikari, *supra* note 22 at 64.
131. *Id.*
132. VCLT, Art. 26; Mineiro, *supra* note 84 at 340.

Recourse to the UN Space Treaties, and to the Outer Space Treaty and the Moon Agreement especially, shows potential to that end. The principles of the former are widely accepted by the international community, whereas the latter specifically integrates environmental considerations into governing space resource activities. In essence, both instruments have the potential to be leveraged to provide a strong sustainability framework for space resource activities. They contain binding principles which capture several facets of sustainable development, such as the principles of "equitable use" and "due regard" to present and future generations. They also require States Parties to authorize and supervise the activities of nongovernmental entities, an obligation which is often implemented at the domestic level through the enactment of licensing regimes and procedural requirements, like reporting on the status of activities. Finally, they also define an environmental regime that aims to protect the outer space environment by limiting its contamination.

However, a common element between these obligations is the use of broad and undefined key expressions. For instance, there is no indication in the treaties as to what amounts to "harmful contamination" of the outer space environment. Yet, determining this element is crucial since the entire environmental regime, in both treaties, is based on it. Indeed, States are only obliged to adopt preventive measures if the risk of harmful contamination is established. Admittedly, approaching "harmful contamination" as a form of "harmful interference" has merits; it opens the way to the consultation mechanism under Article IX of the Outer Space Treaty. Yet, this procedural mechanism does not grant the affected party a veto right against the planned activity. Furthermore, it must be underlined that the consultation mechanism outlined by the Outer Space Treaty has yet to be used by States Parties.

In this perspective, having recourse to principles of international environmental law may provide support to the sustainability framework outlined in the UN Space Treaties, especially regarding the protection of the (outer space) environment.

2 INTERNATIONAL ENVIRONMENTAL LAW

Looking back at 60 years of experience in outer space, one thing is certain: space activities have generated a variety of environmental problems. Some, such as the biological contamination of celestial bodies, were anticipated and therefore addressed by the UN Space Treaties.[133] Others, like space debris, were not. Yet, they have created potentially irreversible damage to the space environment; their number continuously increases, and there is still no international agreement on their remediation.[134] Based on this observation, as well as the history of pollution and environmental damages

133. As seen in the previous section, Article IX of the Outer Space Treaty requires States to avoid causing "harmful contamination" to the outer space environment. This provision has been used, *inter alia,* as a legal basis for the determination of a planetary protection policy by COSPAR. *See* Chapter 3 *infra*, COSPAR.

134. Rada Popova & Volker Schaus, *The Legal Framework for Space Debris Remediation as a Tool for Sustainability in Outer Space*, 5 AEROSPACE 55 (2018).

experienced on Earth, it can be inferred that new ventures—like space resource activities—will present their own unaddressed environmental challenges.[135]

The previous section established that, although the UN Space Treaties incorporate some environmental elements, they do not provide a fully adequate legal framework to address these issues. However, Article III of the Outer Space Treaty opens the possibility to refer to more effective international norms to bridge the gap left by space treaties[136] since it states that space activities must be carried out "in accordance with international law."[137]

This is a promising venue for environmental protection since different parts of international law deal with the protection of the environment. The question, though, is to assess how promising this approach is: the wording of Article III raises the question of whether international law applies *in toto*.[138] The scholars addressing the question lean toward an unequivocal yes, agreeing that relevant norms of other areas of international law apply to space activities.[139] Such consensus can further be inferred regarding the specific applicability of international environmental law,[140] that is, the corpus of international rules relevant to environmental problems.[141] Larsen and Lyall go a step further, arguing that "[the nature of outer space] presents exceptional difficulties, but these are not sufficient to require unique concepts."[142] Thus, they put forward that "[e]nvironmental space law is simply a specialized area of environmental law" and should, accordingly, not be considered as "something separate, distinct and different" from terrestrial environmental law.[143]

The merits of Larsen and Lyall's concept of a "specialized area of environmental law" for space activities are undeniable. It brings some perspective to the application of international environmental law to space activities, even if it would be naïve to

135. Studies already show that some forms of contamination and other environmental impact in outer space are to be expected as a result of space resource activities. Vondrak, *supra* note 61; Lyall, *supra* note 48. For examples of negative impacts on the environment from exploitation activities, *see, e.g.*, CHRISTOPHE BOUILLON & MICHEL HAVARD, *Rapport d'information par la commission du développement durable et de l'aménagement du territoire, en conclusion des travaux d'une mission d'information sur la gestion durable des matières premières minérales*, 49–50 (2011); Impacts environnementaux de l'exploitation des ressources minérales marines profondes. Expertise scientifique collective, 56–70 (CRNS & Ifremer eds., 2014).

136. Claudia Cinelli & Katarzyna Pogorzelska, *The Current International Legal Setting for the Protection of the Outer Space Environment: The Precautionary Principle Avant La Lettre*, 22 REV. EUR. COMP. INT. 186, 194 (2013) DOI: 10.1111/reel.12026.

137. In its entirety, Article III of the Outer Space Treaty provides that "States Parties to the Treaty shall carry on activities in the exploration and use of outer space, including the moon and other celestial bodies, in accordance with international law, including the Charter of the United Nations, in the interest of maintaining international peace and security and promoting international co-operation and understanding."

138. Olivier Ribbelink, *Article III*, 1 *in* COLOGNE COMMENTARY ON SPACE LAW 65, 11 (Stephan Hobe, Bernhard Schmidt-Tedd, & Kai-Uwe Schrogl eds., 2009).

139. *Id.*, at 11–14; Valnora Leister & Lalin Kovudhikulrungsri, *Outer Space: Of the People, by the People and for the People*, 52 *in* IISL PROCEEDINGS (2009).

140. For example, FRANCIS LYALL & PAUL B. LARSEN, SPACE LAW—A TREATISE 120 (2nd ed. 2018); Cinelli and Pogorzelska, *supra* note 136 at 194; VIIKARI, *supra* note 22 at 120.

141. On the definition of "international environmental law," *see* PATRICIA W. BIRNIE, ALAN E. BOYLE & CATHERINE REDGWELL, INTERNATIONAL LAW AND THE ENVIRONMENT 2–6 (3rd ed. 2009).

142. LYALL AND LARSEN, *supra* note 140 at 245.

143. *Id.*

assume that environmental concepts developed in response to terrestrial concerns can apply *as is* to environmental extraterrestrial issues. Some flexibility is required in their application to fit the specific nature of the outer space environment. Indeed, in most cases, environmental (terrestrial) principles are developed to answer different interests and adapted to specific geographical contexts.[144] In a nutshell, activities in the marine environment raise different environmental problems than activities carried out in a desert. By the same token, it is not enough to simply identify international environmental norms; their relevance and applicability to the outer space environment must also be considered.

The section provides a study of three selected principles of environmental law that have been broadly recognized among legal scholars for their contribution to the achievement of sustainable development. Notably, each of these principles was incorporated into the 1992 Rio Declaration. The first principle, addressed in the first subsection, is the precautionary principle (section 2.1). This principle is grounded in the idea that preventive action should not be dependent on the full scientific certainty that without them significant damage to the environment will occur. In other words, a State is required to adopt anticipatory measures even when doubt remains regarding the occurrence of environmental damage. Having regard to the ultra-hazardous nature of space activities and humanity's limited knowledge of outer space, it has seemed unavoidable to consider incorporating the precautionary approach into the framework of space activities, even though attempts in this direction have so far proved unsuccessful.[145] Thus, the merits of the precautionary principle ought to be debated. The second subsection approaches the broader obligation of due diligence (section 2.2). The principle of due diligence finds several expressions under international law, including international environmental law. It is best summarized as the obligation of a State to take all appropriate steps to achieve its obligations under international law. In international environmental law, due diligence is most notably expressed in the principle of prevention which requires States to prevent significant transboundary harm by adopting measures commensurate with the risk. The third subsection discusses a core element of the sustainability framework outlined in Chapter 1: the EIA requirement. This requirement is, as a matter of fact, the most complex to classify since along with the precautionary principle it is part of due diligence. To this extent, the EIA process is more of an environmental mechanism than a principle as such (section 2.3). It still ranks as a high-level requirement of international norms because of its capacity to operationalize broad obligations of international environmental law, such as due diligence and the objective of sustainable development.[146]

144. Neil Craik, The International Law of Environmental Impact Assessment: Process, Substance and Integration 163–164 (2008).
145. Building Blocks for the Development of an International Framework for the Governance of Space Resources Activities: A Commentary, 64 (Olavo de O. Bittencourt Neto et al. eds., 1 ed. 2020).
146. Craik, *supra* note 144 at 164. On the link between EIA and sustainable development, *see* Hugh Wilkins, *The Need for Subjectivity in EIA: Discourse as a Tool for Sustainable Development*, 23 Environmental Impact Assessment Review 401 (2003) DOI: 10.1016/s0195-9255(03)00044-1; Birnie, Boyle, and Redgwell, *supra* note 141 at 116.

2.1 Precautionary Principle

> In order to protect the environment, the precautionary approach shall be widely applied by States according to their capabilities. Where there are threats of serious or irreversible damage, lack of full scientific certainty shall not be used as a reason for postponing cost-effective measures to prevent environmental degradation.
>
> —Principle 15 of the Rio Declaration

"If we err in our decisions affecting the future of our children and our planet, let us err on the side of caution."[147] These words from Gro Harlem Brundtland reflect the intrinsic link between the precautionary principle and sustainable development. That precaution is regarded as a necessary condition for the achievement of sustainable development is now widely accepted,[148] especially in the context of the sustainable use of natural resources.[149]

Like the prevention principle, precaution is a predominantly environmental concept.[150] Both principles call for the adoption of measures to protect the environment from harm. However, they must not be confused for the same. From a theoretical standpoint, prevention occurs when the harmful environmental effects of an activity are known, whereas precaution calls for the adoption of measures if such effects are uncertain.[151] Here, the distinctive element is uncertainty: precautionary measures are anticipatory preventive measures.[152] Then, as Trouwborst underlines, precaution does not apply because of uncertainty but *in spite of* it.[153]

In the context of space activities, and in particular of emerging activities such as space resource utilization, recourse to the precautionary principle appears more

147. As cited in James Cameron & Juli Abouchar, *The Precautionary Principle: A Fundamental Principle of Law and Policy for the Protection of the Global Environment*, 14 B. C. INT'L & COMP. L. REV. 1, 1 (1991).
148. *See, e.g.*, ARIE TROUWBORST, PRECAUTIONARY RIGHTS AND DUTIES OF STATES 34 (2006); Andrew Stirling, *The Appraisal of Sustainability: Some Problems and Possible Responses*, 4 LOCAL ENVIRONMENT 111–135, 125 (1999) DOI: 10.1080/13549839908725588; W. Neil Adger & Andrew Jordan, *Sustainability: exploring the processes and outcomes of governance*, *in* GOVERNING SUSTAINABILITY 3–31, 25–26 (Andrew Jordan & W. Neil Adger eds., 2009); Jaeckel, *supra* note 1 at 31. Separate Opinion of Judge Weeramantry *in* Gabčíkovo-Nagymaros Project (Hungary v. Slovakia) (Judgment), 1997 ICJ Rep. 7 (September 25) ["ICJ, Gabčíkovo-Nagymaros"]; ILA, Resolution 3/2002 on sustainable development, para. 4§1 (2002), which affirms that a "precautionary approach is central to sustainable development."
149. Jaeckel, *supra* note 148 at 31; BIRNIE, BOYLE, AND REDGWELL, *supra* note 141 at 137.
150. For a comprehensive analysis of the relationship between precaution and prevention, *see* Arie Trouwborst, *Prevention, Precaution, Logic and Law: The Relationship between the Precautionary Principle and the Preventative Principle in International Law and Associated Questions*, 2 ERASMUS LAW REVIEW 23 (2009) DOI: 10.5553/elr221026712009002002002. Trouwborst concludes that a rigid segregation of the two concepts—prevention and precaution—is not operable, though a "dividing line" may be drawn in theory to distinguish precautionary logic from preventative logic. *Id.*, at 116–118.
151. Trouwborst, *supra* note 150 at 116.
152. VIIKARI, *supra* note 22 at 157.
153. Trouwborst, *supra* note 150 at 118.

appropriate than to the prevention one, and for this reason, it legitimately draws more attention than the latter. Space activities are classified as ultra-hazardous and, as a consequence, can be very harmful to, *inter alia*, the environment.[154] This is due in part to the combination of new space technology with a lack of knowledge regarding the outer space environment. As a result, there remains a level of scientific uncertainty regarding the potential effects of activities on the fragile extraterrestrial environment.[155]

Beyond its intrinsic theoretical value, the precautionary concept is also a legitimate focus for analysis because of actual attempts to include it in space-related instruments. One such example is the initial inclusion of the precautionary approach in the first versions of the *Building Blocks for the Development of an International Framework on Space Resource Activities*,[156] which were drafted by the Hague Space Resources Governance Working Group (HSRGWG) in 2019.[157] Its application has been also considered by several legal scholars as a means to preserve the outer space environment, especially regarding the proliferation of space debris.[158]

The origins of the precautionary concept are anchored in domestic law: it was first introduced in Sweden toward the end of the 1960s,[159] before being expressly recognized in German Law in the mid-1980s.[160] With regard to treaty law, the principle is first explicitly referred to in the 1985 *Vienna Convention for the Protection of the Ozone Layer*,[161] and subsequently in the 1987 *Montreal Protocol on Substances that Deplete the Ozone Layer*.[162] At this point, it can be considered that the precautionary principle had already been incorporated in nonlegally binding international instruments, such as the 1982 *World Charter of Nature*, which acknowledges it implicitly.[163] The focus, at that time, is obviously the utilization of terrestrial resources. Ultimately, the precautionary principle is globally endorsed by States during the 1992 Rio

154. Thomas Neger & Edith Walter, *Space Law—An Independent Branch of the Legal System*, 7 *in* Outer Space in society, politics and law 234, 342–343 (Christian Brünner & Alexander Soucek eds., 2011).
155. Paul Larsen, *Application of the Precautionary Principle to the Moon*, 71 Journal of Air Law and Commerce 295, 298 (2006).
156. Building Blocks: A Commentary, *supra* note 145.
157. The reference to the "adoption of a precautionary approach with the aim of avoiding harmful impacts" was subsequently removed during the later stage of the discussion. The precautionary approach was seen as too cumbersome by representatives of the industry. *Id.*, at 64.
158. For example, Cinelli and Pogorzelska, *supra* note 136; Viikari, *supra* note 22 at 157–178; Olavo de O. Bittencourt Neto, *Preserving the Outer Space Environment: The "Precautionary Principle" Approach to Space Debris*, *in* IISL Proceedings 341 (2013).
159. Jose Felix Pinto-Bazurco, *The Precautionary Principle*, International Institute for Sustainable Development (2020).
160. Nicolas de Sadeleer, *The Precautionary Principle*, *in* Environmental Principles: From Political Slogans to Legal Rules 135, 146 (2nd ed. 2020).
161. Vienna Convention for the Protection of the Ozone Layer, *entered into force* Sept. 22, 1988, at preamble, §5, 1513 UNTS 293.
162. Montreal Protocol on Substances that Deplete the Ozone Layer, Sept. 16, 1987, *entered into force* Jan. 1, 1989, 1522 UNTS 29 (Montreal Protocol), preamble, para. 6.
163. The Charter states that "where potential adverse effects are not fully understood, the activities should not proceed" and that "[s]pecial precautions shall be taken to prevent discharge of radioactive or toxic wastes." GA Res. 37/7, UNGAOR, 37th Sess., at §§11b and 12b, UN Doc. A/RES/37/7 (1982).

Conference with the adoption of the Rio Declaration.[164] This international endorsement of the precautionary principle is further exemplified by its incorporation in an increasing number of treaties during the 1990s, thus reflecting a widespread and consistent recognition of the principle by States.[165]

A variation in the legal terminology of international norms dealing with precautionary requirements is worth noting: some international instruments refer to the precautionary *principle*, whereas others use the expression precautionary *approach*. The study of several instruments shows that international instruments are more likely to use the expression "approach," whereas regional instruments, particularly European ones, favor the term "principle."[166] The question is whether these two distinct terms produce different effects from a legal standpoint. According to Birnie et al., the confusion between the two expressions coincides with "the difficulty in distinguishing between identification of the risks or how to respond to said risks."[167] Moreover, the concept seems to resonate differently with States depending on which expression is used. For instance, during the negotiations of the Rio Declaration, the United States pushed for the use of a "precautionary approach"—as opposed to a "precautionary principle." "Approach" is perceived as more flexible than "principle" and reflects the idea that the precautionary concept is more a policy orientation than a legal norm.[168] However, it might just be that the distinction is "largely semantic," as Freestone notes it,[169] and the fact is that it is used in an interchangeable fashion by scholars. This is the position adopted in this book, and therefore "precautionary approach" and "principle" will be used indifferently.

Beyond the question of its nature in international law, the precautionary principle raises questions regarding its content and normative basis,[170] despite a large literature attempting to clarify these issues. There exists indeed an overall agreement on the

164. United Nations Conference on Environment and Development, Rio de Janeiro, Brazil, June 3–14, 1992. *See* Rio Declaration, principle 15 *in* Report of the United Conference on Environment and Development, UNGAOR, Annex I, UN Doc. A/CONF.151/26/rev.1 (Vol. 1) (1992) ["Rio Declaration"].
165. Birnie, Boyle, and Redgwell, *supra* note 141 at 157; Trouwborst, *supra* note 150 at 108.
166. "Approach" is used in, *e.g.*, 1992 Convention on Climate Change, Article 3; United Nations Framework Convention on Climate Change, *entered into force* Mar. 21, 1994, Art. 3, 1771 UNTS 107 ["UNFCCC"]; Agreement for the Implementation of the Provisions of the United Nations Convention on the Law of the Sea of 10 December 1982 relating to the Conservation and Management of Straddling Fish Stocks and Highly Migratory Fish Stocks, *entered into force* Dec. 11, 2001, Art. 6, 2167 UNTS 3; Stockholm Convention on Persistent Organic Pollutants, *entered into force* May 17, 2004, preamble, §8 and Art. 1, 2256 UNTS 119; Rio Declaration, Principle 15. On the other hand, "principle" is used in, *e.g.*, European Union, Consolidated version of the Treaty on the Functioning of the European Union, 13 December 2007, Art. 191§2, 2008/C 115/01; Convention on the Protection and Use of Transboundary Watercourses and International Lakes, *entered into force* Oct. 6, 1996, Art. 2§5, 1936 UNTS 269.
167. The former refers to States being more cautious about identifying risks, whereas the latter refers to acting more cautiously by adopting precautionary measures. Birnie, Boyle, and Redgwell, *supra* note 141 at 105.
168. Daniel Bodansky, *Deconstructing the Precautionary Principle*, *in* Bringing New Law to Ocean Waters 381, 381–382 (David D. Caron & Harry N. Scheiber eds., 2004).
169. David Freestone, *The Road from Rio: International Environmental Law after the Earth Summit*, 6 Journal of Environmental Law 193, 212 (1994) DOI: 10.1093/jel/6.2.193.
170. Pierre-Marie Dupuy & Jorge E. Viñuales, International Environmental Law 70 (2nd ed. 2018).

purpose of the concept: it aims to ensure adequate protection of the environment by calling for actions at an early stage to prevent environmental harm, even in a context of scientific uncertainty.[171] Beyond this common understanding, matters are unsettled. What are the implications of the principle? When does the obligation to act arise? Is there an obligation to act, or is it merely an encouragement to be cautious? Is there a threshold of potential environmental harm under which the precaution plays no role?[172] These questions contribute to the obscurity surrounding the principle and call for an investigation.

The canonical formulation of the precautionary principle in Principle 15 of the Rio Declaration is a good starting point for several reasons. First, even though—but also precisely because—the Rio Declaration is a nonlegally binding instrument, it has the paradoxical merit, from a conceptual standpoint, of not being a treaty. Treaties rarely have a universal vocation, especially in the matter of environmental protection. Rather, they are specifically tailored to answer specific issues; as a result, the scope of the precautionary principle, whenever found in a treaty, will reflect a targeted goal. For instance, the 1995 Agreement on Straddling Fish Stocks requires States to "apply the precautionary approach widely to conservation, management and exploitation of straddling fish stocks and highly migratory fish stocks in order to protect the living marine resources and preserve the marine environment" and to be "more cautious when information is uncertain, unreliable or inadequate."[173] In a different context, the 1992 *United Nation Framework Convention on Climate Change* (UNFCCC) encourages States to "take precautionary measures" which should consider "different socio-economic contexts, be comprehensive, cover all relevant sources, sinks and reservoirs of greenhouse gases and adaptation, and comprise all economic sector."[174] It is striking that both examples adopt a precautionary approach with significantly different scopes. The former focuses on the rational use of a natural living resource, whereas the latter calls for the consideration of various socio-economic interests.

Second, the interest of Principle 15 is that the Rio Declaration is the result of a negotiation between States. More precisely, if we consider how the precautionary principle—or rather, in the terms of the Declaration "approach"—made its way into the instrument, we see how it was adopted through a progressive agreement between parties. As mentioned above, the United States' input resulted in the use of the expression "precautionary approach"; however, the adopted text was phrased by the European Community.[175] Most importantly, the consensus regarding the formulation

171. Trouwborst, *supra* note 150 at 108; Christol, *supra* note 61 at 433.
172. Dupuy and Viñuales, *supra* note 170 at 70.
173. Agreement on Straddling Fish Stocks, *supra* note 166, Art. 6. §§1 and 2.
174. UNFCCC, *supra* note 166, Art. 3§3.
175. The proposal submitted by the European Economic Community states that "[...] where there are threats of serious or irreversible damage, lack of full scientific certainty should not be used as a reason for postponing measures to prevent environmental degradation." The final version of Principle 15 is very similar; it adds that the measures shall be "cost-effective." Preparatory Committee for the UN Conference on Environment and Development, Principles on general rights and obligations: Chairman's consolidated draft, UNGA, 3rd Sess., §54, UN Doc. A/CONF.151/PC/WG.III/L.8/Rev.1 (1991).

of the precautionary principle in the Rio Declaration is evidenced by its endorsement, in 1992, by the UN General Assembly.[176]

Third, Principle 15 of the Rio Declaration is a good reference when investigating the content and normative basis of the precautionary principle because its agreed-upon wording has been incorporated in other binding international instruments. It was, for instance, referenced in the preamble of the 1992 *Convention on Biological Diversity*,[177] and incorporated in the main body of the UNFCCC.[178] It provides that:

> [t]he Parties should take precautionary measures to anticipate, prevent or minimize the causes of climate change and mitigate its adverse effects. *Where there are threats of serious or irreversible damage, lack of full scientific certainty* should *not be used as a reason for postponing* such *measures* [italics added].

This second sentence, and particularly the part highlighted above, repeats almost word for word the formulation of the precautionary principle in the Rio Declaration. Indeed, Principle 15 of the Declaration states that:

> [i]n order to protect the environment, the precautionary approach shall be widely applied by States according to their capabilities. Where there are threats of serious or irreversible damage, lack of full scientific certainty shall not be used as a reason for postponing cost-effective measures to prevent environmental degradation.

2.1.1 Components

From the outset, three basic components of the precautionary principle can be identified from the formulation of Principle 15: (1) a potentially serious or irreversible harmful threat to the environment, (2) uncertainty, and (3) regulatory action. These three elements consistently appear in doctrine on the precautionary principle, although phrased differently.[179] They are, as Trouwborst puts it, the "three legs of the precautionary tripod."[180] Accordingly, the following paragraphs will discuss each leg of the tripod in the following order: harm, uncertainty, and action.

2.1.1.a Potentially Serious or Irreversible Harm to the Environment

Discussing the element of harm first is all the more appropriate since it is the condition *sine qua non* for the existence of the precautionary principle.[181] Principle 15 of the Rio Declaration affirms as much in its very beginning: "*[i]n order to protect the environment*, the precautionary approach shall be widely applied by States..." [italics added]. Although the text does not use the word "harm," it refers to the equivalent expressions:

176. GA Res. 47/190, UNGAOR, 47th Sess., at 2, UN Doc. A/RES/47/190 (1992).
177. Convention on Biological Diversity, *entered into force* Dec. 29, 1993, preamble, §9, 1760 UNTS 79.
178. UNFCCC, *supra* note 166, Art. 3§3.
179. For an overview of definitions of the precautionary principle in doctrine, *see* TROUWBORST, *supra* note 148 at 30–31.
180. *Id.*, at 30.
181. Jaeckel, *supra* note 148 at 32.

"threats of serious or irreversible damage" as well as "environmental degradation." This confirms that precaution is not intended to be applied to all changes in the environment, only those which cause a certain level of damage. In this regard, the Group of Legal and Technical Experts on Liability and Redress notes, in the context of the *Convention on Biological Diversity*, that "mere change in the state of biological diversity might not necessarily constitute damage" and that "[t]o constitute damage, the change had to result in an adverse or negative effect."[182] Thus, precaution is required where there is a risk of harmful change in the environment due to an activity of a State. At this stage, it can be concluded that the precautionary principle does not apply to all types of environmental change but to those which specifically have a negative effect.

The next question, then, would be whether the principle applies to all levels of environmental harm.[183] The formulation of Principle 15 would suggest that it is not the case. It refers to "serious or irreversible damage" which implies the existence of a triggering threshold, linked to the gravity of the anticipated harm.[184] In other words, if this threat does not amount to at least serious or irreversible damage, States are not required to adopt precautionary measures. It sets a minimum threshold for the gravity of the harm.

The existence of a triggering threshold is especially important in the context of the precautionary principle as it applies to cases where there is a certain lack of scientific certainty. By determining a minimum threshold when incorporating precaution in normative instruments, States ensure that not every adverse impact or minor concern is meant to trigger precautionary action.[185] Yet, this position is an appropriate answer only insofar as the principle of a threshold is incorporated into the relevant legal norm. This is not the case for all international instruments incorporating the precautionary principle.[186] Applied strictly, and in the absence of a threshold, the precautionary principle could lead to an untenable situation where any potential damage to the environment—even the most insignificant ones or those resulting from everyday activities—would require the adoption of mitigating measures. From an ecocentric perspective, this radical application of the principle would favor the environment by making its protection an absolute priority. However, such practice would not be sustainable since it would impede socio-economic development, which is the main source of environmental harm but is also the very object of sustainability.[187] This is why sustainable development calls for a balance of both socio-economic development

182. Report of the Group of Legal and Technical Experts on Liability and Redress in the Context of Paragraph 2 of Article 14 of the Convention on Biological Diversity, UNEP, 8th Meeting, §19, UN Doc. UNEP/CBD/COP/8/27/Add.3 (2005).
183. TROUWBORST, *supra* note 148 at 43.
184. Trouwborst, *supra* note 150 at 110; Jaeckel, *supra* note 148 at 32.
185. Jaeckel, *supra* note 148 at 32.
186. For an overview of international instruments not defining a threshold of harm, *see* TROUWBORST, *supra* note 148 at 45.
187. The ICJ notes, for instance, that "throughout the ages, [hu]mankind has, for economic and other reasons, constantly interfered with nature." ICJ, Gabčíkovo-Nagymaros, *supra* note 148, §140.

and environmental protection.[188] For this reason, scholars argue that, even in the absence of an explicit threshold, one may be implied when reading between the lines of these instruments.[189]

2.1.1.b *Uncertainty*

Connected to the question of the level of harm and its threshold is the notion of uncertainty. Principle 15 of the Rio Declaration clearly states that when the threshold of harm is reached, a "lack of full scientific certainty" cannot justify a lack of action by the States carrying out the harmful activity. The fact that the text refers to full scientific certainty is noteworthy. It suggests that the duty to adopt precautionary action is triggered somewhere in the middle between a situation where risk is certain—thus requiring preventive action—[190] and a situation where there is no scientific "full" evidence that a damage could occur. Accordingly, not all levels of scientific uncertainty are covered.[191] There is, in Jaeckel's words, "a maximum limit on the level of uncertainty."[192] In practice, it means that there must be "reasonable grounds for concern" or some supporting evidence that damage to the environment will occur.[193]

Similar to the determination of the gravity threshold for the first component of the precautionary principle is the introduction of a probability threshold which acts as a safeguard against absurd situations. Without requiring some level of proof regarding the probability that harm would occur, precautionary action could be triggered for a multitude of risks—including hypothetical ones.[194] This would lead to absurd situations since it is impossible to identify—and thus anticipate—every potential risk caused by an activity. However, the inclusion of the element of uncertainty in the precautionary principle is not without advantages. Its main effect is to lower the standard of proof for environmental threats.[195] The proof that the activity may cause serious or irreversible environmental damage does not have to be conclusive; it is sufficient to demonstrate that it is supported by some scientific evidence.[196]

We understand why, as stated at the beginning of this section, the precautionary principle represents a core value for the protection of the environment in the context of space activities. Humankind is far from having a complete scientific knowledge of outer space; this is why until recently a large part of space activities was scientific in nature and intended to better understand the unknown universe. Added to this lack of general knowledge, the development of new space activities—such as the extraction and utilization of space resources—adds a new layer of uncertainty. It requires developing

---

188. *Id.*
189. Jaeckel, *supra* note 148 at 38; Trouwborst, *supra* note 150 at 47–48.
190. For a comprehensive analysis of the principle, *see, e.g.*, Nicolas de Sadeleer, *The Principle of Prevention*, *in* ENVIRONMENTAL PRINCIPLES: FROM POLITICAL SLOGANS TO LEGAL RULES 61 (2002).
191. Jaeckel, *supra* note 148 at 38.
192. *Id.*
193. Trouwborst, *supra* note 150 at 118–119; BIRNIE, BOYLE, AND REDGWELL, *supra* note 141 at 157.
194. BIRNIE, BOYLE, AND REDGWELL, *supra* note 141 at 157.
195. *Id.*
196. *Id.*, at 154.

and testing new technologies in an environment only partially controllable. Nevertheless, humanity has gained, through several decades of experience, a working knowledge of the outer space environment. It is therefore reasonable to believe that potentially serious or irreversible harm to the environment is foreseeable, and we already see this capacity to identify problems operationalized in certain cases: precautionary measures are already in place to anticipate and prevent planetary contamination and the proliferation of any more space debris.[197]

2.1.1.c Regulatory Action

This leads us to the third component of the precautionary principle, namely regulatory action. Principle 15 of the Rio Declaration requires States to adopt "cost-effective measures to prevent environmental degradation" once the thresholds of gravity and probability of an environmental threat are crossed. This is the operative part of the principle since without it the precautionary approach would be meaningless.[198] From the outset, it can be noted that Principle 15 does not specify which measures should be adopted by States. It can only be deduced by relying on the context: these measures must be "cost-effective" and assist in preventing "environmental degradation." Thus, the first criterion would be the effectiveness of the measures. It means that, regardless of their nature, measures adopted by States must effectively safeguard the part of the environment that is threatened by the activity.[199] By relying on the general condition of effectiveness—rather than setting down precise criteria that may not fit all situations—Principle 15 promotes the adoption of "clear and meaningful, yet flexible" measures.[200] When compared to the subjective language used in the Outer Space Treaty ("appropriate measures"), the criterion of effectiveness promoted by the Rio Declaration allows for an objective assessment of the appropriateness of adopted measures: the measure is appropriate if it actually prevents harm.

The second criterion is that while precautionary measures must be effective, they should also be proportionate: they must be "cost-effective." This is in line with the idea that the precautionary principle contributes to the achievement of sustainable development, i.e., a form of growth, not its negation. While it is an environmental principle and focuses on preserving the environment, it does not call for actions that would impede socio-economic development. Thus, the precautionary measures adopted do not have to be the best for the environment but, instead, reflect a balance of interests, including environmental ones.

In summary, the principle of precaution is triggered by a combination of the gravity of a threat to the environment and its probability. In order to enforce and avoid an untenable application of the principle, both gravity and probability thresholds should be defined clearly in international instruments. An apt example would be the

197. Also *see* Chapter 1 *supra* on potential environmental issues raised by space resource activities.
198. Jaeckel, *supra* note 148 at 39–40.
199. Trouwborst, *supra* note 150 at 110.
200. Jaeckel, *supra* note 148 at 39–40.

MARPOL Convention[201] which contains detailed annexes for preventing and minimizing various types of pollution from ships. It is true that this Convention is more the exception than the rule as many instruments fail to explicitly define a triggering threshold. It is all the more exceptional since there appears to be no universally accepted standard regarding the level of harm that would oblige States to be cautious.[202] Despite the many imperfections of international laws regarding the protection of the environment, the wide application by States of the precautionary principle ensures that, in many cases, regulatory action is taken without waiting for the presentation of more compelling evidence of a harmful threat to the environment. Therefore, the salient point in the enforcement of the precautionary principle is its inherent link to the existence of scientific evidence.

2.1.2 Burden of Proof

Although the evidence does not have to be conclusive, it must help establish the existence of a threat to the environment for the precautionary principle to be enforced. This raises the matter of which party—between the one undertaking the harmful activity and the one opposing it—bears the burden of proof. Neither the Rio Declaration nor international law at large provides a definitive answer on this matter. International jurisdictions seem to generally require the party claiming the existence of a risk of serious or irreversible harm to adduce evidence.[203] Yet, it can be noted that the burden of proof has been reversed in several cases.[204] In this situation, it must be underlined

201. The annexes of the MARPOL Convention regulate different types of polluting substances: oil (Annex I); noxious liquid substances in bulk (Annex II); harmful substances carried by sea in packaged form (Annex III); sewage and garbage from ships (Annexes IV and V, respectively); air pollution from ships (Annex VI). Of these, Annexes I and II are mandatory, whereas the others are optional. Protocol of 1978 relating to the International Convention for the prevention of pollution from ships, *entered into force* Oct. 2, 1983, 1340 UNTS 61.

202. Trouwborst, *supra* note 148 at 45–47.

203. T-13/99, Pfizer Animal Health v. Council, §§136–148, 164–173, 2002 ECR II-3305; Appellate Body Report, EC—Hormones, §§97–109, WTO Doc. WT/DS26/AB/R, WT/DS48/AB/R (adopted Feb. 13, 1998) ["WTO, EC—Hormones"].

204. For an overview of the jurisprudence on the reversal of the burden of proof, *see* Trouwborst, *supra* note 148 at 201–219. Moreover, several international judges have argued that the precautionary principle calls for a reversal of the burden on proof. In his Separate Opinion on the *MOX Plant* case, Judge Wolfrum affirmed that:

> [t]here is no general agreement as to the consequences which flow from the implementation of [the precautionary] principle other than the fact that the burden of proof concerning the possible impact of a given activity is reversed. A state interested in undertaking or continuing a particular activity has to prove that it will result in no harm, rather than the other side having to prove that it will result in harm.

Separate Opinion of Judge Wolfrum, 134 and Separate Opinion of Judge Ad Hoc Székely, §22 *in* MOX Plant (No. 10) (Ireland v. UK), Order of Dec. 3, 2001, 2001 ITLOS Rep. 95 ["ITLOS, MOX Plant"].

In a similar manner, also *see* Separate Opinion of Judge Laing, §14 *in* Southern Bluefin Tuna (Nos. 3 and 4) (New Zealand v. Japan; Australia v. Japan), Provisional Measures, Order of Aug. 27, 1999, 1999 ITLOS Rep. 280 ["ITLOS, Southern Bluefin Tuna"]; Dissenting Opinion of Judge Weeramantry, 502–503 *in* Legality of the Threat or Use of Nuclear Weapons, Advisory Opinion, 1996 ICJ Rep. 226 (July 8) ["ICJ, Nuclear Threat (A/O)"].

that—like the opponent to the activity which claims the existence of risk—the States undertaking the harmful activity do not have to provide absolute evidence of, in this case, harmlessness.[205] Consequently, it can only be concluded that the application of the precautionary principle does not automatically operate as a reversal of the burden of proof.[206]

2.1.3 Legal Status

Another fundamental question, especially in the context of space activities where none of the UN Space Treaties include the precautionary principle, is that of the normative basis. Precaution can clearly be invoked between States Parties to treaties incorporating the approach. But *quid* of other sources of international law? Does the precautionary approach amount to a general principle of international law or to international custom, as defined in Article 38 paragraph 1 of the ICJ Statute? Customary international law binds States without requiring a formal acceptance of a rule, whereas general principles are often used to complement other rules of international law and affect the way in which certain treaty rules are applied.[207] Consequently, in the absence of a reference in the UN Space Treaties, assessing the legal status of the precautionary principle is fundamental: it determines whether States must comply with the principle when carrying out space (resources) activities.

The legal status of the precautionary principle has been discussed on several occasions by international jurisdictions. The World Trade Organization (WTO) underlined several times that the status of the principle in general international law remained uncertain.[208] Particularly, it noted in *Biotech* that "no authoritative decision by an international court or tribunal [...] recognizes the precautionary principle as a principle of general or customary international law."[209] This is, in part, due to the reluctance of international jurisdictions to explicitly recognize the existence of said principle in international law.

The existence of a precautionary principle was invoked by a party before the ICJ in two cases, yet in each occurrence, the majority opinion declined to address the argument and instead ruled the case on other grounds.[210] In the second *Nuclear Tests*

205. Jaeckel, *supra* note 148 at 55.
206. For instance, in *Pulp Mills*, the ICJ affirmed—in response to Argentina's argument that the precautionary principle aims to reverse the burden of proof—that "while a precautionary approach may be relevant in the interpretation and application of the provisions of the Statute, it does not follow that it operates as a reversal of the burden of proof." Pulp Mills (Argentina v. Uruguay) (Judgment) 2010 ICJ Rep. 14, §164 (Apr. 20) ["ICJ, Pulp Mills"].
207. Vincy Fon & Francesco Parisi, *Stability and Change in International Customary Law*, 17 Supreme Court Economic Review 279, 279–281 (2009) DOI: 10.1086/656058; Giorgio Gaja, *General Principles of Law*, Max Planck Encyclopedias of International Law 21–22 (Rüdiger Wolfrum ed., 2020).
208. WTO, EC—Hormones, *supra* note 203, §124; Panel Report, EC—Approval and Marketing of Biotech Products, §7.88, WTO Doc. WT/DS291/R (adopted on Nov. 21, 2006) ["WTO, EC—Biotech"].
209. *Id.*, WTO, EC—Biotech.
210. Sonia E. Rolland, *The Precautionary Principle: Development of an International Standard*, 23 429, 452 (2002).

case, New Zealand argues that France is under an obligation to provide absolute evidence that its activities will not result in radioactive material being introduced into the environment, "in accordance with the "precautionary principle" very widely accepted in contemporary international law."[211] The Court dismissed the case on procedural grounds and thus did not address substantive arguments.[212] In a Dissenting Opinion, Judge Weeramantry shares his "regret" that:

> the Court has not availed itself of the opportunity to enquire more fully into this matter and of making a contribution to some of the seminal principles of the evolving corpus of international environmental law. The Court has too long been silent on these issues.[213]

In a similar manner, Hungary invoked the existence of the "precautionary principle" in *Gabčíkovo-Nagymaros*.[214] The claim was not challenged by Slovakia, with both Parties to the case agreeing on the adoption of a precautionary approach, though they disagreed on its proper implementation.[215] Yet, once more, the ICJ declined to address the argument, preferring to ground its decision in "ecological necessity."[216] Even when the Court affirms the emergence of "new norms and standards" of environmental law which "are relevant for the implementation of the Treaty," it merely acknowledges that prevention is one of them.[217]

In comparison, the International Tribunal for the Law of the Sea (ITLOS) is more open to parties basing their arguments on a precautionary approach. In several cases, the Tribunal encourages States to act with "prudence and caution,"[218] thus implicitly endorsing the precautionary principle.[219] Yet, the fact that the jurisdiction declines to confirm the legal status of the precautionary approach is noteworthy.[220] Indeed, it is not possible to fully ascertain from the Tribunal's jurisprudence whether its application is grounded in a principle of general or customary international law or in the *United Nations Convention on the Law of the Sea* (UNCLOS).[221] According to the jurisdiction in *Bluefin Tuna*, the Convention requires States "to cooperate directly or through appropriate international organizations with a view to ensuring conservation and

211. Request for Examination of the Situation in Accordance with Paragraph 63 of the Court's Judgment of 20 December 1974 in the Nuclear Tests Case (New Zealand/ France.) (Order), 1995 ICJ Rep. 288, §5 (September 22) ["ICJ, Request for Examination"].
212. *Id.*, §68.
213. *Id.*, Dissenting Opinion of Judge Weeramantry, at 362.
214. ICJ, Gabčíkovo-Nagymaros, *supra* note 148, §97.
215. Rolland, *supra* note 210 at 454.
216. *Id.*, at 453–454.
217. ICJ, Gabčíkovo-Nagymaros, *supra* note 148, §§112 and 140.
218. ITLOS, Southern Bluefin Tuna, *supra* note 204, §77 and ITLOS, MOX Plant, *supra* note 204, §84; Land Reclamation in and around the Straits of Johor (No. 12) (Malaysia v. Singapore), Provisional Measures, Order of Oct. 8, 2003, §99, 2003 ITLOS Rep. 10 ["ITLOS, Land Reclamation"]. On the jurisprudence of ITLOS regarding the precautionary approach, *see* Mar Campins Eritja, *L'appréhension jurisprudentielle du principe de précaution par le Tribunal international du droit de la mer*, 46 Revue juridique de lenvironnement 83 (2021).
219. Jaeckel, *supra* note 148 at 34.
220. *Id.*
221. United Nations Convention on the Law of the Sea, *entered into force* Nov. 16, 1994, 1833 UNTS 3 ["UNCLOS"].

promoting the objective of optimum utilization of highly migratory species."[222] Yet, at the same time, the Tribunal's demarche is not without reminding of the precautionary approach. In particular, it justifies the grant of provisional measures based on the lack of scientific certainty concerning the measures to be taken for the conservation of the southern bluefin tuna stocks.[223] Furthermore, both Judge Treves and Judge Laing explicitly refer to the "precautionary approach" in their separate opinions. The former acknowledges "the reluctance" of the Tribunal "to take position" on the customary nature of the precautionary principle,[224] whereas the latter emphasized the impossibility to determine, at the time, whether it has crystallized into a customary norm.[225]

A possible explanation for the reluctance of international jurisdictions to take a position on the precautionary principle's legal status could be its relatively novel character at the time of the ruling. Indeed, the abovementioned cases ruled by the ICJ and ITLOS were all judged within a decade of the adoption of the Rio Declaration.[226] Since then, international jurisdictions have started to address arguments based on a "precautionary approach," though the status of its legal character remains unclear.

In *Pulp Mills*, the World Court concedes, for instance, that "a precautionary approach may be relevant in the interpretation and application of [a treaty]."[227] This explicit reference to a "precautionary approach" constitutes an evolution in the jurisprudence of the World Court, especially when weighted against its findings in *Gabčíkovo-Nagymaros*: in *Pulp Mills*, the jurisdiction singles out the precautionary approach as a norm of environmental law which can be used to implement a treaty whereas it had stayed silent on the matter in *Gabčíkovo-Nagymaros*.[228] However, it must be underlined that the ICJ did not rule on the basis of the precautionary approach. It only referred to it to dismiss Argentina's argument that such an approach shifts the burden of proof to the other party.[229] Hence the lack of decision regarding the legal status of the principle.

In comparison, the ITLOS is more forthcoming in its position; it has abandoned the timid approach to the precautionary approach adopted in *Bluefin Tuna*. Making a reference to the ICJ ruling in *Pulp Mills*, the Tribunal explicitly refers to an obligation to apply a precautionary approach in *Land Reclamation*.[230] In this case, the jurisdiction affirms that precaution is among "the most important [...] direct obligations incumbent on sponsoring States" and that the incorporation of the approach in a growing number

222. ITLOS, Southern Bluefin Tuna, *supra* note 204, §48.
223. *Id.*, §§79–80.
224. *Id.*, Separate Opinion, of Judge Treves, §9.
225. *Id.*, Separate Opinion of Judge Laing, §16.
226. The ruling on the cases referenced above occurred between 1995 and 2003. *See* Nuclear Test (Order of Sept. 22, 1995); ICJ, Gabčíkovo-Nagymaros, *supra* note 148; ITLOS, Southern Bluefin Tuna, *supra* note 204; ITLOS, MOX Plant, *supra* note 204 and ITLOS, Land Reclamation, *supra* note 218.
227. ICJ, Pulp Mills, *supra* note 206, §164.
228. *Id.*, and ICJ, Gabčíkovo-Nagymaros, *supra* note 148, §97.
229. Dupuy and Viñuales, *supra* note 170 at 72.
230. ITLOS, Land Reclamation, *supra* note 218.

of instruments "has initiated a trend towards making this approach part of customary international law."[231]

2.1.4 Conclusion

Eventually, we see that while the importance of the precautionary principle is being increasingly acknowledged by international jurisdictions, these jurisdictions have so far failed to issue a conclusive statement regarding its legal status. This justifies the fact that States are only required to adopt a precautionary approach under treaty law. As a result, since there is no reference to the approach in the UN Space Treaties, it is not possible to enforce the precautionary principle on States carrying out space activities.

However, this is only true at the *international* level. In reality, States remain free to voluntarily incorporate precaution into their *domestic* legal order for space activities. For this reason, the question of the precautionary principle is far from being irrelevant. It may even be *more* relevant at the national level since the enforceability of the precautionary principle actually depends on the definition of clear gravity and probability thresholds; they help identify when to apply the precautionary principle.[232]

Currently, there is no equivalent for outer space. There does exist a sort of threshold in Article IX of the Outer Space Treaty when "harmful contamination" is defined as one that would impede other space activities. But this is too vague to be efficiently leveraged toward the application of a precautionary principle. Thus, a more efficient solution would be for each State to unilaterally define threshold standards in their domestic law.[233] Even if this approach would lead to the adoption of various thresholds across spacefaring nations, it would still achieve its purpose, i.e., preventing environmental degradation of outer space as a result of human activities.

In the context of space resource activities, one last avenue must be considered. In 2021, the UNCOPUOS LSC agreed to establish a *Working Group on Legal Aspects of Space Resource Activities*[234] tasked with, *inter alia*, "assess[ing] the benefits of further development of a framework for such activities, including by way of additional international governance instruments."[235] Although the wording of the mandate was chosen carefully to accommodate different preferences of delegations on the nature of the framework,[236] it presents an opportunity to incorporate the precautionary principle at the international level in future developments.

231. *Id.*, §122.
232. Birnie, Boyle, and Redgwell, *supra* note 141 at 73, 163.
233. Larsen, *supra* note 155 at 304.
234. Report of the Legal Subcommittee on its sixtieth session, held in Vienna from May 31 to June 11, 2021, UNCOPUOS, 64th Sess., §§30–33 UN Doc. A/AC.105/1243 (2021).
235. Report of the Committee on the Peaceful Uses of Outer Space on its 64th Sess., held in Vienna from August 25 to September 3, UNGA, 76th Sess., Supp. No. 20, §53, UN Doc. A/76/20 (2021).
236. Antonino Salmeri, *The Multi-Level System of Space Mining: Regulatory Aspects and Enforcement Options*, July 7, 2022.

2.2 Due Diligence

> States have [...] the responsibility to ensure that activities within their jurisdiction or control do not cause damage to the environment of other States or of areas beyond the limits of national jurisdiction.
>
> —Principle 2 of the Rio Declaration.

The duty of a State to exert due diligence when fulfilling its international obligations is a prominent principle of international law. Sometimes referred to as a "rule," a "principle" or a "standard" by scholars,[237] due diligence has continuously been applied by international jurisdictions.[238] Although it was originally used in relation to State responsibility,[239] the principle has since been extended to several other areas of international law, including international environmental law, maritime law, humanitarian law, and investment law.[240] Since this book considers the reinforcement of environmental rules for the protection of the outer space environment, the focus here is primarily on outlining a due diligence obligation under international environmental law, specifically within the context of transboundary environmental harm, outer space being an area located beyond the borders of any State.

Notwithstanding the environmental perspective adopted in this research, the adaptation of due diligence to distinct areas of international law is noteworthy. It highlights one of the key features of the principle, namely its flexibility.[241] However, these adaptations of due diligence requirements are not necessarily equivalent to a

237. Riccardo Pisillo-Mazzeschi, *The Due Diligence Rule and the Nature of the International Responsibility of States*, 35 German Yearbook of International Law 9 (1992) DOI: 10.4324/9781315242439-12; Robert P. Jr. Barnidge, *The Due Diligence Principle under International Law*, 8 International Community Law Review 81 (2006) DOI: 10.1163/187197306779173194; Giulio Bartolini, *The Historical Roots of the Due Diligence Standard, in* Due diligence in the international legal order 23 (Heike Krieger, Anne Peters, & Leonhard Kreuzer eds., First edition ed. 2020).

238. *See, e.g.*, Alabama Claims Arbitration (United States/Great Britain), 1872, 29 RIAA 125, pp. 125–134 (United Nations ed., 2012) ["Alabama Arbitration"]; Trail Smelter Arbitration (US/Canada), 1941, 3 RIAA 1905; ICJ, Nuclear Threat (A/O), *supra* note 204; ICJ, Pulp Mills, *supra* note 206, §§101, 197, 204 and 223; Certain Activities Carried Out by Nicaragua in the Border Area (Costa Rica v. Nicaragua) and Construction of a Road in Costa Rica along the San Juan River (Nicaragua v. Costa Rica), Judgment, 2015 ICJ Rep. 665, §§104, 153, 168, 228 (Dec. 16) ["ICJ, Costa Rica/Nicaragua"]; PCA, South China Sea (Republic of the Philippines/People's Republic of China) 2016, §755, 33 RIAA 153 ["PCA, South China Sea Award"]; Responsibilities and obligations of States with respect to activities in the Area (No. 17) Advisory Opinion of Feb. 1, 2011, §§110–112, 117–120 and 131–132, 2011 ITLOS Rep. 10 ["ITLOS, Responsibilities in the Area (A/O)"]; Request for Advisory Opinion submitted by the Sub-Regional Fisheries Commission (No. 21) Advisory Opinion of Apr. 2, 2015, §§125–140, 2015 ITLOS Rep. 4.

239. Timo Koivurova, *Due Diligence*, Max Planck Encyclopedias of International Law 2 (Rüdiger Wolfrum ed., 2010). On the history of the concept, *see* Bartolini, *supra* note 237.

240. Koivurova, *supra* note 239 at 2; Alice Ollino, Due Diligence Obligations in International Law 18 (2022). Also *see* ILA first report on due diligence which considers the evolution of the concept in several areas of international law, like international environmental law, investment law, human rights law and transnational criminal law. ILA, *Study Group on Due Diligence in International Law*, First Report (2014) available online.

241. Birnie, Boyle, and Redgwell, *supra* note 141 at 118.

statement about the existence of *due diligences*. As noted by Barnidge, the main characteristic of the principle of due diligence also provides the "underlying legal framework" for its application to particular facts and circumstances.[242] Therefore, the presence of due diligence in international law is less about creating distinct principles of due diligence—each specific to a legal area—and more about applying a general principle to specific situations.[243]

In essence, due diligence describes a standard of behavior States must adopt when fulfilling their obligations toward other States. In this sense, they must act as a "good government" would, by deploying the "best possible efforts" and taking "all the necessary and appropriate" measures when achieving an objective, such as the prevention of transboundary environmental harm.[244] Accordingly, due diligence is an obligation of *conduct*, not of *result*: failure to achieve the objective does not amount to a breach of the duty of due diligence but failure to adopt an appropriate behavior might. Applied to the obligation to prevent transboundary environmental harm, it means that a lack of diligence is not characterized by the existence of actual environmental damage but by the failure of the State to have tried to the best of its capacity to prevent it. This is where the distinction between an obligation of conduct and an obligation of result comes into play. The former looks at the behavior of the State when trying to achieve a result, whereas the latter ascertains whether the result has been achieved.

2.2.1 General Obligation

From a historical perspective, due diligence is rooted in international law in the notion of State responsibility, particularly in relation to the attributability to the State of the behavior of private actors.[245] It was first explicitly applied in international law in the *Alabama Arbitration*[246] of 1872 which opposed the United States to Great Britain.[247] The case raises the question of the interpretation of Great Britain's obligation to exercise due diligence in the application of the *Treaty between Great Britain and the United States of America for the Amicable Settlement of all Causes of Difference between*

242. *Id.*
243. In this regard, Barnidge underlines the necessity for general principles of international law to be "sketched in the abstract." Barnidge, *supra* note 237 at 158.
244. In *Responsibilities in the Area*, the ITLOS elaborates on the responsibility of UNCLOS' States Parties "to ensure" that activities in the deep seabed—i.e., in the "Area"—are carried out in accordance with the Convention. It characterizes the obligation as one of "due diligence," i.e., one which requires States "to deploy adequate means, to exercise best possible efforts, to do the utmost, to obtain this result." ITLOS, Responsibilities in the Area (A/O), *supra* note 238, §110. Also *see*, e.g., UNCLOS, Art. 139.
245. Koivurova, *supra* note 239 at 2.
246. Alabama Arbitration, *supra* note 238, 125–134. For an exhaustive overview of the facts, parties submissions and ruling of the Tribunal, *see, e.g.*, Awalou Ouedraogo, *La Due Diligence en Droit International: De la Regle de la Neutralite au Principe General*, 42 Rev. Gen. 641, 646–656 (2012) DOI: 10.7202/1026909ar.
247. Koivurova, *supra* note 239 at 34.

the Two Countries[248] ("Washington Treaty").[249] In a nutshell, the case pertains to the consequences of Great Britain's declaration of neutrality in the conflict opposing the Confederate States of America to the Union. The duties of a neutral State were laid down in Article 6 of the Washington Treaty which calls for the neutral State to "use" and "exercise" due diligence. The legal dispute arose when Great Britain failed to prevent the construction and partial armament, on its territory, of warships—including the *Alabama*—for the Confederate States of America. While neither party contested the existence of a due diligence obligation, they both hold contrasting views on its interpretation. For Great Britain, due diligence had to be interpreted restrictively: lack of due diligence means "a failure to use, for the prevention of an act which the government was bound to endeavour [sic] to prevent, such care as governments *ordinarily employ* in their domestic concerns, and may reasonably be expected to exert in matters of international interest and obligation" [italics added].[250] The US, however, favored an "active diligence," that is, one "commensurate with the emergency or with the magnitude" of the State's failure to act diligently.[251] The Tribunal agreed with the American position, finding that "the government of Her Britannic Majesty cannot justify itself for a failure in due diligence on the plea of insufficiency of the legal means of action which it possessed."[252] The jurisdiction concluded that "Great Britain has in this case failed, by omission, to fulfill the duties" under the Washington Treaty.[253] As a result, the *Alabama Arbitration* confirmed that the exercise of due diligence was not to be assessed according to how a State works under ordinary circumstances but, rather, in light of the particular facts and circumstances.

The persistence of the principle and its interpretation from this initial case is shown by the 20th-century ruling of the World Court regarding the attributability of the conduct of private individuals to the State in which due diligence played a prominent role. In *United States Diplomatic and Consular Staff in Tehran,*[254] the ICJ addresses aspects of a State's due diligence obligation in the context of the first[255] phase of the

248. Treaty between Great Britain and the United States of America for the Amicable Settlement of all Causes of Difference between the Two Countries, signed May 8, 1871, *entered into force* June 17, 1871, 61 BSP 40.
249. Alabama Arbitration, *supra* note 238, 129.
250. Horst Blomeyer-Bartenstein, *Due Diligence*, 10 ENCYCLOPEDIA OF PUBLIC INTERNATIONAL LAW 138 139 (Rudolf Bernhardt ed., 1987).
251. *Id.*
252. The Arbitral Tribunal notes, *inter alia,* that "with respect to the vessel called the Alabama, it clearly results from all the facts relative to the construction of the ship [...] and its equipment and armament [...], that the British government failed to use due diligence in the performance of its neutral obligations; and especially that it omitted, notwithstanding the warnings and official representations made by the diplomatic agents of the United States during the construction of [said ship] to take in due time any effective measures of prevention, and that those orders which it did give at last, for the detention of the vessel, were issued so late that their execution was not practicable." Alabama Arbitration, *supra* note 238, 130–131.
253. *Id.*, 131.
254. United States Diplomatic and Consular Staff in Tehran (United States of America v. Iran) (Judgment) 1980 ICJ Rep. 3 (May 24) ["ICJ, US Staff in Tehran"].
255. The Court draws a clear distinction between the two phases of the attack on the US embassy. In the first phase, the State failed to effectively protect the US embassy from the militia's actions, whereas, in the second phase, Iranian authorities approved the individuals' conduct. Under the rules of State responsibility codified in the ILC Draft Articles on State Responsibility,

attack on the US embassy by an Iranian revolutionary militia in 1979. In particular, the jurisdiction looks at the behavior adopted by Iranian authorities in response to the attack by private individuals. In this regard, the international jurisdiction notes that the State "failed altogether to take any 'appropriate steps' to protect the premises, staff, and archives of the United States' mission against attack by the militants, and to take any steps either to prevent this attack or to stop it before it reached its completion."[256] In the opinion of the Court, the "inaction" of the Iranian State constitutes in itself a "clear and serious violation of Iran's obligations to the United States."[257] As a result, the jurisdiction "inevitably conclude[s]" that the Iranian authorities:

> (a) *were fully aware of their obligations* under the conventions in force to take appropriate steps to [*inter alia*] protect the premises of the United States Embassy [...];
> (b) *were fully aware*, as a result of the appeals for help made by the United States Embassy, *of the urgent need for action on their part;*
> (c) *had the means* at their disposal to perform their obligations;
> (d) *completely failed* to comply with these obligations [italics added].[258]

With these elements, the ICJ's decision brings forward more elements regarding the content of due diligence: in particular, the State must have "full awareness" of its obligations and of the necessity to take action to fulfill them.[259] This means that a State is not expected to act beyond what can reasonably be expected of a "good government." However, in the present case, the circumstances unequivocally called for the State to act, which it "completely failed" to do.

Although the World Court grounds its findings in the application of a Convention, it also states that "[i]n the view of the Court, the obligations of the Iranian Government here in question are not merely contractual obligations established by the Vienna Conventions of 1961 and 1963, but also obligations under general international

---

the conduct of private individuals is attributable to the State to the extent it acknowledges and adopts it as its own. *See* Articles on State Responsibility, Art. 11 *in* GA Res. 56/83, UNGA, 56th Sess., UN Doc. A/RES/56/83 (2002). In the present case, the ICJ considers that "[t]he policy thus announced by the Ayatollah Khomeini, of maintaining the occupation of the Embassy and the detention of its inmates as hostages for the purpose of exerting pressure on the United States Government was complied with by other Iranian authorities and endorsed by them repeatedly in statements made in various contexts. The result of that policy was fundamentally to transform the legal nature of the situation created by the occupation of the Embassy and the detention of its diplomatic and consular staff as hostages. *The approval given to these facts by the Ayatollah Khomeini and other organs of the Iranian State, and the decision to perpetuate them, translated continuing occupation of the Embassy and detention of the hostages into acts of that State*" [italics added]. *Id.*, §74.

256. The ICJ further notes that "the Iranian Government similarly failed to take appropriate steps for the protection of the United States Consulates at Tabriz and Shiraz. In addition, they show, in the opinion of the Court, that the failure of the Iranian Government to take such steps was due to more than mere negligence or lack of appropriate means." *Id.*, §63.
257. *Id.*, §67.
258. *Id.*, §69.
259. Robert P. Barnidge, *States' Due Diligence Obligations with Regard to International Non-State Terrorist Organisations Post-11 September 2001: The Heavy Burden that States Must Bear*, 16 IRISH STUDIES IN INTERNATIONAL AFFAIRS 103, 108–109 (2005) DOI: 10.1353/isia.2005.0012.

law."[260] In Barnidge's opinion, the statement could be interpreted in favor of the extension of the due diligence obligation defined by the World Court to broader situations, i.e., beyond the application of the Convention. Furthermore, the ICJ underlines that the failure to act was not the result of a lack of means, which *a contrario* could be interpreted as meaning that, had it been the case, the State would not have been in violation of its due diligence obligation.

The question of the relationship between a State's due diligence obligation and the means at its disposal was detailed by the ICJ in *Military and Paramilitary Activities in and against Nicaragua*.[261] In this case, the jurisdiction has to determine whether the Nicaraguan authorities provided armed support to the opposition in El Salvador.[262] To that end, the World Court first looks at the evidence provided by the parties as well as the Statement submitted by El Salvador. The international jurisdiction concludes that, although evidence demonstrates "a certain amount of aid [to the opposition] from Nicaraguan territory,"[263] it is not sufficient, in itself, to conclude the responsibility of the State. In particular, the World Court recalls its decision in *Corfu Channel* where it observed that:

> it cannot be concluded from the mere fact of the control exercised by a State over its territory and waters that that State necessarily knew, or ought to have known, of any unlawful act perpetrated therein, nor yet that it necessarily knew, or should have known, the authors. This fact, by itself and apart from other circumstances, neither involves prima facie responsibility nor shifts the burden of proof.[264]

Nonetheless, the World Court takes an additional step in its assessment of the situation. Namely, it looks at the conduct of the Nicaraguan State in response to the aid provided from and through its territory to the armed opposition in El Salvador. In other words, it ascertains whether the State acted diligently. Accordingly, the ICJ makes several observations, notably with regard to the behavior of other States. It observes, *inter alia*, that "[n]either Honduras or El Salvador or the United States succeed[ed] in preventing [the traffic]," emphasizing the fact that—even with the deployment of "exceptionally extensive resources"—the United States "have been powerless to prevent this traffic from keeping the Salvadorian armed opposition supplied."[265] Therefore, the World Court creates here a reference point—i.e., what preventive actions other affected States in the area were able to take—to which it can confront the conduct adopted by Nicaragua. Notably, it highlights the fact that the State possesses

260. ICJ, US Staff in Tehran, *supra* note 254, §62.
261. Military and Paramilitary Activities in and against Nicaragua (Nicaragua v. United States of America) (Judgment) 1986 ICJ Rep. 14 (June 27) ["ICJ, Military and Paramilitary Activities"].
262. In this case, the ICJ attempts to determine whether US activities in and against Nicaragua were justified under the claim of collective self-defense. To that end, the jurisdiction must first ascertain the facts presented in support of the US claim, namely that Nicaragua provided support to the armed opposition in Nicaragua. *Id.*, §§126–128. On the analysis of the conduct of Nicaragua, *see* §§126–171.
263. *Id.*, §§152–153.
264. *Id.*, §155; Corfu Channel (UK v. Albania) (Judgment) 1949 ICJ Reports 18 (Apr. 9) ["ICJ, Corfu Channel"].
265. *Id.*, ICJ, Military and Paramilitary Activities, §157.

"much smaller resources at its disposal for subduing this traffic" than the US.[266] Consequently, the international jurisdiction concludes that "it would clearly be unreasonable to demand of the Government of Nicaragua a higher degree of diligence than is achieved by even the combined efforts of the other three States."[267] Therefore, "it is scarcely possible for Nicaragua's responsibility for an arms traffic taking place on its territory to be automatically assumed."[268]

The World Court's holding in *Military and Paramilitary Activities in and against Nicaragua* confirms the hypothesis suggested by *United States Diplomatic and Consular Staff in Tehran*: a lack of resources can be used to justify a lack of effective action on the part of a State. More generally, the due diligence obligation outlined by the ICJ is grounded in the possibility for a State to act in response to particular facts and circumstances.[269] To act diligently, a State must first be fully aware that the fulfillment of its obligations may require additional action on its part. Second, a State must be aware of the existence of risk which, without prompt action on its part, may jeopardize the good fulfillment of its obligation. A third element may come into play to soften the due diligence obligation, namely whether the State has the resources to respond adequately to the risk. The jurisdiction could consider, for instance, the financial, economic, and technological resources available to the State, as well as its capacity to exercise effective control of the situation, when assessing the State's behavior.[270] However, it must be underlined that simply because a jurisdiction *may* consider the resources available to a State in its assessment, there is no guarantee that it *will*.[271] Nor does it mean that a State should not try to go "beyond one State's resource capacity."[272]

2.2.2 *ILC's Articles on Prevention of Transboundary Harm*

Another source of development of the due diligence obligation has been the work of the UN International Law Commission (ILC). It is all the more important since its work on the codification of State responsibility has led to a major contribution in the field of environmental protection by articulating a position regarding the due diligence obligation in the context of transboundary environmental harm.

In the 1950s, the Commission debated the role of due diligence in the determination of State responsibility for acts of private individuals. This was in line with the rich jurisprudence, in addition to extensive literature, which links due diligence to the

266. *Id.*
267. *Id.*
268. *Id.*, §158.
269. Ollino, *supra* note 240 at 166.
270. *See, e.g.*, in the context of space activities, Irmgard Marboe, *The Importance of Guidelines and Codes of Conduct for Liability of States and Private Actors*, *in* Soft Law in Outer Space: The Function of Non-binding Norms in International Space Law 119, 138 (Irmgard Marboe ed., 2012); Viikari, *supra* note 22 at 156.
271. The assessment of the resources at the disposal of a State is generally limited to the evaluation of the due diligence obligation of developing countries. Ollino, *supra* note 240 at 166–167.
272. *Id.*

attributability of private conduct to a State as shown before.[273] Yet, while working on the *Draft Articles on Responsibility of States for International Wrongful Acts*[274] ("Articles on State Responsibility"), the Commission had progressively eliminated references to due diligence since no agreement could be reached on its inclusion.[275] It was a severe setback, but the question was not definitively closed.

The topic was discussed once more by the ILC in the 1970s in the framework of the project on *International Liability for Injurious Consequences Arising Out of Acts Not Prohibited*.[276] Where the Articles on State Responsibility would codify a system from which State responsibility arises with the occurrence of an internationally wrongful act—i.e., the breach of international obligation—the *Draft Articles on Prevention of Transboundary Harm from Hazardous Activities*[277] ("Articles on Prevention of Transboundary Harm" or "ILC Articles") would outline a framework for State liability arising from the occurrence of transboundary harm, in cases where the harmful activity was not prohibited under international law.[278] Or, in the words of Article 1, the ILC Articles apply to activities "not prohibited by international law which involve a risk of causing significant transboundary harm through their physical consequences."

Progressively, the Commission's work on transboundary harm shifted to primarily focus on transboundary *environmental* harm. As a result, the Articles on Prevention of Transboundary Harm outline the conditions and procedural requirements of due diligence in the context of environmental protection. The contribution of the ILC in this area is particularly valuable since, as underlined by ITLOS in *Responsibilities in the Area*:

---

273. *See, e.g.*, Pisillo-Mazzeschi, *supra* note 237; OLLINO, *supra* note 240 at 187–231; LE STANDARD DE DUE DILIGENCE ET LA RESPONSABILITÉ INTERNATIONALE (Sarah Cassella ed., 2018).
274. ILC, Draft Articles on Responsibility of States for Internationally Wrongful Acts, with commentaries, 2001 ILC YB II/2.
275. The root of the issue was the close relationship between the concepts of due diligence and "fault," as the ILC could not agree on whether State responsibility should include an element of fault. Regarding the link between the two notions, Special Rapporteur F. V. Garcia Amador notes that:

> the rule of "due diligence" is the expression par excellence of the so-called theory of fault (*culpa*), for if there is any category of cases in which it cannot be said that responsibility arises through the simple existence of a wrong it is surely the category dealt with in [Chapter V. Acts of individuals and internal disturbances].

ILC, International responsibility. Second report by F. V. Garcia Amador, Special Rapporteur, at 122, UN Doc. A/CN.4/106 (1957). More generally, on the role of due diligence in the codification of rules of State responsibility, *see, e.g.*, Helmut Philipp Aust & Prisca Feihle, *Due Diligence in the History of the Codification of the Law of State Responsibility*, *in* DUE DILIGENCE IN THE INTERNATIONAL LEGAL ORDER 42 (Heike Krieger, Anne Peters, & Leonhard Kreuzer eds., 2020).
276. Report of the ILC, GA Res. 3071(XXVIII), UNGA, 28th Sess., UN Doc. A/RES/3071(XXVIII) (1973).
277. Draft Articles on Prevention of Transboundary Harm from Hazardous Activities, GA Res. 56/10, UNGAOR, 56th Sess., Supp. No. 10, UN DOC A/56/10 (2001) ["ILC Articles on Prevention of Transboundary Harm"].
278. 1980 ILC Yearbook I, 248, §9. The ILC had already underlined in 1978 the benefits of studying State liability as a separate topic, Report of the Working Group on International Liability for Injurious Consequences Arising out of Acts Not Prohibited by International Law, 1978 ILC Yearbook II/2 150, §178.

> [t]he content of "due diligence" obligations may not easily be described in precise terms. Among the factors that make such a description difficult is the fact that "due diligence" is a variable concept. It may change over time as measures considered sufficiently diligent at a certain moment may become not diligent enough in light, for instance, of new scientific or technological knowledge. It may also change in relation to the risks involved in the activity.[279]

Although—this will be discussed *infra*—international jurisprudence had confirmed several elements of due diligence which are included in the nonlegally binding Articles on Prevention of Transboundary Harm, it had generally focused on a specific aspect of the obligation. Consequently, recourse to the jurisprudence of international jurisdictions used to require piecing together the evolution and content of due diligence from various sources. In contrast, the Articles on Prevention of Transboundary Harm outline and group them in a single document.

More precisely, the ILC Articles root the due diligence obligation in a core provision and build an entire operationalizing framework on its basis. This core provision is delineated in Article 3, which provides that:

> [t]he State of origin shall take all appropriate measures to prevent significant transboundary harm or at any event to minimize the risk thereof.

Thus, in the context of transboundary harm, due diligence translates into a prevention obligation.

Before moving to a deeper analysis of the due diligence obligation under the Articles on Prevention of Transboundary Harm, some preliminary remarks are necessary. First, the expression "State of origin"—as opposed to the State(s) affected—refers to the party under which territory, or jurisdiction and control, the potentially harmful activity is undertaken.[280] Second, the ILC Articles translate the obligation of due diligence within the context of transboundary harm into an obligation to prevent. The Commission clearly affirms the link between the two obligations in its Commentary, sometimes using them interchangeably.[281] Third, despite a strong environmental element, the ILC Articles are not limited in their application to transboundary *environmental* harm. Indeed, Article 2 (b) defines harm as "harm caused to persons, property or the environment." Nonetheless, it can be noted that the integration of the environmental component in the Articles on Prevention of Transboundary Harm is reflected on several levels. Its inclusion in the scope of the expression "harm" means the State is under an obligation to prevent, or at least minimize the risk of, environmental damage. This obligation is complemented by environmentally oriented procedural requirements, such as the obligation to undertake an EIA and to consider "the risk of significant harm to the environment and the availability of means of preventing such

279. ITLOS, Responsibilities in the Area (A/O), *supra* note 238, §117.
280. ILC Articles on Prevention of Transboundary Harm, *supra* note 277, Art. 2§d.
281. For instance, the Commission refers to the "[d]ischarge of the duty of prevention or due diligence." It further affirms that "[t]he obligation of the State of origin to take preventive or minimization measures is one of due diligence." *See* Draft Articles on Prevention of Transboundary Harm from Hazardous Activities, with commentaries, 2001 ILC Yearbook II/2, General Commentary, p. 148, §2 and Art. 3, p. 154, §7 ["ILC Commentary"].

harm or minimizing the risk thereof or restoring the environment."[282] Furthermore, a noteworthy reference in the preamble to the Rio Declaration emphasizes the necessity to consider the environment when carrying out risky activities. It frames the due diligence obligation in the context of "the general principles incorporated in the Rio Declaration and other considerations that emphasize the close interrelationship between issues of environment and development."[283] Fourth, and last, Article 3 establishes a clear hierarchy between the obligation to prevent and the obligation to minimize the harmful impact of the activity.[284] States must do their utmost to prevent the occurrence of transboundary harm. Failing to achieve this result, they are then required to, at least, take proportionate measures to ensure the risk of transboundary harm is minimized.

These preliminary remarks highlight what is at stake in the operative part of Article 3, namely the obligation of States to "take all appropriate measures" to prevent or at least minimize the risk of transboundary harm. The expression is not dissimilar to the one used by the ICJ in *United States Diplomatic and Consular Staff in Tehran* when observing that the Iranian State had failed to "take appropriate steps for the protection of the United States Consulates."[285] In the same manner, under the Articles on Prevention of Transboundary Harm, the compliance of the State of origin with its obligation to prevent transboundary harm is ascertained by its conduct.[286] Thus, compliance with the prevention obligation is not dependent on the success of the State to prevent transboundary harm, but on the efforts exerted toward that objective.[287] Therefore, the standard of due diligence applied here is one of reasonableness.[288]

Consequently, the obligation to take measures is triggered by the foreseeability of the risk.[289] It would not be reasonable to expect a State to adopt measures tailored to a risk justifiably unknown to it. As established earlier, the exercise of due diligence is intrinsically linked to the capacity of a State to act. Moreover, reasonableness also implies that the measures adopted by the State of origin to prevent transboundary harm are "appropriate," as is required by Article 3. It means that the degree of care shown by the State must be proportionate to the probability and degree of hazard the planned activity involves.[290] Additionally, as underlined by the ILC in its Commentary of the ILC Articles, reasonableness is not a fixed standard in the sense that the degree of care it entails evolves with technological changes and scientific developments.[291] If better

282. ILC Articles on Prevention of Transboundary Harm, *supra* note 277, Arts. 7 and 10§c. It can also be noted that the commentary refers to several documents with a strong environmental component, such as the Brundtland report and the Stockholm Declaration. *Id.*, 148, §4.
283. ILC Articles on Prevention of Transboundary Harm, *supra* note 277, preamble, 146, §2.
284. ILC Commentary, *supra* note 281, Art. 3, p. 153, §3.
285. ICJ, US Staff in Tehran, *supra* note 254, §63.
286. ILC Commentary, *supra* note 281, Art. 3, p. 154, §7.
287. On the necessity for the State of origin to authorize activities involving a risk of causing significant transboundary physical harm, *see* ILC Articles on Prevention of Transboundary Harm, *supra* note 277, Art. 6.
288. For a comprehensive analysis of the standard of reasonableness, *see, e.g.*, Ollino, *supra* note 240 at 168–176.
289. ILC Commentary, *supra* note 281, Art. 3, p. 155, §18.
290. *Id.*
291. ILC Commentary, *supra* note 281, Art. 3, p. 154, §11.

preventive instruments are developed and the State of origin has access to them, then, it is only reasonable to expect it to make use of them.

In addition to requiring the State of origin to take "all appropriate measures," the Articles on Prevention of Transboundary Harm list several complementary obligations for the "States concerned"—i.e., both the State of origin and the State(s) affected by the activity. These obligations are grounded in the duty of the concerned States to "cooperate in good faith" during all phases of the planned activity.[292] To that end, all States involved must "take the necessary legislative, administrative or other action including the establishment of suitable monitoring mechanisms."[293] By requiring both the State of origin and the affected State to adopt measures, the ILC Articles ensure, *inter alia*, that the impact of the risky activity is monitored both by the State undertaking the activity and by the one potentially suffering its harmful effects. Moreover, inter-State cooperation is further operationalized by Articles 8 and 9 which establish, respectively, the duties to notify and consult. Accordingly, once the existence of a risk of causing significant transboundary harm has been established, the State of origin is required to notify, in a timely manner, likely affected States of its intention to undertake a risky activity. This obligation goes beyond simply informing affected States since the State of origin is further required to share "technical and all other relevant information on which the assessment [of the risk] is based."[294] Furthermore, the State of origin must await the confirmation of receipt, by the affected State, of the notification before proceeding to authorizing the conduct of the risky activity.[295] However, Article 8 imparts that the State of origin does not have to wait indefinitely and sets a limit to a waiting period not exceeding six months. The definition of a waiting period allows for the State affected to request consultations on the matter before the start of the planned activity. Indeed, Article 9 of the ILC Articles provides that either State may request consultation "with a view to achieving acceptable solutions regarding measures to be adopted." In order to ensure a balance between the right to hold consultations and the right of the State of origin to undertake the activity, Article 9 specifies that the parties "shall agree, at the commencement of such consultations, on a reasonable time frame for the consultations." In other words, consultations are not intended to be used as a means to delay the beginning of the planned activity. Such an approach would go against the principle of good faith emphasized under Article 4 on inter-State cooperation. In the same manner, it must be underlined that the consultation mechanism is not intended to be used as a veto right by the affected State. In the case where an agreement cannot be reached between the parties, the State of origin is allowed to proceed with the planned activity on the condition that it takes into account the interests of the other State.[296]

The Articles on Prevention of Transboundary Harm further define specific obligations to assist the State of origin in acting diligently. Specifically, the State of

292. ILC Commentary, *supra* note 281, Art. 4, p. 155, §1.
293. ILC Articles on Prevention of Transboundary Harm, *supra* note 277, Art. 5.
294. *Id.*, Art. 8.
295. *Id.*
296. *Id.*, Art. 9.

origin is required to authorize the risky activity prior to its start.[297] This decision is conditioned by the prior realization of a risk assessment, including an *environmental* impact assessment, of the possible harm derived from the activity of the State of origin.[298]

To summarize, the Articles on Prevention of Transboundary Harm outline the content and procedural requirements of due diligence in the (environmental) context of transboundary harm. In addition to the general obligation, under Article 3, to "take all appropriate measures to prevent significant transboundary harm," the ILC Articles expect States to cooperate in good faith,[299] to carry out an (environmental) impact assessment of the risks involved prior to authorizing the hazardous activity,[300] and to notify[301] and consult[302] with potentially affected States.

Despite their nonlegally binding character, the due diligence requirements included in the Articles on Prevention of Transboundary Harm have gained continuous support in the decisions of international jurisdictions. The obligation of a State to prevent transboundary environmental harm was already well established by the time the ILC adopted its Articles, in 2001.[303] In 1996, the ICJ confirmed in its Advisory Opinion on the *Legality of the Threat or Use of Nuclear Weapons*[304] that:

> the existence of the general obligation of States to ensure that activities within their jurisdiction and control respect the environment of other States or of areas beyond national control is now part of the corpus of international law relating to the environment.[305]

Furthermore, a similar obligation had already been affirmed by the Arbitral Tribunal in the *Trail Smelter Arbitration*[306] regarding the pollution by fumes of the State of Washington in the US as a result of Canadian activities.

297. *Id.*, Art. 6.
298. *Id.*, Art. 7.
299. *Id.*, Art. 4.
300. *Id.*, Art. 7.
301. *Id.*, Art. 8.
302. *Id.*, Art. 9.
303. The more general obligation to prevent transboundary harm can be traced back further to the ICJ decision in *Corfu Channel* of 1949. Briefly, the legal dispute arose after Albania failed to inform Great Britain of the presence of mines in the Corfu Channel which, ultimately, resulted in a loss of life and damage to British warships during the crossing. In this case, the World Court enounces the general obligation that a State must not "allow knowingly its territory to be used for acts contrary to the rights of other States." ICJ, Corfu Channel, *supra* note 264, p. 22.
304. ICJ, Nuclear Threat (A/O), *supra* note 204, §29.
305. This obligation was reaffirmed by the World Court on several occasions. ICJ, Gabčíkovo-Nagymaros, *supra* note 148, §53; ICJ, Pulp Mills, *supra* note 206, §§101 and 193; ICJ, Costa Rica/Nicaragua, *supra* note 238, §118.
306. The Tribunal found that "under the principles of international law, as well as of the law of the United States, no State has the right to use or permit the use of its territory in such a manner as to cause injury by fumes in or to the territory of another or the properties or persons therein, when the case is of serious consequence and the injury is established by clear and convincing evidence." Trail Smelter Arbitration, *supra* note 238, 1965.

2.2.3 *Accessory Obligations*

More recently, the development of international environmental law in the jurisprudence of international jurisdictions has further contributed to the recognition of several international obligations flowing from the existence of a broader duty to exert due diligence. In *Pulp Mills*, the World Court confirms the prevention principle as a customary rule of international law that "has its origins in [...] due diligence."[307] It further declared that a State is "obliged to use *all the means at its disposal* in order to avoid activities which take place in its territory, or in any area under its jurisdiction, causing significant damage to the environment of another State" [italics added],[308] a statement which is not without echoing the wording of Article 3 of the Articles on Prevention of Transboundary Harm. It confirms that due diligence implies an obligation for a State to "use all the means at its disposal" to prevent transboundary environmental harm. The World Court continues by affirming that:

> *due diligence*, and the duty of vigilance and prevention which it implies, *would not be considered to have been exercised*, if a party planning works liable to affect the régime of the river or the quality of its waters *did not undertake an environmental impact assessment* [italics added].[309]

Here, the World Court explicitly links the conduct of an EIA to the exercise of due diligence, thus confirming one of the procedural requirements defined in the ILC Articles.[310]

Similarly, the international jurisdiction underlines in *Corfu Channel* the duty of a State to notify potentially affected parties and that such obligation is based "on certain general and well-recognized principles" such as the obligation not to allow its territory to be used to cause harm to other States.[311] Moreover, in the *Lake Lanoux Arbitration*,[312] the Arbitral Tribunal holds that "[c]onsultations and negotiations between the two States must be genuine, must comply with the rules of good faith and must not be mere formalities. The rules of reason and good faith are applicable to procedural rights and duties relative to the sharing of the use of international rivers."

This "customary matrix of international environmental law" is confirmed by the World Court in *Costa Rica/Nicaragua*.[313] First, the international jurisdiction recalls that the prevention principle is a due diligence obligation.[314] Second, it recalls its holding in *Pulp Mills* and expands on the obligation, under general international law, to undertake an EIA prior to the start of a risky activity.[315] In particular, the World Court extends the

307. ICJ, Pulp Mills, *supra* note 206, §101.
308. *Id.*
309. *Id.*, §204.
310. Articles on Prevention of Transboundary Harm, Article 7. It can be noted that the obligation to carry out an EIA is also included in Principle 17 of the Rio Declaration. The EIA mechanism is discussed in more detail in the next section of the work.
311. ICJ, Corfu Channel, *supra* note 264, p. 22.
312. Lake Lanoux Arbitration Award, *supra* note 108.
313. Dupuy and Viñuales, *supra* note 170 at 62.
314. ICJ, Costa Rica/Nicaragua, *supra* note 238, §104.
315. *Id;* ICJ, Pulp Mills, *supra* note 206, §§101 and 204.

requirement of undertaking an EIA—limited until then to "industrial activities"—to all proposed activities which may have a significant transboundary harmful impact.[316] The jurisdiction also uses the opportunity to stress the link between a State's obligation to exercise due diligence in preventing significant transboundary environmental harm and the requirement to carry out an EIA.[317] Third, and last, the ICJ confirms that—when the existence of a risk has been ascertained by the EIA—a State must "notify and consult in good faith with the potentially affected State, where that is necessary to determine the appropriate measures to prevent or mitigate that risk," to conform with its due diligence obligation.[318]

2.2.4 Conclusion

In conclusion, the obligation of States to exercise due diligence in the context of transboundary environmental harm is well established under customary international law. Reference to the ILC's Articles on Prevention of Transboundary Harm and to international jurisprudence shows that the prima facie abstract obligation of due diligence finds its concrete expression in a number of well-recognized principles. Notably, there exists a general obligation for States to ensure that activities under their jurisdiction and control do not cause significant environmental harm beyond their borders. In order to achieve this objective, States are required to: 1) notify and consult in good faith with potentially affected parties and 2) undertake an EIA prior to the start of their activity.

In the context of space activities, the obligation must first be distinguished from another obligation of conduct included in the Outer Space Treaty and the Moon Agreement: due regard.[319] Whereas due diligence requires States Parties to use their best efforts in preventing planned activities from causing damage to other States and their environment, due only requires performing duties and rights reasonably, meaning in a manner that respects other States' competing rights and duties.[320]

With regard to the transposition of the due diligence principle to outer space, we observe that elements of the procedural requirements necessary to the exercise of due diligence can be found in the Outer Space Treaty. Article IX of the Treaty affirms the obligation of the State of origin—i.e., the planning State—to "undertake appropriate international consultations before proceeding" with any activity which may "cause potentially harmful interference" with activities of other States Parties. Accordingly, although the consultation mechanism does not specifically apply to "environmental harm," it could be leveraged to that end. Especially if, as suggested in subsection 1.2.1 *supra*, the notion of "harmful interference" is interpreted as encompassing "harmful contamination" of the outer space environment. Moreover, Article XI of the Outer Space

316. ICJ, Costa Rica/Nicaragua, *supra* note 238, §104; ICJ, Pulp Mills, *supra* note 206, §204.
317. ICJ, Costa Rica/Nicaragua, *supra* note 238, §104.
318. *Id.*
319. Outer Space Treaty, Art. IX and Moon Agreement, Arts. 2 and 4§1.
320. Caroline E. Foster, *Due Regard and Due Diligence, in* GLOBAL REGULATORY STANDARDS IN ENVIRONMENTAL AND HEALTH DISPUTES: REGULATORY COHERENCE, DUE REGARD, AND DUE DILIGENCE 89 (2021).

Treaty provides that the planning State shall "inform the Secretary-General of the United Nations as well as the public and the international scientific community" of its activities. Although the obligation does not particularly target the "affected State," it could be argued that: (1) the duty to inform is in essence an obligation to notify and (2) that since outer space is *res communis*, all States are potentially affected States in the sense of the prevention principle. Lastly, in *Responsibilities in the Area*, ITLOS argues for the extension of the obligation to "activities with an impact on the environment in an area beyond the limits of national jurisdiction," such as outer space.[321] One "important constituent element" of due diligence still requires a closer look: the necessity to undertake an EIA.[322]

2.3 Environmental Impact Assessment

> Environmental impact assessment, as a national instrument, shall be undertaken for proposed activities that are likely to have a significant adverse impact on the environment and are subject to a decision of a competent national authority.
>
> —Principle 17 of the Rio Declaration

One salient mechanism to promote the sustainability of (mining) activities is EIA. Described by the literature as, *inter alia*, a procedural element and crucial tool of sustainable development, the primary objective of conducting an EIA is to provide decision-makers with comprehensive information regarding the potential environmental impact of a proposed activity.[323]

The origins of EIA—or of similar mechanisms aiming to examine, analyze and assess the environmental impact of a proposed activity—can be traced back to the domestic legislation of States and, particularly, one from the United States, passed in 1969.[324] In subsequent years, the practice of conducting EIA was implemented by many States[325] and progressively extended to apply beyond the State and to consider the transboundary environmental impact of proposed activities.[326] It was then incorporated

321. ITLOS, Responsibilities in the Area (A/O), *supra* note 238, §148.
322. Separate Opinion of Judge Owada, §18 *in* ICJ, Costa Rica/Nicaragua, *supra* note 238.
323. Convention on Environmental Impact Assessment in a Transboundary Context, *entered into force* Sept. 10, 1997, Art. 1§vi, 1989 UNTS 309 ["Espoo Convention"]; BIRNIE, BOYLE, AND REDGWELL, *supra* note 141 at 165.
324. National Environmental Policy Act, 42 USC §§4321–4370(f) [NEPA]. On the origins of EIA in domestic legislations, *see* CRAIK, *supra* note 144 at 23–53.
325. For an overview of domestic legislations implementing the EIA mechanism, *see* UN ENVIRONMENT, *Assessing Environmental Impacts- A Global Review of Legislation*, 150 (2018).
326. CRAIK, *supra* note 144 at 45–51. In the context of NEPA particularly, *see* Karen Klick, *Extraterritorial Reach of NEPA's EIS Requirement after Environmental Defense Fund v. Massey*, 44 AMERICAN UNIVERSITY LAW REVIEW (1994); Alexander Gilbert & Monica Vidaurri, *Major federal actions significantly affecting the quality of the space environment: applying NEPA to federal and federally authorized outer space activities*, 44 ENVIRONS 233 (2021).

into several regional[327] and international[328] instruments, including treaties with a universal scope.[329]

Typically, EIAs comprise several phases: screening, information-gathering, notification, and consultation.[330] In some cases, EIA procedures will also involve public participation before the competent authority ultimately delivers its decision regarding whether the proposed activity may proceed and how to regulate it.[331] The assessment itself considers different elements, such as the environmental impact of the activity on ecosystems and its surrounding environment, the diminution of aesthetic, historic, and scientific values as well as the long-term and cumulative effects.[332] Beyond assisting the competent authority in making an informed decision—one that takes into account the environment—the EIA may further result in the adoption of post-project monitoring and environmental measures.[333]

Therefore, the EIA process is a particularly significant tool when integrating environmental concerns into project planning. EIA can be qualified as a "tool" in the sense that it is useful in helping to achieve a goal.[334] EIA results do not determine per se the outcome of the review process—i.e., whether the proposed activity is authorized—but only assist decision-makers in making an informed decision, one that considers environmental concerns. Consequently, as underlined by Birnie et al., a "satisfactory" EIA is not necessarily an EIA which shows the proposed activity will have no environmental impact; a satisfactory EIA is one which provides the competent authority with understandable and adequate information.[335]

Moreover, an EIA carried out in a satisfactory manner can help demonstrate that precaution and due diligence have been exercised by the planning State. It shows that environmental risks were considered and, when appropriate, mitigation measures were adopted. *A contrario*, the ICJ held in *Pulp Mills* that:

> due diligence [...] would not be considered to have been exercised, if a party planning works liable to affect [the environment] did not undertake an environmental impact assessment on the potential effects of such works.[336]

327. Most notably, the European Community adopted an EIA directive in 1985 requiring Member States to assess the environmental effects of public and private projects which are "likely to have significant effects on the environment." Council Directive 85/337/EEC of June 27, 1985 on the assessment of the effects of certain public and private projects on the environment OJ L 175, 5.7.1985, pp. 40–48. Since then, the directive has been amended to, *inter alia*, align with the Espoo Convention, *supra* note 323, on EIA in a transboundary context and the Convention on Access to Information, Public Participation in Decision-Making, and Access to Justice in Environmental Matters, entered into force Oct. 30, 2001, 2161 UNTS 447.
328. Rio Declaration, Principle 17; Espoo Convention, *supra* note 323; UNEP Principles, *supra* note 347.
329. UNCLOS, Art. 206; Protocol on Environmental Protection to the Antarctic Treaty, *entered into force* Jan. 14, 1998, Art. 8 and Annex I, 2941 UNTS 3 ["Madrid Protocol"].
330. For a comprehensive overview of the different phases, *see* CRAIK, *supra* note 144 at 132–174.
331. BIRNIE, BOYLE, AND REDGWELL, *supra* note 141 at 165; CRAIK, *supra* note 144 at 146–150.
332. VIIKARI, *supra* note 22 at 268–269.; also *see, e.g.*, Madrid Protocol, *supra* note 329, Art. 3§2.
333. For example, Espoo Convention, *supra* note 323, Appendix V; ILC Articles on Prevention of Transboundary Harm, *supra* note 277, Art. 5.
334. Cambridge University Press, *Tool*, CAMBRIDGE DICTIONARY (n.d.).
335. BIRNIE, BOYLE, AND REDGWELL, *supra* note 141 at 165.
336. ICJ, Pulp Mills, *supra* note 206, §204.

In *Costa Rica/Nicaragua*, Judge Owada further remarks in a Separate Opinion that EIAs play "an important and even crucial role in ensuring that the State in question is acting with due diligence under general international environmental law."[337] For this reason, Craik believes that EIAs can be used as "action forcing mechanisms" to operationalize abstract principles of environmental law, such as due diligence.[338] Beyond its incorporation in treaties, which apply to Signing Parties only, the obligation to conduct an EIA under international law has been recognized by international jurisdictions. In particular, the ICJ considered in *Pulp Mills*[339] that:

> in recent years [the practice] has gained so much acceptance among States that it may now be considered a requirement under general international law to undertake an environmental impact assessment where there is a risk that the proposed industrial activity may have a significant adverse impact in a transboundary context, in particular, on a shared resource.

The existence of a binding obligation to undertake an EIA was further confirmed by the ITLOS in *Responsibilities and Obligations of States with Respect to Activities in the Area*.[340]

Moreover, in *Costa Rica/Nicaragua*, the World Court broadened the scope of application of the obligation to include "proposed activities which may have a significant adverse impact in a transboundary context."[341] In this regard, ITLOS affirmed that the ICJ's reasoning in a transboundary context could also apply "in an area beyond the limits of national jurisdiction, and the Court's references to 'shared resources' may also apply to resources that are the common heritage of mankind."[342] Therefore, the obligation for States to conduct an EIA under international law equally applies to activities intended to be carried out in areas beyond the limits of national jurisdiction, such as the high seas or outer space. The ITLOS further explicitly considers that the obligation remains applicable in the context of resources "that are the common heritage of mankind," which is the status of space resources under the Moon Agreement.[343] Consequently, by analogy, it can be argued that States are required to conduct an EIA before authorizing, *inter alia*, private space resource activities.[344] This conclusion is further supported by recourse to Article III of the Outer Space Treaty which states that general international law explicitly applies to space activities.

337. Separate Opinion of Judge Owada, §18 *in* ICJ, Costa Rica/Nicaragua, *supra* note 238.
338. Craik, *supra* note 144 at 164. On the link between EIA and sustainable development, *see* Wilkins, *supra* note 146; Birnie, Boyle, and Redgwell, *supra* note 141 at 116.
339. ICJ, Pulp Mills, *supra* note 206, §204.
340. ITLOS considers that the obligation to conduct an EIA exists under both the UNCLOS—as a result of Article 206—and customary international law. ITLOS, Responsibilities in the Area (A/O), *supra* note 238, §145.
341. ICJ, Costa Rica/Nicaragua, *supra* note 238, §104.
342. ITLOS, Responsibilities in the Area (A/O), *supra* note 238, §148.
343. Moon Agreement, Art. 11.
344. The extension of the obligation to conduct an EIA to activities carried out beyond national jurisdiction has further been argued by scholars and recognized by national jurisdictions in the context of the application of the domestic obligation. *See*, in the context of NEPA, Klick, *supra* note 326; Gilbert and Vidaurri, *supra* note 326.

2.3.1 *Implementation*

As showcased in the jurisprudence of international jurisdictions, recognizing the existence of an EIA obligation is not where the issue often lies.[345] The question is rather to define when this obligation is triggered.[346] The interrogation relates to the screening phase of an EIA, where it must be determined whether a formal EIA will be undertaken. For instance, Principle 17 of the Rio Declaration calls for States to undertake an EIA when the proposed activity is "likely to have a significant adverse impact on the environment." In a similar manner, the 1987 UNEP's *Goals and Principles of Environmental Impact Assessment*[347] ("UNEP's Principles") call for an EIA when the proposed activity is "likely to significantly affect the environment," and the 1991 Espoo Convention[348] when it is "likely to cause a significant adverse transboundary impact." The threshold of a "significant risk" was further cemented by the ILC in the 2001 Articles on Prevention of Transboundary Harm.[349] It is safe to conclude that a majority of instruments follow the formulation of the Rio Declaration. At this point, it must be emphasized that the threshold defined by these instruments does not concern whether the proposed activity should be authorized or whether measures should be taken; this will be decided based on, *inter alia*, the results of the EIA. The question of threshold is about whether a planning State is obliged to undertake an EIA.

As a result, the establishment of a threshold to initiate an EIA limits the scope of the obligation in two ways. First, not all proposed activities require the undertaking of an EIA, only those which have a "significant" risk of impacting the environment. Consequently, proposed activities which have been deemed to have a minor environmental impact do not require a prior EIA to be undertaken.[350] Second, it means that the implementation of the EIA mechanism is based on "a threshold of foreseeability" which must be met before undertaking an EIA.[351] According to Birnie et al., "[t]his is both circular and potentially self-defeating if taken literally."[352] The purpose of an EIA is to determine the level of environmental impact a proposed activity may cause. Yet,

345. Birnie et al. underlines, for instance, that international jurisdictions are not typically asked to determine whether the obligation exists but rather if it has properly taken place. Birnie, Boyle, and Redgwell, *supra* note 141 at 170. Also *see, e.g.*, ICJ, Gabčíkovo-Nagymaros, *supra* note 148; ITLOS, MOX Plant, *supra* note 204; ITLOS, Land Reclamation, *supra* note 218; PCA, South China Sea Award, *supra* note 238.
346. For instance, in *Costa Rica/Nicaragua*, the Court determined that the threshold triggering the obligation to carry out an EIA was met. ICJ, Costa Rica/Nicaragua, *supra* note 238, §156.
347. UNEP, Goals and Principles of Environmental Impact Assessment (1987) available online, Principle 1 ["UNEP Principles"].
348. Espoo Convention, *supra* note 323, Art. 2§3.
349. The State of origin must undertake an EIA when its planned activity presents a "significant risk" of transboundary harm. Here, the assessment of the significance of the risk is rather based on factual considerations than legal ones. According to the accompanying commentary, the term "significant" refers to "something more than "detectable" but need not be at the level of "serious" or "substantial." ILC Commentary, *supra* note 281, Arts. 1, 2§a, and 7.
350. For instance, the Madrid Protocol does not require States to undertake an EIA for proposed activities in Antarctica that are foreseen to have "less than a minor and transitory impact." Madrid Protocol, *supra* note 329, Arts. 1§2, 8, and Annex 1.
351. Birnie, Boyle, and Redgwell, *supra* note 141 at 171.
352. *Id.*

as seen above, most instruments only require States to undertake an EIA when it is known that the environmental impact is likely to be significant. In other words, States conduct an informal EIA to determine if they must undertake a formal EIA under international law.

This approach weakens the EIA mechanism since, while the primary assessment must be conducted in good faith, it does not formally require the compilation of information. One key feature of the EIA is its participatory nature. Indeed, many instruments require the planning State to allow affected parties to make observations about the project. For instance, Principle 7 of the UNEP Principles recommends that interested parties be allowed "appropriate opportunity to comment on the EIA" before any decision is taken. Similarly, Article 3 of the Espoo Convention requires the planning State to notify potentially affected parties about the proposed activity and to ensure they are "provided with possibilities for making comments or objections on, the proposed activity." In the context of an activity taking place in an area beyond national jurisdiction, Article 206 of UNCLOS demands the planning State "publish[es] reports of the results obtained" or communicate them so that other States may be informed. However, these rules only apply when the obligation to undertake an EIA is triggered. It does not extend to the foreseeability test which determines whether such EIA has to be undertaken. As a result, a State potentially affected by the transboundary activity could find challenging the need for an EIA, as it would not have access to relevant information.[353]

A possible alternative would be to follow the example of the *Protocol on Environmental Protection to the Antarctic Treaty*[354] ("Madrid Protocol"). It requires States to conduct an EIA for all activities in Antarctica—governmental and nongovernmental—except for *de minimis* cases.[355] The model is based on three levels of environmental impacts, with a baseline set at the determination of a "minor or transitory impact" on the environment. "Less than" the baseline means that no EIA is required. At the baseline level, the planning State must undertake an initial EIA, and above the baseline level—i.e., "more than" a minor or transitory impact—the State is required to conduct both an initial and a comprehensive EIA.[356] This distinction between two levels of EIAs depending on the extent of the environmental impact of the proposed activity was also included in the UNEP Principles. They recommend States—including their "competent authorities"—assess the environmental impact of the activity "at an early stage."[357] If the circumstances of the activity are "likely to significantly affect the environment," then the planning State must undertake a "comprehensive environmental impact assessment."[358] However, contrary to the Madrid Protocol which defines clear elements of the EIA,[359] the UNEP Principles only

353. *Id.*
354. Madrid Protocol, *supra* note 329.
355. *Id.*, Art. 8 and Annex I.
356. *Id.*, Annex I.
357. UNEP Principles, *supra* note 347, Principle 1.
358. *Id.*
359. *Id.*, Annex I.

call for States to clearly define criteria and procedures "by legislation, regulation or other means" so that "subject activities can be quickly and surely identified."[360]

In this regard, the UNEP Principles are in line with the practice of States. Indeed, as underlined by the ILC, "most existing international conventions and legal instruments do not specify the content of assessment."[361] Rather, they leave it to the discretion of States. Exceptions, however, exist, and a further distinction between sources of international law must be done. With regard to treaties, it can be noted that the second annex to the Espoo Convention provides a description of the minimum content elements that the EIA should include.[362] Accordingly, the EIA undertaken by the States Parties shall include, *inter alia*, a description of the proposed activity and its purpose, a description of reasonable alternatives to the activity and of the mitigation measures adopted, information regarding the method used to determine the potential impact of the activity and identified gaps in knowledge as well as an outline of the monitoring program when appropriate.[363] In a similar manner, the Madrid Protocol contains a detailed procedure for the EIA to be performed. It must "contain sufficient detail to assess whether a proposed activity may have more than a minor or transitory impact."[364] In particular, the instrument requires different levels of information for the initial and the comprehensive EIA.[365] The second EIA operates as an enhanced EIA; it requires the same information and more. Both require a description of the proposed activity and of alternatives. The comprehensive EIA, however, requires, *inter alia*, information regarding the methods used to assess the potential impact of the activity, the identification of mitigation measures, and monitoring programs. It also requires States to consider the indirect or second-order impact of the activity. It can also be noted that both conventions call for States to conduct an EIA prior to the start of the proposed activity.[366]

In comparison, the obligation to undertake an EIA in a transboundary context—and for activities carried out in an area beyond national jurisdiction—under customary international law is more general. There is no predetermined content. Indeed, as emphasized by the ICJ in *Pulp Mills*:

> it is for each State to determine in its domestic legislation or in the authorization process for the project, the specific content of the environmental impact assessment required in each case, having regard to the nature and magnitude of the proposed development and its likely adverse impact on the environment as well as to the need to exercise due diligence in conducting such an assessment.[367]

---

360. *Id.*, Principle 2.
361. For this reason, the Draft Articles do not include details regarding the content of the EIA; even in the commentary of Article 7, it only refers to the assessment including "the effects of the activity not only on persons and property, but also on the environment of other States." ILC Commentary, *supra* note 281, Art. 7, §§6–8.
362. Espoo Convention, *supra* note 323, Art. 4§1 and Annex II.
363. *Id.*, Annex II.
364. *Id.*, Annex I Art. 2.
365. *See in general id.*, Annex I.
366. Espoo Convention, *supra* note 323, Art. 2§3; *Id.*, Art. 8§2.
367. ICJ, Pulp Mills, *supra* note 206, §205.

Nonetheless, minimum requirements can be identified from the jurisprudence of international jurisdictions. For instance, the EIA must be undertaken prior to the start of the proposed activity.[368] Furthermore, as noted by the World Court in *Gabčíkovo-Nagymaros*, in the field of environmental law, it is important to apply new standards to both new activities and "activities begun in the past."[369] As such, States may be required to monitor their activities once authorized if the circumstances call for it.[370] In that sense, the obligation to carry out an EIA is a "continuous one"; it is not enough to simply undertake an initial EIA.[371] Monitoring of the authorized activity is particularly important as it allows us to confront the estimations made regarding the potential impact in the initial EIA with the reality of the situation. It enables adjustments when necessary. This is particularly important because, as emphasized by the requirements in the abovementioned conventions, there may be gaps in the knowledge or existing uncertainties regarding the environmental impact of the activity. Therefore, although not detailed, the obligation to carry out an EIA under international law also includes a duty to conduct an EIA that is appropriate to the circumstances of the situation.[372] Moreover, while international jurisdictions do not pronounce themselves on the content per se of an EIA, they do, however, assess whether the EIA undertaken by a State is adequate in light of the circumstances.[373]

2.3.2 Conclusion

The obligation to undertake an EIA in a transboundary context—or when operating in an area beyond national jurisdiction—is not absolute. Its application is dependent on the definition of an initiating threshold by States. In many instruments, this threshold has been set to the level of a "significant" environmental impact resulting from the proposed activity on the environment. However, it must be underlined that this threshold is not universal; the Madrid Protocol for Antarctica requires the conduct of an EIA for all activities except *de minimis* cases. The practice of States further shows that implementing rules for EIA are often drafted in general terms to allow competent authorities the necessary leeway to adapt the procedure to the circumstances of the case. However, similarly to the definition of a threshold, States are free to determine how detailed the rules framing the EIA should be. For instance, the Espoo Convention provides a description of the minimum content elements that the EIA should include, whereas the Madrid Protocol is very specific. In any case, the implementation of an EIA

368. *Id.*, §205; Costa Roca/Nicaragua, para. 161.
369. ICJ, Gabčíkovo-Nagymaros, *supra* note 148, §140.
370. ICJ, Pulp Mills, *supra* note 206, §205.
371. ICJ, Costa Rica/Nicaragua, *supra* note 238, §161.
372. In *Costa Rica/Nicaragua*, the Court held that "determination of the content of the environmental impact assessment should be made in light of the specific circumstances of each case." ICJ, Costa Rica/Nicaragua, *supra* note 238, §104.
373. *Id.*, §§157–161. For instance, Permanent Court of Arbitration deemed deficient the EIAs undertaken by China in the South China Sea Arbitration. PCA, South China Sea Award, *supra* note 238, §§988–990.

procedure could be used to operationalize the general obligation under Article IX of the Outer Space Treaty to avoid causing harmful contamination to the environment.

It can already be remarked that certain elements of EIA have been included in nonlegally binding space instruments promoting better care of the outer space environment. Although these instruments are discussed in depth in Chapter 3 *infra*, the inclusion in them of EIA-like standards calls for a few immediate remarks. For instance, paragraph 4 of the 1996 NPS Principles[374] preamble recognizes that:

> the use of nuclear power sources in outer space should be based on a *thorough safety assessment*, including probabilistic risk analysis, with particular emphasis on reducing the risk of accidental exposure of the public to harmful radiation or radioactive material [italics added].

The assessment mechanism itself is encompassed in Principle 4 and requires the launching State to ensure that, prior to the launch, a "thorough and comprehensive safety assessment" is conducted. Furthermore, similarly to the EIA requirement under general international law, the results of the safety assessment must be made "publicly available prior to each launch," notably through their communication to the UN Secretary-General.[375]

Another example is the development of nonlegally binding guidelines for space debris mitigation.[376] They recommend operators draw a "mitigation plan" which shall include, among other elements, "a plan for the assessment and mitigation of risks related to space debris."[377] Guideline 5.1 of the Inter-Agency Space Debris Coordination Committee (IADC)'s instrument further states that "[a]ny program, project or experiment that will release objects in orbit should not be planned unless an adequate assessment can verify that the effect on the orbital environment, and the hazard to other operating spacecraft and orbital stages, is acceptably low in the long-term." Hence, similarly to an EIA, the guidelines encourage States to consider the environmental impact of activities in Earth orbit and to, when appropriate, adopt mitigation measures.

Moreover, it must be noted that a small number of national space legislations already require, in their licensing process, the conduct of an EIA which considers both the terrestrial and extraterrestrial environmental consequences of the planned space activity. This is the case, for instance, of Belgium and, more recently, Finland.[378]

Although EIAs may, in some instances, be seen as a "cumbersome and expensive" process which also causes delay, it is not without advantages.[379] According to Viikari, adopting such practice could allow space actors to minimize the long-term costs of projects as well as the delay in reaching decisions because "the assessment

374. Principles Relevant to the Use of Nuclear Power Sources in Outer Space adopted by Resolution 47/68 of the General Assembly in 1992.
375. *Id.*, Principle 4§3.
376. *See* IADC, IADC Space Debris Mitigation Guidelines, IADC Steering Group and Working Group 4, IADC-02-01 Rev. 3 (2021); Report of the Committee on the Peaceful Uses of Outer Space, UNGAOR, 62nd Sess., Supp. No. 20, at 117–118 and Annex, UN Doc. A/62/20 (2007).
377. *Id.*, IADC, Guideline 4(2).
378. The environmental mechanisms adopted by Belgium and Finland are discussed in Chapter 4 *infra*.
379. Birnie, Boyle, and Redgwell, *supra* note 141 at 165.

identifies and evaluates also those potential consequences which might require expensive pollution abatement technology or potentially substantive compensation for damage."[380] In her opinion, these arguments should make adopting EIAs into their practice "increasingly appealing" even to space commercial entities.[381]

However, EIAs are not without limits. The fact remains that EIAs rely on scientific knowledge, and there is still a great deal that is unknown about the outer space environment. As emphasized by Viikari, "[s]cientists are usually expected to produce information that is as unambiguous as possible for the use of decision-makers."[382] Yet, the combination of constantly evolving technology with the knowledge gaps regarding the natural extraterrestrial environment can "considerably increase uncertainty about the conclusions."[383] As a consequence, the assessment of the environmental impact of activities in outer space could be expensive to implement and more time-consuming than it usually is for terrestrial activities.[384] Therefore, the EIA process needs to be adapted to not only the specificities of space activities but also to the degree of uncertainty which comes with operating in an unknown environment.

2.4 Conclusion

International environmental law provides a deeper insight into the management of activities and their impact on the surrounding environment. The legal area is the sum of decades of legal instruments addressing specific issues on different levels. The outcome is the identification of broad principles which can be applied to a broad range of circumstances. For instance, the principle of due diligence was initially developed in relation to State responsibility before being used to define rules within the context of transboundary environmental harm. Similarly, the precautionary principle has been used in many environmental instruments.

Another benefit of referring to international environmental law is the extensive practice of States. Environmental principles have been used, implemented, studied, and interpreted by a diversity of actors, including international jurisdictions. Consequently, despite their broad character, these principles are backed up by a strong practice that allows for clearly envisaging means of application. For instance, international jurisprudence clearly establishes a correlation between acting diligently and carrying out an EIA. It has also allowed international jurisdictions to identify constitutive elements of these principles. Accordingly, due diligence implies notification of and consultation with States potentially affected by the planned activity and undertaking an EIA. Similarly, these jurisdictions have remarked that although there is an

380. Lotta Viikari, *Environmental Impact Assessment in the Space Sector*, *in* THEORY AND PRACTICE OF TRANSBOUNDARY ENVIRONMENTAL IMPACT ASSESSMENT 265, 285 (C. J. Bastmeijer & Timo Koivurova eds., 2007); also *see* Chung, *supra* note 73 at 12.
381. Viikari, *supra* note 381 at 285.
382. Lotta E. Viikari, *Environmental impact assessment and space activities*, 34 ADVANCES IN SPACE RESEARCH 2363, 2365 (2003).
383. *Id.*
384. *Id.*

obligation to conduct an EIA prior to the start of an activity, this obligation is not absolute; it is conditioned by a threshold below which an EIA is not necessary.

As customary norms of international law, the obligations of due diligence and of undertaking an EIA are legally binding upon States, regardless of their noninclusion in the UN Space Treaties. This is advantageous since it permits extending the realm of obligations applicable to States without having to amend existing treaties. It is about reusing existing rules to fill the gaps left by the UN Space Treaties.

Yet, establishing the existence—and *a fortiori* the binding character—of a customary rule of international law with certainty is a complex exercise. It requires ascertaining separately the existence of two constituent elements: general practice and its acceptance by States as law (*opinio juris*).[385] For instance, although the precautionary approach is widely known in the field of international environmental law, the absence of a uniform practice among States means it cannot be counted as a binding customary principle, even if it may be voluntarily integrated by States in their domestic space legislation. In this regard, treaties offer more legal certainty as they leave no doubt regarding the existence of an obligation.

3 CONCLUSION

One of the fundamental criticisms of the UN Space Treaties is the ambiguity of the language they use. This is, however, a typical issue of treaties: to remain relevant, they must withstand time and the evolution of the area they govern. A possible solution would be to amend existing treaties as needed or to adopt new binding instruments. From a legal standpoint, these options would allow for the use of precise language and to address specific issues. The consequence, however, is the multiplication of instruments, as is the case in the field of environmental law.

Furthermore, amending multilateral treaties, or drafting new ones, is time-consuming. They require a group of States to (re-)negotiate their rights and obligations and to reach a consensus. For instance, the amendment of the 1967 Outer Space Treaty to explicitly integrate space debris issues would require that the majority of its States Parties reach a consensus on the text of the proposed amendments.[386] As of January 2022, it would mean that at least 57 States would have to consent to these changes.[387]

A less burdensome solution—and the one adopted in the UN Space Treaties—is to use broad language. It allows for an open interpretation of the rights and obligations of the Parties, which permits, in turn, keeping relevant dated international agreements in a constantly evolving field, like the space sector. In practice, this solution enables us to interpret the expression "harmful contamination" in Article IX of the Outer Space Treaty as encompassing space debris. A direct consequence of this interpretation is that we can argue that States Parties are obliged to adopt measures to avoid the generation of space debris, as they create harmful contamination of, *inter alia*, Earth orbit.

385. Report of the International Law Commission, UNGAOR, 73rd Sess., Supp. 10, UN Doc. A/73/10 (2018).
386. Outer Space Treaty, Art. XV.
387. 2022 Status of the UN Space Treaties, *supra* note 15, at 10.

Yet, the absence of a common agreement regarding the interpretation of broad provisions—such as the ones in Article IX of the Outer Space Treaty—grants States a wide margin of appreciation in the execution of their obligations. So is the case with the obligation to authorize and supervise nongovernmental space activities; not all States Parties to the treaties have adopted licensing regimes.

As international binding written instruments, treaties nonetheless provide a stable common framework. They create common rights and obligations among States Parties, thus allowing other Parties to operate with an understanding of what other Parties can or cannot do. In a nutshell, treaties have the considerable advantage of engaging inter-human mutual obligations.

However, when it comes to the protection of the outer space environment, both the concept of sustainable development and these obligations need to be operationalized. This can only be done by having recourse to other legal fields of study and instruments. Indeed, while several principles of international space law provide a basis for the implementation of space sustainability-related obligations, they do not as such provide a clear path to this goal.

It is at this point that customary norms of international law show their full interest as they may provide much-needed clarity. Such general rules are binding upon States as a result of a combination of established State practice and the existence of *opinio juris*. As a result, though they are general in their scope, i.e., not specific to the field of the protection of the outer space environment, or even to space resource activities, they are also supported by strong practice and examples of implementation. For this reason, they may be preferable to more specific provisions in treaties that are not really leveraged. This is the case, for instance, of the mechanism for consultation provided under Article IX of the Outer Space Treaty. The assessment of its efficiency as a procedural obligation is difficult, all the more so since it appears to have never been used in the past.

A comparison between the principle of due regard, specific to space law, and the broader principle of due diligence sheds light on the discrepancy. The latter has been interpreted by international jurisdictions and scholars on several occasions and in diverse contexts. Comparatively, the principle of due regard, which is also an obligation of conduct like due diligence, has only been interpreted once, by a party to a case, in front of an international jurisdiction.[388] Furthermore, due diligence has been consistently interpreted—in the field of environmental law—as including a customary obligation to conduct an EIA, a core element of the conceptual sustainability framework. Therefore, recourse to principles of international environmental law allows for complementing the sustainability framework outlined in the UN Space Treaties since they are based on extensive practice.

388. The obligation of "due regard" was defined by Panama in the context of article 87 of the UNCLOS as the obligation of States, when exercising their freedoms, to consider the interests of other States and refrain from interfering with other States exercising the same freedoms. Although the ITLOS did not confirm or infirm the interpretation of the applicant, it must be underlined that Italy did not argue against Panama's interpretation. M/V "Norstar" (No. 25) (Panama v. Italy), Judgment of Apr. 10, 2019, §§199, 231, 2019 ITLOS Rep. 10.

CHAPTER 3

Nonlegally Binding International Instruments

Historically, when discussing the protection of the outer space natural environment, the primary concern has been its potential biological contamination. As seen in Chapter 2, this particular issue was envisaged, *inter alia*, in the Outer Space Treaty.[1] Yet, with the continued development of space technology, new environmental challenges have arisen, ones that were not foreseen by the drafters of the UN Space Treaties.[2] Most notable is the lack of reference, in these treaties, to one of the greatest current environmental challenges of space activities: the proliferation of space debris.[3] Although a dynamic interpretation of Article IX of the Outer Space Treaty can be used as a legal basis to promote environmental protection in outer space, such a situation makes it obvious that it is not sufficient to ensure the effective management of unforeseen environmental issues.[4] The flexibility Article IX offers for interpretation purposes is paid for by a lack of clearly defined and objectively applicable environmental measures.

Since part of the problem in finding an effective solution in the space treaties is the broadness of the language used, it seems that working on more precise terms would be the way to solidify discussions and practical outcomes between States. Why not, then, tailor the treaties to the (environmental) issue at hand? Answering this question is neither easy nor impossible. It requires being aware of a fundamental problem when

1. Article IX, Sentence 2 of the Outer Space Treaty refers to both forward and backward contamination, demanding that States prevent the "harmful contamination" of outer space and "adverse changes" in the terrestrial environment from "the introduction of extraterrestrial matter." The Moon Agreement makes similar demands in article 7§1.
2. David Tan, *Towards a New Regime for the Protection of Outer Space as the "Province of all Mankind,"* 25 YALE J. INT'L L. 145, 157 (2000).
3. None of the five UN Space Treaties include the word "debris" or a synonym in their text. Ruth Holmes, *UK "space junk" project highlights threat to missions*, PHYS.ORG (2016), accessible online.
4. The broad terms used in the treaties allow for a dynamic interpretation of what constitutes "harmful contamination" and "harmful interference" in the Outer Space Treaty, thus, potentially applying to different sorts of environmental issues. *See* Chapter 2 *supra*.

regulating space activities: the lack of comprehensive knowledge about the outer space environment. It is arguably difficult to create standards to effectively protect the natural environment of a faraway land about which not much is known. Added to the lack of knowledge is the necessity to balance environmental protection with the development of space activities in order to achieve their long-term sustainability. The former should not impede the latter. Hence, the first step in finding workable solutions is access to knowledge and basing any action on reliable data. This is the work of space scientists. The second step—and the one that is of interest here—is how to export this scientific knowledge into the legal realm. It is good to know what should be done, it is better if it can be enforced or, at the very least, backed up by political entities like States. Therefore, the question of what *can* States do to address new environmental issues becomes: what are States *willing* to do about it?

Retrospective consideration of States' behavior, as regards their involvement in space developments, gives us some indication about the answer to such an interrogation. It has now been over 40 years since a binding multilateral instrument has been provided to regulate space activities.[5] In that time, UNCOPUOS' Member States have shown a clear reluctance to adopt new space treaties.[6] Instead, the international community has been favoring the adoption of "soft law" instruments, which could be described as written "non-binding principles, norms, standards or other statements of expected behavior."[7]

Contrary to "hard" law, soft law instruments host "normative commitments" which do not have the legally binding force of formal treaties or customary international law.[8] They "expres[s] a preference and not an obligation that States should act, or should refrain from acting, in a specific manner."[9] As a consequence, soft law instruments do not imply a responsibility for a breach of an international obligation.[10] Their purpose is not to be enforced but to "achieve functional cooperation among States to reach international goals."[11] That is not to say soft law is utterly deprived of law-like consequences. On the contrary, it is particularly relevant as a precursor to a

5. The last treaty was adopted in 1979. Responses to the set of Questions provided by the Chair of the Working Group on the Status and Application of the Five United Nations Treaties on Outer Space, UNCOPUOS, 56th Sess., at 2, UN Doc. A/AC.105/C.2/2017/CRP.17 (2017); Jack Beard, *Soft Law's Failure on the Horizon: The International Code of Conduct for Outer Space Activities*, 38 Univ. Pa. J. Int. 335, 342 (2016).
6. Freeland comments on how an "ideological divide" between spacefaring nations and non-spacefaring nations resulted in the low ratification of the Moon Agreement and, *a fortiori*, made it impossible to negotiate new multilateral, legally binding, space instruments within the UNCOPUOS. Steven Freeland, *The Role of 'Soft Law' in Public International Law and its Relevance to the International Legal Regulation of Outer Space, in* Soft Law in Outer Space: The Function of Non-binding Norms in International Space Law 9, 17–18 (Irmgard Marboe ed., 2012).
7. Beard, *supra* note 5 at 138 citing Marco Ferrazzani, at 342. Frans von der Dunk, Handbook of Space Law 379 (2015); more generally on the relevance of soft law for space activities, *see* Freeland, *supra* note 6.
8. Dinah Shelton, *Soft Law, in* Routledge Handbook of International Law 68, 68 (David Armstrong ed., 2009).
9. Joseph Gold, Interpretation: The IMF and International Law 301 (1996).
10. Cynthia Crawford Lichtenstein, *Hard Law v. Soft Law: Unnecessary Dichotomy?*, 35 The International Lawyer 1433, 1433–1434 (2001).
11. Shelton, *supra* note 8 at 69.

treaty negotiation, as evidenced by the 1963 Declaration of Principles which paved the way to the 1967 Outer Space Treaty. Moreover, soft law instruments are also useful in addressing new topics of regulation, such as environmental issues in outer space.[12] Notably, the adoption by the UN General Assembly of resolutions as well as the various reports produced by the UNCOPUOS have heavily contributed to the constant development of international cooperation between Member States and space law.

Though strikingly different, the continuous recourse to soft law leads to one conclusion: the efficiency of space law to regulate environmental sustainability in space for, *inter alia*, space resource activities does not solely rest on treaties.[13] For the legal scholar, it also means that it would be a mistake to restrict the analysis to the study of formal sources of international law only. Such a limited approach would exclude any international instrument discussed by the international community after 1979. Accordingly, Chapter 3 reflects on the positive contribution of selected international nonlegally binding instruments and technical standards to the protection of the outer space environment. The first instrument discussed is the planetary protection policy published by the International Council for Science (ISC)'s[14] Committee on Space Research (COSPAR), i.e., the first international organization to attempt coordinating international efforts to preserve the outer space environment from interplanetary contamination (1). The other instruments have been developed by, *inter alia*, the UNCOPUOS: the *Principles Relevant to the Use of Nuclear Power Sources in Outer Space*[15] ("NPS Principles") adopted by Resolution 47/68 of the General Assembly in 1992 (2), the two sets of SDM Guidelines adopted respectively by the IADC in 2002 and the UNCOPUOS in 2007 (3),[16] and the *Guidelines for the Long-Term Sustainability of Outer Space Activities*[17] ("LTS Guidelines") adopted by the UNCOPUOS in 2019 (4).

1 COSPAR's POLICY ON PLANETARY PROTECTION

COSPAR is an NGO which aims to promote scientific research in space, on an international level, by, *inter alia*, establishing an independent forum for the exchange of results, information, and opinions among scientists.[18] In addition to organizing and

12. *Id.*, at 76.
13. Freeland, *supra* note 6 at 13–15.
14. The International Science Council is a nongovernmental organization that brings together over two hundred ISUs and associations as well as national and regional scientific organizations. Established in 2018, it combines two historical international scientific organizations: the International Council for Science and the International Social Science Council. ISC, *An introduction to the International Science Council* (2022).
15. Principles Relevant to the Use of Nuclear Power Sources in Outer Space adopted by Resolution 47/68 of the General Assembly in 1992 ["NPS Principles"].
16. IADC, IADC Space Debris Mitigation Guidelines, IADC Steering Group and Working Group 4, IADC-02-01 Rev. 3 (2021) ["IADC SDM Guidelines"]; Report of the Committee on the Peaceful Uses of Outer Space, UNGAOR, 62nd Sess., Supp. No. 20, at 117–118 and Annex, UN Doc. A/62/20 (2007) ["UNCOPUOS SDM Guidelines"].
17. Report of the Committee on the Peaceful Uses of Outer Space, UNGAOR, 74th Sess., Supp. No. 20, at 163 and Annex II, UN doc. A/74/20 (2019).
18. COSPAR Charter, Art. 1 (1998) available online. COSPAR was established during the Cold War; thus, it was important to create an independent forum to overcome political tension and allow

participating in various events to encourage the flow of information between countries, COSPAR acts as an advisor to the United Nations and other international organizations on space matters.[19] However, though its global role as an international forum and its cooperation with the United Nations is far from being negligible when considering environmental matters, it is more precisely the organization's development of scientific and technical standards to prevent interplanetary contamination that is of particular interest here.

1.1 History and Evolution of COSPAR's Policy

It is worthy of note that the foundations of COSPAR and its planetary protection policy predate the beginning of the Space Age: far from being a concern rising from new activities, the question of the protection of the outer space environment has haunted space activities even before their inception.[20] One of the earliest attempts to coordinate international efforts to avoid interplanetary contamination by microorganisms actually took place in 1956, during the seventh meeting of the International Astronautical Federation (IAF).[21] With the successful launch of Sputnik 1 in 1957, initiatives to preserve the natural environment of celestial bodies began to be institutionalized. For instance, the US National Academy of Sciences adopted, in early 1958, a set of resolutions that urged scientists to "plan lunar and planetary studies and with great care and deep concern so that initial operations do not compromise and make impossible forever after critical scientific experiments."[22] It further beseeched the ISC—then known as the International Council of Scientific Unions—"to encourage and assist the evaluation of such contamination and the development of means for its prevention."[23] This ended up being the push the ISC needed to establish a dedicated body, with the creation of the ad hoc Committee on Contamination by Extraterrestrial Exploration (CETEX) the same year.

CETEX held its first meeting in May 1958 and produced a report which highlighted the dangers of contaminating the natural environment of celestial bodies.[24] The ad hoc Committee also releases recommendations for the creation of a code of conduct for space activities. Although acknowledging its own inability to issue a specific proposal that would "embod[y] a reasonable compromise between the desire to start lunar and planetary exploration at the earliest possible moment and the need to

---

information about space to flow within the international community. Jean-Louis Fellous, *COSPAR, a young 62-years old space research organization*, 43 2447 (2021).

19. COSPAR Charter, Art. 1.
20. Traditionally, the "Space Age" is considered having started with the successful launch in orbit of the Soviet satellite Sputnik, in 1957. Anne Millbrooke, *History of the space age*, *in* Handbook of Space Engineering, Archaeology, and Heritage 195 (Ann Darrin & Beth L. O'Leary eds., 2009).
21. Morton Werber, *Objectives and Models of the Planetary Quarantine Program*, NASA General Technical Series 140, 1 (1975); Andrew G. Haley, *Space Medical Jurisprudence*, 1 *in* Space Law and Government 274, 287–288 (1963).
22. Werber, *supra* note 21 at 2.
23. A Review of Space Research, 257 (National Academy of Sciences ed., 1962).
24. Haley, *supra* note 21 at 290; Charles R. Phillips, *The Planetary Quarantine Program: Origin and Achievements*, NASA General Technical Series 58, 3 (1974).

safeguard future research,"[25] CETEX identifies four "primary objectives," the rationale being that celestial bodies must be considered "scientific preserves."[26] These objectives are: (1) the freedom to explore celestial bodies, subject to limitations linked to planetary protection measures; (2) the disclosure, to COSPAR and the ISC, of information concerning space activities and experiments; (3) the restriction of experiments to those only which are likely "to yield useful scientific data"; and (4) nuclear explosion should not take place near the surface of celestial bodies.[27] Additionally, CETEX outlines quarantine and sterilization standards for the Moon, Mars, and Venus. For instance, CETEX recommends avoiding soft landings on Mars "unless all precautions have been taken to exclude living organisms from them."[28]

The recommendations of CETEX were accepted by the ISC which, in turn, decided to establish a more permanent committee: COSPAR.[29] The idea is that COSPAR would help expand and coordinate space research worldwide.[30] Making use of the newly created ISC committee, CETEX suggests that COSPAR takes over overseeing the research on methods of sterilization and generally assumes responsibility for contamination issues.[31] With this decision, COSPAR officially takes over all aspects of space research, including biological contamination.[32]

The next step in COSPAR's planetary protection efforts occurred in 1961 with the adoption of Resolution 10 on *Space Experiments with Undesirable Effects* by the ISC. The resolution states that:

> all countries launching space experiments with possible adverse effects on other scientific research should provide ICSU and COSPAR with information about those intended experiments sufficient to evaluate the potential for contamination, adverse or not.[33]

In order to help evaluate the potential adverse effects of these experiments, COSPAR creates a Consultative Group on Potentially Harmful Effects of Space Experiments.[34] Together, this series of decisions lay the foundation for COSPAR's key role in developing planetary protection standards at the international level.[35]

In 1964, COSPAR adopted an interim quantitative framework for the development of planetary protection standards in the form of another resolution.[36] The aim is

25. Haley, *supra* note 21 at 290.
26. Leslie I. Tennen, *Evolution of the Planetary Protection Policy: Conflict of Science and Jurisprudence?*, 34 Advances in Space Research 2354, 2355 (2004) DOI: 10.1016/j.asr.2004.01.018.
27. *Id.*
28. Haley, *supra* note 21 at 291.
29. Committee to Review the Planetary Protection Policy Development Processes et al., *Chapter 2. Historical Origins of Planetary Protection Policies, in* The Goals, Rationales, and Definition of Planetary Protection: Interim Report (2017).
30. A Review of Space Research, *supra* note 23 at 258.
31. Phillips, *supra* note 24 at 4.
32. *Id.*
33. George S. Robinson, *Interplanetary Contamination: The Ultimate Challenge for Environmental and Constitutional Lawyers*, 31 J. Space L. 117, 122 (2005).
34. *Id.*
35. Committee to Review the Planetary Protection Policy Development Processes et al., *supra* note 29.
36. Robinson, *supra* note 33 at 122; Tennen, *supra* note 26 at 2355.

to implement decontamination techniques to reduce the probability of biological contamination of the natural environment of celestial bodies.[37] To that end, the probability of contamination is to be determined by a mathematical formula, "which multipli[es] the initial microbial burden, after decontamination, of an interplanetary probe at launch, by factors relating to the probability of survival of the rigors of launch, transit, entry, release and growth in the target alien environment."[38] This framework stayed in place until 1982.[39] Its importance was emphasized by the UNCOPUOS soon after its publication in 1964. For the first time since its establishment, the Scientific and Technical Subcommittee (UNCOPUOS STC) made direct reference in its report to a COSPAR resolution. COSPAR was also expressly mentioned by the UNCOPUOS Chairman in his opening speech in 1964, and the resolution was added as an annex to the UNCOPUOS' report.[40]

The major revision of the policy in 1984 is of particular importance as it structures COSPAR's policy in the shape it exists today.[41] From now on, the policy is organized around "categories." Each category carries out different planetary requirements based on the combination of the targeted celestial body and the mission type—i.e., orbiter, lander, etc. A separate category is also created specifically for missions that include the return of samples. Through continuing review and revision by relevant stakeholders and scientific commissions, COSPAR guidelines have progressively been relaxed with the overall probabilistic contamination model eventually being discarded.[42] The updated policy in 1994 pays particular attention to Mars missions. For these missions, the revisited version ties decontamination measures to, *inter alia*, whether detecting life is part of the mission objectives.[43] In 1999, COSPAR extended its reach and chartered a Panel on Planetary Protection ("PP Panel") to develop, maintain and promulgate a planetary protection policy ("PP policy").

It so happens that the PP Panel soon tackled the problem of consolidating COSPAR's recommendations regarding planetary protection. Over time, despite considerable transformations in COSPAR's policies, no single document reflected those changes.[44] Hence, the necessity for the PP Panel to work on a draft to consolidate the policy. This draft, approved by COSPAR in 2002,[45] is based on a target body/mission type combination, following the model of the 1984 framework. The policy, as stated in the preamble of the document issued from the draft, intends to be a reference for spacefaring nations:

37. Tennen, *supra* note 26 at 2355. For an explanation of the implementation of the mathematical formula, *see* Leslie I. Tennen, *The Role of COSPAR for Space Security and Planetary Protection, in* HANDBOOK OF SPACE SECURITY 1559, 1563–1564 (Kai-Uwe Schrogl ed., 2020).
38. Tennen, *supra* note 26 at 2355.
39. Robinson, *supra* note 33 at 122.
40. Report of the Committee on the Peaceful Uses of Outer Space, UNGA, 26th Sess., UN Doc. A/5785 (1964), *see* p. 11 and Annex II.
41. Tennen, *supra* note 26 at 2355.
42. *Id.*
43. *Id.*
44. J. D. Rummel et al., *COSPAR's Planetary Protection Policy: A Consolidated Draft*, 30 ADVANCES IN SPACE RESEARCH 1567, 1568 (2002) DOI: 10.1016/s0273-1177(02)00479-9.
45. COSPAR Planetary Protection Policy, available online ["COSPAR PP Policy"].

> both as an international standard on procedures to avoid organic-constituent and biological contamination in space exploration, and to provide accepted guidelines in this area to guide compliance with the wording of this UN Space Treaty and other relevant international agreements.[46]

The policy itself is carefully framed in the broader context of international law: particular reference is made to Article IX of the Outer Space Treaty. As was the case with previous COSPAR works, the document is not meant to remain static. As a result, the PP policy was last updated in June 2021 to include, within Category II, two new subcategories for lunar surface missions.[47]

1.2 COSPAR's Planetary Protection Policy, as Approved in 2021

As it stands after the 2021 revision, the PP policy is divided into five categories[48] which determine which documentation a space operator must fill, depending on the mission type, target body, and degree of concern for contamination. Category I applies to any mission to a target body that is not of direct interest in understanding the process of chemical evolution or the origin of life. As such, COSPAR considers there is no need to protect these celestial bodies, and, thus, no planetary protection requirements are imposed. It applies to "undifferentiated, metamorphosed asteroids."[49] Thus, from a planetary protection perspective, Category 1 non-requirements would apply to space mining activities taking place on "undifferentiated" asteroids.

Category II includes all types of missions to target bodies that are of significant interest but where the potential for contamination compromising future research is remote. Accordingly, space operators are only required to submit simple documentation about their planetary protection plan, pre- and post-launch reports, a post-encounter report, and an end-of-mission report. It concerns, *inter alia*, missions to Venus, the Moon, Jupiter, Saturn, Uranus, and Neptune as well as Callisto and comets. The two new subcategories introduced in 2021, Categories IIa and IIb, apply to missions taking place on the lunar surface, whereas Category II standards continue to apply to flyby and orbiter lunar missions. Category IIb regards missions to the Moon's Permanently Shadowed Regions (PSRs) and the lunar poles, "in particular latitudes south of 79°S and north of 86°N." For these missions, a full organic inventory is recommended in addition to Category II documentation. As for Category IIa, it regards lunar surface missions occurring outside PSRs and the lunar poles. They require Category II documentation and a more limited inventory than Category IIb missions; the inventory is limited to "organic products that may be released into the lunar environment by the propulsion system." The requirements developed under these two new subcategories could apply to missions aiming to commercially exploit lunar resources.

---

46. *Id.*
47. COSPAR, *COSPAR updates its Planetary Protection Policy for missions to the Moon's surface*, Press Release (2021).
48. COSPAR PP Policy.
49. *Id.*

Category III concerns flyby and orbiter missions to target bodies that present a significant interest regarding the process of chemical evolution or the origin of life and an increased chance of contamination that would compromise future investigations. It applies to flyby and orbiter missions to Mars, Europa, and Enceladus. The requirements for Category III missions include reinforced Category II documentation and the implementation of procedures, including trajectory biasing, the use of cleanrooms, and possibly bioburden reduction. They could apply to a satellite orbiting Mars to control mining operations on the Martian ground.

Category IV applies to missions involving direct contact with the target body, like lander and probe missions. Planetary protection requirements comprise consolidated Category III documentation and the implementation of additional procedures, such as the partial sterilization of contacting hardware. So far, it applies to lander missions to Mars, Europa, and Enceladus. With regard to mining activities on Mars, Category IV requirements could apply to, *inter alia*, rovers and space objects designed to extract the planet's *in situ* resources.

Lastly, Category V comprises all Earth-return missions. The concern with these missions is backward contamination. In addition to preserving the Earth's environment, Category V deals with the prevention of backward contamination from other celestial bodies to the Moon. The goal, here, is to specifically allow for unrestricted returns of lunar samples to Earth. The category is divided into two subcategories: unrestricted Earth return and restricted Earth return. Unrestricted Earth return concerns returning samples from celestial bodies with no indication of indigenous life forms, like the Moon and Venus. The planetary protection requirements only apply to the outbound phase and correspond to that phase. All other Category V missions are defined as "restricted Earth return," such as missions to Mars. It prohibits destructive impact upon return and requires the containment of any sample and the sterilization of all returned hardware that directly contacted the target body. Additionally, enhanced Category II documentation should be submitted, and procedures implemented, like trajectory biasing and project advanced studies and research. These requirements could be relevant in missions that will consist in bringing back, from outer space, natural resources that are scarce on Earth.

1.3 Organizational Structure

The bulk of the legal efforts to protect the outer space environment is narrowly linked with the work of COSPAR. This means that the design of such protective norms and—crucially—their validity for legal purposes are themselves tied to the organization and its standing among international bodies. From an organizational perspective, COSPAR is governed by a Council composed of a President, the representatives of its institutional members, the elected chairs[50] of the Scientific Commissions, and the Chair

50. The chairs of the Scientific Commissions are elected by their peers, i.e., the scientists and individuals which have joined the Commission. COSPAR, By-Laws, Arts. IX and XI (2021) available online.

of COSPAR's Finance Committee.[51] The Council's main duty is to formulate, approve and execute all COSPAR plans and policies.[52] When not in session, the Council's work is carried out by a Bureau in charge of the administering and conducting of the organization's affairs, like the implementation of policies.[53] The Bureau is composed of COSPAR's President and Vice Presidents, as well as six other members elected by the Council from a list of candidates selected among the institutional members.[54]

As an organization aiming to encourage the flow of scientific information at the international level, COSPAR naturally turned toward scientific institutions in order to recruit its first members. They are of two kinds: (1) national scientific institutions (NSIs) which are engaged in space research and (2) international scientific unions (ISUs) federated in ISC.[55] Their work is supported by "Associates"—scientists or individuals interested in space research.[56] Each category entails its own list of rights and duties. For instance, COSPAR Associates can gain their status by attending a biennial COSPAR Assembly or by participating in the organization's activities. They are required to join at least one—but no more than three—COSPAR Scientific Commissions.[57] In return, their status grants them access to information about COSPAR scientific activities and the right to participate in discussions as well as vote in their affiliated commission. However, only the Chairs of the Scientific Commissions may vote on the Council.[58] Institutional members—i.e., the NSI and ISU—are further tasked with "evaluating and disseminating scientific information resulting from space research," to facilitate the flow of information between COSPAR and the institutional members via their representatives and vote on their behalf.[59] Moreover, "each [ISU] shall be allowed one liaison representative to each Scientific Commission."[60] Thus, in addition to their involvement in the functioning of the organization, COSPAR members are expected to take an active part in the scientific activities of the organization by joining the Scientific Commissions and Panels.

Pursuant to the COSPAR *Charter* approved in 1998, the Scientific Commissions are tasked with all scientific activities of the organization. The subject is covered in just six sections,[61] which means that the Charter does not concern itself with the practical details of the establishment, rights, and duties of these bodies. These are referred to in the establishment of *By-Laws and Procedures*,[62] but the Bureau retains the prerogative

51. COSPAR Charter, Arts. II and IV.
52. *Id.*, Art. IV.
53. *Id.*
54. *Id.*
55. COSPAR Charter, Art. II.
56. COSPAR By-laws, Art. IX. 1.
57. *Id.*, Art. IX. 2.
58. *Id.*, Art. IV. 2.
59. *Id.*, Art. II. 2–3.
60. *Id.*, Art. II. 5.
61. The Charter defines the purpose of the organization (I) and its members—both institutional and individual (II-III), attributes general roles to its governing body—i.e., the Council, Bureau and Scientific Commissions (IV), sets the framework for the development of procedures (V) and makes provisions for the amendment of the instrument (VI).
62. COSPAR By-laws, Art. XI.

to assess the necessity to establish, modify and discontinue scientific commissions.[63] They are set up for an indefinite period and mainly consist of the Associates who have expressed a particular interest in following the work these commissions are tasked with. COSPAR's Scientific Commissions are responsible for the organization of meetings and events and for the preparation of scientific papers and their publication after they have been approved; they must regularly report to the governing entities, i.e., the Bureau and Council.[64] Currently, there are eight Scientific Commissions established under COSPAR, each discussing a different area of space research.[65]

Beyond the Commissions, the Charter and By-Laws allow for the creation of subsidiary bodies whose role is to examine "special issues."[66] Like the Commissions, these subsidiary bodies are established by the Bureau for an indefinite period. They take the form of Task Groups or Subcommissions and exist under the umbrella of the Scientific Commissions. Another type of subsidiary body created by COSPAR is the Panels. It is at this level that planetary protection has been discussed and policies promoted, showing that despite the relative flexibility of their inception, panels can play a significant role.

As a matter of fact, they are—with the Scientific Commissions—the primary active bodies within the organization.[67] Where the tasks groups and subcommissions are established to investigate specific topics of scientific interest to Associates, the Panels focus on "topics of interdisciplinary interest, or involving participation from experts from disciplines not represented within Scientific Commissions."[68]

Among the 12 currently active panels established by COSPAR,[69] the PP Panel remains the most important as regards environmental protection measures, since it is the one in charge of drafting COSPAR's policy on planetary protection.[70] The PP Panel is concerned with the matter of "biological interchange in the conduct of solar system

---

63. *Id.*
64. *Id.*, Arts. VI and IX.
65. As of 2022, the active Scientific Commission (SC) are SC-A on space studies of the Earth's surface, meteorology, and climate; SC-B on space studies of the Earth-Moon system, planets, and small bodies of the solar system; SC-C on space studies of the upper atmospheres of the Earth and planets including reference atmospheres; SC-D on space plasmas in the solar system, including planetary magnetospheres; SC-E on research in astrophysics from space; SC-F on life sciences as related to space; SC-G on Materials Sciences in Space; and SC-H on Fundamental Physics in Space. COSPAR, Scientific Commissions, available online.
66. COSPAR Charter, Art. V; COSPAR By-Laws, Art. XIII.
67. COSPAR, Scientific Commissions, *supra* note 65.
68. COSPAR By-Laws, Art. XIII.
69. COSPAR, Panels, available online.
70. Two additional panels, in particular, are relevant from the perspective of planetary protection: the Panel on Potentially Environmentally Detrimental Activities in Space (PEDAS) and the Panel on Exploration (PEX). The former, PEDAS, acts on an ad hoc basis and focuses on "perturbations of the terrestrial and planetary environments resulting from space activities," such as space debris in Earth orbit or the perturbation of the lunar environment by manned activities. The latter, PEX, provides, *inter alia*, "independent scientific advice to support the development of exploration programs, [...] to safeguard present and potential scientific [space] assets and to understand the consequences of proposed and ongoing [space activities]." Mahulena Hofmann, *COSPAR Recommendations in a New Context? Environmental Aspects of Space Mining*, *in* Proceedings of the International Institute of Space Law 2016 (P.J. Blount et al. eds., 2017).

exploration and use," namely forward and backward contamination.[71] There are specific constraints to the policies developed in the panel. In particular, they must be based on the "most current, peer-reviewed scientific knowledge." This explains the successive revisions of policies, following a process which is carefully organized: the process of revising the policy involves several entities, starting with the Panel's members. They consist of equal numbers of appointed members representing national or international space agencies, and of representatives of COSPAR Scientific Commissions B and F.[72] The intent is to have the policy benefit from the insight of scientific institutions and individual scientists but also from practitioners in the form of space agencies' representatives. The pool of expertise has even been extended with the recent appointment of the current Active Director of the UN's Office for Outer Space Affairs, Niklas Hedman as one of the two PP Panel's Vice-Chairs,[73] adding to the panel expertise in space law.

A second requirement for the revision of the policy is a consensus condition. Only after the members of the panel have reached a consensus, can they formulate a proposal to update the existing PP policy. The proposal is then submitted for review and approval to the Bureau and the Council.[74] They will, eventually, be the ones to authorize the publication of the consolidated policy.

COSPAR also dedicates resources to the dissemination of its panels' work and relies on two main approaches: through direct publication or through the organization's members' networks. For this reason, the PP policy is made available to the public at large via its publication in open access on the COSPAR's website and in the COSPAR's information bulletin *Space Research Today*.[75] As for the involvement of COSPAR members, disseminating scientific information is one of their main duties.[76] This is done through feedback to home institutions or nations (for instance, in the case of NSIs) or through events COSPAR members are expected to organize and participate in to ensure the dissemination of the information in different fora.[77]

1.4 Legal Status of COSPAR's Policy

The legal outcomes of the considerable work of COSPAR are encapsulated in the preamble of its PP policy:

71. COSPAR, Panel on Planetary Protection, available online ["COSPAR PP Panel"].
72. Sub-Commission B focuses on space studies of the Earth-Moon system, planets, and small bodies of the solar system and Sub-Commission F on life sciences as related to space. COSPAR, Scientific Commissions, *supra* note 65.
73. The Vice-Chairs current term started in 2022 and will last until 2026. COSPAR PP Panel, *supra* note 71.
74. Hofmann, *supra* note 70.
75. COSPAR's information bulletin is published three times a year by *Elsevier Science*. It provides, *inter alia*, reports on COSPAR activities, scientific space mission news, and research articles from space organizations. *See, e.g.*, COSPAR, *COSPAR Policy on Planetary Protection*, 211 SPACE RESEARCH TODAY 12 (2021) DOI: 10.1016/j.srt.2021.07.010.
76. COPSAR By-Laws, Art. II.
77. *Id.*

> COSPAR maintains and promulgates this policy on planetary protection for the reference of spacefaring nations, both as an international standard on procedures to avoid organic-constituent and biological contamination in space exploration, and to provide accepted guidelines in this area to guide compliance with the wording of the UN Outer Space Treaty and other relevant international agreements.

Yet, this reference to international agreements—and in particular to Article IX of the Outer Space Treaty—must not be mistaken for an indication that COSPAR's policy is legally binding under international law. The language used in the policy clearly reflects the voluntary character of the document. For instance, it "*recommends* that COSPAR members inform COSPAR when establishing planetary protection requirements for planetary missions."[78] It also "*recommends* the use of the best available clean-room technology."[79] It further "*suggest[s]* that the lead partner *should* take the lead in submitting these reports" [italics added] for multinational missions.[80] This collection of excerpts from the policy shows how cautious COSPAR is when formulating its guidelines: they generally do not exceed the form of a recommendation.[81] Furthermore, the policy remains silent on how to implement the requirements, leaving it to the discretion of users.[82]

The legal standing of the policy, and more generally of key elements of COSPAR's recommendations, is ambiguous. Indeed, under certain conditions, a policy based on recommendations may evolve into norms of customary international law, which would effectively make the instrument's content legally binding upon States. In this regard, there are two constitutive elements to international custom: the settled practice of States and *opinio juris*—that is, the "belief that this practice is rendered obligatory by the existence of a rule of law requiring it."[83] The question, here, is whether COSPAR's policy fulfills these conditions, and it comes as no surprise that it has been debated by legal scholars.

In practice, COSPAR's policy has been widely accepted by States.[84] Furthermore, it could be argued that the normative reference[85] to COSPAR standards in national legislations as well as their implementation by national space agencies reflects an obviously established *opinio juris*. Yet, asserting that COSPAR's PP policy has evolved to a norm of customary international law based on these elements may be premature, according to Hofmann.[86] The States implementing the policy do not directly transpose

78. COSPAR PP Policy.
79. *Id.*
80. *Id.*
81. Hofmann, *supra* note 70.
82. Gerhard Kminek et al., *The International Planetary Protection Handbook*, 205 Space Research Today e1, 38 (2019) DOI: 10.1016/j.srt.2019.09.001.
83. Continental Shelf (Libyan Arab Jarnahiriya/Malta) (Judgment) 1985 ICJ Rep. 13 §§27, 77 (June 3).
84. Hofmann, *supra* note 70.
85. On the use of normative reference in space law, *see* Alexander Soucek & Jenni Tapio, *Normative References to Non-legally Binding Instruments in National Space Laws: A Risk-Benefit Analysis in the Context of Domestic and Public International Law*, 2018 *in* Proceedings of the International Institute of Space Law 553 (2018).
86. Hofmann, *supra* note 70.

the document in their national order. They sometimes refer to an obligation to comply with existing international standards: this is the case with Kazakhstan's national legislation.[87] They may also create their own planetary protection requirements, based on COSPAR's findings, like the United States.[88] Some national space legislations do not refer to COSPAR altogether but to Article IX of the Outer Space Treaty or use similar phrasing to the treaty provisions, like the *Austrian Outer Space Act of 2011*.[89] Moreover, not all States address environmental concerns in their national space act; this is the case, for instance, of South Africa.[90] Hence, in consideration of these elements, it is difficult to affirm that there exists a consistent practice in the implementation of COSPAR recommendations. Nor have States, according to Hofmann, "express[ed] their *opinio juris* in this area."[91]

It remains that COSPAR's recommendations are widely used by spacefaring nations even if their national legislation does not always refer to them directly. To this extent, the lack of binding force of the planetary protection requirements does not erase their importance in the continued efforts to preserve the outer space environment. States and space agencies generally endeavor to satisfy the requirements set by COSPAR.[92] Moreover, several space agencies have incorporated substantial elements of the policy into their processes. For instance, the European Space Agency (ESA) has adopted COSPAR's policy and acts "on behalf of its Member States to ensure that the requirements are met for all missions the Agency is flying or contributing to."[93] The Council of the Agency has adopted an overall planetary protection management requirement.[94] It includes "technical planetary protection requirements for robotic and human missions," "requirements related to procedures," and "descriptions of necessary documentation."[95] Contrary to COSPAR's policy, the Agency has not made these documents available to the public, but the European Cooperation for Space Standardization has published specific standards.[96] Moreover, the Agency's policy does not solely apply to ESA space missions. Typically, it applies to all ESA-related space activities, i.e., missions launched by ESA or from ESA facilities for other entities, like States or the private sector. Ultimately, this represents a considerable impact of the work of COSPAR as regards the protection of the outer space environment.

87. Law of the Republic of Kazakhstan on Space Activities, Jan. 6, 2012, Art. 30§4, No. 528-IV (KAZ).
88. *See* Chapter 4 *infra* on the US planetary protection policy.
89. Austrian Federal Law on the Authorisation of Space Activities and the Establishment of a National Registry of 2011, Art. 4§1.5 (AU).
90. Space Affairs Act, No. 84 (1993) (ZA).
91. Hofmann, *supra* note 70.
92. *See infra* the example of the United States, Japan, Finland, and the United Arabic Emirates.
93. ESA? *Planetary Protection*, available online.
94. Tennen, *supra* note 37 at 1572–1573; Gerhard Kminek, *ESA planetary protection requirements. Technical Report ESSB-ST-U-001* (2012).
95. Tennen, *supra* note 37 at 1572–1573; Kminek, *supra* note 94.
96. ECSS, *ECSS-U-ST-20C—Space sustainability—Planetary protection* (2019).

1.5 Conclusion

Since the beginning of space activities, the continuous development of a planetary protection policy has contributed to the protection of the natural environment of celestial bodies from biological contamination. Though voluntary, the broad and international acceptance of the requirements reflects the importance of setting international standards, even nonlegally binding ones. Outer space does not belong to one; it belongs to all. As such, everyone needs to do their part to ensure it is preserved to the best of our capacity. Far from intending to impede the development of space activities, COSPAR's policy contributes to the long-term sustainability of space exploration and use. Without the establishment of guidelines, humankind runs the risk of creating irremediable environmental damage that could negatively impact scientific investigation in space and space activities altogether.

Yet, the more we learn about the outer space environment, the less we seem to protect it. Tennen argues that the subsequent revisions by COPSAR of its PP policy have "erode[d] and limit[ed]" the application of the requirements.[97] It is difficult not to agree to an extent with such a statement. Objectively, there is little ground to argue that the overall requirements have not lessened throughout the years. This is, however, only part of the truth. In some cases—such as for Mars missions in the 1994 revision—the planetary protection requirements have increased. It is also important to consider the evolution of the requirements as a whole: at the beginning of space activities, everything had to be sterilized when approaching a celestial body, a requirement that is now only emphasized for certain types of missions. This change reflects the fact that over the course of the years, the policy has been adjusted to reflect a more specific concern: the search for evidence of extraterrestrial life. The entire policy is built around avoiding biological contamination that could have a negative impact on the research for life forms in outer space and the need to avoid backward contamination. Encouraging a stronger PP policy would therefore require extending the scope of the PP Panel's interest, currently focused on biological contamination.

Another aspect has to be considered: the applicability of COSPAR's policy to space resource missions, especially if these are of a commercial nature. Now, COSPAR's policy is built around the determination of categories that are based on a target body and mission type combination. They are also taking into account the probability of finding evidence of extraterrestrial life. Consequently, the nature of the mission—whether commercial or scientific—has no impact on the application of the recommendations. Thus, there is no apparent reason justifying their exclusion when carrying out space resource activities. These activities could fall under the scope of several planetary protection categories. Missions to extract resources from asteroids and the Moon would fall respectively under Categories I and IIa, or b, depending on where on the lunar surface the mission would take place. Category I requires no documentation as asteroids are of no significant interest in understanding the origin of life, whereas simple documentation would have to be submitted for lunar missions, in

97. Tennen, *supra* note 26 at 2361.

addition to either a limited organic inventory (Category IIa) or a full one (Category IIb). Lastly, missions aiming to return space resources to Earth would fall under Category V of the policy. Depending on the origin of the extracted resources, space operators could have to comply with containment procedures, in addition to having to implement procedures and submit complete documentation. Thus, COSPAR's PP policy could be relevant for space resource activities, especially in controlling the risk of backward contamination when bringing back space resources to Earth.

2 THE UN NUCLEAR POWER SOURCE PRINCIPLES

For the sake of completeness, the *Principles Relevant to the Use of Nuclear Power Sources in Outer Space* ("NPS Principles")[98] adopted by the UNCOPUOS in 1992 should be briefly considered here. They mark a positive step forward in the UNCOPUOS using nonlegally binding instruments to further the protection of the outer space environment.[99]

The NPS Principles contain "goals and guidelines to ensure the safe use of nuclear power sources in outer space" by minimizing the number of radioactive materials present in space and the accompanying risks, such as accidental collision or explosion.[100] These incidents could result in the creation of radioactive debris spreading in orbit and uncontrollably reentering Earth's atmosphere or crashing into other celestial bodies,[101] thus contaminating the surrounding environment. The crash of the Soviet nuclear-powered Cosmos 954 satellite in Canada in 1978 certainly proved that the risk is real.[102]

The complexity of the situation with nuclear power sources (NPS) is that they present the risk of leaking radioactive materials in both the terrestrial and extraterrestrial environments, yet at the same time, their applications "have played a critical role in the exploration of space."[103] According to MacAvoy, NPS offer "potential benefits"

98. NPS Principles, *supra* note 15.
99. Lotta Viikari, The environmental element in space law assessing the present and charting the future 83 (2008).
100. NPS Principles, Preamble, §5, and Principle 3; Francis Lyall & Paul B. Larsen, Space Law: A Treatise 261 (2nd edition ed. 2017).
101. Working Paper submitted by the Russian Federation "Collisions between nuclear power sources and space debris, UNCOPUOS STC, 38 Sess., UN Doc. A/AC.105/C.1/L.246 (2001).
Viikari, *supra* note 99 at 45-48; Daniel A. Porras, *The United Nations Principles Relevant to the Use of Nuclear Power Sources in Outer Space: the Significance of a Soft Law Instrument after nearly 20 Years in Force, in* Soft Law in Outer Space: The Function of Non-binding Norms in International Space Law 205, 221 (Irmgard Marboe ed., 2012).
102. Initially, the USSR believed that the satellite and radioactive materials it contained would burn up upon reentry and safely disperse in the atmosphere. When it did not, highly radioactive debris crashed into an uninhabited region in Canada, thus contaminating the ground. *See* Stephen Gorove, *Cosmos 954: Issues of Law and Policy*, 6 J. Space L. 137 (1978); Canada: Claim Against the Union of Soviet Socialist Republics for Damage Caused by Soviet Cosmos 954, 18 International Legal Materials 899 (1979).
103. US Mission UNVIE, *2022 COPUOS STSC–US on the Use of Nuclear Power Sources in Outer Space* (2022) available online; for an analysis of the benefits, dangers, and legality of NPS use in outer

in several space activities like planetary science, deep space exploration, and astronomy.[104] Today, many satellites are equipped with solar power or rely on chemical propulsion. However, these sources of power limit space operations to the immediate vicinity of the Earth.[105] Further and longer use and exploration of outer space, such as interplanetary missions, are simply not possible with these means.[106] This is where NPS come into play: they open the way for "cheaper, more expansive, more effective space travels."[107] For instance, a fixed, long-term lunar base would need to be powered by NPSs "to provide the heavy electrical needs of the base."[108]

In this context, the NPS principles aim to strike a balance between the necessity to use NPS and the minimization of nuclear risk. In practice, this minimization translates into the restriction of NPS use to space activities that could not reasonably be carried out without it.[109] Their application is exclusively limited to non-propulsive NPS that are used for the generation of electric power onboard space objects.[110] In substance, the NPS Principles are based on the well-accepted practice of States, with some innovations.[111] They cover the safe use of NPS,[112] safety assessment,[113] notification of reentry of radioactive materials,[114] emergency assistance to States,[115] responsibility,[116] liability, and compensation.[117]

The cornerstone of the NPS Principles, however, is found in the innovative nature of Principle 3.[118] It sets guidelines forming technical criteria for the safe use of NPS in outer space and contributes to the protection of the outer space environment. Principle 3 aims to "protect individuals, populations and the biosphere against radiological hazards" by limiting the use of nuclear power in space to "those space missions which cannot be operated by non-nuclear energy sources in a reasonable way." It calls for the fueling of nuclear reactors with "highly enriched uranium 235" only.[119] It also prescribes that "nuclear reactors shall not be made critical before they reach their

space, *see* Joseph MacAvoy, *Nuclear Space and the Earth Environment: The Benefits, Dangers, and Legality of Nuclear Power and Propulsion in Outer Space*, 29 WM. & MARY ENVTL. L. & POL'Y REV 191, 191 (2004).

104. *Id.*, 233.
105. *Id.*
106. Porras, *supra* note 101 at 205.
107. MacAvoy, *supra* note 103 at 233.
108. MICHAEL D. CAMPBELL ET AL., *The Role of Nuclear Power in Space Exploration and the Associated Environmental Issues: An Overview*, 47 22 (2009).
109. NPS Principles, Principle 3.
110. *Id.*, Preamble 6.
111. VIIKARI, *supra* note 99 at 83.
112. *Id.*, Principle 3.
113. *Id.*, Principle 4.
114. *Id.*, Principle 5.
115. *Id.*, Principle 7.
116. *Id.*, Principle 8.
117. *Id.*, Principle 9. For a comprehensive analysis of the NPS Principles, *see* Marietta Benko, Gerhard Gruber & Kai Uwe Schrogl, *The UN Committee on the Peaceful Uses of Outer Space: Adoption of Principles Relevant to the Use of Nuclear Power Sources in Outer Space and Other Recent Developments*, 42 ZLW 35 (1993).
118. MacAvoy, *supra* note 103 at 228.
119. NPS Principles, Principle 3 §2c.

operating orbit or interplanetary trajectory."[120] Furthermore, Principle 3 requires that the design and construction of the nuclear reactors be such that they "cannot become critical before reaching the operating orbit during all possible events, including rocket explosion, re-entry, impact on ground or water, submersion in water or water intruding into the core."[121]

Although not legally binding, the NPS Principles have been considered "a topic of the highest priority" by UNCOPUOS' Member States, with a view to "maintaining constant assessment, in a multilateral framework, of existing safety regulations on that subject."[122] Though they represent an essentially voluntary engagement, some States, like Finland,[123] have adhered to the principles by referring to them in their domestic space legislation, therefore ensuring the principles are enforced at the national level. More recently, the United States reiterated its commitment to "the safety intent of the [NPS] Principles" during the 59th session of the UNCOPUOS STC.[124] It further:

> call[ed] on Member States and international intergovernmental organizations that are considering the use of [NPS] to implement the joint Safety Framework developed in 2009 by this Subcommittee, in partnership with the International Atomic Energy Agency.[125]

Here, the United States refers to the *Safety Framework for Nuclear Power Source Applications in Outer Space* ("NPS Safety Framework"):[126] a self-standing voluntary instrument which lays down "a foundation for the development of national and international intergovernmental safety frameworks" by providing guidance for governments and management and technical elements to mitigate nuclear risks.[127] Together, these rules contribute to avoiding the nuclear contamination of outer space, including celestial bodies which may be sought for their natural resources. Moreover, the NPS Principles could be relied upon to interpret Article IX of the Outer Space Treaty, notably regarding the "necessary measures" States shall adopt to avoid the harmful contamination of outer space.

120. *Id.*, §2d.
121. *Id.*, §2e.
122. Since the adoption of the NPS Principles, the use of NPS in outer space has been regularly discussed in the UNCOPUOS. Report of the Legal Subcommittee on the work of its forty-third session, held in Vienna from Mar. 29 to Apr. 8, 2004, UNCOPUOS, 47th Sess., §64, UN Doc. A/AC.105/826 (2004); Report of the Scientific and Technical Subcommittee on its fifty-ninth session, held in Vienna from Feb. 7 to 18, 2022, UNCOPUOS, 62nd Sess., §229, UN Doc. A/AC.105/1258 (2022).
123. Act on Space Activities, 63/2018, Art. 10 (FI).
124. US Mission UNVIE, *2022 COPUOS STSC–US on the Use of Nuclear Power Sources in Outer Space* (2022).
125. *Id.*
126. Safety Framework for Nuclear Power Source Applications in Outer Space, UNCOPUOS, UN Doc. A/AC.105/934 (2009).
127. *Id.*, §1. For a comprehensive analysis of the Safety Framework for Nuclear Power Source Applications in Outer Space and its application, *see* Ulrike M. Bohlmann & Leopold Summerer, *The STSC/IAEA Safety Framework for Space Nuclear Power Source Applications—Influence of Non-binding, in* SOFT LAW IN OUTER SPACE: THE FUNCTION OF NON-BINDING NORMS IN INTERNATIONAL SPACE LAW 233 (2012).

3 SPACE DEBRIS MITIGATION GUIDELINES[128]

As soon as 1965, Hall takes note of "the mounting accumulation of debris in orbit" and how it "has already begun to create traffic congestion in this near-earth region."[129] When Hall makes this observation, less than a decade has passed since the launch of the first artificial satellite into space in 1957, and the Outer Space Treaty has not yet been adopted. It will take another 40 years for the international community to adopt instruments including space debris mitigation measures.[130] In the meantime, space debris has become, without a doubt, the most immediate threat to the sustainability of space activities.

The creation of debris has dramatically increased by way of launches, in-space collisions, and breakups of space objects,[131] continuously filling the Earth's orbital environment with functional and nonfunctional human-made objects, most of which are debris. According to the latest estimations of ESA's Space Debris Office,[132] there are currently about 5,700 functioning satellites and 31,380 debris in orbit cataloged. Over 80% of the objects currently orbiting Earth are nonfunctional, discounting non-cataloged objects.[133]

In addition to their great number, space debris—like any other objects in space—has a high orbital velocity: about 7 km/s.[134] At this speed, even the tiniest debris could cause a significant amount of damage when colliding with another object and disturb normal operations. Indeed, debris smaller than one centimeter in size "could disable an instrument or a critical flight system on a satellite."[135] Furthermore, "[a]nything above 1 centimeter could penetrate the shields of the [International Space] Station's crew modules, and anything larger than 10 centimeters could shatter a satellite or spacecraft into pieces."[136]

This is especially problematic since space debris are primarily found in LEO, where most human activities take place.[137] This is where Earth observation satellites, some

128. This subsection focuses on nonlegally binding instruments developed by three entities for space debris mitigation purposes: IADC, the UNCOPUOS and ISO. The selection was realized based on their widespread use and citation in space law practices. They also offer an analysis of three different types of nonlegally binding instruments. However, it is understood that the selection of these three instruments alone is not comprehensive and that there are other nonbinding instruments contemplating the matter, directly or indirectly.
129. R. Hall, *Comments on Traffic Control of Space Vehicles*, 31 Journal of Air Law and Commerce 327, 329 (1965).
130. IADC SDM Guidelines and UNCOPUOS SDM Guidelines, *supra* note 16.
131. Nicolas M. Matte, *Environmental Implications and Responsibilities in the Use of Outer Space*, 14 Ann. Air & Space L. 419, 422–423 (1989).
132. The values were updated by ESA in May 2022. ESA, *Space debris by the numbers* (2022), available online.
133. Current technologies are not yet capable of tracking and cataloguing all objects in orbit. Nonetheless, using statistical models, ESA estimates that there are about 36,500 space debris greater than 10 centimeters, about 130 million measuring less than a centimeter and a million varying between 1 and 10 centimeters in size. *Id.*
134. Rada Popova & Volker Schaus, *The Legal Framework for Space Debris Remediation as a Tool for Sustainability in Outer Space*, 5 Aerospace 55, 56 (2018) DOI: 10.3390/aerospace5020055.
135. ESA, *Impact chip* (2016), available online.
136. *Id.*
137. Popova and Schaus, *supra* note 134 at 56.

telescopes as well as the habited ISS are positioned.[138] Debris can further be found in great amounts in GEO, which is used primarily for communications and broadcasting.[139] These specific activities are better carried out in GEO due to the orbit's specific: it allows a satellite to rotate around Earth at the same speed the planet rotates on itself; hence, it allows it to continuously transmit a signal to a precise position on the ground without interruptions.[140] To manage to stay in a fixed position above ground, GEO has to be aligned with the Earth's equator. Consequently, there is only one GEO which makes it a relatively limited natural resource. As such, having nonfunctioning objects in GEO is a waste of potential. Lastly, debris can be found in smaller amounts in medium-Earth orbit (MEO) which is essentially used for navigation, geodetic and communication satellites.[141] Therefore, no matter in which orbit they are located—LEO, GEO, or MEO—space debris hold the potential to disrupt activities from which humankind as a whole benefits greatly; satellites are used every day to monitor climate change and natural disasters, agriculture, global health, education, etc.[142]

But beyond the disruption of our activities, space debris also pose a risk to human crews in outer space and on Earth. For instance, in 2016, the European-built observation module *Cupola*—which was added to the ISS in 2010—was hit by a space debris which left a 7-millimeter-diameter circular chip impact on one of the windows.[143] According to ESA, the debris was "possibly a paint flake or small metal fragment no bigger than a few thousandths of a millimeter," hence the limited damage.[144] Yet, when comparing the size of the flake to the size of the damage, it is not difficult to picture the destructive potential of bigger debris on other objects in space. Incidentally, the ISS has had to be maneuvered over 25 times since being placed in orbit to avoid collision with bigger debris.[145]

Another risk is that one space debris may also pose to the Earth's environment when not fully disintegrated upon reentry into the atmosphere. The crash of the Soviet Cosmos 954 satellite into Canadian territory in 1978 certainly illustrates this fact. The satellite was carrying a nuclear reactor with highly radioactive materials. After losing control of Cosmos 954, the Soviets believed that it would burn up and disintegrate completely upon reentry into Earth's atmosphere.[146] Unfortunately, this was not the case, and the satellite crashed into a remote area of Canada. The crash did not cause any personal or property damage. However, it resulted in highly radioactive material

138. *Id.*
139. *Id;* Adam Mudge, *Incentivizing "Active Debris Removal" Following the Failure of Mitigation Measures to Solve the Space Debris Problem: Current Challenges and Future Strategies*, 2020.
140. Aurebleyde, C'est quoi l'orbite géostationnaire? YouTube (2018) available online.
141. Popova and Schaus, *supra* note 134 at 56. Major Global Navigation Satellite Systems (GNSS) like the United States' Global Positioning System (GPS), Europe's Galileo, Russia's GLONASS, and China's BeiDou constellations are positioned here. Lesley Jane Smith, *Legal aspects of satellite navigation, in* HANDBOOK OF SPACE LAW, 556–566 (Frans von der Dunk & Fabio Tronchetti eds., 2015).
142. UNOOSA, *Benefits of space*, available online.
143. Impact chip, *supra* note 135.
144. *Id.*
145. Franceinfo, *La Station spatiale internationale a dû manœuvrer pour éviter une possible collision avec un débris*, FRANCEINFO (2020) available online.
146. Gorove, *supra* note 102 at 137.

being spilled on Earth. This event caused the international community to realize the danger of using nuclear power sources in space activities and incidentally led to the adoption of the NPS Principles. Until then, it was assumed that nuclear material sent into outer space could not reach the surface of the Earth in case of reentry.[147]

Therefore, the question is: how do we limit those risks? How do we prevent the creation of more debris? The first step is to turn to the UN Space Treaties to see if they directly address the problem of space debris; as already stated, they do not. This can be explained by the fact that, at the time the treaties were drafted, the nature and practical effects of space debris as well as their legal implications were relatively unknown to the drafters in the UNCOPUOS.[148] This is why the second step—leveraging these treaties—only offers limited success. As shown in Chapter 2, the Outer Space Treaty outlines a general framework against "harmful contamination" and "harmful interference" in outer space which could apply to issues of space debris. Space debris certainly disturb normal operations of space activities and pollute the outer space environment. However, the content and the binding force of Article IX of the Outer Space Treaty are still debated at the international level,[149] notably because of the lack of definition for key terms and clearly established obligations.[150] Similarly, could a debris be considered a "space object"? Once more, the definition of a space object provided in Article I of the Liability Convention lacks clarity; it "includes component parts of a space object as well as its launch vehicle and parts thereof." For instance, could fragmentation debris be considered component parts? In the affirmative, space debris could fall within the scope of the Liability Convention which addresses the liability regime for damage caused by a space object—here a debris—to another space object or on the surface of the Earth.[151]

In the absence of definite answers or clear obligations in the treaties, the international community moved to create specific soft law instruments to address the increased presence of debris in orbit. Discussions about the dangers they pose started to rise at the national and international levels toward the end of the 1980s and early 1990s.[152] Domestically, the United States were the first to adopt space debris mitigation measures with NASA in the mid-1990s. The new policy required, *inter alia*, that all new NASA programs conduct orbital debris assessments during the designing phase of the project and submit a debris assessment to the NASA Administrator for review and

147. *Id.*, at 137–139.
148. Nandasiri Jasentuliyana, *Space debris and international law*, 26 JOURNAL OF SPACE LAW: A JOURNAL DEVOTED TO THE LEGAL PROBLEMS ARISING OUT OF MAN'S ACTIVITIES IN OUTER SPACE 139, 145 (1998).
149. Finland, Government proposal to Parliament for the approval and implementation of the Convention on Registration of Objects Launched into Outer Space and for the Act on Space Activities and the Act on the Amendment of Section 2 of the Lost and Found Objects Act. Unofficial translation, section 10 (2017) (FI) available online.
150. *See* Chapter 2 *supra*.
151. Liability Convention, Arts. II and III. Also *see* Jasentuliyana, *supra* note 148 for a study of the space treaties in relation to the space debris issue.
152. Henry T. Scott, *Improving the Shield: Mitigating the Danger of Space Debris by Enforcing and Developing Already Existing Space Law Section II: Space Law: Part A: Leading Articles*, 34 ANNALS AIR & SPACE L. 713, 723 (2009).

approval.[153] Eventually, the topic of space debris was addressed by the United Nations; space debris were added as a new recurring item on the UNCOPUOS STC agenda in 1994.[154]

3.1 The Development of Guidelines by the IADC

In parallel, the United States also started discussing the problem of space debris with ESA, Japan, and the Soviet Union through a series of conferences and bilateral meetings in the late 1980s. This series of exchanges between different space players made apparent "the need for a more formal and possibly more inclusive organization."[155] As a result, the four parties created the IADC and progressively extended it to include new space agencies.[156]

The primary purpose of the international forum is to exchange information on space debris research and mitigation options as well as to facilitate cooperation between agencies on this matter.[157] With regard to deliverables, the IADC focuses on mitigation guidelines that can be considered during the entire lifecycle of a space object—i.e., from the design and planification phase to the end-of-life phase.[158] Accordingly, the IADC developed and published the first version of its *Space Debris Mitigation Guidelines* ("IADC's SDM Guidelines") in 2002.[159]

From the outset, it must be emphasized that the IADC was established by a handful of space agencies, not governments, and not in a universal manner. As such, the IADC guidelines have a limited political impact on spacefaring nations. First, since they are not adopted by governments, they are voluntary; i.e., they do not have a legally binding force. Second, since the guidelines are drafted by space agencies—i.e., space experts—they are very technical and provide operators and space program managers with clear directives. These guidelines are based on the practice of IADC members and are the result of consensus among them.[160] Hence, they reflect current best practices. Furthermore, the lack of involvement from political entities, such as

153. For more details on the policy, *see* Robert Reynolds, Peter Eichler & Nicholas Johnson, *An Overview of Revised NASA Safety Standard 1740.14, in* Second European Conference on Space Debris 721 (1997).
154. Report of the Scientific and Technical Subcommittee on the Work of its Thirty-first Session, UNCOPUOS, §§63-74, UN Doc. A/AC.105/571 (1994).
155. Nicholas Johnson, *Origin of the Inter-Agency Space Debris Coordination Committee*, ARES Biennial Report 2012 Final (2014).
156. Members of the IADC are the Italian Space Agency, Centre National d'Etudes Spatiales (France), China National Space Administration, Canadian Space Agency, German Aerospace Center, European Space Agency, Indian Space Research Organisation, Japan Aerospace Exploration Agency, Korea Aerospace Research Institute, National Aeronautics and Space Administration (U.S.), Russian State Space Corporation, State Space Agency of Ukraine, and United Kingdom Space Agency.
157. IADC, SDM Guidelines, 4.
158. *Id.*
159. These guidelines were then revised in 2007, 2020 and 2021 for clarification purpose and to adapt to new developments in space activities, *id.*, 2.
160. *Id.*, 6.

governments, means that the guidelines can more easily be updated as needed as they do not require consensus among a hundred Member States, like in the UNCOPUOS.[161]

In substance, the IADC guidelines apply to "mission planning and the operation of newly designed spacecraft and orbital stages and, if possible, to existing ones."[162] They include measures regarding (1) the limitation of debris released during normal operations, (2) the minimization of potential for breakup during operational phases, (3) the limitation of the probability of accidental collision in orbit, (4) the avoidance of intentional destruction and other harmful activities, (5) the minimization of potential post-mission breakups resulting from stored energy, and (6) the limitation of long-term presence of space objects in the LEO region after the end of their mission.[163]

In order to limit the release of debris during normal operations—meaning outside of uncontrollable events—operators are encouraged to design their project with the aim of not releasing any debris. If this is not possible, due to the nature of the mission or of technological capabilities, they should minimize the number of debris generated and avoid crowding a congested area, like LEO. Regarding the minimization of potential on-orbit breakups, the IADC divides its recommendations into three subsections: (a) post-mission breakup from stored energy, in which case passivation measures are recommended;[164] (b) breakups during the "operational phase" which would require operators to demonstrate that the project has a probability of occurrence at least below 1/1000;[165] and (c) the avoidance of intentional destruction, via, for instance, self-destruction and direct-ascent anti-satellite (ASAT) tests.

This last point is particularly topical in the context of Russia's ASAT test in November 2021 and the United States' response to this regrettable event.[166] ASAT tests are particularly bad for the outer space environment as they consist in destroying a satellite in orbit, an action that generates a large amount of space debris. According to the United States, Russia's ASAT test "generated over fifteen hundred pieces of trackable orbital debris and will likely generate hundreds of thousands of pieces of smaller orbital debris."[167] For this reason, the United States banned on April 18, 2022, ASAT missile tests that create orbital debris. US Vice President Harris was reported saying that "these tests are dangerous and [the United States] will not conduct them"

161. Angola, Bangladesh, Kuwait, Panama and Slovenia joined COPUOS in 2021, thus raising the number of Member States to hundred. UNOOSA, *COPUOS Membership Evolution* (2021) available online.
162. Popova and Schaus, *supra* note 134 at 66.
163. I IADC, SDM Guidelines, 11–15.
164. Passivation refers to the elimination of stored energy on a space object by, *inter alia*, venting high pressured spacecraft, burning excess propellant and other fluids or discharging batteries. *Id.*, 9.
165. The requirement of a probability below 1/1000 is based on what would be necessary to have a positive noticeable effect on the space debris environment. *Id.*, 5.2.2.
166. US Department of State, *Russia Conducts Destructive Anti-Satellite Missile Test* (2021) available online; US White House, *Vice President Harris Advances National Security Norms in Space: New U.S. Commitment on Destructive Direct-Ascent Anti-Satellite Missile Testing* (2022) available online.
167. *Id.*, *Russia Conducts Destructive Anti-Satellite Missile Test.*

because it is "reckless and irresponsible."[168] According to the IADC guidelines, if these activities cannot be avoided, then they should at least be conducted in a lower orbit to avoid congested areas—which could endanger other satellites or the ISS—and limit the long-term presence of fragments in outer space.

Furthermore, the guidelines also recommend post-mission disposal measures to decongestion occupied areas, especially in GEO and LEO, and avoid on-orbit collisions. This could be achieved in two ways: (1) by re-orbiting an object away from congested areas—this is the so-called graveyard orbit approach[169]—or (2) by deorbiting an object, with a preference for reentry in the Earth's atmosphere.[170] Lastly, States and international organizations should adopt collision avoidance procedures. These can be achieved by assessing the probability, during the design phase, of accidental collisions, by conducting conjunction assessments, and by coordinating launch windows.[171]

From a legal standpoint, despite their lack of binding nature—the IADC guidelines do not create norms of international law—they can be considered a "standard for the responsible space operator."[172] They have also been used as models for the development of national space legislations[173] and international instruments, like the UNCOPUOS' SDM Guidelines adopted in the UN General Assembly in 2007.

3.2 The Adoption of Guidelines by the UNCOPUOS

The UNCOPUOS officially starts discussing space debris in 1994 when it is added as a new recurrent item on the agenda of the STC.[174] During the next five years, the subcommittee worked on accumulating knowledge on space debris and space debris mitigation options, an action which led to the publication of a *Technical Report on Space Debris* in 1999.[175] This report notes in its conclusion that "because of the difficulty of improving the space environment with existing technologies, the implementation of some debris mitigation measures today is a prudent step towards preserving space for future generations."[176]

168. Sandra Erwin, *U.S. declares ban on anti-satellite missile tests, calls for other nations to join*, SpaceNews (2022) available online.
169. The "graveyard approach" involves re-orbiting an object in an orbit away from operational space objects. In the case of objects operating in GEO, they should be moved, at the end of mission, to an orbit above GEO which guarantees the object will not cross the GEO protected region for at least a hundred years. For activities in LEO, they should be relocated to an orbit with an expected residual lifetime of 25 years or shorter. IADC SDM Guidelines, 5.3.
170. In case of reentry, the planned maneuver should demonstrate a 90% probability of disposal. Additionally, the probability of human casualty upon reentry should be less than 1/10000 per reentry. IADC, *supra* note 160 at 5.2.2; Popova and Schaus, *supra* note 134 at 57.
171. IADC SDM Guidelines, 5.2.3.
172. Steven A. Mirmina, *Reducing the Proliferation of Orbital Debris: Alternatives to a Legally Binding Instrument*, 99 The American Journal of International Law 649, 661 (2005) DOI: 10.2307/1602296; Popova and Schaus, *supra* note 134 at 56.
173. *See* for instance Finland, *Act on Space Activities* (2018).
174. Report of the Scientific and Technical Subcommittee on the Work of its Thirty-first Session, UNCOPUOS, §§63–74, UN Doc. A/AC.105/571 (1994).
175. Technical Report on Space Debris, UNCOPUOS STC, UN Doc. A/AC.105/720 (1999).
176. *Id.*, §136.

After agreeing to widely circulate the report among key space actors in order to raise awareness about space debris-related issues,[177] the Subcommittee decides to adopt a multiyear plan that would ultimately result in a proposal for SDM guidelines.[178] To that end, the UNCOPUOS STC invites the IADC in 2003 to present the mitigation guidelines it adopted the previous year. These guidelines are used as a basis for the work of the Subcommittee, and members of the organization are invited to contribute to the drafting of the UNCOPUOS' own mitigation guidelines.[179] The task of drafting the guidelines is given to a dedicated Working Group with the idea of updating the existing IADC guidelines. The work is concluded in 2005, and the guidelines are circulated in the hope of gathering consent from UNCOPUOS members and, ultimately, the UN General Assembly.[180] This goal is achieved in 2007 with the subsequent adoption of the voluntary *Space Debris Mitigation Guidelines of the Committee on the Peaceful Uses of Outer Space* (UNCOPUOS' SDM Guidelines") by the STC and their endorsement the same year by both the UNCOPUOS and the General Assembly in Resolution 62/217.[181] In particular, the General Assembly agrees that the UNCOPUOS' "voluntary guidelines for the mitigation of space debris reflect the existing practices as developed by a number of national and international organizations"; it further "invites Member States to implement those guidelines through relevant national mechanisms."[182]

Although the two sets of SDM guidelines—the IADC's as revised and the UNCOPUOS'—are very similar, several discrepancies can be noted. It has already been emphasized that the IADC guidelines were drafted by experts—not governments—and are, as a result, clear and technical. In comparison, the UNCOPUOS' guidelines are the result of necessary compromises between several Member States to achieve consensus.[183] As such, they are not only broader in nature but also embody a consensus at the international level of what practical measures individual States should adopt to mitigate the increasing space debris population in orbit. It further means that the IADC Guidelines can be updated more easily—as exhibited by the three revisions the guidelines went through so far—[184] than the ones adopted by the UNCOPUOS in 2007; it would require achieving consensus again. Other than their political impact, differences can also be seen in the content of the recommended measures. Indeed, when considering drafting its own set of guidelines, the UNCOPUOS decided early on they

177. Report of the Scientific and Technical Subcommittee on its thirty-seventh session, held in Vienna from Feb. 7 to 18, 2000, UNCOPUOS, 43rd Sess., §39, UN Doc. A/AC.105/736 (2000).
178. Report of the Scientific and Technical Subcommittee on its thirty-eighth session, held in Vienna from Feb. 12 to 23, 2001, UNCOPUOS, 44th Sess., §130, UN Doc. A/AC.105/761.
179. UNCOPUOS SDM Guidelines, *supra* note 16, iii–iv, 1–2 (2010). Report of the Committee on the Peaceful Uses of Outer Space, UNGAOR, 60 Sess., Supp. No. 20, §126, UN Doc. A/60/20 (2005).
180. Report of the Scientific and Technical Subcommittee on its forty-second session, held in Vienna from Feb. 21 to Mar. 4, 2005, UNCOPUOS, 48th Sess., Annex II, §§5–6, UN Doc. A/AC.105/848 (2005).
181. UNCOPUOS SDM Guidelines, *supra* note 16.
182. GA Res. 62/217, UNGA, 62 Sess., §27, UN Doc. A/RES/62/217.
183. Towards Long-term Sustainability of Space Activities: Overcoming the Challenges of Space Debris, UNCOPUOS STC, 48th Sess., §§28–29, UN Doc. A/AC.105/C.1/2011/CRP.14 (2011).
184. These guidelines were then revised in 2007, 2020 and 2021, *supra* note 159.

"would not be more technically stringent than the [IADC's] space debris mitigation guidelines."[185] Incidentally, the UNCOPUOS' Space Debris Mitigation Guideline No. 6—which refers to the use of graveyard orbits post-mission to avoid congesting LEO—abstains from indicating a maximum orbital lifetime, whereas the IADC clearly sets the limit at 25 years.[186] Lastly, the UNCOPUOS openly recognizes that "exceptions [to the implementation of individual guidelines or elements thereof] might be justified."[187] Therefore, although both sets of guidelines address the main issues, the approach adopted differs. One is technical and clearly aims to be used by space operators, whereas the other takes on the subject from a policy perspective.

3.3 The Creation of ISO Standards

A last actor in the development of SDM Guidelines is the International Organization for Standardization (ISO), which has sought to propose its own standards, encouraged in this undertaking by the efforts of both the IADC and the UNCOPUOS. This international NGO operates as a forum for national standardization bodies.[188] Each country is allowed one representative body, though it does not act as a delegation for the national government.[189] Members are therefore a mix of governmental bodies and appointed representatives from the private sector. ISO aims to develop and promote "standards,"[190] drafted on a consensus basis, with the purpose of unifying best practices in specific fields.[191] These standards are not legally binding under international law and encompass a series of voluntary recommendations and requirements.[192]

With regard to space debris, ISO determined that the topic deserved the attention of its own working group, whose purpose would be to "transform guidelines and best practices from the IADC, the United Nations, spacecraft operators, and regulatory bodies into a comprehensive set of international standards on space debris mitigation."[193] The organization adopted its first standard on space debris mitigation in 2010:

185. Report of the Scientific and Technical Subcommittee on its forty-second session, held in Vienna from Feb. 21 to Mar. 4, 2005, UNCOPUOS, 48th Sess., Annex II, §5b, UN Doc. A/AC.105/848 (2005).
186. IADC, *supra* note 160 at 5.3.2.
187. UN doc. A/AC.105/848, *supra* note 185; UN Doc. A/AC.105/C.1/2011/CRP.14, *supra* note 183, §28.
188. ISO Statutes, at 22, available online.
189. Since 2012, only States which are recognized by the United Nations may seek membership for a representative body. *Id.*, at 3; ISO, *Membership Manual*, 6 (2015) available online.
190. A standard can be understood as "a collection of technical requirements." Soucek and Tapio, *supra* note 85 at 563.
191. ISO Statutes, 2; ISO, *Consumers and Standards: Partnership for a Better World*, available online.
192. ISO Statutes, 4. The distinction between recommendation and requirement is signaled by the respective use of the word "should" and "shall" in the ISO standards text. ISO, *Foreword—Supplementary information*, available online.
193. H. Stokes et al., *Evolution of ISO's Space Debris Mitigation Standards*, 7 Journal of Space Safety Engineering 325, 325 (2020) DOI: 10.1016/j.jsse.2020.07.004; Camille Toussaint & Hervé Dumez, *Gérer un méta-problème: le cas des débris spatiaux*, 141 Annales des Mines: Gerer et comprendre 3, 5 (2020) DOI: 10.3917/geco1.141.0003.

ISO 24113.[194] It is a top-level ISO standard covering "all the high-level debris mitigation requirements."[195] It is supplemented by a series of lower-level standards based on the UNCOPUOS and IADC guidelines.[196]

3.4 Conclusion

Although the implementation of these diverse instruments on space debris mitigation remains voluntary, their impact is not negligible. Over the last two decades, several States have implemented these guidelines into their national legal order.[197] For instance, the UNCOPUOS guidelines are indirectly implemented through authorization and licensing mechanisms for private[198] space activities.[199] This is the case, for instance, of France,[200] the United States,[201] Austria,[202] and Denmark.[203]

As such, the development of SDM Guidelines and standards is the result of a plurality of efforts of diverse nature (technical experts, NGOs, States, industry) and levels of implementation (national and international). Although these efforts are concentrated on solving the immediate problem of orbital debris, it would be a mistake to leave it at that. With the development of new space ventures beyond Earth orbit, such as space resource activities, space debris may very well become a problem there too. Some of the current guidelines would not be applicable. For instance, the Moon has no tangible atmosphere; thus, reentry measures would not work out in the circumstances of lunar operations. For this reason, preparing new measures or adapting to the current ones may become necessary.

Furthermore, even the SDM Guidelines—as useful as they are—do not entirely solve the issue at hand: they are more focused on containment than, simply put, cleaning outer space from all the "junk" humankind has left behind.[204] In other words, they are

194. So far, ISO 24113 has been revised three times since its first publication in 2010. A fourth revision is underway and ISO 24119/2019—year of the last revision—should ultimately be replaced by ISO/DIS 24113. The new standard is currently under review for approval.
195. Stokes et al., *supra* note 193 at 325–326.
196. For a summary of ISO's standards on space debris mitigation, *see* ISO: Standards and technical reports, *in* Compendium of space debris mitigation standards adopted by States and internatio nal organizations, UNCOPUOS LSC, 61st Sess., UN Doc. A/AC.105/C.2/2022/CRP.17 (2022).
197. For a detailed overview of mitigation guidelines adopted by States and international organizations, *see id.*
198. Article VI of the Outer Space Treaty requires States Parties to "authorize" the activities of nongovernmental entities. Consequently, governmental entities are often not subjected to the licensing regime provided by national space legislations. Then, the application of space debris mitigation standards for governmental entities will generally depend on the policy of governmental agencies. Towards Long-Term Sustainability of Space Activities, *supra* note 183, §30. Also *see* Chapter 4 *infra* on the environmental component of States' space law domestic framework.
199. *Id.*
200. Loi N° 2008-518 du 3 juin 2008 relative aux opérations spatiales, No. 2008-518 Art. 5 (2008) (FR).
201. American Space Commerce Free Enterprise Act of 2019, H. R. 3610, 116th Cong. (2019) (US) ["ASCFEA"].
202. Austrian Outer Space Act, adopted by the National Council on 6 December 2011, §§4.1.4. and 5 (2011) (AT) translation available online.
203. Danish Outer Space Act of 2016, Act No. 409 of May 11, 2016, Art. 6§1.4 (2016) (DK) translation available online.
204. Frans von der Dunk, Advanced Introduction to Space Law 39.

mitigation guidelines, not *mitigation and remediation* guidelines.[205] This severe limitation entails an important lesson: it is a clear indication that, in outer space, the environmental impact of space activities should be considered from the outset; waiting for the problem to materialize endangers the sustainability of the venture. The problem of space debris proliferation does teach us that waiting for more knowledge about the outer space environment and the consequences of new activities is not a viable option. We need to anticipate problems because cleaning up afterward proves to be very difficult and—when dealing with the (definitive) extraction of natural resources—potentially irremediable. This is precisely the purpose of adopting a precautionary approach, as discussed in Chapter 2 *supra*. Environmental damage may be permanent. As such, waiting for full scientific certainty is rarely wise.

Nonetheless, the three instruments studied above provide valuable insight into how to legally address environmental problems in outer space in general and as a result of space mining efforts in particular. First, the interrelated nature of the IADC, the UNCOPUOS, and ISO instruments shows the value of an interdisciplinary approach. All three texts are of distinct origins and were developed in distinct circumstances. Considered together, they consolidate insights from governments, technical experts and standard bodies, the industry as well as academics on the subject.[206] Second, their differences further promote their utilization on different levels: whereas the UNCOPUOS guidelines address "Member States and international organizations,"[207] ISO's standards do not single out an overall addressee and focus on transforming the guidelines into "engineering practices."[208] Third, these sets of SDM Guidelines assert the importance of environmental integration from the very beginning of a mission. In the case of space debris, it means considering the end-of-life cycle of a satellite and integrating solutions in the design of the technology, and drawing upon the mission plan. For space resource activities, it could mean carrying out an EIA and designing the technology and mission to create the least environmental impact possible.

4 THE LTS GUIDELINES

In addition to the adoption by the UNCOPUOS of SDM Guidelines, the work of the UNCOPUOS STC on the subject brought about the realization that "a safe environment for space activities is no longer a given if one takes a long-term view."[209] With an increasing number of States, international organizations, and private entities engaging in space activities, new risks have emerged, ones that may affect the long-term sustainability of outer space exploration and use. The proliferation of space debris, the increased risk of collision and interference, the development of satellite constellations, and the emergence of space tourism make compelling examples of such risks.

205. For an assessment of the limit of the space debris mitigation guidelines in cleaning outer space, *see* Popova and Schaus, *supra* note 134.
206. ISO, *Membership Manual*, *supra* note 189, 6.
207. UNCOPUOS SDM Guidelines, 3.
208. Soucek and Tapio, *supra* note 85 at 562.
209. Future role and activities of the Committee on the Peaceful Uses of Outer Space, UNCOPUOS, 50th Sess., §26, UN Doc. A/AC.105/L.268 (2007).

Throughout the years, the topic of the long-term sustainability of space activities has progressively gained importance among the international community. Ultimately, the UNCOPUOS decides to formally adopt the topic as a new agenda item. As a result, the UNCOPUOS STC setups in 2010 a working group dedicated to the matter: the *Working Group on the Long-Term Sustainability of Outer Space Activities* ("LTS Working Group"). It is tasked with examining and proposing voluntary measures to ensure the safe and sustainable use of outer space. By 2018, it manages to reach a consensus on a preamble and 21 voluntary guidelines. These LTS Guidelines are adopted by the UNCOPUOS in June 2019, though they have yet to be endorsed by the UN General Assembly.

4.1 History and Evolution

The topic of the long-term sustainability of space activities is first introduced within the framework of the UNCOPUOS in 2004 when UNCOPUOS STC Chair Karl Doetsch delivered a speech on the issue.[210] In 2007, a year after the adoption of the UNCOPUOS' SDM Guidelines, UNCOPUOS Chair Gérard Brachet contributes a working paper reflecting on a range of initiatives, including the long-term sustainability of space activities. He notes that it has become "imperative to agree on some kind of 'rules of the road' to avoid interference, collisions and other mishaps that may hamper the use of outer space by all."[211] Such action, however, would not require amending existing treaties "but instead to develop recommendations to deal with the new realities of space operations." Thus, cementing the approach, the UNCOPUOS had already adopted to mitigate the proliferation of space debris.[212]

Fortified by this first introduction of the topic, the French delegation announces the following year, during the UNCOPUOS STC session, its intention to formally propose to UNCOPUOS the inclusion of a new agenda item entitled "the long-term sustainability of space activities."[213] The proposal, which includes a multiyear work plan spanning over three years, was to be introduced during the UNCOPUOS' next plenary meeting in June 2008.[214]

210. Unedited transcript, UNCOPUOS, 536th Meeting, §§23–26, COPUOS/T.536 (2005).
211. UN Doc. A/AC.105/L.268, *supra* note 209, §26.
212. The same year, Brachet was invited to give a presentation to the First Committee of the UN General Assembly. During his presentation, Brachet emphasized "the need to acknowledge the lack of a consensus on reopening the Outer Space Treaty, or to design a new international convention" and noted that "there was, however, a shared feeling that a bottom-up approach, based on technical guidelines, would make it possible to produce recommendations." Similarly, in 2008 when discussion the agenda item on space debris, a delegation noted "a cooperative approach to solving emerging problems could productively serve in the future as a model for the development of other rules or guidelines addressing the need to ensure the safety of space traffic." United States says discussing merits of treaties to prevent "weaponization" of outer space "pointless," as first committee continues thematic debates, UNGA, 62nd Sess. UN Doc. GA/DIS/3349 (2007).
213. Information on a proposal by France for a new item to be included on the agenda of the Committee on the Peaceful Uses of Outer Space, UNCOPUOS STC, 45th Sess., UN Doc. A/AC.105/C.1/2008/CRP.11 (2008); Gérard Brachet, *The Origins of the "Long-term Sustainability of Outer Space Activities" Initiative at UN COPUOS*, 28 Space Policy 161, 163 (2012) DOI: 10.1016/j.spacepol.2012.06.007.
214. *Id.*, Information on a proposal by France.

According to Brachet, the proposal was met with "strong support" by some of the delegations, such as the one from the United States.[215] However, discussion within the UNCOPUOS STC revealed that an introduction of the item during the UNCOPUOS' next plenary session—i.e., only a year after the introduction of Brachet's working paper—might be premature. Rather, France is advised to organize consultations with a variety of space actors outside the formal framework of the Committee.[216] The intention, here, is to allow time to build international support for the initiative and to gather a group of experts who would agree to draft a report describing the stakes on the LST of space activities.[217] Accordingly, France set ups an Informal Working Group which meets in Paris the same year. The group consists of representatives from 25 spacefaring nations, ESA, four of "the most significant commercial telecommunications satellite operators," as well as UNOOSA.[218]

Following the recommendations of the UNCOPUOS STC, the French delegation presents to the UNCOPUOS the preliminary findings of the Informal Working Group in 2008 and waits an additional year before formally proposing the topic of the "long-term sustainability of outer space activities" during UNCOPUOS' session in 2009.[219] After several exchanges, notably regarding the definition of space sustainability and the assurance that the effort would not be redundant with other initiatives, like space debris mitigation, "[the UNCOPUOS] finally agre[es] to include this item on its agenda from 2010 onwards."[220]

The agenda item is considered for the first time by the UNCOPUOS STC in 2010 during its 47th session.[221] During the session:

> the Subcommittee agre[es] that any best-practice guidelines that may be developed should be implemented on a voluntary basis and be focused on practical and prudent short- and medium-term measures that could be implemented in a timely manner.[222]

It is during that same session that the UNCOPUOS STC formally establishes the LTS Working Group and elects its Chair, Peter Martinez, from South Africa.[223]

The next year, in 2011, the UNCOPUOS STC reaches a consensus on the terms of reference and methods of work of the Working Group on the Long-Term Sustainability of Outer Space Activities of the Scientific and Technical Subcommittee as well as on a

215. Brachet, *supra* note 213 at 163.
216. *Id.*
217. *Id.*
218. *Id.*; Unedited transcript, UNCOPUOS, 593rd Meeting, at 12, UN Doc. COPUOS/T.593 (2008).
219. *Id.* Brachet, at 164.
220. *Id.*, at 162.; Report of the Committee on the Peaceful Uses of Outer Space, UNGAOR, 64th Sess., at 23, UN Doc A/64/20 (2009); Peter Martinez, *Development of an International Compendium of Guidelines for the Long-Term Sustainability of Outer Space Activities*, 43 Space Policy 13, 14 (2018) DOI: 10.1016/j.spacepol.2018.01.002.
221. Report of the Committee on the Peaceful Uses of Outer Space Scientific and Technical Subcommittee on its forty-seventh session, UNCOPUOS, 53rd Sess., §174, UN Doc A/AC.105/958 (2010).
222. *Id.*, §179.
223. *Id.*, §§181–182.

four-year work plan spanning from 2011 to 2014.[224] In order to carry out its work, the LTS Working Group decides to divide the work between four groups of experts; each group is expected to draft a series of voluntary guidelines. The expert groups are divided as such:[225]

- Expert Group A on sustainable space utilization supporting sustainable development on Earth;
- Expert Group B on space debris, space operations, and tools to support collaborative space situational awareness;
- Expert Group C on space weather; and
- Expert Group D on regulatory regimes and guidance for actors in the space arena.

Over the span of the four-year calendar, the LTS Working Group meets five times, following the progress of each Expert Group.[226] In 2014, it decides that, moving forward, the central role in the deliberations on the set of drafted guidelines would be assumed by the LTS Working Group rather than the separated groups of experts. During that time, the Working Group reports to and has consultations with the UNCOPUOS LSC.[227] Finally, in 2016, the LTS Working Group reaches a consensus on 12 initial guidelines, which are adopted by the UNCOPUOS during its following plenary session.[228] These voluntary guidelines are completed, two years later, with a preamble and an additional nine guidelines. The final compendium of 21 voluntary LTS Guidelines is formally adopted by the UNCOPUOS during its 62nd session in June 2019.[229] Incidentally, the Committed further decides to establish a new LTS working group ("LTS Working Group 2.0") to, *inter alia*, "conside[r] possible new guidelines for the long-term sustainability of outer space activities" within a five-year work plan.[230]

4.2 Content of the LTS Guidelines[231]

In substance, the finalized instrument comes in two parts: a preamble and the actual guidelines. The preamble elaborates on the context of the guidelines. It reflects on the

224. Terms of reference and methods of work of the Working Group on the Long-Term Sustainability of Outer Space Activities of the Scientific and Technical Subcommittee, UNCOPUOS, UN Doc. A/AC.105/C.1/L.307/Rev.1 (2011).
225. Long-Term Sustainability of Outer Space Activities, UNCOPUOS, 54th Sess, UN Doc. A/AC. 105/2011/CRP.15/Add.1 (2011).
226. For example, Working report of expert group A: Sustainable Space Utilization Supporting Sustainable Development on Earth, UNCOPUOS STC, 51st Sess., UN Doc. A/AC.105/C.1/2014/CRP.13 (2014).
227. Report of the Legal Subcommittee on its fifty-third session, held in Vienna from Mar. 24 to Apr. 4, 2014, UNCOPUOS, 57th Sess., UN Doc. A/AC.105/1067 (2014).
228. COPUOS Report 2016, A/71/20, para. 130.
229. A/AC.105/1167, Annex III and A/73/20.
230. Report of the Committee on the Peaceful Uses of Outer Space, UNGAOR, 74th Sess., Supp. 20, UN Doc. A/74/20 (2019); Report of the Scientific and Technical Subcommittee on its fifty-ninth session, held in Vienna from Feb. 7 to 18, 2022, UNCOPUS, 65th Sess., at Annex II, §7 and appendix UN Doc. A/AC.105/1258 (2022).
231. Report of the Committee on the Peaceful Uses of Outer Space, UNGAOR, 74th Sess., Supp. No. 20, at 163 and Annex II, UN Doc. A/74/20 (2019) ["LTS Guidelines"].

background of the adoption of the LTS Guidelines; their definition, objectives, and scope; their status under international law; voluntary implementation; and, lastly, the necessity in the future to review and update them.

The Guidelines themselves are found in the second part of the instrument and divided into four sections. Each guideline provides detailed guidance regarding their implementation. Accordingly, Section A considers the long-term sustainability of space activities from the perspective of policy and regulatory frameworks for space activities. Section B focuses on the safety of space operations. Section C highlights the importance of international cooperation, capacity-building, and awareness. Lastly, Section D looks toward the future by encouraging further scientific and technical research and development.

Accordingly, this section first provides an analysis of the preamble before addressing each section separately. Having regard to the approach adopted in this research—i.e., a legal perspective on space sustainability—the subsection pays particular attention to Section A.

4.2.1 Preamble

As a starting point, the preamble informs the reader—and users—of the LTS Guidelines about the rationale behind their adoption.[232] In the first paragraph of the preamble, the drafters—that is, the LTS Working Group—make note of Earth orbits being:

> [a] finite resource that is being used by an increasing number of States, international intergovernmental organizations and non-governmental entities.

This first sentence, read from the perspective of future space resource activities, brings two primary conclusions: first, the LTS Guidelines do not consider all aspects of space sustainability. They are primarily focused on space activities taking place in Earth's orbital environment. It means that *a contrario*, they are not intended prima facie to apply to future space resource exploitation activities. Second, and perhaps paradoxically, the sentence summarizes one of the main concerns that come with exploitation activities: space resources are limited in number, and an increasing number of space actors are looking forward to their utilization.[233]

The paragraph continues by emphasizing the fact that addressing the risks and developments that come with orbital activities—i.e., space debris, collisions, and mega constellations, "requires international cooperation by States and international intergovernmental organizations to avoid harm to the space environment and the safety of space operations." This sentence deserves to be highlighted, for it gives away two key elements of space sustainability. First, the sentence stresses the need for international cooperation. The sustainability of space activities cannot be achieved on one's own; it is a collective effort from the international community. Second, there are at least two dimensions to space sustainability according to the drafters: the preservation of the outer space environment and the safety of space operations.

232. LTS Guidelines, Background §§1-4.
233. As explained in the introduction, *supra*, though there exists an indefinite number of asteroids, the resource is limited when considered on a human scale.

The preamble carries on with a reminder that space activities are essential for the achievement of the SDGs. Adopted in 2015 by the United Nations, they are a collection of 17 goals to improve the planet and human life by 2030. Consequently, space sustainability must be ensured because it contributes, *inter alia*, to sustainability on Earth, not because the outer space environment should be preserved per se. In other words, the LTS Guidelines consider sustainability from an anthropocentric approach. This is not particularly surprising: the environment is rarely protected for its intrinsic value. As a matter of fact, concerns for the natural environment—terrestrial as extraterrestrial—increased when it started being articulated with other preoccupations, like human health or the safety of space operations.[234]

The preamble further notes that UNCOPUOS has not waited until the adoption of the LTS Guidelines in 2019 to contribute to the sustainability of space activities. Over the years, it has considered different facets of the topic. For this reason, the LTS Guidelines were not built from scratch. Rather, the LTS Working Group relied on "previous efforts" to "develo[p] a set of voluntary guidelines with a view to setting out a holistic approach to promoting the long-term sustainability of outer space activities."[235] Consequently, the "guidelines comprise a compendium of internationally recognized measures for, and commitments to, ensuring the long-term sustainability of outer space activities and, in particular, enhancing the safety of space operations."[236] More precisely, they are based on a "substantial body of knowledge" as well as on the experience of States, international intergovernmental and nongovernmental entities.[237] Therefore, the LTS Guidelines aim to consolidate and harmonize the best practice of States to promote a global and rational effort in ensuring the sustainability of space activities.

Interestingly, the rationale of the LTS Guidelines provided in paragraph 4 is phrased in a manner that mixes both the language of sustainable development and the UN Space Treaties. It states that:

> outer space should remain an operationally stable and safe environment that is maintained for peaceful purposes and open for exploration, use and international cooperation by current and future generations, in the interest of all countries, irrespective of their degree of economic or scientific development, without discrimination of any kind and with due regard for the principle of equity.

The expression "in the interests of all countries, irrespective of their degree of economic or scientific development" is a direct partial transposition of Article I paragraph 1 of the Outer Space Treaty. Further references to "peaceful purposes," "due regard," "international cooperation," and the freedom of exploration and use of outer space are also not without echoing Articles I, III, IV, and IX of the Outer Space Treaty. As for the "principle of equity" and reference to "current and future generations," they

234. France Inter, *Quand l'alimentation est politique: dis-moi ce que tu manges et je te dirais pour qui tu votes?*, LE TÉLÉPHONE SONNE (2022).
235. LTS Guidelines, 3.
236. *Id.*
237. Preamble, §11.

are typical elements associated with the concept of sustainable development, as seen in Chapter 1 *supra*.

Sustainability is similarly reflected in the statement regarding the purpose of the LTS Guidelines. Indeed, "[t]he purpose of the guidelines is to assist States and international intergovernmental organizations, both individually and collectively, to mitigate the risks associated with the conduct of outer space activities so that present benefits can be sustained and future opportunities realized." Thus, the main addressees of the LTS Guidelines are States and international intergovernmental organizations; though, it does not preclude them from being relevant for nongovernmental actors as well.[238]

It is not until paragraph 5 of the preamble that the instrument provides a definition of the long-term sustainability of space activities. For the LTS Working Group, space sustainability is defined as:

> the ability to maintain the conduct of space activities indefinitely into the future in a manner that realizes the objectives of equitable access to the benefits of the exploration and use of outer space for peaceful purposes, in order to meet the needs of the present generations while preserving the outer space environment for future generations.

There appears to be a qualitative element to the definition of space sustainability: humankind must be able to maintain a certain standard of activities throughout time. This is the very finality of ensuring space sustainability. Additionally, the idea of preserving the outer space environment for future generations is not without reminding the definition of sustainable development adopted in the Brundtland report.[239] Read together, the last part of the definition can be understood as the current generation not being able to foresee what the future generation will need from outer space. Thus, caution must be exercised to avoid closing doors humankind might need to open in the future. Here, the continuity of space activities is seen as a "basic need" by the drafters.

It is necessary to keep in mind that the definition adopted in the LTS Guidelines only applies for the purpose of the instrument. As established in Chapter 1, there is no international consensus on the meaning of "space sustainability." Although the definition of sustainability provided in the LTS Guidelines is being increasingly used by scholars, it still reflects individual choices of the LTS Working Group, as illustrated by paragraph 6 of the preamble. It refers to "the objective of ensuring and enhancing the long-term sustainability of outer space activities, *as understood at the international level* and *as set out in the guidelines*" [italics added]. These choices are necessary in order to give some substance to sustainability. Sustainability, even narrowed to "space" sustainability, is a broad concept. In order to be effectively implemented, it requires identifying key issues to find appropriate solutions. The congestion of Earth orbits does not raise the same issues as the extraction of space resources. Hence, as

238. *Id.*
239. Brundtland report, *supra* Chapter 1.

established in Chapter 1, there are different problems, different solutions, and different definitions.

Despite the limitation of its scope, the preamble still provides a measure of potential generalization that could be of interest when considering the sustainability of space resource activities. The sustainability of space activities should be thought out throughout the life cycle of the activities, i.e., "while developing, planning and executing" space activities.[240] Sustainability further requires the promotion of "international cooperation and understanding" to properly address the risks—man-made or natural—that could compromise humankind's ability to continue carrying out activities in outer space. The fact that—on several occasions—the preamble refers to not only "ensuring" the long-term sustainability of space activities but also its "enhancement" shows that States and international organizations are expected to play an active role in developing sustainable space activities.[241] They should not rest on their laurels but strive to do even better.

Another significant aspect of the LTS Guidelines is the fact that they are intended to support the development of both national and international practices "while allowing for flexibility in adapting such practices" to specific national circumstances.[242] Accordingly, achieving sustainability in outer space requires a two-speed process. The (potentially slow) work of States at the international level will ensure that the practice is harmonized and coherent, whereas, at the domestic level, they will be able to have a better vision of what works or not and be quick to react, hence, the flexibility of the system. Ultimately, the goal is to "reduc[e] to a minimum or, as feasible, avoi[d] causing harm to the outer space environment and the safety of space operations." The order of the two goals—"minimizing" and "avoiding"—is telling. It shows that while avoiding causing harm to the environment is the ultimate goal, managing to minimize it is much more realistic. In this, the LTS Guidelines have not emancipated themselves from the logic guiding previous efforts as regards the protection of the outer space environment: the reflection is still dominated by the preoccupation to mitigate damages rather than fully avoid them.

In addition to these substantial elements, the preamble further considers the status of the guidelines.[243] It refers to the UN Space Treaties and Principles as the "fundamental legal framework" of the LTS Guidelines.[244] Yet, in the subsequent paragraph, the LTS Working Group strongly emphasizes the voluntary nature of the guidelines; they are "not legally binding under international law."[245] It further adds that:

> [n]othing in the guidelines should constitute a revision, qualification or reinterpretation of those principles and norms. Nothing in the guidelines should be interpreted as giving rise to any new legal obligation for States. Any international

240. LTS Guidelines, Preamble, §6.
241. For example, *id.*, §§3, 6, 15 and 17.
242. *Id.*, §9.
243. *Id.*, §§14–20.
244. §14.
245. *Id.*, §15.

treaties referred to in the guidelines apply only to the States parties to those treaties.[246]

At the same time, the LTS Working Group explicitly encourages States and international intergovernmental organizations to implement the Guidelines.[247] The text reflects a certain consciousness of the drafters regarding the fact that their implementation "requires certain capacities and capabilities" that not all spacefaring nations may have.[248] Consequently, it encourages entities to implement the measures through national "or other applicable mechanisms" and "to the greatest extent feasible and practicable, in accordance with *their respective needs, conditions and capabilities*" [italics added].[249] The idea is that everyone should work toward space sustainability to some extent. States with greater capabilities should put a "greater emphasis" on implementing the guidelines. States without such capabilities should work toward developing their own capacity to implement the guidelines, and if they cannot, they should seek support from other entities to help them reach a position where they are capable of meeting the goals of the LTS Guidelines.[250]

Lastly, the preamble addresses the evolving nature of the initiatives. It underlines the value of a "continuous institutionalized dialogue" on issues linked to space sustainability and the implementation of the LTS Guidelines, notably during the UNCOPUOS, which is held as the favored forum.[251] In particular, the UNCOPUOS may be tasked with periodically reviewing and revising the LTS Guidelines "to ensure that they continue to provide effective guidance."[252] In practice, as previously mentioned, UNCOPUOS has already established a new working group—LTS Working Group 2.0—to work on identifying new guidelines and addressing implementation issues regarding existing ones.[253]

4.2.2 Section A on Policy and Regulatory Framework for Space Activities

Section A hosts the first collection of guidelines agreed upon by the members of the Working. It focuses on "policy and regulatory framework for space activities" and hosts five guidelines. The first one encourages States to "adopt, revise and amend, as necessary, national regulatory frameworks for outer space activities."[254] The guideline is based on States' obligations under the UN Space Treaties to, *inter alia*, bear responsibility for and supervise national space activities.[255] It advises States "to ensure

246. *Id.*
247. *Id.*, §16.
248. *Id.*, §19.
249. *Id.*, §16.
250. *Id.*, §17.
251. *Id.*, §21.
252. *Id.*, §24.
253. *See* Report of the Scientific and Technical Subcommittee on its fifty-ninth session, held in Vienna from Feb. 7 to 18, 2022, *supra* note 230.
254. LTS Guidelines, A.1.
255. Outer Space Treaty, Arts. VI and VII.

the effective application of relevant, generally accepted international norms, standards, and practices for the safe conduct of outer space activities," like the SDM Guidelines and the NPS Principles. Moreover, when reviewing their policy, States should take into account both existing space activities and potential future activities their space sector may want to explore. As stressed in the preamble, the long-term sustainability of space activities requires States and international organizations to look to the future to preserve the outer space environment for future generations. Accordingly, this approach should ideally be reflected in their policy.

The second guideline—Guideline A.2—reflects on a number of elements policymakers should consider. These elements include the implementation by States of their international obligations under the UN Space Treaties as well as the implementation of international practices and standards. In particular, Guideline A.2 refers to, *inter alia*, the SDM Guidelines, the guidance contained in the NPS Safety Framework, ISO standards, and the work of the IADC. It further recommends weighing "the costs, benefits, disadvantages and risks of a range of alternatives and ensur[ing] that such measures have a clear purpose and are implementable and practicable in terms of the technical, legal and management capacities of the State imposing the regulation."

Guideline A.3 reflects on the supervision of nongovernmental space activities. It puts a particular emphasis on the necessity for States to ensure that private entities have appropriate structures and procedures for planning and conducting space activities and have the means to comply with various national and international relevant requirements. To that end, States should encourage each entity to, *inter alia*, "establish and maintain all the necessary technical competencies required" to carry out space activities in "a safe and responsible manner" and to "develop specific requirements and procedures to address the safety and reliability" of space activities during all phases of the mission life cycle. The commitment to ensuring the long-term sustainability of space activities should also be a high-level priority for space actors, and this should be reflected in their management structures and procedures. They could also designate a point of contact to keep in communication with relevant authorities "to facilitate efficient and timely sharing of information and coordination of potentially urgent measures."

The fourth guideline under Section A aims to "ensure the equitable, rational and efficient use of the radio frequency spectrum and the various orbital regions used by satellites." Guideline A.4 refers first to States' international obligations pursuant to the Constitution and the Radio Regulations of the ITU. In this regard, States are reminded of the fact that radio frequencies and "any associated orbits" are a limited natural resource. Accordingly, States must use this resource "rationally, efficiently and economically" in order to ensure their equitable access among countries.[256] Furthermore, States should facilitate the prompt resolution of identified harmful radio frequency interferences. The guideline emphasizes the fact that avoiding harmful interference with the reception and transmission of radio signals contributes to the safe and sustainable use of outer space. Thus, States and international organizations are called

256. LTS Guidelines, A.4.

to implement the radio regulation procedures developed by ITU and to avoid the congestion of Earth orbits.

Last but not least, Guideline A.5 encourages "the development and/or implementation of effective and comprehensive registration practices" since "proper registration of space objects is a key factor in the safety and the long-term sustainability of space activities." For this purpose, the LTS Working Group recommends that the States which could qualify as the "launching State" jointly consider who should register the space object prior to its launch. They should also ensure they request "all necessary information from space launch service providers and users under their jurisdiction and/or control to meet all registration requirements under the Registration Convention." In addition, States should consider the content of UN General Assembly resolution 62/101 on *Recommendations on enhancing the practice of States and international intergovernmental organizations in registering space objects.*[257] The resolution recommends, *inter alia,* providing information about any change of status in operations or in orbital positions and encouraging the harmonization of the information provided to the UN Secretary-General about registered space objects. It could be achieved, for instance, by using "Coordinated Universal Time as the time reference for the date of launch" and "kilometers, minutes and degrees as the standard units for basic orbital parameters."[258]

4.2.3 Section B on Safety of Space Operations

With 10 guidelines under its umbrella, Section B on the safety of space operations is composed of close to half of the total amount of guidelines drafted by the LTS Working Group. The guidelines recommend, first, that States and international organizations provide updated contact information and share information on space objects and orbital events (B.1). In particular, they should exchange information on "on-orbit spacecraft operations, conjunction assessments and the monitoring of objects and events in outer space." The aim is to, *inter alia,* "enable timely coordination to reduce the probability of and/or to facilitate effective responses to orbital collisions, orbital break-ups and other events that might increase the probability of accidental collisions or may pose a risk to human lives, property and/or the environment, in the case of uncontrolled re-entries of space objects." They should further "improve accuracy of orbital data on space objects and enhance the practice and utility of sharing orbital information on space objects" since spaceflight safety "strongly depends" upon the accuracy of collected data (B.2). Moreover, the collection, sharing, and dissemination of space debris monitoring information should be encouraged (B.3).

The LTS Working Group further considers how performing conjunction assessment during all orbital phases of controlled flight (B.4) contributes to the safety of space operations. Specifically, these measures should be performed for all space objects which are capable of adjusting their trajectories during orbital phases of

257. GA Res. 62/101, UNGAOS, 62nd Sess., UN Doc. A/RES/62/101 (2007).
258. *Id.*

controlled flight. To that end, States—and when appropriate, international intergovernmental organizations—are encouraged to develop and implement "approaches to and methods for" conjunction assessment that could include: "(a) improving the orbit determination of relevant space objects; (b) screening current and planned trajectories of relevant space objects for potential collisions; (c) determining the risk of collision and whether an adjustment of trajectory is required to reduce the risk of collision; and (d) sharing information on the proper interpretation and usage of the conjunction assessment results, as appropriate." They should also develop practical approaches for pre-launch conjunction assessment (B.5).

The LTS Working Group also addresses the topic of space weather and agrees that States, as well as international intergovernmental organizations, should "share operational space weather data and forecasts" (B.6) and develop space weather models and tools as well as collect established practices on the mitigation of space weather effects (B.7).

Lastly, the LTS Working Group encourages States to promote design approaches that "increase the trackability of space objects, regardless of their physical and operational characteristics" (B.7).[259] It would require, *inter alia*, pushing manufacturers and operators to design objects which implement the SDM Guidelines to limit their presence in outer space once they reach the end of their life. States and international organizations should also take measures to address risks associated with the uncontrolled reentry of space objects (B.9) and observe measures of precaution when using sources of laser beams passing through outer space (B.10).

4.2.4 *Section C on International Cooperation, Capacity-Building, and Awareness*

Section C looks at how States could be enabled to implement the LTS Guidelines, with the understanding that not all countries are equal in terms of space capabilities and means. The LTS Working Group comes to the conclusion that international cooperation is key in achieving these objectives, especially for "developing and emerging spacefaring countries." Thus, international cooperation must be not only promoted but also facilitated (C.1). It should not be limited to intergovernmental cooperation. Rather, when appropriate, cooperation should include "the public, the private and then academic sectors"; it could include "the exchange of experience, scientific knowledge, technology and equipment for space activities." To that end, new procedures should be developed, when appropriate, to facilitate the exchange of information, experience, and expertise regarding the long-term sustainability of space activities (C.2). In this regard, the experience and expertise acquired by seasoned spacefaring nations should be regarded as "instrumental."

Additionally, capacity-building should be promoted and supported in developing and emerging spacefaring countries (C.3). This could be achieved by helping these

259. Guideline B.7 Design and operation of space objects regardless of their physical and operational characteristics.

countries find human and financial resources and establish regulatory frameworks. According to the LTS Working Group, capacity-building includes a wide range of activities, like "education, training and sharing of appropriate experience, information, data, tools and management methodologies and techniques, as well as the transfer of technology." Lastly, achieving long-term space sustainability requires raising awareness about the social benefits of space activities and the ensuing necessity to preserve outer space for future generations (C.4).

4.2.5 Section D on Scientific and Technical Research and Development

The last Section of the LTS Guidelines focuses on the future and how to continue to improve space sustainability. Section D contains only two guidelines. Briefly, the first guideline looks at how to "promote and support research into and the development of ways to support sustainable exploration and use of outer space" (D.1). It suggests States to consider, *inter alia*, the three dimensions of sustainable development: social, economic, and environmental. It further promotes the development of technologies that "minimize the environmental impact of manufacturing and launching space assets and that maximize the use of renewable resources and the reusability or repurposing of space assets." Interestingly, Guideline D.1. is the only guideline to make direct reference to the protection of the outer space environment from "harmful contamination."[260] The last guideline of the instrument, Guideline D.2, recommends that States "investigate and consider new measures to manage the space debris population in the long term."

4.3 Implementation of the LTS Guidelines

As stated in the preamble of the LTS Guidelines, "the guidelines are voluntary and not legally binding under international law."[261] However, as with other "soft law" instruments like COSPAR's PP policy or the different sets of SDM Guidelines, "voluntary" does not mean deprived of any legal consequence. It simply means that the instrument, in itself, cannot be enforced directly; instead, it relies on the implementation of its normative content by relevant authorities for it to be enforceable. Thus, in order to assess the legal impact of the LTS Guidelines, it is necessary to look at States and their behavior: have they implemented the measures? If so, how?

Some of the UNCOPUOS' Member States, like the United Kingdom (UK) and Belgium, have directly reported to the Committee on their advancement and approach to implementing the LTS Guidelines.[262] There does not appear to be a given template

260. Paragraph 4 of the guidelines provides that "States and international intergovernmental organizations should consider appropriate safety measures to protect the Earth and the space environment from harmful contamination, taking advantage of existing measures, practices and guidelines that may apply to those activities, and developing new measures as appropriate." LTS Guidelines, D.1, §4.
261. LTS Guidelines, preamble, §15.
262. United Kingdom Update on its Reporting Approach for the Voluntary Implementation of the Guidelines for the Long-Term Sustainability of Outer Space Activities, UNCOPUOS STC, 59th Sess., UN Doc. A/AC.105/C.1/2022/CRP.22 (2022); Implementation of the Guidelines for the

for the report, though both countries have chosen to comment on their progress following the structure of the guidelines rather than write an overall report on their implementation. Both approaches bring valuable insights into the implementation of the instrument. The Belgian report, for instance, takes the form of a table with two columns. The column on the left reproduces the text of the LTS Guidelines, with each line corresponding to a different paragraph. In the column on the right, the State explains how the corresponding recommendation is implemented. The format of the report gives almost a play-by-play implementation of the guidelines, clearly indicating which provision in Belgian policy or legal framework for space activity addresses the given point.

The UK's report shares some similarities with the Belgian report in the sense that it also contains a table in an appendix. However, rather than commenting on each recommendation, the report focuses on how the government has implemented the objective set in the text. After reporting on the general progress regarding the implementation of the LTS Guidelines, the UK report provides a filled table that aims at "capturing the implementation of the guidelines." To that end, each guideline is presented in a table with four "implementation categories." The first line regards the "thoughts or approach to implementation." When reporting on Guideline A.1, it notes, for instance, that "the Space Industry Act 2018 (SIA) is being used as an opportunity to update and further develop the UK regulatory regime for authorizing outer space activities."[263] The second line in the table reports on "current progress and/or proposed future activities." Lines 3 and 4 respectively consider "experiences, challenges and lessons learnt" and allow for "comments on specific needs for capacity building necessary to support implementation." For instance, for Guideline A.2 on the elements a State should consider when revising its policy, the UK notes in the experience section that:

> [its] non-prescriptive, outcome-based authorisation regimes provide flexibility by design. This flexibility, alongside proactive engagement with the space industry and community will be key to ensuring that the rapid pace of change in technology and operational practice can be adequately taken into account.

Eventually, while Belgium acts as a good student, pointing out where and how it has implemented the LTS Guidelines, the UK adopts a more pedagogical approach.

In addition to States directly reporting to the UNCOPUOS on their progress, UNOOSA created a website dedicated to awareness-raising and capacity-building related to the implementation of the Guidelines for the Long-Term Sustainability of Outer Space Activities.[264] The project aims to "showcase how the LTS Guidelines of the [UNCOPUOS] materialize in practice through a multi-stakeholder approach." To that end, UNOOSA has created a template for case studies of various entities—i.e., governments, intergovernmental and NGOs, the private sector, and national space

Long-Term Sustainability of Outer Space Activities of the Committee on the Peaceful Uses of Outer Space: Belgium, UNCOPUOS STC, 58th Sess., UN Doc. A/AC.105/C.1/2021/CRP.12 (2021).

263. Guideline A.1. concerns the adoption, revision, and amendment, as necessary, of national regulatory frameworks for outer space activities.

264. UNOOSA, *Case Studies*, Spacesustainability.unoosa.org (2021) available online.

agencies—to briefly report on their implementation of the LTS Guidelines. This voluntary process resolves around three axes: (1) a brief description of the activity, (2) the connection with the LTS Guidelines, i.e., what has been implemented and not, and (3) the lessons learned. These reports can then be used by the public to assist them in their implementation of the Guidelines. The website allows, for instance, filtering the results by guideline, topic, or by the nature of the entity which submitted the case study. There are currently over 30 case studies available online.

However, while these case studies and the direct reporting to the UNCOPUOS are useful to assess the level of implementation of the LTS Guidelines, it would also require more than one person or a separate project to filter through all the data, analyze it and draw an informed conclusion. Thankfully, in November 2020, the *Space Law & Policy Project Group* of the Space Generation Advisory Council (SGAC) assembled a research team to take on a similar project.[265] The project aims to, *inter alia*, publish a report on the LTS Guidelines' implementation "across continents accounting for various sources of State practice" in order to establish whether trends can be identified.[266] To that end, the SGAC team selected 20 countries across six continents, having the care to include both major and developing spacefaring nations.[267] They based their analysis on various sources, like policy, legislation, expert interviews, and documented initiatives.

The team presented its preliminary findings during the 60th session of the UNCOPUOS LSC, in June 2021. They found that—to an extent—all selected countries had implemented the five guidelines of Section A, i.e., on policy and regulatory frameworks for space activities. More precisely, 80% of the surveyed countries have "legislated and/or have substantial practical implementation." The remaining 20% have "partially implemented" the guidelines under Section A or already "planned their implementation."[268] According to the research team, "States appear to be producing comprehensive and detailed space legislations beyond *de facto* regulation and basic legislations implementing treaty provisions."

With regard to the other three sections of the LTS Guidelines, they found that "a substantial number of countries have launched initiatives to develop space weather monitoring capabilities and data sharing" (Guidelines B.6 and B.7). Out of the 20 surveyed countries, 16 are working on space weather to a certain extent. The SGAC team further concluded the existence of "strong support" from surveyed countries regarding the promotion and facilitation of international cooperation and raising awareness on space activities (Guidelines C.1 and C.4). States are, for instance, participating in international intergovernmental and nongovernmental organizations, like the IADC or the Asia-Pacific Space Cooperation Organization (APSCO). With

265. Chan Yuk Chi, *SGAC Report on the LTS Guidelines National Implementation*, *in* Technical Presentations Made at the UNCOPUOS LSC (2021) available online.
266. *Id.*
267. In alphabetical order, the surveyed countries are Australia, Belarus, Belgium, Brazil, Canada, China, Finland, Germany, India, Japan, Kazakhstan, Luxembourg, New Zealand, Russia, South Africa, Spain, the United States of America, Ukraine, the United Arab Emirates, the United Kingdom. *Id.*
268. A slight decrease can be noted for the implementation of Guideline A.5 on the enhancement of practice of registering space object. Nonetheless, the guideline has been implemented in over 75% of the sampled countries according to the graph. *Id.*, at 9.

regard to Section D, the two guidelines on research and development have been implemented by around 40% of the surveyed countries, and an additional equal number of States are considered in the process of implementing them.

However, the results are more mitigated in other areas. For instance, while States perform conjunction assessments, they rarely share their practice with other States. Consequently, there is a lack of consensus among States on what the measure entails in practice. Another example of low implementation is Guideline B.10 on laser beams passing through space; it has been implemented by less than 20% of the surveyed countries.

Overall, the SGAC team has been able to identify "best practices"—i.e., practices shared by most of the surveyed countries—regarding the long-term sustainability of space activities. They include:

- the early enacting of national space legislation;
- international and domestic capacity-building;
- the implementation of debris mitigation standards in States' licensing process;
- object trackability and Space Situational Awareness (SSA) data sharing; and
- international space weather data sharing.

On the other end, the adoption of domestic space legislation and the enforcement of end-of-life procedures need to be improved along with conjunction assessments, laser notification, consultation, and coordination, as well as the sharing of space object design.

Although the SGAC team has only surveyed 20 countries—in comparison to over one hundred Member States in the UNCOPUOS in 2021—their findings still demonstrate a trend in the implementation of the LTS Guidelines. Less than three years after their endorsement, it is already possible to see trends emerge. First, the results of the SGAC team's investigation showcase common practices among States. Second, they highlight the implementation of Section A guidelines on policy and regulatory frameworks for space activities. It shows that when trying to achieve sustainability, building or adapting a framework is the most used approach. Last, the result of the survey shows that the implementation of the LTS Guidelines is not uniform.

Overall, the LTS Guidelines are being implemented at various levels, as shown by the case studies published by UNOOSA. Not only States and international organizations but also the private sector are paying attention and progressively working toward more sustainable practices. Sustainability in space has also become a topic of interest in various fora, with multiple events being organized around the world,[269] thus, contributing to the necessity to raise awareness and capacity building.

269. For instance, the Secure World Foundation organized the 4th Summit for Space Sustainability in London, UK in June 2022. Similarly, the 11th SES Workshop organized by the SES Chair of the University of Luxembourg and SES, in 2022, focused on space sustainability in orbit, addressing the topics of life cycle assessment, space traffic management and space situational awareness.

4.4 Conclusion

It is not an overstatement to consider that the LTS Guidelines are a success. First, the LTS Working Group managed to create what other multilateral space efforts have failed to achieve: produce a "tangible result."[270] Already, the LTS Guidelines are being implemented to various extents by a diversity of space actors.[271]

Second, they represent a consensus at the international level. As previously stated, the UNCOPUOS works on the basis of consensus among its Member States. Consequently, any decisions made in the Committee—and by extension on these guidelines and their content—are indicative of the international community's views and agreements on these issues. Moreover, the LTS Guidelines find their origin in the best practice of States; they were not created out of thin air. Thus, beyond providing insights on how to ensure and enhance space sustainability, they are a proof of concept. They have already proven to be effective in contributing to the long-term sustainability of the exploration and use of outer space. Their consolidation in a single, consensus-based, document contributes to enhancing their efficiency by creating common goals at the international level and raising awareness about existing solutions.

Third, the LTS Guidelines are a success because of their inclusiveness. This inclusiveness is twofold. The process itself of their creation was inclusive. The guidelines were initially developed by scientific, technical, legal, and policy experts nominated by the UNCOPUOS members and permanent observers.[272] They were then finalized by the LTS Working Group which made a conscious effort to gather a wide range of inputs from a variety of sources.[273] The inclusiveness of the measures adopted by the UNCOPUOS further extends to their addressees. As a UNCOPUOS instrument, the natural addressees are States and international governmental organizations. Yet, the LTS Guidelines were designed to be used by both governmental and nongovernmental entities.[274] Their implementation by private entities, for instance, shows that the LTS Guidelines can be implemented on multiple levels, from top to bottom.[275] The reference to developing and emerging spacefaring nations further exhibits that the LTS Working Group considered the space sector in its diversity. The LTS Guidelines are designed so that even the smallest space actor can contribute, within the boundaries of its capabilities, to the sustainability of space activities.

270. For an overview of other similar initiatives, *see* Brian Weeden, *New UN Guidelines For Space Sustainability Are A Big Deal*, Breaking Defense (2018), available online.
271. *See*, for instance, the case studies submitted to UNOOSA regarding the implementation of Section A guidelines by ISO, the Chilean Air Force, the company D-Orbit which provides space logistics and transportation services, the intergovernmental Asia-Pacific Space Cooperation Organization (APSCO) and the Philippine Space Agency. UNOOSA, *Case Studies*, *supra* note 264.
272. Martinez, *supra* note 220 at 15.
273. The Working Group received contributions from several entities, including, *inter alia*, COPUOS Member States, the ITU, the Office for Disarmament Affairs of the UN Secretariat, the International Astronautical Federation, the Secure World Foundation and the Space Generation Advisory Council. *Id.*
274. LTS Guidelines, Preamble, §11.
275. *See, e.g.*, ispace, Inc. case study on the relevance of the LTS Guidelines for lunar exploration and use. ispace, Inc., *Case Studies*, UNOOSA (2021) available online.

Lastly, although it has been noted that the scope of the LTS Guidelines does not address all aspects of space activities—it focuses on activities in Earth orbits—they remain relevant for other types of activities. In 2021, the Japanese startup ispace, Inc. filed a case study report with UNOOSA on the LTS Guidelines,[276] even though its activities focus on lunar exploration and the use of its natural resources. The company notes that, although "[d]iscussions on sustainability in lunar exploration and development have yet to begin seriously," "utilization of lunar resources improves the sustainability of space activities and is linked to the concept of LTS Guidelines in many ways."[277] In particular, ispace, Inc. emphasizes the importance of "maintain[ing] the safety of activities on the lunar surface or in the lunar orbit."[278]

More generally, the LTS Guidelines provide a direction toward achieving the sustainability of future exploitation activities. The development and adoption procedure of the instrument demonstrate once more the value of adopting a multidisciplinary approach when considering environmental issues in outer space. We need the knowledge of scientific and technical experts to understand the circumstances we are working with. We further need legal and policy experts to understand how to maneuver international and national frameworks without creating a conflict with existing obligations. We need access to a variety of actors, like the private sector, to understand their needs and ensure the measures are flexible.

Ultimately, each of the four sections of the LTS Guidelines can be used to an extent for space resource activities. Section A encourages States to adopt, revise and amend their domestic regulatory framework to "ensure and enhance" the long-term sustainability of space activities. It promotes minimizing the environmental impact of human activities in outer space. This is in line with the integration element of the sustainable development concept;[279] it consists in integrating environmental considerations in decision-making processes. Section A further advises States on implementing their international obligation to continuously supervise the activities in outer space of national nongovernmental entities,[280] notably by implementing structures and procedures "for planning and conducting space activities."[281] It also encourages States to consider space debris mitigation measures and implement the NPS Safety Framework. Section B promotes the safety of operations which, as emphasized by ispace, Inc., is also a relevant topic beyond Earth orbits. Section C stresses the importance of capacity-building and raising awareness, notably through international cooperation. With several States planning to conduct missions to the Moon, coordination of activities to avoid interference will be essential. Lastly, Section D promotes continued research and development to enhance sustainability and minimize the environmental impact of our activities in outer space.

Altogether, many elements of the sustainability framework outlined by the LTS Guidelines fit the requirements of the conceptual sustainability framework used in this work. It integrates the environmental component, encourages States to regulate and

276. *Id.*
277. *Id.*, at. 2.
278. *Id.*
279. *See* Chapter 1 *supra*.
280. Outer Space Treaty, Art. VI.
281. LTS Guidelines, A.3, §1.

monitor their activities at the domestic level, and promotes the implementation of soft law instruments, like the NPS Safety Framework and the SDM Guidelines of UNCOPUOS, ISO, and the IADC. In this sense, the LTS Guidelines provide insights of a general nature. Nevertheless, it does not explicitly delineate a detailed sustainability framework, especially from an environmental perspective.

5 CONCLUSION

The successive study, in this chapter, of COSPAR's PP policy, the NPS Principles, and three sets of SDM Guidelines as well as the LTS Guidelines allows us to make several observations of the crucial role played by nonbinding instruments in the governance of space activities.

First, they offer great flexibility. Soft law instruments are easier to revise than treaties. This flexibility allows to quickly adapt space law to new scientific discoveries and technological developments. In practice, amending a treaty is a long process. Taking the example of the Outer Space Treaty, Article XV provides that amending the instrument would require the "acceptance by a majority of the States Parties to the Treaty." Accordingly, over 50 States Parties would have to agree to the amendment. This is partly why, whereas the 1967 Outer Space Treaty has not been amended in the last 25 years, the IADC's SDM Guidelines have been revised three times so far. It is partially due to soft law instruments having lower stakes internationally than treaties; they do not create international obligations and, thus, refrain from limiting States' exercise of their sovereignty. From an administrative perspective, these instruments further create fewer hurdles as they do not, for instance, require ratification by the State. They also do not oblige States to potentially amend their domestic legislation to ensure compliance with the amended text.[282]

Moreover, nonbinding instruments enable addressing issues which were unanticipated by the UN Space Treaties. This is particularly in technical areas, as evidenced by the adoption of the NPS Principles which set down clear requirements regarding the use of NPS in outer space.

Second, in addition to being flexible, soft law allows for detailed instruments. This is not possible with treaties because, to be a flexible and long-lasting instrument, they must rely on the use of vague and ambiguous language.[283] Indeed, the key to the perennity of binding instruments is to remain open for interpretation, as seen with the Outer Space Treaty. As argued in Chapter 2, a dynamic interpretation of the expression "harmful contamination" in Article IX of the Outer Space Treaty would allow considering its application to unanticipated environmental issues, such as space debris.[284] There is, however, no certainty that such an interpretation would be accepted widely by States.

282. Brian Wessel, *The Rule of Law in Outer Space: The Effects of Treaties and Nonbinding Agreements on International Space Law*, 35 HASTINGS INT'L & COMP L REV 289, 315 (2012).
283. *Id.*, at 316.
284. On the possibility to interpret the Outer Space Treaty by relying on soft law instruments, also *see* Alan E. Boyle, *Soft Law in International Law-Making, in* INTERNATIONAL LAW 119, 124–125 (Malcom Evans ed., 5th ed. 2018).

Third, contrary to treaties, nonlegally binding instruments can be adopted by private actors, like a body of experts or practitioners. Having regard to COSPAR's PP policy, the three sets of SDM Guidelines, and the UNCOPUOS LTS Guidelines, their drafting involved a diversity of actors, from scientists to politicians and space practitioners. The analysis of the IADC, UNCOPUOS, and ISO SDM Guidelines shows the value of adopting an interdisciplinary approach when elaborating technical rules. In particular, the subtle difference between the IADC and UNCOPUOS Guidelines is noteworthy, the latter being less stringent and abstaining from using scientific language.

Fourth, the absence of binding force is not an end, in itself, to the implementation of soft law standards. These instruments were adopted for a purpose: they answer issues left answered by treaties by outlining a standard of behavior. Thus, it would be irrational for UNCOPUOS Member States to spend time discussing proposals on how to ensure the long-term sustainability of space activities or on the mitigation of space debris if, ultimately, they had no intention to align their practice with the standard that they, themselves, have adopted. If they negotiated the instrument, it is because they have an interest in it.

This is especially evidenced by States' voluntary adoption of the instrument—or most often of their content—in their domestic order. As will be further demonstrated in Chapter 4 *infra*, space debris mitigation measures have been adopted by several States, notably through their inclusion in the authorization process for nongovernmental space activities. Similarly, the analysis of the LTS Guidelines shows that the instrument is being implemented by States. Moreover, beyond State's implementation of the instrument at the national level, it must be underlined that several practitioners, like space agencies, have made a commitment to either implement or align their practice on international standards, like COSPAR's PP policy.

Finally, the instruments analyzed in this chapter are a collection of best practices in diverse technical areas. As such, they set out a standard of behavior that space actors should aim to achieve. According to Wëssel, nonbinding space law instruments, like the SDM Guidelines, are a tool that helps determine the standard to which space actors' behavior will be judged.[285] In this manner, COSPAR's PP policy, or the SDM Guidelines, could be used to define the standard of due diligence expected of actors carrying out space activities.

To conclude, from the perspective of space resource activities, a soft law approach has a lot to offer. It could help articulate a complex regulatory framework based on the interaction between the UN Space Treaties and a dedicated soft law instrument on space mining. In this configuration, the Outer Space Treaty would be used as the floor below which certain behaviors become unacceptable—i.e., they breach the treaty. The soft law instrument would, *inter alia*, outline sustainable practices for space resource activities, notably by recommending the adoption of environmental measures, like the implementation of EIA. These measures would further benefit from being drafted based on the input of a diversity of actors, like practitioners, politicians, and scientists.

285. Wessel, *supra* note 283 at 316.

CHAPTER 4

National Laws

Another facet of space law is the voluntary adoption by States of domestic regulatory frameworks to govern the conduct of space-related activities falling under their jurisdiction. There is a measure of irony in the history of the development of such laws. Initially regarded—and often criticized—as a way to move away from, or even avoid, international binding agreements, the enactment of national space laws is now often perceived by States as a means to fulfill these very international obligations.[1] It is certainly true that the UN Space Treaties create no obligation for States Parties to take such regulatory steps; however, they do require the compliance of national space activities with their provisions and, more generally, with international law.[2] Beyond the issue of abiding by international law, national legislations also prove, in some aspects, to be at the forefront of legal norms as regards space activities. This is particularly the case with the protection of the outer space environment.

In the same fashion, the UNCOPUOS' *Working Group on National Legislation Relevant to the Peaceful Exploration and Use of Outer Space* ("NL Working Group") identifies two additional reasons States commonly enact domestic legislation:[3] first is the need for States "to achieve consistency and predictability in the conduct of space

1. Report of the Working Group on National Legislation Relevant to the Peaceful Exploration and Use of Outer Space on the work conducted under its multiyear workplan, UNCOPUOS LSC, 51st Sess., §15, UN Doc. A/AC.105/C.2/101 (2012).
2. Art. VI of the Outer Space Treaty only requires States Parties to ensure that national space activities comply with the provisions of the Treaty, and to authorize and supervise the activities of nongovernmental entities. The provision leaves the means of implementation to the discretion of the States Parties. Michael Gerhard, *Article VI*, 1 *in* COLOGNE COMMENTARY ON SPACE LAW 103, 117–119 (Stephan Hobe, Bernhard Schmidt-Tedd, & Kai-Uwe Schrogl eds., 2009). On the compliance of national space activities with international law, *see* Outer Space Treaty, Art. III.
3. The Working Group was established in 2009 by the UNCOPUOS LSC to "develop an understanding of the manner in which Member States had regulated [governmental and non-governmental space] activities." The outcome of the work is a set of recommendations, which were adopted by the UN General Assembly in 2013. Report of the Legal Subcommittee on its forty-eighth session, held in Vienna from Mar. 23, to Apr. 3, 2009, UNCOPUOS, 52nd Sess., at Annex III, UN Doc. A/AC.105/935 (2009); GA Res. 68/74, UNGAOR, 68th Sess., UN Doc. A/RES/68/74 (2013).

activities under [their] jurisdiction."[4] Second, enacting a national legislation "provide[s] a practical regulatory system for private sector involvement" in space-related activities.[5]

In this regard, the significant increase in the participation of nongovernmental entities in space activities has led to deliberate efforts, at the international level, to promote the adoption of national space legislation. Two initiatives, in particular, deserve mention. The first is the adoption of the UNCOPUOS' *Recommendations on National Legislation Relevant to the Peaceful Exploration and Use of Outer Space* ("UNCOPUOS' Recommendations") in UN General Assembly Resolution 68/74.[6] These recommendations were drafted by the NL Working Group in the form of paragraphs, where each paragraph considers a different legal aspect of space activities.[7] From an environmental perspective, these recommendations only touch lightly on the matter when considering the drafting process of national instruments. Excluding the reference to the UNCOPUOS' SDM Guidelines and "other relevant instruments," Paragraph 4 only makes a brief allusion to "minimize[ing] the risks [...] to the environment" as an authorization requirement. It is unclear, however, whether the expression refers to the terrestrial or extraterrestrial environment. Similarly, the preamble notes the need to maintain the "sustainable use of outer space" by, *inter alia*, mitigating debris and minimizing the potential harm to the outer space environment. Though devoid of a will to detail necessary steps or delineate clear goals, the UNCOPUOS' Recommendations are not entirely without utility. They actually provide useful elements of reflection for States when contemplating the enactment, or amendments, of a domestic space law instrument.

At any rate, other sources prove to include more precise orientations. This is the case of the second initiative: the ILA's guidelines on the enactment of national space legislation adopted by the Space Law Committee in 2012.[8] Strikingly contrasting with the timidity of the UNCOPUOS, these guidelines take a practical approach to the task. Commonly referred to as the *Sofia Guidelines for a Model Law on National Space Legislation* ("Model Law"),[9] ILA Resolution 6/2012 takes the form of a template for the drafting of national legislation. In "General Remarks," the Rapporteur claims there are "indispensable requirements underlying any future model law," namely the duty to authorize space activities and to detail the authorization and licensing procedures, the duty to supervise activities, as well as to ensure private operators are properly insured. This Model Law is articulated around 14 provisions[10] and explicitly integrates concerns for

4. UNCOPUOS Working Group on National Legislation, *supra* note 1, §15.
5. *Id.*
6. UNCOPUOS' Recommendations on national legislations, *supra* note 3.
7. The UNCOPUOS' Recommendations consider, *inter alia*, the scope of application of the legislation, authorization conditions and supervision processes, the registration of space objects, the liability of operators under the UN Space Treaties and the transfer of ownership. *Id.*
8. ILA Res. 6/2012, 75th ILA Conference (2012).
9. *Id.* Information on the activities of international intergovernmental and non-governmental organizations relating to space law, UNCOPUOS LSC, 52nd Sess., UN Doc. A/AC.105/C.2/2013/CRP.6 (2013).
10. The Model Law includes provisions regarding the scope of the law, the definition of terms, the obligation to authorize space activities and its conditions, the duty to supervise, issues of

the environment in the template. Furthermore, that this concern is not limited to an allusion to Article IX of the Outer Space Treaty—i.e., the avoidance of harmful contamination—or to space debris mitigation measures is noteworthy.[11] Where the UNCOPUOS' Recommendations made the environmental element a part of the authorization process, the Model Law dedicates an entire provision to the protection of the environment. Article 7 of the Model Law states that space activities shall not cause "environmental damage," directly or indirectly, to "outer space or parts thereof." Additionally, the provision recommends that domestic space legislations implement the requirement of conducting EIAs prior to the beginning of the planned space activity, the details of which are to be addressed in an "implementing decree/regulation." Ultimately, the purpose of conducting an initial EIAs is to ensure private space actors "meet the highest environmental standards."[12]

Although the UNCOPUOS' Recommendations and the ILA's Model Law are in stark contrast as regards the length to which they go in about the protection of the environment, it must be noted that, at this stage, the purpose is the same: guiding States in the enactment of domestic space legislation. Furthermore, considering that the two instruments were adopted within a year of one another, it is not difficult to understand that they were developed within the same legal context: the UNCOPUOS' Space Debris Mitigation Guidelines were adopted, and the LTS Working Group had started its task. They also have common grounds. Most notably, they both refer to the mitigation of space debris.[13] The real divergence lies in the weight the question of the environment carries in each instrument: barely an allusion in the UNCOPUOS' recommendations and a full provision for the ILA's Model Law.

This variation in the level of environmental protection for outer space is reflected in practice in national space legislation. Some domestic space legislations do not include environmental clauses;[14] others incorporate them in the licensing process;[15] few have separate provisions addressing the matter in itself.[16]

---

withdrawal and suspension of authorization, the protection of the environment and mitigation of space debris, the transfer of space activity, the registration of space object, issues of liability and insurance, procedure-related issues, and sanctions. ILA's Model Law, *supra* note 8.

11. space debris mitigation measures are addressed in the subsequent provision. *Id.*, Art. 8.
12. ILA's Model Law Commentary, *supra* note 9, Art. 7.
13. UNCOPUOS' Recommendations, §4; ILA's Model Law, *supra* note 8, Art. 8.
14. Luxembourg, for instance, does not include a reference to the environment in the 2017 Law regulating space resource activities. It does, however, make a brief reference to the environment when defining the term "damage" in the 2020 Law on space activities. *See* Loi du 20 juillet 2017 sur l'exploration et l'utilisation des ressources de l'espace, Mémorial A No 674, 28 juillet 2017 (LU) [SRL]; Loi du 15 décembre 2020 portant sur les activités spatiales, Art. 2, Mémorial A No 1086, 28 décembre 2020 (LU) [2020 Law on space activities]. For a comprehensive analysis of the Luxembourgish laws, *see generally* M. HOFMANN ET AL., THE SPACE LEGISLATION OF LUXEMBOURG: A COMMENTARY (2022)[HOFMANN ET AL. (2020)].
15. *See, e.g.*, the Austrian Space Act which provides that an authorization shall be issued only if, *inter alia*, appropriate space debris mitigation measures are adopted and if the activity does not cause "harmful contamination" of outer space. Austrian Federal Law on the Authorisation of Space Activities and the Establishment of a National Registry, as adopted by the Parliament on 6 December 2011, Art. 4§1 (4) and (5) (AT).
16. Loi N° 2008-518 du 3 juin 2008 relative aux opérations spatiales, Art. 5, No. 2008-518 (2008) (FR); Act on Space Activities, Art. 10, 63/2018 (2018) (FI) [Finnish Space Act]; Law of Sept. 17,

Chapter 4 aims to assess the environmental element—and by extension, the consideration given to sustainability—in the domestic space legislation which explicitly governs space resource-related activities. To that end, the chapter considers several national regulatory frameworks, with specific attention being paid to the scope of the law, the authorization process, and, ultimately, the environmental rules at play. In particular, the study of the scope of the law aims to determine the extent to which the law applies and, *a fortiori*, the impact of its environmental measures. The specific interest in the authorization procedure is threefold; first, it allows to understand how private actors—the most common ones for space resource activities—are monitored by the State, which is itself an international actor bound, at various levels, by international law instruments which include environmental provisions. Second, as it has been noted above, since the environmental aspect of the law is often incorporated into the authorization mechanism, focusing on the authorization process is a way to understand how a State intends to integrate such concerns into its spatial developments. Third, the adoption of a licensing process is one of the elements identified in the sustainability framework outlined in Chapter 1 to promote sustainable space resource activities. Accordingly, Chapter 4 first considers domestic space legislations which have adopted advanced environmental mechanisms to ensure the protection of the extraterrestrial environment (1). Then, having established the feasibility of advanced environmental mechanisms, the chapter provides a study of domestic legislations that have been adopted to explicitly govern space resource activities (2).

1 GENERAL NATIONAL SPACE LEGISLATIONS PROTECTING THE OUTER SPACE ENVIRONMENT

A complete examination of all national current space legislations from an environmental perspective, in their details and nuances, would require a—and probably more than one—separate and voluminous study. To adopt a better-focused approach, rather than engaging in a high-level survey of such legislation, it seems more efficient to focus on domestic space legislations which leverage the question of environmental protection with particular interest. In this spirit, the legislations of Belgium and Finland have been selected for the originality and advanced environmental approach adopted to ensure the outer space environment is protected from the negative impact of humans' activities. In particular, Belgium's regulatory framework implements one of the key elements identified in the sustainability framework developed in Chapter 1: the obligation for operators carrying out space activities, under the State's jurisdiction, to conduct a mandatory EIA. The Finnish legislation not only incorporates an EIA requirement but also includes an independent section specifically dedicated to the protection of the environment and makes a normative reference to nonlegally binding instruments. Additionally, both frameworks have further been developed—or

2005 on the Activities of Launching, Flight Operation or Guidance of Space Objects, consolidated text as revised by the Law of 1 December 2013, Art. 8, B.O.J. of Jan. 15, 2014 (2014) (BE) [Belgian Space Act].

revised—within the last five years, thus benefiting from the discussion at the international level on the long-term sustainability of outer space. Accordingly, this section first provides a review of the Belgian regulatory framework for space activities (1.1) before examining the Finnish space legislation (1.2).

1.1 Belgium

Often called "the largest of Europe's minor space powers,"[17] Belgium has no launch capacity and few space activities registered in its name.[18] For the most, its involvement in the space sector consists of continuous investment in cooperative space research and development.[19] In this regard, Belgium works closely with ESA.[20] Coupled with its annual financial contribution to the organization, Belgium participates in ESA missions by, *inter alia*, designing and manufacturing small satellites.[21] For instance, since the early 2000s, Belgium has been contributing small satellites to the Agency's *Project for On-Board Autonomy*, a technology demonstration mission.[22]

As seen in Chapter 3, ESA has implemented in its practice several provisions originating from nonbinding instruments, like the SDM Guidelines and COPSAR's PP policy. As such, governmental and nongovernmental entities must comply with these requirements when working with the Agency. Similarly, Belgium has signed several bilateral cooperation instruments with emerging spacefaring nations, which create its own set of obligations.[23] Moreover, the Belgian State is a party to the five UN Space Treaties.[24] As a result, it is bound by several international instruments which it must uphold.

17. BELSPO, *The Belgian Space Law* (2022) available online.
18. Belgium does not have any launch service operator under its jurisdiction or launch facility located on its territory. Belgium, *Implementation of the Guidelines for the Long-term Sustainability of Outer Space Activities of the Committee on the Peaceful Uses of Outer Space: Belgium*, 8 (2021).
19. BELSPO, *The Belgian Space Law* (2022) available online.
20. For an overview of Belgium's associated activities with ESA, *see* ESA, *L'ESA & la Belgique*, ESA (2021), available online.
21. As a (founding) Member State of ESA, Belgium is required to contribute to the financing of the Agency's activities. In 2021, the State contributed EUR 255.8 million to the international organization's annual budget for activities and programs, thus, making Belgium the fifth largest Member State investor behind France, Germany, Italy, and the United Kingdom. This monetary contribution is all the more important when it is evaluated in relation to the overall annual budget of EUR 270 million that the country allocates to public support for space research and development. Jean-François Mayence, *Experiences with Implementing the LTS Guidelines from the Belgian Perspective*, *in* ENSURING THE SUSTAINABILITY OF OUTER SPACE: THE ROLE OF SPACE LAW AND POLICY (NPOC Space Law Austria, 2022) available online. *See also* BELSPO, *The Belgian Space Law* (2022) available online.
22. So far, Belgium has contributed three small satellites to the Project: PROBA-1 launched in 2001, its successors PROBA-2 and PROBA-V launched respectively in 2009 and 2013, as well as PROBA-3 which is scheduled to be launched in 2023. ESA, *Proba Missions* (2021), available online.
23. *Implementation of the Guidelines for the Long-term Sustainability of Outer Space Activities of the Committee on the Peaceful Uses of Outer Space: Belgium*, *supra* note 18 at 23.
24. BELSPO, *The Belgian Space Law* (2022) available online.

With the rapid development of the space industry, the number of space actors likely to engage in space activities falling under the jurisdiction of the Belgian State has multiplied.[25] So far, six private entities have been authorized to carry out activities in outer space, and 36 objects have been registered under the national space legislation.[26] Pursuant to Article VI of the Outer Space Treaty, Belgium is internationally responsible for space activities carried out by national nongovernmental entities. This includes ensuring they comply with the provisions of the ratified UN Space Treaties. More generally, it is the State's responsibility to ensure its nationals comply with its international obligations. By developing a national regulatory framework for space activities, Belgium ensures the compliance of its private operators with the State's international obligations.

To that end, the State adopted, in 2005, a national *Law on The Activities of Launching, Flight Operation or Guidance of Space Objects*, which was revised in 2013 ("Belgian Space Act").[27] The 2013 revision takes into account, *inter alia*, the special case of non-maneuverable satellites, which constitute most of Belgium's space activities.[28] It is completed by a regulation in the form of a royal decree[29] to implement the provisions of the law. A first decree was adopted in 2008, but it has since been abrogated and replaced by a new royal decree adopted in March 2022 ("Royal Decree").[30] According to the drafters, "the decree must be seen as an instrument ensuring the flexibility and responsiveness of the Belgian regulatory framework to the evolution of international standards."[31] It aims to assess the experience Belgium has gained since the first licensing application for space activities under its regulatory framework and to encourage the development of new activities under Belgian jurisdiction.[32] Additionally, the adoption of a royal decree presented an opportunity for Belgium to implement international standards, like the NPS Principles, the SDM Guidelines, and LTS Guidelines in its regulatory framework.[33]

25. BELSPO, *The Belgian Space Law*, BELSPO (2022), https://www.belspo.be/belspo/space/belaw_en.stm (last visited January 2024).
26. BELSPO, *Directory of authorizations delivered in application of the law of 17/09/2005* (2022) available online; Mayence, *supra* note 21.
27. Law of Sept. 17, 2005 on The Activities of Launching, Flight Operation or Guidance of Space Objects, consolidated text as revised by the Law of 1 December 2013 (B.O.J. of Jan. 15, 2014) (BE).
28. The revised Belgian legislation was adopted in December 2013 and published in the Belgian Official Gazette in January 2014. Mayence, *supra* note 21.
29. In Belgium, a royal decree is an act of the federal executive power. It is signed by the King, countersigned by one or more Ministers or Secretaries of State who assume responsibility for it. 1994 Const. (Belg.) Art. 37 and 106.
30. Royal Decree implementing certain provisions of the Law of Sept. 17, 2005 on the activities of launching, flight operations and guidance of space objects, C–2022/31435, 2022 (BE) ["Belgian Decree"]. *See* Art. 16§1 on the abrogation of the Royal Decree of 2008.
31. *Id.*, 42372.
32. *Implementation of the Guidelines for the Long-term Sustainability of Outer Space Activities of the Committee on the Peaceful Uses of Outer Space: Belgium*, *supra* note 18, 2.
33. It is interesting to note that, contrary to other States, Belgium implements standards by *reception* rather than adoption. In other words, the State does not create its own standards but rather align itself on standards and guidelines recognized at the European and international level. Hofmann, Mahulena, *Sustainability Aspects in the UN Space Treaties and the LTS Guidelines*, *in* Ensuring the Sustainability of Outer Space: The Role of Space Law and Policy (NPOC Space Law Austria,

The Belgian Space Act is divided into seven chapters, each addressing a specific aspect of the law. Chapter I discusses general provisions such as the scope of the law and definitional issues. Chapters II and III set the framework for the authorization and supervision framework of the activities, as well as the content of, and procedure for, the application. From our standpoint, this first group of chapters is of particular importance as they incorporate, *inter alia*, the rules relating to the protection of the outer space environment. These sections will be addressed in separate subsections after a brief synthesis of Chapters IV to VII.

Chapter IV anticipates, in a single provision, the transfer of activities from one operator to another, such as the case of an authorized operator under Belgian law desiring to transfer the ownership of a satellite which has already been placed in orbit. In a nutshell, the process must be authorized by the Minister in charge of space research, i.e., the Minister in charge of the scientific policy of the State. For this purpose, the transferee must fill in an application. If granted, the authorization may be accompanied by conditions for either or both the transferor and the transferee.[34]

Chapter V sets down the obligation to register space objects launched by Belgian nationals. However, the conditions of implementation are undetermined in the body of the law. This is precisely a novelty of the 2022 Royal Decree to decide on the requirements: until then, Belgium had no legal basis to demand private operators register their space objects.[35] For this purpose, Belgium created a national electronic registry which is—out of a desire for transparency—accessible online in open access.[36] The list of information that must be communicated to the Minister is aligned with Article 4 of the Registration Convention.[37] The operator is further asked to identify both the manufacturer and operator of the object and to list the "constituent elements and instruments on board." Lastly, should it be the case, the mention "NPS" must be appended on the registry to indicate that the space object carries a nuclear power source onboard. Once the space object is registered under Belgian Law, the Minister sends all relevant information to the UN Secretary-General for the object's inscription on the UN registry.

2022), online. With regard to the LTS Guidelines themselves, Belgium reported on their implementation to the COPUOS' STC in 2021. It underlined, *inter alia*, that "until now, the concept of the long-term sustainability of space activities may not have been explicitly integrated in the managerial culture of the concerned Belgian entities" because "all operational activities conducted by Belgian authorities have been carried out on the basis of projects reviewed or assessed by ESA [which takes care of their compliance with international standards like the LTS Guidelines]." *Implementation of the Guidelines for the Long-Term Sustainability of Outer Space Activities of the Committee on the Peaceful Uses of Outer Space: Belgium*, *supra* note 18, 5; Mayence, *supra* note 21.

34. Belgian Space Act, Art. 13.
35. BELSPO, *The Belgian Space Law* (2022) available online.
36. Belgian Space Act, Art. 14. The online registry can be accessed through the Belgian space law webpage of the Belgian Science Policy Office (BELSPO). BELSPO, *Directory of authorizations delivered in application of the law of 17/09/2005* (2022) available online.
37. Accordingly, the operator must indicate to the Minister: (1) the name of the other launching State, if applicable; (b) the object's registration number; (c) the date and territory or location of launch; (d) the main orbital parameters, including the nodal period, inclination, apogee and perigee; as well as (e) the general function of the space object. Convention on Registration of Objects Launched into Outer Space, *entered into force* Sept. 15, 1976, VI, 1023 UNTS 15.

It is worth noting that Article 14 paragraph 7 of the Belgian Space Act implements one particularly significant element: the registration on the national registry must "be effective at the time of the launch of the space object," i.e., prior to the launch.[38] This requirement is included in neither Article VIII of the Outer Space Treaty nor the Registration Convention[39] but is directly transposed from the LTS Guidelines, which have particular importance, as we have seen it, for the protection of the outer space environment.

Chapter VI is entitled *Liabilities, counterclaims and measures in the event of falling space objects*. It implements the provisions of the 1972 Liability Convention and defines the rules of liability for the operator who caused the damage.[40] In essence, Chapter VI ensures that when Belgium is held liable pursuant to the UN Space Treaties—i.e., Article VII of the Outer Space Treaty and the Liability Convention—as well as under its national law, it can file a counterclaim against the operator "up to the amount of compensation determined [by the law]." This expression refers to the possibility of the operator involved in the damage to benefit from cap liability, a possibility offered by the Royal Decree. Article 11 of the Royal Decree limits the amount of the compensation at 10% of the operator's average annual turnover or its average annual budget "calculated on the base of three financial years preceding the year in which the authorization request was submitted." However, if the operator is found having, *inter alia*, violated the conditions of the authorization license, the cap on liability does not apply, and the operator has to bear the full financial consequences of the damage it caused. Furthermore, the operator is required to inform "immediately" the National Crisis Center of "any maneuver, any malfunctioning or any anomaly of the space object" that may cause damage.[41]

Lastly, Chapter VII contains the "final provisions" of the revised Law of 2005. In particular, it refers to the Royal Decree for the fixation of the administrative fee covering the application process; Article 13 of the Royal Decree fixes the amount at EUR 1,000. The Law also provides that the costs for the service of technical experts are borne by the operator. However, in cases where such expertise is needed, the Belgian Science Policy Office (BELSPO) is required to provide operators with a quotation so that they may withdraw their application for authorization.

Chapter VII further considers the sanction regime should the operator conduct space activities without having obtained proper authorization prior to the start of operations. Similarly, the operator may be sanctioned if they willfully provided false information for the purpose of obtaining authorization. In both cases, the sanction may include a fine and a period of imprisonment of up to a year. Likewise, the guilty operator shall also be deprived of the cap on liability. Last, the chapter concludes with two provisions regarding the entry into force of the law and sets a transition period.

38. *Implementation of the Guidelines for the Long-Term Sustainability of Outer Space Activities of the Committee on the Peaceful Uses of Outer Space: Belgium*, *supra* note 18, 8.
39. According to Art. IV §1 of the Registration Convention, the object must be registered "as soon as practicable."
40. Belgian Space Act, Arts. 15–17.
41. Belgian Space Act, Art. 16 §1.

A simple overview of the Belgian Space Act gives already an idea of the willingness of Belgian authorities to follow more stringent guidelines in certain areas of their domestic space law than their strict international obligations. However, it is in the first group of chapters—Chapters I to III—that core principles are adopted pertaining to the question of the outer space environment and its protection. Chapter I deals with the scope of application of the Law, while Chapters II and III delineate the authorization process, which involves provisions pertaining to the question of environmental protection. The following three subsections will accordingly review the scope of the law (1.1.1) before examining the authorization and supervision regime for the space activities carried out by nongovernmental operators (1.1.2). Lastly, a last subsection evaluates the environmental element of the Law (1.1.3).

1.1.1 Scope of the Law

The analysis of the scope of a law is generally threefold. It must consider:

- the material scope of the law, i.e., the space activities it targets;
- the territorial scope of the law, i.e., where it applies; and
- the personal scope of the law, i.e., to whom the law applies.

The Belgian Space Act is not different in this regard, and its scope can be understood from the standpoint of this multifaceted approach.

1.1.1.a Material Scope

Significantly, the material scope of the Belgian law was at the core of its revision in 2013. Both versions of the law apply to the same three space activities: launching, flight operations, and guidance of space objects. However, with the emergence of new activities, Belgium felt the need to clarify the scope of its regulatory framework by, *inter alia*, remedying the problems inherited from using the UN Space Treaties' ambiguous language.[42]

One such example is the tautological definition of "space debris" used in the 1972 Liability Convention.[43] In a similar manner, the original text of the Law of 2005 defined a space object as an object "launched or attempted to be launched into outer space, including their components."[44] Following the revision of the law, the definition no longer includes a reference to "outer space," instead preferring the notion of "orbital

42. Chambre des représentants belges, *Projet de loi modifiant la loi du 17 septembre 2005 relative aux activités de lancement, d'opération de vol ou de guidage d'objets spatiaux*, 3 (15 mai 2013).
43. In essence, Art. I of the Liability Convention defines a space object as an object that is launched into outer space. Liability Convention, *supra*.
44. *Trans.* "tout objet lancé ou destiné à être lancé dans l'espace extra-atmosphérique, y compris les éléments matériels qui le composent." Chambre des représentants belges, *supra* note 42 at 18.

trajectory around the Earth" and of "a destination beyond the Earth orbit."[45] Thus, space activities are covered by the law, both in orbit and beyond, like space resource activities.[46]

The amended definition further recognizes that a launching vehicle is, in itself, a space object.[47] This explicit recognition was brought by the fact that if a space object is defined by the fact it must be launched, as it is usually done, then the launcher itself is no such object since it is not—by definition—a space object. As confusing as it may sound, it simply means that a launch vehicle, as a means of launching, is not launched per se. Additionally, the new definition considers that a launch vehicle remains a space object even in the absence of a payload when it is operated "solely for its development and validation phase."

Similarly, the revision of the Law of 2005 expands the definition of "flight operations and guidance of space object" to explicitly include activities related to non-maneuverable space objects, like nanosats. To that end, flight and guidance operations include "delivering an object in orbit," and selecting the object's orbit and trajectory is expressly assimilated to the operation of flying one.[48]

To summarize, from a material standpoint, the Belgian space legislation applies to:

- activities in Earth orbit and beyond;
- the launching of a space object, i.e., its attempt, procurement, and preparation; as well as
- the control and operation of said object, i.e., flight and guidance operations, including the selection of its orbit and trajectory.

1.1.1.b Territorial Scope

On the matter of the territorial scope, the Belgian Space Act is in line with the national space legislations of other States. It applies to space activities conducted from the Belgian territory and from its "quasi-territory," i.e., on vessels or platforms on the high seas.[49] Article 2 paragraph 1 provides that the Law applies to space activities:

- carried out in "the zones placed under the jurisdiction or control" of the Belgian State; or

45. The rationale was that there is no international consensus on the delimitation of outer space and that the lack of clarity could potentially exclude from the scope of the law suborbital flights. For a discussion on the definition of the expression "outer space," *see supra* Chapter 1.
46. With regard to space mining activities specifically, Belgium and Luxembourg signed in 2019 a joint declaration committing to collaborate on the development of an international framework for the exploration and utilization of space resources. LSA, *Luxembourg and Belgium Join Forces to Develop the Exploration and Utilisation of Space Resources*, LSA (2019), available online.
47. Chambre des représentants belges, *supra* note 42 at 9.
48. *Id.*, at 12.
49. Laurent Chassot et al., *Droit spatial national—Etude portant sur l'analyse de différentes législations spatiales nationales, en vue d'une réflexion de lege ferenda*, 39 (gbf Avocats SA ed., 30 juin 2021).

- using "installations, personal or real property, owned by the Belgian State or which are under its jurisdiction or its control."[50]

The phrasing itself of the provision is interesting since, rather than refer to its "territory," Belgium decided to use two criteria to delimit its territorial scope: jurisdiction and control. This is in line with Belgium's tendency to mirror the language of treaties to implement its international obligations; and here, of Article VIII of the Outer Space Treaty. The aim of the provision is to ensure that the Belgian Space Act covers the full scope of activities that could trigger the Belgian State's international responsibility in the sense of Article VI of the Outer Space Treaty.[51]

The element of "jurisdiction" is the primary criterion used in the Law. It means that Belgium is internationally responsible for all space activities conducted in places where the State has sovereign power.[52] As such, the Belgian Space Act ensures that all persons—legal or natural—exercising these activities under the jurisdiction of the Belgian States are subjected to the provision of law.

The element of "control" acts as a complementary criterion. It brings under the scope of the Law activities conducted outside the territory of Belgium yet still under its control, such as a launching platform that would be placed on the high seas. It further excludes from the scope of the Belgian Space Act entities located on the Belgian territory but not owned or controlled by it.[53] This is the case, for instance, of ESA's *European Space Security and Education Centre* which is situated in Redu, Belgium.

1.1.1.c Personal Scope

One particularity of the Belgian Space Act is that it excludes the application of personal jurisdiction. The Law applies to both natural and legal persons, but beyond that, its scope is determined by the territorial jurisdiction of the State. Thus, foreign entities carrying space activities on Belgian territory are as bound by the Belgian Space Act as Belgian nationals.

Here again, the decision of the State coheres with the obvious intention to align its regulatory framework with the UN Space Treaties. As the Outer Space Treaty makes no reference to the nationality of an entity, preferring to use the criterion of territory, so does the Belgian Law. Beyond this legal parallelism, other reasons have to be considered. According to Mayence,[54] the choice was also guided by the desire to ensure legal security. If the scope was extended to include the personal jurisdiction of the State, it would mean that Belgium could be held responsible for activities carried out by Belgian persons from a place under the jurisdiction of another State while having little ability to control the actions of its nationals.

50. Belgian Space Act, Art. 2 §1.
51. Projet de loi relative aux activités de lancement, d'opération de vol ou de guidage d'objets spatiaux, Doc. Parl., Chambre, 2004-2005, 14 février 2005 n° 51-1607/001, pp. 7-8.
52. *Id.*, 8.
53. Jean-François Mayence, *La Belgique se dote d'une législation sur les activités spatiales. Pourquoi?*, Droit & Technologies (2008) available online.
54. *Id.*

The revised Law of 2005, however, makes an exception in paragraph 2 and extends the scope of the law to include the criterion of nationality when it is "provided under an international agreement."[55] In that case, the law may apply "irrespective of the location where [the] activities are carried out." There is no contradiction between the redefinition of the criterion and its general formulation: the condition of the existence of an international agreement "neutralizes" potential conflicts in law between two or more States.[56] Here, the exercise of the State's jurisdiction can be defined in the agreement so that Belgium can control the extent of its responsibility in the sense of Article VI of the Outer Space Treaty.

1.1.2 Authorization Mechanism

Eventually, Chapters II and III of the Belgian Space Act lay down the operator's obligation to obtain authorization from the Minister in charge prior to the start of the space activities, as well as the procedure for its procurement. They also represent the bulk of the provisions regarding environmental protection. The term "operator" refers to the person who carries out—or plans to carry out—the space activity and has effective control over the space object.[57]

The authorization may be delivered for an indefinite or specific period,[58] but it must be underscored that the authorization is personal and cannot be transferred to another operator without the prior consent of the Minister.[59]

In order for the operator's application for authorization to be approved, they must meet several conditions laid down in the Belgian Space Act and the implementation of the Royal Decree. The first condition is obvious to an extent: the planned activity must not violate international law. This means that the activity must be in line with Belgium's international obligations under, *inter alia*, the UN Space Treaties.[60] Additionally, the King as well as the Minister may also supplement the authorization with specific conditions. The conditions imposed by the Minister take into account "the specific case," while those set by the King take into account "the legal or factual circumstances that are required for any authorization."[61] In practice, the Minister may impose the technical assistance of a third party—like ESA—or require the operator to

55. Belgian Space Act, Art. 2 §2.
56. Mayence, *supra* note 53.
57. Paragraph 2 of the Law further clarifies that "operator" also refers to the person who has "ordered the delivery in orbit of the space object," in cases where said object cannot be maneuvered. Belgian Space Act, Art. 2. "Effective control" means that the person must have the authority to decide on "the activation of the means of control or remote control and the related means of supervision." In other words, it is the person who has the authority to push the right button when it matters. Belgian Space Act, Art. 2 §3.
58. Belgian Space Act, Art. 5 §2.
59. Belgian Space Act, Art. 4 §2. On the matter of transfer, the transfer of the authorization implies the transfer of the effective control from one operator to another. In such case, the transferee must request an authorization for transfer of the space activity to the Minister. Belgian Space Act, Art. 13.
60. Belgian Space Act, Art. 4 §3.
61. *Trans.* Projet de loi 2005, p. 18., Belgian Space Act, Art. 5.

be insured in case damage occurs.[62] It may also impose conditions "relating to the location of the activities or the location of the main establishment of the operator."[63] The Minister also has the right to:

> call for a reasoned opinion, to be provided by experts to be designated by [them] for that purpose, on the basis of legal, technical and economic criteria, concerning in particular the reliability, know-how and experience of the operator, the reliability of the manufacturer in the areas concerned and their capacity to comply with the rules applying to the activities carried out, as well as the operator's solvency and the legal and financial guarantees that he provides.[64]

In other words, the Minister must be in a position to make an educated decision on whether or not to grant the operator the authorization to carry out its planned activity.[65]

In the same fashion, the King has the possibility to lay down—in a royal decree—conditions to ensure Belgium's national interests are respected. This includes not only imposing conditions regarding the safety of people and property but also protecting the environment and ensuring the "optimal use" of outer space.[66] Like the Minister, the King may also set down conditions relating to the control and supervision of space activities.[67]

The operator's duties include providing information related to the identity of the persons involved, on various levels, in the space activity, as well as about the activity itself. In particular, the application must identify the operator, their collaborators, and the manufacturers. The application must further provide a description of the activity and precisely identify the space object. For this reason, BELSPO has created a template, available online in open access, to guide operators in the application process. BELSPO also publishes online the authorization delivered by the Minister—i.e., a ministerial decree—as well as the application and annexes completed by the applying operator.[68]

Briefly, the application template is divided into three sections: (1) identification of the operator, (2) information about the planned space activity, and (3) information about the space object. The first section requires the operator to input their personal data as well as their principal shareholders'. They must also indicate whether the activity is being carried out for a third party and whether they have any experience in designing, manufacturing, or operating a space object. Furthermore, the form has a subsection fully dedicated to the respect, by the operator, of standards relating to the safety and long-term sustainability of space activities. In particular, the operator is asked to indicate whether they apply the standards adopted by ESA and the IADC. Section 2 asks for, *inter alia*, a description of the space activity, such as the purpose of

62. Mayence, *supra* note 21.
63. Belgian Space Act, Art. 5, §2.
64. Mayence, *supra* note 53., Art. 7 §6.
65. Projet de loi belge, 2005, *supra* note 51, 19.
66. Belgian Space Act, Art. 5 §1.
67. Mayence, *supra* note 53, Arts. 6 and 7 §4.
68. The directory of delivered authorization is available on BELSPO's website. BELSPO, *supra* note 26. Although the documents are made public, the operator retains the capacity to ask the Minister to withdraw confidential information from public access.

the activity—i.e., scientific, governmental, or commercial—the number of space object involved, their orbital parameters, the launching location, and the radio frequencies used. Finally, section 3 concerns, *inter alia*, the type of space object used—such as a CubeSat, its components, its manufacturers, and whether there is an NPS onboard.

Moreover, the operator must attach to the application form the study of EIA they had to conduct in accordance with Article 8 paragraph 2 of the Law. The precise content of the EIA will be elaborated on *infra*.

Altogether, the Belgian Space Act is designed to ensure the Minister can make an educated decision on whether authorization should be delivered to the operator. The Belgian legislation intends to give the Minister the necessary means to adopt an informed decision regarding the advisability of issuing authorization to an operator to exercise a space activity. To this end, the Law defines several conditions with which the operator must comply to ensure that the information is communicated to the Minister. Far from being rigid, the Belgian Space Act further gives the Minister the possibility of requesting additional information when necessary. Similarly, the operator can voluntarily communicate to the Minister information that they consider important for the process.

Lastly, the refusal, by the operator, to comply with the conditions determined by the King and the Minister is grounds for refusal of the application. Furthermore, according to Article 9 paragraph 3 of the Law, the absence of deliverance of authorization by the Minister within the allotted time signifies the rejection of the operator's application.

1.1.3 Environmental Component

As shown in the previous section, the authorization procedure for space activities falling under Belgian jurisdiction requires the operator to carry out an EIA.[69] Although Belgium is not the only country to require the operator to conduct an EIA,[70] its inclusion in the Belgian Space Act is noteworthy. It is also in line with the sustainability framework outlined in Chapter 1, which recommends the adoption of a licensing process incorporating environmental systems management, such as an EIA.

In 2005, Belgium had not yet launched a satellite in orbit, and the UNCOPUOS had yet to adopt its SDM Guidelines. Nonetheless, despite its involvement in space activities being limited to their financing—and in spite of a relative lack of interest in the environmental protection of outer space at the international level—Belgium decided to integrate this environmental mechanism into its national space law.[71] The emphasis was conscious and clearly expressed: Belgium considered that, in view of the nature of space activities, it was "indispensable" to plan for environmental protection.[72] At the time, the

69. Belgian Space Act, Art. 7 §5.
70. *See*, for instance, Finland *infra* section 1.2.
71. Mayence, *supra* note 53. LOTTA VIIKARI, THE ENVIRONMENTAL ELEMENT IN SPACE LAW ASSESSING THE PRESENT AND CHARTING THE FUTURE 276 (2008).
72. Projet de loi belge, 2005, *supra* note 51, 12.

main concern for the drafters was the environmental terrestrial risks associated with space activities. They highlighted that:

> [d]amage to the environment can manifest itself in different ways: recurrent damage due, for example, to repetitive launches from the same site, or even occasional damage following an accident, for example the fallout of a spacecraft.[73]

These risks also inherently have "a very important ecological component."[74] Therefore, the drafters concluded that "it is entirely justified to include provisions allowing the evaluation, both *a priori* and *a posteriori*, of the possible environmental consequences of these activities."[75]

Accordingly, Article 8 paragraph 1 of the Belgian Space Act creates an obligation for operators to have experts assess the environmental impact of the planned activity. These experts are designated by the Minister, but the costs of the EIAs they conduct must be borne by the operator.[76] In practice, Belgium relies on ESA to carry out the technical review of the planned activity.[77]

Moreover, paragraph 1 further provides for the possibility of multiple EIAs being carried out, as they may occur "at different stages of the activities." Eventually, the Belgian Space Act includes two types of EIAs: the mandatory EIAs that must be attached to the application and the optional EIAs during and at the end of the activities that may be requested by the Minister.[78]

The content of the initial EIA is determined by the King.[79] It aims to assess both the environmental impact of the planned activity on Earth and in outer space.[80] According to the Royal Decree, the mandatory EIA is divided into four parts.[81] The first part must contain:[82]

(a) "a description of the activity and its objectives, and the use of the data and derivatives generated by the activity;
(b) a description of the technologies, components, system design and Critical Design Review;
(c) a report of the functional tests of the infrastructure and software performed as part of the Flight Model and the Flight Readiness Review; and
(d) a description of the technical and operational characteristics of the activity and purpose by which the operator demonstrates its compatibility with, [*inter alia*, the UNCOPUOS recommendations] insofar as these recommendations are applicable to the activities concerned."

73. Author's translation. The drafters also used the Cosmos 954 incident to illustrate the problem of the environmental risk associated with space activities. *Id.*, 12–13.
74. *Id.*, 20.
75. *Id.*, 20.
76. Belgian Space Act, Art. 8 §§1 and 8.
77. Mayence, *supra* note 21.
78. Belgian Space Act, Art. 8 §§4–5 and 7.
79. *Id.*, Art. 8 §3.
80. *Id.*, Art. 8 §2.
81. Belgian Decree, *supra* note 30, Art. 8 §1.
82. *Id.*, Art. 8 §1.

The UNCOPUOS recommendations referred to by the Royal Decree are listed in the *Operator Handbook* available on BELSPO's website.[83] In practice, the expression "recommendations" refers to the UNCOPUOS' SDM Guidelines, the LTS Guidelines, and the NPS Principles. With regard to the use of NPS, Article 8 paragraph 4 of the Royal Decree states that if they are used onboard the space object, the EIA must include a specific annex, detailing the safety measures adopted by the operator to mitigate the nuclear risk. Additionally, the use of NPS onboard must also be indicated in the application form itself.

The second and third parts of the mandatory EIA concern respectively the potential impact of the planned activity on the terrestrial and extraterrestrial environment. The assessment should address the short, medium, and long-term consequences of the activity, "in particular from the point of view of the risks in the event of the space object falling back to earth and with regard to the compliance of the activities with the applicable international standards intended to limit space debris."[84] The EIA should also provide a description of the measures taken or planned to reduce or limit the environmental impact.

Regarding the Earth's environment specifically, special emphasis is put on the natural and human environment of the place of launching. In cases where the launch does not occur on Belgium's territory, the operator is required to attach to the application "all available information or documentation relating to the environmental protection measures applicable to these locations."[85] As for the environmental impact in outer space, the measures adopted to minimize the environmental impact of the activity should "ensure the sustainable and rational use of the natural resources" of the outer space environment.[86]

This reference to, *inter alia,* space resource activities shows the intention of the drafters of the Royal Decree to take into account emerging space activities. More importantly, it creates a legal basis to minimize the environmental impact in outer space of mining activities. Furthermore, the fact that the Belgian law provides a stronger environmental protection mechanism for the sustainable exploitation of space resources than national space legislations explicitly allowing space mining activities must be highlighted.[87]

Finally, the fourth section of the mandatory EIA contains:

- a nontechnical summary of the activity;
- a description of the expertise available to the applicant in carrying out the activities; and
- a descriptive summary of activities similar to that for which the application was made and in which the operator has participated in the three years preceding the application for authorization.

83. *See* BELSPO, *The Belgian Space Law* (2022) available online.
84. Belgian Decree, *supra* note 30, Art. 8 §2.
85. *Id.*, Art. 8 §3.
86. *Id.*, Art. 8 §§3 and 5.
87. The four domestic legislations expressly governing space resource activities are discussed *infra* section 2.

In contrast, neither the Belgian Space Act nor the Royal Decree set down detailed requirements for the optional EIAs. Since they are only conducted at the request of the Minister, they are the ones to decide on the studies' content.[88] The Belgian Space Act only provides general guidelines as to the purpose of such EIAs. Accordingly, the Minister may request an intermediate EIA be carried out after the launch of the space object or during its operation. The aim of the study is to assess the "real consequences" on the terrestrial or extraterrestrial environment of the activity.[89] In a similar manner, the Minister may further decide that an EIA should be conducted "when the space object returns to the earth's atmosphere."[90] It can be noted that the Minister's request to carry out an intermediate EIA does not automatically lead to the conduct of a final EIA. The Minister may request either or both, depending on the circumstances.

Finally, Belgium takes an additional step in the protection of the environment—terrestrial as extraterrestrial—to ensure that the EIAs are not solely a procedural requirement. Pursuant to Article 9 of the Royal Decree:

> [w]here applicable, when the description of the environmental impact of the activity under Article 8 reveals a substantial risk to the safety of persons, property or the environment despite compliance with the standards and conditions applicable under the law, the applicant shall attach to the impact study referred to in Article 8, §2 of the law [i.e., the mandatory initial EIA] a description of the alternatives to the activity that can reasonably be considered, particularly with regard to the location, parameters or manner of carrying out the activity, and the protection of the environment.

Considering that Article 8 paragraph 2 refers to both the impact of the space activity on the environment on Earth and in outer space, Article 9 can be interpreted as meaning that the operator shall, *inter alia*, provide alternatives in the case where there exists a "substantial risk" to the outer space environment. Similarly, the alternative presented should pay particular attention to, *inter alia*, the protection of the outer space environment. Although the Royal Decree does not elaborate on what constitutes a "substantial" risk, it sets a threshold *ad minimum*; the risk remains substantial even though the planned activity complies with, *inter alia*, the NPS Principles and the SDM Guidelines. Both instruments intrinsically attempt to mitigate the risk of a different nature—i.e., the proliferation of space debris and nuclear contamination. Furthermore, it is necessary to keep in mind that, once submitted, the EIA will be reviewed by experts, within institutions like ESA. Thus, it is in the interest of the operator to propose acceptable alternatives rather than risk the application being rejected. These alternatives must also be "reasonable," meaning that the operator is not expected to adopt drastic, costly measures. A balance must be struck.

88. Belgian Space Act, Art. 8 §6.
89. Belgian Space Act, Art. 8 §4.
90. Belgian Space Act, Art. 8 §5.

1.1.4 *Conclusion*

Several conclusions regarding the Belgian domestic framework for space activities can be drawn from an environmental perspective. First, the environmental mechanism does not put the protection of the terrestrial environment above that of the extraterrestrial environment. Most of the time, the Law and the Royal Decree simply refer to "the environment," without further details.[91] In some cases, the Belgian Space Act refers to both in the same paragraph, as if to emphasize that both environments must be considered.[92] Where these instruments make a distinction, one is directly followed by the other. For instance, Article 8 paragraph 2 of the Royal Decree refers to the terrestrial environment and is immediately followed by paragraph 3 on the extraterrestrial environment. The distinction between the two does not reflect a difference in the level of environmental protection to be achieved but, rather, a direction aimed toward the adoption of concrete measures.[93]

Second, the obligation to conduct an EIA integrates environmental considerations in the designing and operation phase of the space activity. Operators must think about the environmental consequences that, for instance, launching—repeatedly or not—an object into space has on the launching site, the atmosphere, and Earth orbits. It means that the technology used and component elements of the space object must be carefully considered.

Third, the Belgian regulatory framework, and especially the EIA requirement, integrate into the system the environmentally related standards adopted by the international community. In particular, the guidelines regarding the mitigation of space debris and safety measures regarding the use of nuclear power sources must be followed.

Fourth, it must be concluded that, at the same time, the regulatory framework allows for flexibility. For instance, if the operator does not comply with the environmental policy of ESA, the application must provide a brief description of the alternative measures adopted. Thus, the framework does not so much set rules than it establishes standards to be met. In the end, it does not matter how the goal is achieved so long as it is achieved.

Fifth, and last, the Belgian framework showcases a noteworthy concern for the environmental protection of outer space. The Royal Decree adopted in 2022 intends to be as up-to-date as possible by addressing future potential environmental issues. Notably, it makes provisions for the rational and sustainable use of outer space natural resources, even though space resource utilization activities have yet to be planned by Belgium.

Ultimately, the Belgian regulatory framework incorporates several elements of the sustainability framework. In essence, the Belgian Space Act includes rules on the protection of the outer space environment. It, *inter alia,* incorporates in its licensing process—i.e., the authorization regime—environmental management systems such as

91. For example, Belgian Space Act, Art. 8 §1.
92. For example, Belgian Space Act, Art. 8 §§2 and 4.
93. Protecting the Earth environment means paying particular attention to the impact on the atmosphere and on the natural and human environment of the launching sites. Belgian Decree, *supra* note 30, Art. 8 §2. As for outer space, its protection should focus on the sustainable and rational use of its natural resources, like the one that can be extracted and the geostationary orbit. *Id.*, Art. 8 §§3 and 5.

mandatory EIAs and compliance with international recommendations, like the SDM Guidelines and NPS Principles. Moreover, the possibility to request the conduct of an intermediary EIA allows to monitor and audit the activity to assess the actual environmental impact of activities. It must further be underscored that, as previously noted, Belgian Law promotes the sustainable use of natural resources in outer space, such as the ones found on celestial bodies. These elements notwithstanding, one area of improvement should Belgium undertake space mining activities would be the promotion of reciprocal mining agreements with other mining entities to limit the pollution of celestial bodies. Nonetheless, overall, it can be concluded that the Belgian Space Act is in line with the sustainability framework outlined in Chapter 1 and that, as a result, the Belgian regulatory framework for space (resources) activities is conducive to sustainable space mining.

1.2 Finland

Following the launch of its first satellite into space in 2017,[94] Finland decided to quickly equip itself with a national space legislation to support its developing space industry. After less than a year at work, the State adopted on January 23, 2018, two documents regulating national space activities: the *Act on Space Activities* ("Finnish Space Act") and Decree 74/2018 of the Ministry of Economic Affairs and Employment on Space Activities ("Decree 74/2018") which supplements the Act.[95]

Finnish Space Act addresses common issues in space, namely the scope of the law, the licensing process and its requirements, the registration process for space objects, liability and the need for insurance, as well as the consequences of violating the provisions of the Act. The law further precises the extent to which the Finnish Space Act applies to "defense administration" in section 3, with the Ministry of Defense being responsible for these specific activities. For any other space activity falling under the scope of the 2018 Act, the competent authority is the Ministry of Economic Affairs and Employment ("Ministry"). According to section 2, it shall be "responsible for the overall guidance, monitoring and development of [said] activities."

The particular relevance of the Finnish Space Act regarding the protection of outer space is to be found in section 10 which pertains to *Environmental protection and space debris*. It is characterized by a remarkably progressive and inclusive demarche in its approach to environmental issues and sustainability in outer space. The overall

94. Until the launch of the student nanosatellite Aalto-1, Finland was primary involved in the space sector through its contribution in programs of the European Space Agency and the European Union. The nanosatellite was developed by students at Aalto University to design, "build and operate the first Finnish Earth Observation nanosatellite." The Aalto-1 project is Finland's first student satellite project. Started in 2010, the project aimed to have students at Aalto University design, build and operate an Earth Observation nanosatellite by students in collaboration with other Finnish universities and institutes. After encountering some delays, Aalto-1 was launched in 2017 from India. EO, Aalto-1: The Finnish Student Nanosatellite (2012) available online.
95. Finnish Space Act, *supra* note 16; Decree of the Ministry of Economic Affairs and Employment on Space Activities, 74/2018 (FI).
See also Jenni Tapio, *The Finnish Space Act: En Route to Promoting Sustainable Private Activities in Outer Space*, 43 Air and Space Law, 387–388 (2018) DOI: 10.54648/aila2018027.

environmental framework of Finland will be assessed in the last subsection (1.2.3) after the review of the scope of the law (1.2.1) and the licensing process for Finnish space activities (1.2.2).

1.2.1 Scope of the Law

The Finnish Space Act applies to space activities that fall under the territorial, personal, and quasi-territorial jurisdiction of Finland. In this regard, Finland follows the UNCOPUOS' Recommendations on national legislation and the ILA's Model Law.[96] As such, the Act applies to space activities carried out "within the territory of the State of Finland" or over nationally registered objects—like vessels and aircraft—or "by a Finnish citizen or a legal person incorporated in Finland."[97]

The scope of the law is particularly broad considering that, to this date, Finland does not have the infrastructures required to launch space objects into space from its territory or from a registered object, like a platform, outside of its territory. According to the "detailed rationale" ("Explanatory Note")[98] included in the Government proposal for, *inter alia*, the Finnish Space Act, this broad approach to jurisdiction is linked to Finland's international obligations under the Outer Space Treaty.[99] Pursuant to Article VI of the Outer Space Treaty, Finland is indeed internationally responsible for space activities carried out by nongovernmental entities. Furthermore, as a launching State, Finland is also internationally liable under Article VII of the Treaty for damage caused by a space object for which a Finnish nongovernmental entity is responsible. In accordance with the same provision, the notion of "launching State" refers, *inter alia*, to the State from which territory the space object is launched or to the State that "procured" the launch. Considering the fact that Finland does not currently possess the infrastructures required to launch space objects into outer space, procurement appears to be the most likely occurrence. The Explanatory Note also considers cases where the operation of the space object takes place outside of Finland.[100]

Beyond the (quasi-)territorial application of the Finnish Space Act, the law also applies to "a Finnish citizen or a legal person incorporated in Finland"[101] carrying out space activities. To fully appreciate the strength of the provision, it must be linked to the definition of the notion of "operator" included in section 4 of the Finnish Space Act:

96. UNCOPUOS' Recommendations on national legislations, *supra* note 3; ILA's Sofia Model *supra* note 8.
97. Finnish Space Act, *supra* note 16, Art. 1.
98. According to Tapio, the "detailed rational" included in the Government proposal "acts as an explanatory and supplementary guideline for the application and use of the Space Act." Tapio, *supra* note 95 at 388.
99. In addition to submitting the Space Act for approval and implementation, the Government proposal executes three additional actions: (1) it implements into the domestic order the provision of the Registration Convention; (2) it "repeals the existing Act on the return and rescue of astronauts" and (3) it "amends the Act on lost and found objects." Finland, *Government proposal to Parliament for the approval and implementation of the Convention on Registration of Objects Launched into Outer Space and for the Act on Space Activities and the Act on the Amendment of Section 2 of the Lost and Found Objects Act* (2017); Tapio, *supra* note 95 at 388.
100. Finnish Space Act, *supra* note 16, Art. 1.
101. *Id.*

a space operator is "a natural or legal person who carries on or intends to carry on space activities or is effectively responsible for such activities." More precisely, the operator is the person that "may launch the space object or operate it itself or it may procure the launch or operation as a service."[102] Under the Finnish framework, to determine if a person is also an "operator," the key element is to assess whether "the party [...] exercises effective power over the space activity."[103] This person would be the party who, *inter alia*, has the authority to demand a change of trajectory to avoid a collision or, in cases where the object cannot be controlled, the one that can discontinue the operation of the space object.[104] However, the Finnish Space Act would not apply in cases where the Finnish person is employed by a foreign entity and carrying out space activities for said entity.[105]

The broad scope of the law can be justified by Finland's interpretation of its international obligations under the UN Space Treaties; according to the Explanatory Note, "[the State] may [...] be deemed to be a responsible State if a Finnish operator is responsible for the space activity and procures the launch and operation of a space object from abroad."[106] The broad scope of application also offers the benefits of flexibility: though Finland cannot launch from its territory presently, it might in the future. If this situation were to occur, the launch would fall under the scope of the Finnish Space Act.

Related to this point is the question of the material scope of the law, namely, which "space activities" are covered under the Finnish Space Act? Following section 4 (1), "launching a space object into outer space, operation and other control of the space object in outer space, as well as measures to return the space object and its return to the earth" are covered by the law. This definition is further expanded on in the Explanatory note.[107] First, the notion of "launch" must be understood as also including operating launching infrastructures and procuring a launch from a launch provider. The law would further apply to failed launches and nonfunctioning space objects because the State could still potentially be held liable if they were to create damage.

Second, the reference to "operation and other control of the space object" refers to the Finnish Space Act's attachment to the concept of effective control. Consequently, "operating" the space object includes placing the object in space, its use, and conducting its operation. "Other control" means "other influencing of the space object, such as responding to collision warnings and discontinuation of the operation [of] the space object." It would however exclude the manufacturing of space objects and their parts or software.[108]

Lastly, although not evident from the text, Tapio relates that the Working Group who drafted the Finnish Space Act considered that the broad definition of "space

102. Finnish Governmental proposal, *supra* note 99, Art. 4§3.
103. *Id.*
104. *Id.*
105. *Id.*
106. *Id.*, Art. 1.
107. *Id.*, Art. 4§1.
108. *Id.*

activities" could include—in theory—space mining activities in its scope.[109] However, Tapio continues:

> in case an application for a license with a purpose to extract minerals in outer space would be made under the Space Act, the Ministry would need to consider whether it deems such activity to be in accordance with its international obligations[110] and whether it is perceived to have jurisdiction over the subject matter in the context of a national license application.[111]

1.2.2 Authorization Mechanism

The obligation to obtain authorization from the Ministry to carry out space activities and the general conditions for it are encompassed in section 5 of the Finnish Space Act. It further grants to the Ministry the possibility to attach additional requirements to the application through the adoption of a decree, like in practice Decree 74/2018.[112]

As is regularly the case in national space legislations, the adoption of a written authorization process by Finland for space activities stems from Article VI of the Outer Space Treaty. A particularity of the Finnish Space Act, however, is that the obligation to obtain prior authorization applies to both (civil)[113] governmental and nongovernmental entities.[114] This is a significant addition to the international obligations of the country since the Outer Space Treaty only makes it mandatory for nongovernmental entities. The extension of the obligation to governmental operators is seen as a means to promote transparency and information exchange in Finland.[115] It is also expected to contribute to the development of a uniform practice for space activities.[116]

In substance, the operator—who can be different from the owner depending on who exercises effective control—is required to submit a written application to the Ministry.[117] The authorization then may be granted for a definite or indefinite period. It must be sought at least six months prior to the planned date for the launch.[118] However, the six-month period may be increased or decreased in the future by the Ministry, depending on the nature of the activity pursued as well as the impact of the development of new technologies.[119] Furthermore, the requirement of prior authorization is not limited to "launches" only; it extends to the acquisition of space objects

109. Tapio, *supra* note 95 at 393.
110. Finland is not Party to the Moon Agreement but has ratified the other UN Space Treaties.
111. Tapio, *supra* note 95 at 393.
112. Finnish Decree 74/2018 pertains to operational issues regarding the licensing and registration process for space objects. *See supra* note 95.
113. Pursuant to Art. 3 of the law, the authorization process detailed in section 5 does not apply to space activities carried out by the "Defence Forces." These activities are authorized and supervised by the Ministry of Defense.
114. Finnish Governmental proposal, *supra* note 99, Art. 5.
115. *Id.*
116. *Id.*
117. Finnish Space Act, *supra* note 16, Art. 5.
118. Finnish Decree 74/2018, *supra* note 95, Art. 1.
119. Finnish Governmental proposal, *supra* note 99, Art. 5.

that have already been placed in outer space.[120] This rule specifically aims at ensuring that Finland continues to comply with its international obligations in cases where ownership and control of a space object is transferred to a Finnish operator.[121] It means the operator must seek approval from the Ministry before it acquires the object;[122] otherwise, it would be in violation of the Finnish Space Act.[123]

For cases where the operator's main activity can be broken down into several small "space activities," one application encompassing all stages is sufficient.[124] The rationale is to lower the administrative burden on all parties involved by not requiring several applications from a single entity when it operates several space objects or needs to launch several of them together or uses a single operating system for all. In practice, it would mean that the operator only needs to obtain one authorization to launch and/or operate a constellation of satellites.

The conditions per se of the authorization are laid down in section 5 subsection 2 of the Finnish Space Act and supplemented by Decree 78/2018. Accordingly, the operator must present "reliable evidence" that it has the "necessary technical expertise and financial capacity" to carry out the planned activity. To that end, it must provide, *inter alia*, a "description of [its] earlier space activities," "financial statements for the three previous financial years," an estimate of the costs of the planned activity, and how these costs will be covered. The application must also be accompanied by a risk assessment of the activity regarding the risk of personal injury and material damage it may pose on Earth, in the atmosphere, or in outer space. It means that the operator must demonstrate it has carried out tests and any other necessary measures on the space object to ensure its safety and durability.[125] Furthermore, the Finnish Space Act requires the operator to show proof of proper insurance[126] and compliance with Finland's export control provisions and with ITU rules.[127]

120. *Id.*
121. In cases where the transfer of space activities occurs from a foreign operator to a Finnish operator, Finland may request from a prior agreement with the foreign State regarding liability for damage caused by the object. Finnish Space Act, *supra* note 16, Art. 11.
122. The Ministry may only approve the transfer of control and/or ownership if the space activity complies with the requirements of section 5 subsection 2. Finland, *Act on Space Activities*, section 11 (2018).
123. Section 21 of the Finnish Space Act outlines the sanction regime for failing to obtain the Ministry's prior authorization or approval.
124. Finnish Governmental proposal, *supra* note 99, Art. 5.
125. Finnish Decree 74/2018, *supra* note 95, Art. 2§3.
126. In practice, the operator must be insured against damage caused to third parties at least up to EUR 60 million, i.e., up to the State's right of recourse maximum amount. The insurance must cover "at least the stage of launching the space object and the related operations until the time when the space object has settled in orbit." However, upon decision of the ministry, the obligation may be waived "if the risk of collision between the space object and another space object in the orbit is lower than 1/1000" and if the probability that the space object will not burn upon reentry into Earth atmosphere is lower than 1/10,000. *Id.*, Art. 5 and Finnish Space Act, *supra* note 16, Art. 8.
127. In practice, it means that the deliverance of the authorization is dependent on passing, *inter alia*, the ITU coordination process implemented nationally by the Finnish Communications Regulatory Authority (FICORA). This procedure is separate from the authorization procedure laid down in the Finnish Space Act. Consequently, when necessary, the operator must first seek approval from FICORA before applying for an authorization under the Finnish Space Act.

Additionally, Decree 74/2018 expands on the information the operator must provide the Ministry with in order to assess the eligibility for authorization.[128] Accordingly, the operator is required to provide, *inter alia*, information on its identity, the technical details and a description of the planned activity, information about the launch, and about majority shareholders.[129]

Finally, the operator shall "see[k] to prevent the generation of space debris and adverse environmental impacts on the earth, in the atmosphere and in outer space in accordance with section 10." This is where some key issues regarding environmental protection, which are discussed *infra*, lie.

1.2.3 Environmental Component

Although not specifically stated in the Finnish Space Act, Tapio explains, environmental protection is "high on the political agenda in Finland."[130] In particular, she stresses the issues raised by the congestion of Earth orbit with space debris and how it might impede both State and private space activities in the future.[131] She advances—rightfully in my opinion—that removing, mitigating, and preventing space debris could "be seen as interesting business opportunity" and that, as a consequence, enhancing environmental protection through regulation could "foster creation of new private endeavors [and] promote investment enabling technologies."[132] In other words, rather than being a burden on space operators, regulating the protection of the outer space environment is good for business.

For this reason, Finland decided to make the prevention of environmental damage caused by space activities in, *inter alia*, outer space a "special objective" of the Finnish Space Act.[133] As a result, the law includes "a general obligation to conduct space activities in an environmentally sustainable way."[134] Indeed, section 10 provides that "space activities shall be carried on in a manner that is environmentally sustainable and promotes the sustainable use of outer space."

The declared intention of the Finnish Space Act to promote sustainability and environmental protection has few equivalents among other national space legislations. In most cases, these topics are not addressed directly but rather included as a requirement for authorization and often in the context of space debris or by replicating the wording of Article IX of the Outer Space Treaty on "harmful contamination."[135] While using the authorization process as a means to implement environmental

---

Without the proof that the operator complies with ITU rules, the activity will not be authorized. Finland, *supra* note 99 at section 5.

128. Finnish Decree 74/2018, *supra* note 95, Art. 2.
129. Finland, *Decree of the Ministry of Economic Affairs and Employment on Space Activities*, section 2 (2018).
130. Tapio, *supra* note 95 at 401.
131. *Id.*
132. *Id.*
133. Finnish Governmental proposal, *supra* note 99, Art. 10.
134. Tapio, *supra* note 95 at 401.
135. For instance, to obtain an authorization under Denmark's 2016 Outer Space Act, the operator is required to, *inter alia*, take "appropriate measures regarding space debris management" and

measures has merits—it forces operators to take necessary measures—it also puts them on the back burner. They become an element on a checklist, the same as providing a description of the planned activity, and are often not particularly developed, Belgium being the exception as seen *supra*. Although the Belgian Space Act incorporates environmental concerns in its regulatory framework through the licensing process, it also outlines a detailed EIA.[136]

In comparison, Finland includes environmental requirements both as a general obligation and as a requirement for authorization. By having a full section dedicated to these issues—i.e., section 10—the Finnish Space Act places environmental matters in space on the same level of importance as issues of authorization and liability. In this instance, the reference to section 10 and the inclusion of environmental requirements in the authorization process do not diminish the environmental protection regime the law promotes. On the contrary, it strengthens it by using the authorization process in section 5 as a tool to operationalize the general obligation encompassed in section 10.

Subsection 1 of section 10 focuses on environmental protection; it demands the operator assess the environmental impact of its space activities not only on Earth and its atmosphere but also in outer space. To that end, the operator shall provide information on the technology components and products used in the planned activity.[137]

The operator is also asked to specify in the application whether its space object will be using nuclear or other radioactive materials. This requirement refers to the nonbinding NPS Principles[138] which provide that, to the extent feasible, the use of nuclear power sources in outer space shall be restricted.

Furthermore, section 8 of Decree 74/2018 requires the operator to submit an annual report to the Ministry about its space activities. This report must describe, *inter alia*, "the state of the space activities, the functionality and any failures of the space object [...], any environmental impacts and a plan for continuing, altering or discontinuing the activities." Consequently, the operator must first establish a plan and then report on its application. In Tapio's opinion, this is a step forward to ensure that space activities are carried out in "a deliberated manner," notably by considering and anticipating risks.[139] She further argues that by first planning and then reporting, the operator is in a better place to prove it acted diligently should the need arise, particularly in cases where damage is caused to a third party.

---

to conduct activities "in an environmentally safe manner." The "Executive Order on requirements in connection with approval of activities in outer space, etc." brings more precisions in this regard. No reference to sustainability is made. Danish Outer Space Act of 2016, Act No. 409 of May 11, 2016, Art. 3 (DK) translation available online. The French law of 2008 on space operations also refers to potential additional requirements for authorization, including for mitigating space debris. French Space Act, *supra* note 16, Art. 5. Also *see infra* the analysis pertaining to the protection of the outer space environment under the United States, Luxembourg and the United Arab Emirates' laws regulating space mining activities.

136. *See* Belgium, *supra* section 1.1.
137. Finnish Governmental proposal, *supra* note 99, Art. 10.
138. *See* NPS Principles, *supra* Chapter 3.
139. Tapio, *supra* note 95 at 401.

This two-step process could also be a compromise between too stringent or lax rules to regulate the protection of the outer space environment. It could be argued that the operator knows the most about its planned activity and the impact it could have on the environment. Thus, by having the operator draft a plan, it can decide to which extent measures are necessary. In this configuration, the law guides the operator by indicating what issues it should look for—space debris mitigation, planetary protection, etc.—and the competent authority then reviews the plan to assess if it is up to the standard of care the law demands. This approach could be a means to balance a legislation that is detailed to the point it burdens operators unreasonably and keeps quiet on the matter to not impede the development of the space industry.

With regard to space debris specifically, subsection 2 finds its basis in the "generally accepted international guidelines" on space debris mitigation, namely the IADC and the UNCOPUOS instruments.[140] Accordingly, the operator is asked to "seek to ensure" that its activities do not generate debris.[141] In particular:

> the operator shall restrict the generation of space debris during the normal operations of the space object, reduce the risks of in-orbit break-ups and in-orbit collisions and, after the space object has completed its mission, seek to move it into a less used orbit or into the atmosphere.

Consequently, the measures pertaining to space debris mitigation apply through the entire life cycle of the activity: from planning to "retiring" the space object. Although not in the Finnish Space Act, the supplemental Decree 74/2018 incorporates in its section 3 the "25 years rule" from the IADC guidelines. Accordingly, once the space object has fulfilled its purpose, it should be moved—within 25 years—either to a less congested orbit so it does not pose any danger to other activities or into the Earth's atmosphere where it will burn upon reentry.

1.2.4 Conclusion

From an environmental perspective, the Finnish Space Act is one of the most advanced domestic space legislations. It specifically calls for space activities to be carried on "in a manner that is *environmentally* sustainable" [italics added].[142] The emphasis on the environmental dimension of sustainability serves as a reminder that, without environmental considerations, there is no sustainability. The importance of ensuring the protection of, *inter alia*, the outer space environment is further stressed by the Finnish Space Act specifically dedicating a separate provision to the matter. Often, as seen in the Belgian Space Act, these considerations are relegated to a requirement in the authorization process. Here, although the authorization requirements include, *inter alia*, avoiding creating space debris, it makes express reference to the environmental

140. *See supra* Chapter 3.
141. According to Tapio, the expression "to seek to ensure" was a compromise between promoting the values of these nonbinding instruments and the technical and economic responsibility of operators. Tapio, *supra* note 95 at 401 note 50.
142. Finnish Space Act, section 10.

provision for the details. As a result, authorization of activities and environmental protection of outer space are on the same level; one is not subjected to the other.

Moreover, the Finnish Space Act adopts a balanced approach which is noteworthy. In addition to requiring compliance with international standards, such as the NPS Principles and SDM Guidelines, it further places operators at the heart of the process by granting them freedom in their achievement of the environmental standards. Thus, operators are first required to carry out an EIA and to "present a plan for measures to counter and reduce adverse environmental impacts."[143] They are, then, in charge of reporting annually on their activity, including the actual environmental consequences of their activity and corresponding response measures. Ultimately, this approach allows operators to be creative in how they balance costs, economic benefits, and environmental protection of outer space. This balance of interests is the essence of sustainability.

Therefore, it is not surprising to observe that the Finnish Space Act incorporates several elements of the conceptual sustainability framework. In addition to requiring operators—both governmental and nongovernmental—to carry out an EIA, the law also calls for an alignment on best international practices. While it is yet undetermined whether the framework would apply to space resource activities, it provides an example of how domestic space legislation could integrate environmental concerns into their national space law framework.

2 SPECIFIC NATIONAL LEGISLATIONS REGULATING SPACE RESOURCE ACTIVITIES

Among the nations having adopted domestic legislations pertaining to their space activities, or potential space activities, as of 2022, only four States have adopted national legislations precisely addressing space resource activities: the United States of America (US) in 2015 (2.1), Luxembourg in 2017 (2.2), the United Arab Emirates (UAE) in 2020 (2.3) and, more recently, Japan in 2021(2.4). This section deals with this cluster of countries. Each framework is analyzed separately, with particular attention being paid to the scope of the law, the authorization mechanism, and, lastly, the environmental component.

2.1 United States of America

In November 2015, the United States made the headlines when President Barack Obama signed into law the US *Commercial Space Launch Competitiveness Act* (CSLCA).[144] This event officially made the United States the first country in the world to

143. *Id.*

144. US Commercial Space Launch Competitiveness Act, 129 STAT. 704 (2015) (CSLCA). *See, e.g.*, Frédéric Bianchi & Pierre Kupferman, *Obama a donné le top départ de la ruée vers l'or spatial*, BFM BUSINESS, December 14, 2015; Andrew Griffin, *It's now legal to own and mine asteroids*, THE INDEPENDENT, Nov. 26, 2015; Marion Degeorges, *Les Etats-Unis peuvent-ils s'emparer des matières premières de l'espace?*, LES ECHOS, Nov. 22, 2015.

adopt a national regulatory framework for the commercial exploration and utilization of space resources.

Divided into four titles, the real novelty of the CSLCA comes from the last section of the law: Title IV. Whereas Titles I to III are dedicated to amending existing provisions on the licensing regime for launches and commercial remote sensing and to the renaming of the office of space commerce,[145] Title IV—also known as the *Space Resource Exploration and Utilization Act of 2015*—[146] explicitly authorizes space mining.

Accordingly, this section provides an overview of the US regulatory framework for space resource activities. To that end, the section first discusses the scope of Title IV (2.1.1). Second, it addresses the authorization processes considered by Congress to comply with the State's international obligation—under Article VI of the Outer Space Treaty—to authorize and supervise space activities carried out by nongovernmental entities (2.1.2). Lastly, this section considers the US approach to environmental protection in outer space (2.1.3).

2.1.1 Scope of Title IV of the Law[147]

Title IV builds on the aspirations of a previous, discarded, bill dating back from 2014: the US *American Space Technology for Exploring Resource Opportunities in Deep Space Act* ("ASTEROIDS Act").[148] The bill, introduced by Representative Bill Posey, constitutes Congress' first attempt at "[promoting] the development of a commercial asteroid resources industry for outer space in the United States" in order "to increase the exploration and utilization of asteroid resources in outer space."[149] In essence, the purpose of the ASTEROIDS Act is to explicitly recognize American entities' property rights over obtained asteroid resources.[150]

The bill was welcomed with perplexity—its tentative compliance with the Outer Space Treaty principles remaining dubious in many eyes. For instance, Kfir and Perry deem that the ASTEROIDS Act was "rife with problematic language and ambiguities," and Tronchetti considers that the bill would have "collide[d] with international space law."[151] Nonetheless, the ASTEROIDS Act represented a "useful first step" in its

145. *Id.*, Titles I to III.
146. CSLCA, *supra* note 144, §401.
147. This section is based on the previous published work of the author. Gabrielle Leterre, *Providing a legal framework for sustainable space mining activities*, 37–45 (2017).
148. *American Space Technology for Exploring Resource Opportunities in Deep Space Act*, H. R. 5063, 113th Cong. (2014) (US).
149. *Id.*
150. *Id.*, at 51302 (a).
151. Sagi Kfir & Ian Perry, *Title IV of the US Commercial Space Launch Competitiveness Act of 2015: A Critical Step Forward in Facilitating the Development of a Viable Space Infrastructure*, 5 New Space 163–169, 164 (2017); Fabio Tronchetti, *Private property rights on asteroid resources: Assessing the legality of the ASTEROIDS Act*, 30 Space Policy 193–196 (2014) DOI: 10.1016/j.spacepol.2014.07.005.

attempt to adopt a regulatory framework for emerging space resource activities,[152] even if it needed considerable additional work, which was the very goal of the CSLCA.[153]

In comparison to its doomed antecedent, Title IV has been qualified "a dramatic improvement over its legislative predecessor."[154] Of the 2014 bill, only a shared purpose remains: to "facilitate commercial exploration for and commercial recovery of space resources by United States citizens."[155] As we will see at greater length *infra*, authorizing US citizens "to possess, own, transport, use, and sell" space resources they obtain is the cornerstone of Title IV.[156] The drafters also showed increased mindfulness regarding the US international obligations, in virtue of the Outer Space Treaty, by addressing potential issues raised with Article VI and Article II of the Treaty.

2.1.1.a Definitional Issues Addressed in Title IV

Title IV starts by defining three key terms: "asteroid resources," "space resources" and "U.S. citizen."[157]

First, the definition of "asteroid resources" underscores the evolution between the 2014 ASTEROIDS Act and Title IV of the CSLCA: unlike the former, the application of Title IV is not restricted to the exploitation of "asteroid resources" solely but covers more broadly "space resources." It certainly remains apparent that the space industry's predominant interest, at the time of the drafting, is to seek resources from asteroids. This is illustrated by the fact that "asteroid resources" are defined in two different manners. The expression not only appears immediately in Title IV as a stand-alone term requiring no further clarification but is also defined in function of the broader term "space resources." The intertwined definitions of "asteroid resources" function as follows: an "asteroid resource" is *also* a "space resource" "found on or within an asteroid."[158] This added precision means an extension of the law to include any "space resource"—that is, "an abiotic resource *in situ* in outer space"—[159] and we should understand that one is not only found in an asteroid. This is particularly welcome today, with the US Artemis program anticipating a return to the Moon.[160] Regarding the definition of the term "space resource" per se, Title IV explicitly excludes resources containing biological life while making it clear that minerals and water can be exploited.[161]

152. Charles Stotler, *The Space Review: The ASTEROIDS Act and hearing: some observations on international obligations*, THE SPACE REVIEW (2014), https://www.thespacereview.com/article/2604/1 (last visited January 2024).
153. Kfir and Perry, *supra* note 151 at 164.
154. *Id.*
155. CSLCA, §51302(a).
156. *Id.*, 51303.
157. *Id.*, 51301.
158. *Id.*, §51301(1).
159. *Id.*, §51301(2).
160. Artemis Accords: Principles for Cooperation in the Civil Exploration and Use of the Moon, Mars, Comets, and Asteroids for Peaceful Purposes (2020) available online.
161. Title IV of the CSLCA, *supra* note 144, §51301(2)(B); K. G. Orphanides, AMERICAN COMPANIES COULD SOON MINE ASTEROIDS FOR PROFIT WIRED UK (2015), available online.

Second, Title IV only applies to US citizens. For this reason, the law clarifies the expression by way of reference to Title 51 of the US Code.[162] Accordingly, clauses (A) and (B) of paragraph 51301 give an ordinary definition of "U.S. citizens" which includes natural persons with American citizenship and legal entities directly submitted to US Law.[163] So far, Title IV would only apply within the strict confines of the territory of the United States if the definition of a "U.S. citizen" provided by clause (C) were not to considerably broaden the pool of entities concerned by the law. It considers that entities "organized or existing *under the laws of a foreign country*" [italics added] can be seen as US citizens under specific circumstances.[164] These circumstances are that the "controlling interest" of said entities is held by a US citizen as defined in clauses (A) and (B), i.e., a natural person or legal entity directly under the jurisdiction and control of the US.[165] Consequently, it becomes apparent that the notion of "controlling interest" is the key element to define the scope of application of Title IV.

Pursuant to the US Code of Federal Regulations,[166] a "controlling interest" in an entity is reflected by the "ownership of an amount of equity [...] sufficient to direct management of the entity or to void transactions entered into by management," an interest of 51% being presumed sufficient.[167]

Therefore, the personal scope of Title IV extends to: (1) a natural person with US citizenship, (2) a legal entity organized and existing under the laws of the United States, and (3) a foreign "corporation, partnership, joint venture, association, or other entity"[168] with at least 51% of equity owned by a natural or legal American person. In practice, it means that investors and partners in companies owned by at least 51% of US citizens will benefit from the provision of Title IV. This approach considerably extends its scope of application since the law has the potential to benefit non-US citizens too, so long as they do not constitute more than 49% of the commercial entity.

2.1.1.b Commercial Purpose of Title IV

According to paragraph 51302, the purpose of Title IV is to "facilitate commercial exploration and commercial recovery of space resources by the US citizens" by "discourage[ing] government barriers to the development [...] of economically viable, safe, and stable industries for commercial [space mining]."[169] This emphasis on the commercial character of the space activity is particularly forward, especially in 2015 when no equivalent law existed yet. With Title IV, the United States clearly affirms its intention to provide a regulatory framework adapted to the new landscape of the space industry, namely the development of private commercial ventures in outer space.

162. *See* National and Commercial Space Programs, 51 U.S.C. §51301(3) (1996) (U.S.).
163. Legal entities directly submitted to US Law include American companies as well as governmental and State entities.
164. Title 51 U.S.C, *supra.* note 162.
165. *Id.*
166. *See* Aeronautics and Space, 14 CFR 401.5 (US).
167. *Id.*
168. *Id.*
169. Title IV, §51302 (a) (1) and (2).

The commercial nature of the activity was initially a point of contention at the international level. As pointed out by Luxembourg's former Deputy Prime Minister and Minister of Economy Etienne Schneider, the "United Nations' Space Treaty of 1967 [i.e., the Outer Space Treaty] does not touch upon [the] question about who can do what in space, economically speaking."[170] As a matter of fact, the Outer Space Treaty does not expressly refer to commercial activities, only making explicit mention of "scientific investigations" in Article I.[171] One of the most significant evolutions in recent years is that the commercial character of activities in outer space has eventually been accepted by the international community. As a result, the focus of the debate has changed and now moves toward discussing the "legal aspects of space resource activities."[172]

2.1.1.c Relation of Title IV to Article II of the Outer Space Treaty

As part of the questions raised by the United States' adoption of a law about space resources, another source of contention appeared among legal scholars regarding the prohibition—under Article II of the Outer Space Treaty—of appropriating outer space. The response of American law to such concerns is to be found in section 403 of Title IV, which provides a "disclaimer of extra-terrestrial sovereignty" stating that:

> it is the sense of Congress that by the enactment of this Act, the United States does not thereby assert sovereignty or sovereign or exclusive rights or jurisdiction over, or the ownership of, any celestial body.

Adding a "disclaimer" at the end of Title IV may seem peculiar, but it is important to consider the background of the law and, in particular, the time of its drafting. In 2015, when the law is signed by President Obama, no similar national legislation exists in the world. There is no regulatory basis to get inspired from and space resource activities are still considered science fiction by many. The only point of reference was the rejected ASTEROIDS bill, which had already raised questions among legal scholars about its compliance with US's international obligations.[173] Hence, Title IV had to balance two needs: (1) providing legal certainty to US space mining entrepreneurs and (2) compliance with the provisions of the Outer Space Treaty, to which the US is a State Party.

The former was fulfilled by paragraph 51303 recognizing US citizens' rights over asteroid and space resources. It entitles US citizens engaged in space mining activities to "any asteroid resource or space resource obtained, including to possess, own, transport, use, and sell the asteroid resource or space resource obtained." In other

170. LSA, *Etienne Schneider about the importance of the legal and regulatory framework of Luxembourg* (2017) available online.
171. Also *see* Stephan Hobe, *Article I*, I *in* COLOGNE COMMENTARY ON SPACE LAW 25, 33–36 (Stephan Hobe, Bernhard Schmidt-Tedd, & Kai-Uwe Schrogl eds., 2009). IISL Statement by the Board of Directors of the IISL on Claims to Property Rights Regarding the Moon and Other Celestial Bodies (2004) available online; IISL, Statement of the Board of Directors of the IISL (2009).
172. Report of the Legal Subcommittee on its sixtieth session, held in Vienna from May 31 to June 11, 2021, UNGA, 64th Sess., UN Doc. A/AC.105.1243 (2021).
173. Kfir and Perry, *supra* note 151; Hao Liu & Fabio Tronchetti, *The American Space Commerce Free Enterprise Act of 2017: The Latest Step in Regulating the Space Resources Utilization Industry or Something More?*, 47 SPACE POLICY SPACE POLICY 1 (2019) DOI: 10.1016/j.spacepol.2018.02.004.

words, it grants the full extent of property rights to US citizens. Yet—and this is where the disclaimer comes into play—Article II of the Outer Space Treaty clearly states that:

> [o]uter space, including the moon and other celestial bodies, is not subject to national appropriation by claim of sovereignty, by means of use or occupation, or by any other means.

Reading paragraph 51303 of Title IV in view of Article II, two main concerns can be raised: (1) can resources from celestial bodies be appropriated and, in the affirmative, (2) could their exploitation create titles based on means and use?

The first issue refers to the "area versus resources" problem.[174] Whereas Article II explicitly rejects the appropriation of asteroids, for instance, it remains silent regarding its resources. The question is thus whether the prohibition extends to extracted resources. For some States, this absence of explicit prohibition is a sign that space resources can be appropriated.[175] This interpretation of Article II of the Outer Space Treaty was acknowledged by the International Institute of Space Law (IISL) in 2015 in a position paper on space mining.[176] The IISL stated that the lack of explicit prohibition could be understood as allowing the appropriation of space resources under the Outer Space Treaty.[177]

The second issue raised is linked to the lengthy presence in one area that carrying out mining activities would require. Following State practice, the prerogative to "use" is a component of the right of property.[178] Similarly, under international law effective "occupation" is a means for a State to acquire sovereignty over *terra nullius*, i.e., over a territory that no one has claimed.[179] Consequently, the US disclaimer serves as a means to express clearly to the international community that Title IV does not signal the US's ambition to claim sovereignty over parts of the Moon or other celestial bodies. In that regard, the IISL affirmed that the intent of the United States to entitle its citizens to space resources was "independent from the claim of sovereign rights over celestial bodies, which the United States explicitly does not make."[180]

2.1.2 Authorization Mechanism

Concerns with Article II of the Outer Space Treaty are not the only aspects posing problems as regards international law and Congress also touched upon its international

174. *See* Leterre, *supra* note 147 at 30–32.
175. *See*, for instance, the example of the United States and Luxembourg which adopted a national law expressly allowing the appropriation of natural resources in space: Title IV of the CSLCA, *supra* note 144 and SRL, *supra* note 14.
176. IISL Board of Directors, *IISL Position Paper on Space Resource Mining*, International Institute of Space Law (2015) available online.
177. *Id.*
178. Protocol 1 to the European Convention for the Protection of Human Rights and Fundamental Freedoms, *entered into force* May 18, 1954, Art. 1, 213 UNTS 262; American Convention on Human Rights, *entered into force* July 18, 1978, Art. 21(1) 1144 UNTS 123; African Charter on Human and Peoples' Rights, *entered into force* Oct. 21, 1986, §186, 1520 UNTS 217.
179. Island of Palmas Case (US v Netherlands) (1928) II RIAA 829, §§30–31, 160.
180. IISL Position Paper (2015), *supra* note 176.

obligations under Article VI of the Treaty. Pursuant to this provision, the United States bears international responsibility for national governmental and nongovernmental space activities. As such, the State must ensure that such activities comply with its international obligations. Specifically, in the case of nongovernmental activities, they must be authorized and continuously supervised by the State.

In practice, the Outer Space Treaty leaves the means to implement these obligations to the discretion of the States Parties. Some States favor the adoption of a general national legislation encompassing a "one-fit-all" authorization procedure applicable to a variety of space activities.[181] In the United States, the approach to authorization is different. The authorization of nongovernmental space activities is accomplished through "a constellation of detailed statutes and regulations governing different aspects of [said] activities."[182] In Sundahl's words, "[US] space law has arisen as a patchwork of statutes involving multiples agencies."[183] Namely, licensing for launches and reentries is processed through the Department of Transportation's Federal Aviation Administration (FAA) Office of Commercial Space Transportation,[184] whereas remote sensing activities are licensed by the Department of Commerce[185] and satellite communications by the Federal Communication Commission (FCC).[186] This approach to authorizing and supervising space activities thus raises the question of how to regulate unprecedented US commercial space activities, like space mining.

2.1.2.a Proposal of the White House Office of Science and Technology Policy

The complex architecture of the authorization of space activities is the basis for Congress' request, through section 108 of the CSLCA, to require the Director of the White House Office of Science and Technology Policy (OSTP) to submit to Congress a report identifying which—if any—governmental authority is competent to authorize nontraditional space activities. Cases of launching and reentries, telecommunication satellites, and remote sensing are clearly regulated under the national legislation; activities such as space mining are not.

In practice, US companies planning to engage in nontraditional space activities reached out to the FAA to better understand how the existing regulatory framework would apply in these circumstances. While the FAA tried to accommodate and offer some legal certainty to support emerging space activities, it also recognized that its authority did not currently extend to commercial space activities in low-Earth orbit and

181. For instance, the OSTP letter refers to the UK's framework.
182. Mark J. Sundahl, *Regulating Non-traditional Space Activities in the United States in the Wake of the Commercial Space Launch Competitiveness Act*, 42 Air and Space Law, 30 (2017) DOI: 10.54648/aila2017003.
183. *Id.*
184. 51 U.S.C. Ch. 509.
185. 51 U.S.C. Ch. 601.
186. 47 C.F.R. 151.

beyond, like space mining operations.[187] Thus, having a clear overview of what processes exist and could be leveraged became all the more important.

Accordingly, in addition to requiring the OSTP to identify whether there already exists a competent entity, section 108 of the CSLCA tasks it, in the negative, to recommend any legislative action necessary, and preferably ones based on existing systems. The purpose of the Section is to ensure that the United States is compliant with its international obligation to authorize nongovernmental space activities.

To that end, the OSTP issued a 5-page letter, with a legislative proposal in an appendix, to the Senate and the House of Representatives' respective space committees on April 4, 2016.[188] The letter outlines a mission authorization process for nontraditional space activities and is made up of three sections.[189] In section 1, the OSTP broadly identifies three categories of "unprecedented commercial space activities": (1) private missions beyond Earth orbit (e.g., to the Moon and Mars; "space" colonization), (2) new on-orbit activities (e.g., satellite repair and refueling; orbital habitat), and (3) space resource utilization. Section 2 of the letter reflects on the need for licensing processes, notably in view of Article VI of the Outer Space Treaty, and establishes that "existing arrangements [...] are designed to serve a range of public policy interests," such as public safety and foreign policy. This reflection leads the OSTP to conclude that:

> [w]hile existing licensing frameworks provide clear means to address certain aspects of these activities, they do not, by themselves, provide the [US] Government with a straightforward means to fulfill its treaty obligations to ensure the conformity of these activities with the provisions of the Outer Space Treaty.

Lastly, section 3 considers the suitability of a legislative proposal. It emphasizes the "early stage in the development of these [non-traditional] activities" which consists "primarily of experimental technology development and demonstration." For this reason, the OSTP believes that it would be "premature to establish a comprehensive regulatory framework mirroring those of mature commercial space activities," such as the ones expressly regulated by the FAA. Rather, the OSTP favors delimiting a "clear path" for the authorization and supervision of nontraditional space activities. To that

187. Sundahl, *supra* note 182 at 31. Although the FAA was able to make a favorable payload determination for the Moon Express MX-1E mission in 2016 under 51 U.S.C. 50904, it is important to note that the determination does not extend to other similar cases or future mission of Moon Express Inc. Additionally, it is necessary to emphasize that the payload review is only one part of the FAA's overall launch licensing process. Emily Calandrelli, *Moon Express becomes first private company to receive permission to go to the moon*, TECHCRUNCH (2016), available online. The system was tested in 2016 when Moon Express Inc., an American company, submitted a request to the FAA for a Payload Review. While both the FAA and the Department of State agreed to deliver the company a mission authorization, it was stressed that the authorization did not extend to future missions by the company, making it clear that the current process for authorization is done on a case-by-case basis until such a time a law is passed to establish an authorization regime. *See* Gabrynowicz, Title IV of the 2015 U.S. Commercial Space Launch Competitiveness Act, UNCOPUOS LSC (2017) available online.

188. The OSTP's proposal was delivered to the Senate's Committee on Commerce, Science and Transportation and the House of Representatives' Committee on Commerce, Science and Technology.

189. OSTP Letter 2016.

end, it recommends Congress to create a "Mission Authorization" process, modeled on the FAA's existing Payload Review process, one of the elements of the overall FAA's licensing process for launching.

The Payload Review process consists of the FAA reviewing whether a payload proposed for launch would "jeopardize public health and safety, safety of property, US national security or foreign policy interests, or international obligations of the United States."[190] To that end, the FAA engages in interagency consultations with, *inter alia*, the Department of Defense for matters of national security or the Department of State for foreign policy.[191] Additionally, the operator must provide the FAA with information regarding the payload's name, class, physical dimensions and weight, orbital parameters, hazardous materials, intended payload operations, and delivery point in flight at which the payload will no longer be under the licensee's control, as well as the identity of the payload's owner and operator—if different from the party requesting the review.[192]

Noticeably, the OSTP's proposal—spelled out in a 2-page appendix—uses statutory language and puts forth amendments to Title 51 of the United States Code to adapt the proposal to circumstances.[193] In particular, it introduces in section 50902 a definition for "mission" and creates a section 50924 detailing the conditions of the Mission Authorization. The legislative proposal, as such, is not intended to prescribe "substantive, generally applicable regulations", only a procedural "outline" for a case-by-case interagency review.[194]

In practice, the Mission Authorization process would grant the authority to license nontraditional activities to the FAA. The Agency would have to "coordinate" with other federal agencies prior to delivering an authorization, a consultation process it is well used to.[195] The FAA would have the authority to demand the operator meet any conditions that are "deemed necessary for compliance" with the US's international obligations, foreign policy, and national security. Furthermore, the operator would have to provide updated information about the operation on a periodic basis and in cases of any "material change [...] that would affect the affirmations and information that were originally submitted in support of the authorization."[196]

A noticeable divergence from the Payload Review process is the creation of a "mission authorization registry" of all mission authorization delivered for nontraditional space activities. The registry would be maintained by the FAA and constantly updated as new information is received from operators. However, as Sundahl notes, the registry would be limited in scope; it would only apply to operators required to seek a mission authorization—i.e., to US citizens and other entities under the United States' "jurisdiction and control."[197]

190. *See* 14 C.F.R. 415 Subpart D. On the FAA's competence to make payload review determination, *see* 51 U.S.C. 50904.
191. 51 U.S.C. 50918.
192. 14 C.F.R. 415.59.
193. Precisely, it amends 51 U.S.C. Chapter 509 which regulates commercial space launch activities in the United States.
194. OSTP Letter, 4.
195. 51 U.S.C. 50918.
196. OSTP Letter, Appendix, 2.
197. Sundahl, *supra* note 182 at 35.

Overall, the OSTP's proposal was positively received by the space industry. Sundahl attributes this success to three elements.[198] First, the proposal centralizes the authority in the FAA which "streamlines the licensing process." Second, the fact that the proposal is modeled on an existing one means that operators will be familiar with it. Lastly, the proposal is not restrictive since it does not impose specific requirements, which leaves it open for all types of missions, a flexibility that is lacking in the current regulatory framework. Yet, it became apparent during the Space Committees' hearings of spring 2017 held in both chambers that the OSTP's Mission Authorization was losing support. In the words of Liu and Tronchetti, the general feeling was that the OSTP's proposal "created unnecessary administrative burdens to the nascent private space (mining) industry."[199] This change of perception led to the emergence of a new approach in Congress regarding the licensing of US nontraditional space activities.

2.1.2.b The American Space Commerce Free Enterprise Act of 2019

On June 6, 2017, the House of Representatives introduced a bill entitled the *American Space Commerce Free Enterprise Act* (ASCFEA).[200] The bill is rather extensive compared to the small amendments suggested by the OSTP to establish its Mission Authorization process. This supports the idea of a shift in approaching the regulatory framework for nontraditional space activities. Whereas the OSTP intended to avoid prescribing "substantive, generally applicable regulations" and limits itself to outlining a procedure,[201] the ASCFEA aims to "[establish] a general authorization and supervision certification authority for non-governmental outer space activities."[202]

The purpose of the bill is to relieve obstacles and to facilitate the realization of private space activities, like space mining.[203] Section 1 of the ASCFEA also emphasizes the need "to minimize regulations and limitations on the freedom of United States non-governmental entities to explore and use space" in order to "relieve administrative burdens on new and innovative non-governmental space actors." That is not to say that the absence of regulations would be the most favorable outcome. Beyond the issue of compliance with Article VI of the Outer Space Treaty, the bill notes that "[i]t serves the

198. *Id.*
199. Liu and Tronchetti, *supra* note 173 at 2.
200. The ASCFEA bill was introduced in 2017 during the 115th session of the US Congress. However, the text was never passed by Senate during the session and was thus re-introduced as the "American Space Commerce Free Enterprise Act of 2019" during the next congressional session, on July 2, 2019. Unless indicated otherwise, the analysis of the "ASCFEA" in this section refers to the latest bill, i.e., American Space Commerce Free Enterprise Act of 2019, H. R. 3610, 116th Cong. (2019) (US) ["2019 ASCFEA"]. The bill of 2019 underwent some small amendments compared to its earlier version. For instance, the latest bill saw the section on radiofrequency be removed (section 11 of the 2017 bill). The US President also lost its ability to extend the 90-day period for approval "to further evaluate the national security implications of the application." §80202 (4) (A) and (B). *See* US American Space Commerce Free Enterprise Act, H.R. 2809, 115th Cong. (2017) (US) ["2017 ASCFEA"].
201. OSTP Letter, 4.
202. 2017 ASCFEA, *supra* note 200, 2.
203. 2019 ASCFEA, *supra* note 200, 1.

national interest to address misperceptions of legal uncertainty through the establishment of [a regulatory framework]."[204] Among other things, space operators need legal certainty before engaging larger amounts of money and time into a new activity as well as to attract potential investors. The best way to do that is to know in advance whether the planned activity will raise some legal red flags when the time comes to request authorization from the government.[205]

The ASCFEA focuses on two facets of space activities: (1) the creation of a new authorization procedure—under the authority of the Secretary of Commerce—for nongovernmental commercial space activities carried out by US citizens, and (2) the rationalization of the existing procedure for commercial remote sensing activities.[206] Ultimately, the goal is to "enhance the existing [...] framework to provide greater transparency, greater efficiency, and less administrative burden" for US citizens engaging in nontraditional space activities.[207]

In the case of space resource activities—the only one expressly covered by the bill—[208] the operator would have to file a request for authorization with the Secretary of Commerce, acting through the Office of Space Commerce (OSC).[209] This is the first noticeable difference with the OSTP's proposal; it granted the authority to license these activities to the FAA. In practice, the Secretary of Commerce is already responsible for authorizing nongovernmental remote sensing activities.[210] The ASCFEA would thus extend its existing authority to include the certification of emerging private commercial space activities like space mining and human spaceflight.[211]

The decision to grant the authority to the Secretary of Commerce rather than to the FAA raised a few eyebrows. For instance, Liu and Tronchetti highlight the fact that "[the OSC] does not have a level of expertise comparable to [the FAA] in dealing with activities occurring beyond Earth's orbit."[212] It "has no experience in addressing operations taking place on the Moon or other celestial bodies," whereas the FAA has already leveraged its authority to perform payload review and determination for envisioned private commercial missions to the Moon.[213] The relatively small size and budget of the OSC were equally underlined by commentators.[214]

---

204. *Id.*
205. This is the reason why Bigelow Aerospace entered reached out to the FAA for instance.
206. 2019 ASCFEA, *supra* note 200, 4.
207. *Id.*, 1.
208. The bill expressly refers to "the utilization of outer space and resources contained therein" but remains silent about other potential nontraditional activities that could fall within its scope. *See, e.g.*, 2019 ASCFEA, *supra* note 200.
209. *Id.*, §§80101 and 80102.
210. 51 U.S.C. 60121.
211. Latham & Watkins Aerospace, Defense & Government Services Industry Group, *House Passes Space Commerce Free Enterprise Bill to Increase US Support for Commercial Spaceflight, in* Client Alert Commentary (2018) available online.
212. Liu and Tronchetti, *supra* note 173 at 4.
213. *Id.*, at 4; FAA, *Moon Express Payload Review Determination* (2016)available online.
214. Smith, Marcia, *Draft Bill Would Give Commerce, Not FAA, "Mission Authorization" Function*, SpacePolicyOnline (2017) available online. Loren Grush, *House bill would regulate bold commercial space missions—but not very closely*, The Verge (2018), available online.

Although the OSC will not be operating entirely alone in this matter—it must engage in interagency consultation when reviewing applications for certification—ultimately, the authority to authorize, supervise, and place conditions leans exclusively on the Secretary of Commerce.[215] The OSC might accept or deny an application for certification of a nontraditional space activity based on the respect of the conditions and timetable set in the bill. For instance, the application must describe the proposed space activity and inform about the specifics of the space object used, indicate the launch provider, explain the debris mitigation plan, and inform about third-party liability insurance.[216] The applicant must also show proof that it is a US entity, meaning that they are an entity operating under the "jurisdiction and control" of the United States, and attest it complies with the Outer Space Treaty provisions on nuclear and mass destruction weapons.[217]

Upon reception, the OSC then has 90 days to review and approve or deny the issuance of a certification for the proposed activity.[218] Quite strikingly, the bill includes provisions which clearly restrict the OSC's competence to assess the suitability of the activity it must decide on. It provides in section 80103 (c) (3) (A) and (B) that the:

> Secretary shall presume, absent clear and convincing evidence to the contrary, that (A) any attestation made by an applicant pursuant to sub-section (a)(3) is sufficient to meet the international obligations of the United States pertaining to non-governmental entities of the United States under the Outer Space Treaty [...]

and that:

> (B) reasonably commercially available efforts are sufficient to be in conformity with [such] international obligations of the United States.

This provision is softened to an extent by the Secretary's competence to impose conditions necessary to ensure the activity complies with the Outer Space Treaty.[219] Nonetheless, it is clear that the OSC must interpret the Treaty in a practical fashion, that is—one that is favorable to the operator.[220]

Furthermore, to lessen the administrative burden on both the OSC and the space industry, the ASCFEA provides for automatic approval of the application in cases where the OSC does not act within the 90-day timeframe provided by the bill.[221]

It is difficult not to consider that Congress' approach to compliance with the Outer Space Treaty appears quite paradoxical. On the one hand, the intention behind

215. 2019 ASCFEA, *supra* note 200, §§80304 and 80305.
216. *Id.*, §80103.
217. *Id.* Art. IV of the Outer Space Treaty prohibits the placement or the carrying of nuclear weapons or weapons of mass destruction in outer space, as well as their use, including for testing purpose, on celestial bodies.
218. *Id.*, §80103 (b).
219. *Id.*, §80103 (c) (1) (A).
220. *Id.*, at 80103 (c) (1) (B) and (C). The Federal Government must interpret the Treaty "in a manner that minimizes regulations and limitations on the freedom [of US space operators]." Even more controversial, the ASCFEA states that not all the international obligations of the United States under the Outer Space Treaty shall be presumed as extending to nongovernmental entities. It further claims that "outer space shall not be considered a global common." *Id.*, §80309.
221. *Id.*, §80103 (b) (3).

the ASCFEA—and before the OSTP Letter—is to ensure that the US fully fulfills their international obligations, including the one hosted by Article VI of the Outer Space Treaty. Yet, on the other hand, the bill clearly attempts to shield private operators from those very same obligations. While the Treaty is binding upon States, not individuals, Article VI explicitly provides that States Parties bear international responsibility for "assuring that national activities are carried out in conformity with the provisions set forth in the present Treaty." As such, should a US space operator violate a provision of the Outer Space Treaty, the United States would be internationally responsible. Therefore, the US statement that "all obligations of the United States under the Outer Space Treaty [shall not be presumed to be] obligations to be imputed upon United States non-governmental entities"[222] is—to say the least—questionable.

In any event, since the ASCFEA has not yet been adopted by Congress, the determination of the competent authority to authorize, *inter alia*, space resource activities remains open. Indeed, the definition of an authorization and supervision framework for activities not presently licensed by other agencies remains a dynamic aspect of US space policy, one that undergoes continuous evolution, with regular proposals being submitted to US Congress. A recent example is the draft bill presented by the US National Space Council in November 2023, which proposes the division of authority for authorizing and overseeing novel activities between the US Department of Transportation and the US Department of Commerce.[223] The integration of the concept of "space sustainability" into this legislative proposal is particularly noteworthy; the concept was noticeably absent in the 2019 ASCFEA bill. It underscores how, in just a few years, space sustainability has become a key concern of the space sector.

The presence of such legislative proposals certainly represents an effort toward regulation. Even in the absence of a definitive authorizing framework, the US ensures that nontraditional space activities do not occur outside of a regulatory framework, with the FAA leveraging its authority—as the launching regulatory authority—to license missions beyond Earth orbit. However, the orientations of ASCFEA do indicate, if not a will, at least a temptation to lessen the administrative burden of space resource activities on private operators. Hence, there are legitimate concerns about environmental protection, which is usually one of the most neglected aspects when the emphasis is put on business flexibility. This is why the necessity to comply with international norms plays a particular role in balancing out the orientations of domestic law.

222. *Id.*, §80103 (c) (1) (C).
223. National Space Council, *Authorization and Supervision of Novel Private Sector Space Activities Act* (US) (2023) available online. Furthermore, on December 20, 2023, the Biden-Harris Administration announced the adoption of a new executive policy aiming to complement the National Space Council's legislative proposal. For instance, it requests the two departments in charge of authorizing novel space activities to "consider whether to require measures to protect the sustainable use of outer space in their regulations, to include the mitigation and remediation of orbital debris and consideration of impacts to the space operational environment." White House, *United States Novel Space Activities Authorization and Supervision Framework* (US) (2023) available online.

2.1.3 *Environmental Component*

The process of licensing space activities reflects the necessity to comply with Article VI of the Outer Space Treaty; it also serves indirectly another important purpose: to provide a basis to control environmental damage in outer space. It is not an uncommon approach. States often condition the issuance of a license to its compliance with certain environmental guidelines.[224] Generally, two main environmental issues are addressed: space debris mitigation and planetary protection. Incidentally, it can further be noted that the United States recently reiterated its commitment to "the safety intent of the [NPS] Principles" and called "Member States and international intergovernmental organizations that are considering the use of [NPS] to implement the joint Safety Framework developed in 2009."[225]

2.1.3.a *Space Debris Mitigation*

In a recent statement to the UNCOPUOS STC, the United States "call[ed] on all space-faring nations, emerging space nations, international organizations, and non-government organizations to implement the [UNCOPUOS SDM Guidelines] and the [LTS Guidelines] to limit the generation of orbital debris and preserve the near-Earth space environment."[226]

Beyond these entities, the United States emphasizes its belief that "the [SDM Guidelines] must apply to the full range of governmental and *private sector* space activities" [italics added].[227] This extract of the statement is to be understood with two important elements in mind: first, the SDM Guidelines are voluntary; thus, States are not obligated to comply with or implement them. Second, the United States' statement promotes the enforcement of the SDM Guidelines in the private sector. When read in the context of the debated ASCFEA—a bill which aims to, *inter alia*, shield the private sector from US international obligations—the statement is perplexing. On the one hand, the United States wants to soften international obligations resulting from the Outer Space Treaty to ease the burden on nongovernmental entities; on the other hand, it calls for hardening voluntary guidelines to make them legally binding upon the private sector. This paradox, however, can be explained by the same rationale which justifies nongovernmental entities not complying with the United States' international obligations: it is a matter of efficiency. Now, while it is true that some international obligations may appear to impede the development of the space industry, the SDM Guidelines have the opposite effect as they promote space sustainability and facilitate its progress by diminishing the risk of accidents in Earth orbit.

224. This is the case, for instance, of the Belgian Space Act and the Finnish Space Act analyzed *supra*.
225. US Mission UNVIE, *2022 COPUOS STSC–US on the Use of Nuclear Power Sources in Outer Space* (2022) available online.
226. US Mission UNVIE, *2022 COPUOS STSC–US on Space Debris* (2022) available online.
227. *Id.*

In practice, the United States commits space operators to space debris mitigation measures by making their application a requirement for the obtention of a license—or "certification" as it is called in the ASCFEA. Section 80104 of the bill makes the inclusion of a "space debris mitigation plan" a condition of eligibility for the space entity to obtain a certification. In accordance with the ASCFEA, "mitigation" entails preventing on-orbit breakups, removing spacecraft that have reached the end of their mission operation from orbit, and limiting the amount of debris released during the mission.[228] In order to guide space operators regarding the standard they will be held to during the review process, the ASCFEA requires they "take into account best practice guidelines promulgated by the United States and the Interagency Debris Coordinating Committee."[229] Furthermore, in order for the OSC to properly supervise the activities of authorized US nongovernmental entities—as required by the Outer Space Treaty—the authorized entity must report on its implementation of the plan. More precisely, the certified operator must inform the OSC before it begins implementing the disposal phase of the mitigation plan as well as update the authority on implementation results.[230] Most recently, the FCC took its first space debris enforcement action against a private entity for failing to properly dispose of its satellite. Indeed, on October 2, 2023, the Commission's Enforcement Bureau announced the results of its investigations into the American television provider DISH. It found that the company had not complied with the orbital debris mitigation plan it had filed regarding its EchoStar-7 satellite.[231] The plan, as approved by the FCC in 2012, provided that, at the end of its mission, the satellite would be retired at a disposal orbit approximately 300 kilometers above its operational geostationary arc rather than the 122 kilometers it achieved in February 2022. As a result, the television provided was fined USD 150,000 and had to agree to adhere to a compliance plan.

Moreover, on October 31, 2023, the US Senate unanimously passed the *Orbital Sustainability Act of 2023* (ORBITS Act).[232] A similar bill had already passed the Senate in 2022—the "ORBITS Act of 2022"—[233] but it was not taken up by the US House of Representatives before the end of the 117th session of the Congress; hence the re-introduction, in 2023, of a near identical bill. Both bills were introduced by US Senator John Hickenlooper who chaired, in July 2021, the Subcommittee on Space and Science on *Space Situational Awareness, Space Traffic Management, and Orbital Debris: Examining Solutions for Emerging Threats*.[234] The ORBITS Act aims to "establish a demonstration program for the active remediation of orbital debris and to require the development of uniform orbital debris standard practices in order to support a safe and sustainable orbital environment, and for other purposes."[235] The "first-of-its-kind

228. 2019 ASCFEA, §80101.
229. *Id.*, §80104 (a).
230. *Id.*, §80104 (b).
231. FCC, *In the Matter of DISH Operating L.L.C.*, Order, DA-23-888 (October 2, 2023) (US).
232. *ORBITS Act of 2023*, 118th Congress, S.447 (2023) (US) [ORBITS Act].
233. *Orbital Sustainability Act of 2022*, 117th Congress, S.4814 (2022) (US).
234. US Senate Committee on Commerce, Science, & Transportation, *Space Situational Awareness, Space Traffic Management, and Orbital Debris: Examining Solutions for Emerging Threats* (2021) available online.
235. ORBITS Act, *supra* 232.

program" contains provisions on, *inter alia*, the publication of a list of space debris which pose the greatest risk to the safety of orbiting spacecraft and on-orbit activities, as well as a demonstration program for remediating space debris through repurposing or removal from orbit.[236] The ORBITS Act further encourages the FAA and FCC to use the updated standards and practices as the basis for federal regulations applicable to all space activities. At this stage, the bill has yet to pass the US House of Representatives.

2.1.3.b The US Planetary Protection Policy

In addition to requiring an space debris mitigation plan in its licensing process, the United States also recently spent time reviewing its existing policy on planetary protection. To initiate this process, NASA convened a group of experts in 2019—the Planetary Protection Independent Review Board (PPIRB)—for the purpose of:

> assess[ing] how its Planetary Protection (PP) policies can be improved and streamlined, and how those policies should adapt to the entry of new planetary mission opportunities and new players, particularly in the private sector.[237]

In brief, the PPIRB concludes that the context in which we conduct planetary protection today is "profoundly and rapidly changing" due to the swift advancement of the private space sector in planetary mission capabilities.[238] It further notes that planetary protection requirements and implementation processes exhibit a "general lack of clarity," especially for "non-NASA missions."[239] For these reasons, the PPIRB recommends that NASA "reasses[s] its [planetary protection] guidelines at least twice per decade with an IRB-like body that includes representatives of all major stakeholder communities" and clarifies its planetary protection policy for private US space missions carried out with a degree of involvement from NASA.[240] Lastly, the PPIRB observes that, although NASA is not a regulatory agency, it is competent to determine the conditions of its participation in space activity. Thus, the Agency could make compliance with planetary protection rules a condition for its support in current and future space operations.[241]

These findings and recommendations of the PPIRB were implemented in the new NASA Procedural Requirements policy (NPR 8715.24) on *Planetary Protection Provisions for Robotic Extra-terrestrial Missions*.[242] The purpose of the policy is to clarify

236. *Id.*
237. NASA Planetary Protection Independent Review Board, Final Report to NASA/SMD, 3 (Oct. 2019), available online ["PPIRB"].
238. *Id.*, 8–10.
239. *Id.*
240. NASA may, for instance, get involved in private missions by providing the US entity resources like hardware, services, funding, deep-space communication, etc. *See, e.g.*, NASA, NPR 8715.24, 1.3.
241. PPIRB, *supra* note 237, 8–10.
242. NASA, NPR 8715.24. The new NPR became effective as of Sept. 24, 2021, and will remain in place until September 2026, at which time it will be reviewed and potentially revised based on the necessity to update planetary protection policies. The new NPR streams from the retired

practice by providing the industry with a sole document listing the planetary protection requirements for these missions and to define NASA's roles and responsibilities.[243]

NPR 8715.24 introduces risk-informed decision-making to balance different communities' needs.[244] It also describes how mission categories are based on current scientific consensus over the destination and mission operations and guided by COSPAR's PP policy.[245] Section 1.3 of the NASA policy explicitly addresses the issue of ensuring private entities' compliance with planetary protection requirements. First, the NPR identifies which partner is responsible for compliance; it states that, regardless of the partner's governmental or nongovernmental nature, the responsibility falls on the lead partner. Should the lead partner not be NASA,[246] it must then show compliance with Article IX of the Outer Space Treaty. For clarity purposes, the NPR emphasizes that applying COSPAR's PP policy meets the compliance threshold. Furthermore, the policy equally plans for cases where NASA's involvement is limited to providing resources to non-NASA robotic extraterrestrial missions. Then, the "recipient organization" must use "reasonable efforts to implement planetary protection measures" which are generally consistent with COSPAR or NASA's planetary protection measures.[247]

The NPR further defines key roles and responsibilities for executing the planetary protection policy. It creates four new positions at the Programmatic and Technical Authority level of NASA in the Office of Safety and Mission Assurance (OSMA).[248] The purpose of this restructuration is to merge planetary protection into the regular mission and project management structure rather than keep managing planetary protection as a separate discipline.[249]

NASA Policy Directive on Biological Contamination Control for Outbound and Inbound Planetary Spacecraft (NPD 8020.7G). NPR 8715.24 does not cover planetary protection for human missions; these are covered in a separate policy document. NID 8715.129. Nick Benardini, and Elaine Seasly, *Planetary Protection: NPR 8715.24 Update and Discussion* (2021), available online.

243. Before NPR 8715.24, practitioners had to refer to both the NPR 8020.12D of 2011 and the interim directive NID 8020.109A of 2017 to get an understanding of the planetary protection requirements for robotic extraterrestrial missions.
244. NPR 8715.24, 1.3. Risk-informed decision-making (RIDM) is defined in NPR 8000.4 and addresses informed selection of decision alternatives to assure effective approaches to achieving objectives. Notably, the process helps balance the needs of scientific discovery, space exploration, commercial activities, and safety. According to NASA Deputy Planetary Protection Officer Elaine Seasly, RIDM allows for more flexibility in the structure as opposed to having to establish prescriptive requirements. Benardini and Seasly, *supra* note 242.
245. *See* COSPAR PP policy, *supra* Chapter 3.
246. The determination of the lead entity is part of the negotiation process when establishing partnerships. NPR 8715.24, section 1.3.1.
247. NPR 8715.24, 1.3.2.
248. From an organizational standpoint, NASA separates the roles for Programmatic and Technical Authorities. At the programmatic level, the NPR sets up a Mission Directorate Associate Administrator (MDAA) who delivers the planetary protection categorization in concurrence with the Planetary Protection Officer (PPO). At the institutional level, the PPO now appears as part as the Office of Safety and Mission Assurance (SMA) technical authority. Its role is to concur on mission categorization proposals, advise projects on planetary protection approaches and oversee the implementation of planetary protection. *See* NPR 8715.25 Chapter 2, and Benardini and Seasly, *supra* note 242.
249. *Id.*

Regarding the actual procedural requirements and mission categorization, the process has vastly changed. The determination of the mission's planetary protection categorization is now developed by the project. The idea is that the project owns the eventual responsibility of implementing appropriate planetary protection.[250] The NPR intends to make the process more transparent for practitioners so that it can articulate mission-specific needs. Furthermore, the NPR focuses on streamlining the planetary protection documentation required for the project. In a nutshell, the level of documentation that the operator must provide increases proportionally to the level of risk of biological contamination, from only needing the concurrence of the Planetary Protection Officer (PPO) to needing the concurrence from the Chief of Safety and Mission Assurance, based on recommendations from the PPO.[251]

Ultimately, NPR 8715.15 reflects NASA's new approach to planetary protection: it aims to establish a flexible process able to easily adapt to space mission-specifics without overburdening the industry. It further takes into account the development of the space sector, from its new (private) participants to the technological and scientific advancements it generates. However, it must be noted that NPR 8715.15 is only the first step in NASA's review of its planetary protection policy documents, as evidenced by the fact that the new policy's validity is limited to five years. This is in line with the PPIRB's desire to see planetary protection policies reevaluated "at least twice per decade"[252] to ensure they remain up-to-date as new scientific inputs come into play.

Regarding space resource activities specifically, the level of planetary protection documentation required will depend on the targeted body, similar to the guidelines defined by COPSAR in its revised PP policy of 2021.[253]

2.1.4 Conclusion

Altogether, the adoption by the United States, in 2015, of a legal framework for space resource activities was a gamble. It had never been done before. As a result, Title IV of the CSLCA is primarily focused on establishing space mining as a legitimate activity within the US systems. The price for novelty, however, is a lack of clarity regarding procedural aspects, like the licensing regimes.

Eight years after its adoption, the United States has yet to decide on a strong authorization and supervision mechanism to support the activity. This is partially due to the nature of the American regulatory framework for space activities; it takes the form of a patchwork of laws and regulations which govern different aspects of different space activities. The consequence is that the State must now decide between integrating space resource activities into an existing procedural framework—as suggested by the OSTP—or creating a new, separate, regulatory framework, as anticipated by the

250. *Id.*, Chapter 3.
251. *Id.*, Chapter 3, table 3.1.
252. PPIRB, *supra* note 237, 8.
253. NPR 8715.24 includes in its appendix COSPAR's 2021 revised policy on planetary protection which sets different requirements depending on location of the activity on the Moon. *See supra* COSPAR's policy on the new subcategories under Category II.

ASCFEA. In the meantime, the authorization of nontraditional activities, like space resource activities, is handled by the FAA, which has proven capable of leveraging its competence to that end.

From an environmental perspective, the commitment of the United States to (environmental) nonlegally binding space law instruments is noteworthy. In this regard, the State issued two statements in 2022 encouraging the implementation of the NPS Principles and of the SDM Guidelines and took its first space debris enforcement action against a private entity in 2023. It can also be observed that the ASCFEA makes space debris mitigation measures a requirement for the obtention of authorization to conduct a space activity. Moreover, the bill intends to create a Private Space Activity Advisory Committee that will oversee, *inter alia*, the "review[ing][of] existing best practices for United States entities to avoid the harmful contamination of the Moon and other celestial bodies."[254] Similar efforts have also been undertaken by NASA with regard to its planetary protection policy. So far, the planetary protection policy devised for space mining activities is aligned with COSPAR's own policy and thus, articulated around a target body/mission type combination to determine the level of documentation. Since NASA's policies are currently under review, it is not excluded that the Agency may adopt more specific rules for this purpose.

Overall, the US regulatory framework is conducive to sustainable space (resources) activities. It clearly integrates the environmental dimension of sustainability and seeks to implement the most up-to-date best practices. Furthermore, the review of nonbinding instruments in Chapter 3 *supra* shows that the United States is at the forefront of the development of (environmentally) sustainable practices. In particular, the State was actively involved in the setup of COSPAR, and its space agency was one of the four founding members of the IADC.

Ultimately, the United States' commitment to the long-term sustainability of space (resources) activities can be summarized by reference to the *Artemis Accords*.[255] The multilateral document constitutes a political commitment toward certain "Principles for Cooperation in The Civil Exploration and Use of The Moon, Mars, Comets, and Asteroids for Peaceful Purposes."[256] The Accords builds upon the legacy of the US Apollo program and aims to operationalize the Outer Space Treaty in view of returning humans to the Moon.[257] Specifically, the *Artemis Accords* directly addresses space resource activities, providing that they should be executed "in support of safe and sustainable space activities."[258] The document further commits its Signatories[259] to conduct space activities with "due consideration to the United Nations [LTS Guidelines] adopted bythe COPUOS in 2019, with appropriate changes to reflect the nature of

254. 2019 ASCFEA, §80109(e)(5).
255. Artemis Accords: Principles for Cooperation in the Civil Exploration and Use of the Moon, Mars, Comets, and Asteroids for Peaceful Purposes (2020).
256. *Id.*, section 1.
257. *Id.*, preamble, and section 1.
258. *Id.*, section 10.
259. As of December 13, 2022, the Artemis Accords have 23 signatories, office of the Spokesperson, US Department of State, *Nigeria and Rwanda: First African Nations Sign the Artemis Accords* (2022), available online.

operations beyond low-Earth orbit."[260] Incidentally, on December 11, 2022, NASA successfully completed its first mission within the Artemis program—i.e., Artemis 1—with the safe return to Earth of the Orion spacecraft after a flyby around the Moon.[261]

Lastly, the outreach of Title IV of the CSLCA deserves to be briefly addressed. Indeed, it must be underlined that the adoption of the 2015 Law by the United States spurred a series of discussions about space resource activities at the highest levels. After several years of discussions on the subject, the UNCOPUOS LSC ultimately agreed, in 2021, on the establishment of a *Working Group on Legal Aspects of Space Resource Activities*[262] ("SR Working Group").[263] In essence, the SR Working Group is tasked, *inter alia*, with collecting relevant information regarding space resource activities—e.g., scientific and technological developments—studying the existing legal framework provided, *inter alia*, by the Outer Space Treaty and assessing the benefits of adopting additional international governance instruments.[264] Finally, as will be shown *infra*, the United States' gamble prompted three other States to adopt their own regulatory framework for space resource activities.

2.2 Luxembourg[265]

It was a surprise when Luxembourg became, in 2017, the second State in the world—and first in Europe—to enact a law governing private space resource activities carried out under its jurisdiction. The government's decision was all the more unexpected since Luxembourg had not passed legislation regulating private space-related activities since the early 1990s.[266] The intention to develop "a series of measures to position Luxembourg as a European hub in the exploration and use of

260. Artemis Accords, section 11.
261. NASA, *Artemis I—Flight Day 26: Orion splashes down, concluding historic Artemis I mission—Artemis* (2022), available online.
262. Although the subcommittee agreed to the establishment of a working group on space resource activities in 2021, its official title was only agreed upon in 2022. Report of the Chair and Vice-Chair of the Working Group established under the Legal Subcommittee agenda item entitled "General exchange of views on potential legal models for activities in the exploration, exploitation and utilization of space resources," UNCOPUOS LSC, 61st Sess., at 1 and 5, UN Doc. A/AC.105/C.2/2022/SRA/L.1 (2022).
263. Report of the Legal Subcommittee on its sixtieth session, held in Vienna from May 31 to June 11, 2021, UNCOPUOS, 64th Sess., at 30–33, UN Doc. A/AC.105/1243 (2021).
264. *See* Mandate of the SR Working Group *in* Report of the Committee on the Peaceful Uses of Outer Space, UNGAOR, 76th Sess., Supp. 20, at Annex III, §3, UN Doc. A/76/20 (2021).
265. This section is based on the previous published work by the author. *See* Leterre, *supra* note 142; M. Hofmann et al., The Space Legislation of Luxembourg: A Commentary (2022).
266. Luxembourg adopted a law in 1991 to regulate the use of Luxembourgish electronic media. It provided, *inter alia*, for a framework for the State to authorize SES telecommunication satellites, the main space operator in Luxembourg. Loi du 27 juillet 1991 sur les médias électroniques, modifiée par Loi du 2 avril 2001, Mémorial A No 88, 1er août 2001, Art. 1 (1991 Electronic Media Law); Chambre des Députés, Commission de l'Economie, Procès-verbal de la réunion du 11 mai 2017; Mahulena Hofmann, *Entered into force: The 2020 Space Law of Luxembourg*, 46 Air and Space Law, 588 (2021) DOI: 10.54648/aila2021033.

space resources" was announced in February 2016;[267] it came to reality on August 1, 2017, with the entry into force of the *Law of July 20th 2017 on the exploration and use of space resources* (SRL).[268]

The SRL has two primary goals: first, it aims to develop a legal and regulatory framework establishing the right for private operators to own space resources, thus, giving operators legal security on the matter.[269] Second, it lays down the regulations for an authorization and supervision process for said activities.[270]

In this sense, the SRL differs from the law adopted by the United States in 2015. It operates a shift from the question of the legality of appropriation to the question of authorization and supervision of the activity.[271] This is especially apparent from the structure of the Law. Out of 18 provisions, only 1 briefly addresses the appropriability of space resources, whereas a set of 10 provisions builds the administrative framework for operators to obtain the required authorization. The remaining 7 provisions concern issues of liability and insurance,[272] the supervision of activities,[273] the withdrawal of authorization,[274] other authorizations operators may require,[275] and sanctions.[276]

Notwithstanding its limitation to a single article, the assertion that space resources can be appropriated should not be undervalued. To a large extent, Article 1 operates as the most important provision of the SRL. Indeed, the entire regime of authorization is based on the prior recognition that space resources can legally be owned.[277] Interestingly, the wording of Article 1 originally included an express

267. GOUVERNEMENT.LU, Luxembourg to launch framework to support the future use of space resources (2016), available online.
268. Loi du 20 juillet 2017 sur l'exploration et l'utilisation des ressources de l'espace, *supra* note 15 [SRL].
269. Projet de loi sur l'exploration et l'utilisation des ressources de l'espace, Saisine du Conseil d'Etat, 15 novembre 2016, p. 2 ["2016 Draft Law"]. In an interview, Luxembourg's Former Deputy Prime Minister Etienne Schneider emphasized the "extrem[e] importance" to have a legal framework to govern private space resource activities on the country. Not only does it establish a legal basis for operators to conduct their activity but it also further provides investors and companies with legal security. SpaceResources Initiative, *Etienne Schneider about the legal and regulatory framework of the SpaceResources.lu initiative*, YOUTUBE (2017), available online.
270. The rules developed by the government regarding the authorization and the supervision of space resource activities were inspired by those applicable to the financial sector. 2016 Draft Law, p. 2. On the rules applicable to the financial sector, *see* Loi du 5 avril 1993 relative au secteur financier telle qu'elle a été modifiée, Mémorial A, No 27, 10 avril 1993 (LU).
271. Leterre, *supra* note 147 at 48.
272. SRL *supra* note 15, Arts. 10 and 16.
273. *Id.*, Art. 15.
274. *Id.*, Art. 14.
275. *Id.*, Art. 17. In particular, operators may have to seek a license under Art. 20 of the Electronic Media Law if they intend to use frequencies allocated to Luxembourg during their space resource activity. M. HOFMANN ET AL., THE SPACE LEGISLATION OF LUXEMBOURG: A COMMENTARY 17–18, 80 (2022).
276. *Id.*, Art. 18. For a comprehensive analysis of the abovementioned provisions, *see* HOFMANN ET AL., *supra* note 14.
277. In this regard, the parliamentary Commission of Economy considered that the unequivocal recognition of the appropriability of space resources was "the very key" to establishing the legal framework. Chambre des Députés, Commission de l'Economie, Amendements parlementaires (May 24, 2017), p. 2.

reference to international law which was removed in later drafts;[278] the Conseil d'État having judged the inclusion superfluous.[279]

As a result, Article 1 SRL makes a rather blunt statement. It reads: "space resources are capable of being appropriated." The utilization of the term "appropriated"—"appropriation" in the original language—is noteworthy. It mirrors the wording of Article II of the Outer Space Treaty which affirms that "outer space [...] is not subject to national appropriation."[280] In comparison, both the American CSLCA and the Emirati Law of 2019 discussed *infra* carefully avoided the expression. Rather, they refer to words reflecting property rights, like the acquisition, possession, ownership, purchase, sale, etc.[281]

It is thus apparent that, for Luxembourg, the question of the appropriation of space resources is not an issue; the clarification in Article 1 of the Law has less to do with affirming an opinion and more to do with providing interested parties with an unambiguous regulatory framework.[282]

Therefore, the section first looks at the scope of the law (2.2.1) before evaluating the authorization regime it establishes (2.2.2). Last, the section reflects on the absence of an environmental component in the Luxembourgish regulatory framework developed for space resource activities (2.2.3).

2.2.1 Scope of the Law

Pursuant to Article 3, the SRL applies to activities related to the "exploration and use of space resources for commercial purposes" only. *A contrario*, the Law excludes from its scope space resource activities carried out for scientific or fully "private" purposes.[283] In other words, the legal framework developed by Luxembourg only applies to "business activities."[284]

In addition, Article 2 paragraph 4 explicitly excludes from the material scope of the law satellite communication, orbital positions, and use of frequency bands. Indeed, these activities are already covered by the 1991 Law on Electronic Media ("1991

278. The provision originally read "space resources are capable of being appropriated *in accordance with international law* [emphasis added]." Draft Law of 2016, Art. 1.
279. In its Opinion of Apr. 7, 2017, the Conseil d'Etat argues that, in the absence of "an international normative framework" regulating space resource activities, the reference to international law "removed all value" to the provision since international law is hierarchically superior to domestic law. Consequently, the State cannot alone interpret international law. Avis du Conseil d'État (Apr. 7, 2017), pp. 6–8. However, Salmeri argues that "fundamental norms of both international space law and general international law would have called for the opposite decision" of the Conseil d'Etat. Antonino Salmeri, *The Multi-Level System of Space Mining: Regulatory Aspects and Enforcement Options*, July 7, 2022.
280. Outer Space Treaty, Art. II.
281. CSLCA, *supra* note 144, §51303; Emirati law of 2019, *infra* 318, Art. 18 §1.
282. Leterre, *supra* note 147 at 48.
283. In practice, this would exclude, for instance, sample-return missions used to further scientific research. Also *see* Hofmann et al., *supra* note 14 at 21–24.
284. 2016 Draft Law, p. 7. This was further confirmed by the government, *see* Chambre des Députés, Commission de l'Economie, Procès-verbal de la réunion du 11 mai 2017, p. 8, accessible online.

Luxembourgish Law").[285] Thus, if an operator plans to use frequencies allocated to Luxembourg during the course of their space resource mission, they will have to apply for a concession under Article 20 of the 1991 Luxembourgish Law.

With regard to the personal and territorial scopes of the SRL, Article 4 determines that only companies—by opposition to individuals—can be granted mission authorization. This is a notable difference from the American law which considers first individuals with American citizenship. Luxembourg is not attached to the companies being owned by Luxembourgish citizens. Rather, Article 4 refers to two conditions for its applicability: the nature of the company and its presence on Luxembourg's territory. Here, the priority is to ensure the operator applying for authorization under the SRL effectively falls under the jurisdiction of the Grand Duchy of Luxembourg.[286] Accordingly, companies taking the form of a *société anonyme* or a *société en commandite par action*, or a *société à responsablité limité*[287] under Luxembourgish Law—or a *société européenne* with a registered office in Luxembourg—can be granted a mission authorization by the government. Consequently, Article 4 provides normative support to the government's objective to make Luxembourg Europe's space resource hub. On the one hand, it allows foreign companies to seek authorization under the favorable regulatory framework of the State, while, on the other, it ensures their foreign nature does not dispense them to comply with Luxembourg law and international obligations.[288]

2.2.2 Authorization Mechanism

As if to emphasize the necessity of an authorization regime, the SRL bases its mechanism on the provision of Article 2, hence, directly after having established a right to own space resources. The provision comes before even the scope of the law. It states that:

> [n]o person can explore or use space resources without holding a written authorization from the minister or ministers in charge of the economy and space activities.

Accordingly, the company—since the SRL does not apply to individuals—must seek authorization from the administration prior to the start of their activity. This authorization must be in written form. The precision may appear superfluous as authorizations are often conceived as written documents. However, it must be underscored that Article VI of the Outer Space Treaty—which contains States Parties' obligation to authorize private space activities—remains silent on the form of the authorization. Consequently, verbal authorization could have been a valid possibility.

285. 1991 Electronic Media Law, *supra* note 266.
286. HOFMANN ET AL., *supra* note 14 at 26.
287. *Trans*. Public company limited by shares, corporate partnership limited by shares and private limited liability company. Here, the author uses the translation of the SRL provided by the government of Luxembourg.
288. Under the framework of the SRL, operators are required to ensure their activities comply with Luxembourg's international obligations. *See infra*.

Similarly, the operator should submit a written application to the minister for the purpose of obtaining authorization.

The operator must further ensure that the authorized activity respects "the conditions of the authorization and the international obligations of Luxembourg."[289] The provision refers notably to the respect of Luxembourg's obligations under the UN Space Treaties.[290] Article 2 paragraph 3 also introduced the term "operator" in the SRL, though no definition is provided. However, it can be implied—by reference to the second national space legislation adopted by Luxembourg in 2020—that the term means "any person who, on [their] own behalf, carries out or undertakes any space activity, alone or jointly with others."[291] This definition is in line with Article 2 paragraph 2 which excludes the possibility for a "person" to seek authorization "through another person or as an intermediary." In the same line, Article 5 further clarifies that the authorization delivered is "personal and non-assignable." Thus, it is impossible for an operator to sell their authorization to a third party. This is understandable considering that the authorization review process attaches as much importance to the operator carrying out the activity as it does to the planned activity itself.[292]

In practice, Article 6 of the SRL requires operators to provide a mission program in addition to "all such information as may be useful for the assessment of [the authorization application]." The specific details of the authorization requirements are further laid down in Articles 7 to 13 of the Law. Accordingly, the operator must show proof that their central administration and office are in Luxembourg.[293] They must further demonstrate the existence of a "robust scheme of financial, technical and statutory procedures" to support the planning and the operation of the authorization activity.[294]

Additionally, the structural organization of the operating entity must also have "effective processes" in place "to identify, manage, monitor and report" risks it may be exposed to during the mission.[295] Risk management is particularly emphasized throughout the SRL in recognition of the hazardous nature of (new) space activities. Thus, in addition to processes, the authorization regime also requires applying operators to give evidence of sufficient financial means to cover these risks. The financial coverage can be proved either by "personal financial means" or by external means, such as insurance.[296]

Moreover, as the SRL aims to ensure the "sound and prudent" conduct of the authorized space resource activities, it also pays particular attention to the character of the operator.[297] As such, the identity of the main shareholders must be communicated

289. SRL, Art. 2 §3.
290. As of January 2022, Luxembourg is a Signing Party to three of the five UN Space Treaties: the Outer Space Treaty, the Liability Convention, and the Registration Convention. Luxembourg is also working on becoming a Party to the Return and Rescue Agreement.
291. 2020 Law on space activities, *supra* note 15.
292. Leterre, *supra* note 147 at 49.
293. SRL, Art. 7.
294. *Id.*
295. *Id.*
296. *Id.*, Art. 10.
297. *Id.*, Art. 8.

in the application for authorization.[298] To that end, the minister in charge of delivering the authorization must assess, *inter alia*, the good repute of the operator and shareholders, as well as their knowledge, skills and experience in the field.[299]

The authorization may further include conditions on the planned activity itself, such as which activities will be carried out on Luxembourgish territory, the definition of potential limits to the activity, modalities regarding its supervision, and conditions aiming to ensure the operator's compliance with their obligations.[300]

Lastly, the SRL identifies the minister in charge of delivering the authorization as the authority in charge to oversee the continuous supervision of the authorized activity.[301] Said minister shall further determine the amount of the fee covering the administrative expenses incurred; it could range from EUR 5,000 to EUR 500,000.[302]

2.2.3 Environmental Component

From an environmental standpoint, the SRL is the least advanced—not to say, lacking—compared to comparable domestic legislations governing space resource activities. The words "environment," "debris" and "sustainability" are not mentioned once. Nor is there a reference to international standards.

However, according to Schiltz, not everything is lost.[303] Indeed, the second space legislation adopted by the State, in 2020, makes a direct reference to the environment; it provides that the term "damage" includes "environmental damage."[304] Although the Luxembourgish Law of 2020 explicitly excludes space resource activities from its scope,[305] Schiltz remains "firmly convinced" that the SRL framework developed in 2017 would encompass environmental damage as well.[306] The emphasis, during the drafting phase, on aligning the general Law of 2020 on the SRL would support this argument.[307] Furthermore, Schiltz notes that the lack of inclusion of the environmental

298. *Id.*
299. *Id.*
300. *Id.*, Art. 12.
301. *Id.*, Art. 15.
302. *Id.*, Art. 13.
303. Schiltz, Jean-Louis, *Preserving Space Environment—Law & Regulations, in* Space Resources Week 2022 (ESRIC, 2022) available online.
304. 2020 Law on space activities, *supra* note 15, Art. 2§3.
305. The 2020 Law on space activities applies to activities falling under the jurisdiction of the Grand Duchy of Luxembourg, with the exception of activities governed by the SRL, i.e., space resource activities. *Id.*, Art. 1§2.
306. Schiltz argues that the potential harmful impact of space activities is indirectly addressed in the authorization procedure of Luxembourg's regulatory framework. Notably, in addition to the inclusion of "environmental damage" in the 2020 Law on space activities, both legislations contain references to the notion of "risks" and the necessity to guarantee a "sound and prudent operation" of the space activity. *Id.*, Art. 6; SRL, Art. 8; Jean-Louis Schiltz, *Preserving Space Environment—Law & Regulations* (2022), https://www.youtube.com/watch?v=FH88-MR1uOg&list=PLNUvZweBqVAT5g9KCcsuhKR9zVDmlGaq7&index=9 (last visited January 2024).
307. During the drafting phase of the 2020 Law on space activities, the Conseil d'État noted on several occasions that the draft law was diverging from the regulatory framework established under the Law of 2014. It further emphasized the need to harmonize the two legislations in

damage in the SRL could be a simple case of being "smarter" the second time around.[308]

Yet, the sole inclusion of a reference to "environmental damage" may be too thin to claim that Luxembourg's regulatory framework for space (resources) activities supports the protection of the outer space environment. As underlined by Hofmann, the extent to which "environmental damage" applies to the outer space environment and encompasses the creation of space debris is unclear.[309] Furthermore, the Luxembourgish government did attempt during the drafting of the Law of 2020 to include a more advanced environmental provision in the text but ultimately renounced it.

Indeed, originally, Article 4 of the Law read:[310]

> [a]n operator shall adopt necessary measures to limit the harmful degradation of the terrestrial and extra-terrestrial environments or their contamination as well as space debris risks.[311]

The provision was particularly welcomed by the Chamber of Commerce and Conseil d'État, both emphasizing the importance of sustainability in space and environmental protection.[312] However, the Conseil d'État also noted the wording of the provision raised several issues, notably regarding the nature of the obligation created.[313] Ultimately, the Commission of Economy concluded that the comments received by the administrative authority would strip the provision of its value. Additionally, it underlined the fact that no equivalent to the proposed article existed in the SRL and, thus, decided to adopt a provision on liability similar to the one applicable to space resource activities.[314]

From the outset, the backtracking of the Luxembourgish government on the matter of a strong environmental provision can be interpreted as a missed opportunity. However, while it is undoubtedly a loss from an environmental standpoint, it could still be leveraged when interpreting the notion of "environmental damage." Accordingly, operators could be held liable under the Law of 2020—and *a fortiori* under the 2017

order to ease the burden of procedure on operators, especially in cases where an operator would seek an authorization under both legislations. For example, HOFMANN ET AL., *supra* note 14 at xiv, 95,159–162.

308. Schiltz, *supra* note 304.

309. Hofmann, *supra* note 264 at 597; *see also* P. J. Blount, *Article 2 Definitions, in* SPACE LEGISLATION OF LUXEMBOURG: A COMMENTARY 97 (2022).

310. On the evolution of the drafting history and value of the provision, *see* Gabrielle Leterre, *Article 4 Liability for Damage, in* SPACE LEGISLATION OF LUXEMBOURG: A COMMENTARY 109 (2022).

311. Projet de loi sur les activités spatiales et portant modification de la loi modifiée du 9 juillet 1937 sur l'impôt sur les assurances, Parliamentary document. No. 7317 (May 19, 2018).

312. Avis de la Chambre de Commerce (Nov. 19, 2018) 7; Avis du Conseil d'État (Feb. 15, 2019) 3.

313. The Conseil d'Etat regretted, *inter alia*, the vague phrasing of the provision and underlined the fact that, since all space activities have an environmental impact, the obligation to take measures was an obligation of means, not results. As a compromise, the administrative authority suggested making reference to the environment in the definition of damage. Avis du Conseil d'État (Feb. 15, 2019) 3. Leterre, *supra* note 308 at 4.

314. Rapport de la Commission de l'Economie, de la Protection des Consommateurs et de l'Espace (December 2, 2020) 4–5.

SRL—for the "harmful degradation of the terrestrial and extra-terrestrial environments,"[315] including planetary contamination and the production of space debris.

With regard to planetary protection and space debris, it can be observed that Luxembourg is not represented in COPSAR.[316] It is however a member of the UNCOPUOS and ISO,[317] both of which have contributed guidelines on the mitigation of space debris.

2.2.4 Conclusion

Altogether, Luxembourg makes a valid effort to provide operators with a regulatory framework for space resource activities. While supplementary regulations are in the process of being drafted, the SRL already lists detailed conditions for the obtention of authorization. It further determines the authority in charge of supervising the progress of the authorized activity. From this perspective, the SRL is not devoid of concerns regarding environmental protection. It appears more advanced than the framework developed by the United States, where the debate over the allocation of responsibilities is not yet closed.

However, it must be underlined that the SRL only addresses administrative aspects of carrying out space resource activities. Other crucial aspects are left asides such as the protection and long-term sustainability of outer space. There is also no provision on the practical aspects of the mission, such as its length or perimeter. Evidently, this is partially due to a general lack of knowledge regarding practical aspects of space resource activities; technology, for instance, is still being developed. Yet, from an environmental perspective, it can be noted that other national legislations—like Belgium and Finland—have not waited for activities to start laying down environmental requirements. Thus, in the absence of comparable requirements, the Luxembourgish regulatory framework for space resource activities does not currently meet the sustainability criteria outlined by the conceptual framework.

Nonetheless, it can be observed that, since the adoption of the SRL in 2017, Luxembourg's position on sustainability has evolved; the subject is now at the core of the State's Space Strategy for 2023–2027.[318] In particular, when presenting its Strategy to the public in December 2022, Luxembourg highlighted four main priorities, including the sustainable use of space resources.

315. *See* original wording of Art. 4 of the Law on space activities, *supra* note 311.
316. As of 2022, no Luxembourgish national scientific institution is a member of COSPAR. COSPAR, *Members* (2022) available online.
317. Luxembourg became a member of COPUOS in 2014. GA res. 69/85, UNGAOR, 69th Sess., §32UN Doc. A/RES/69/85 (2014). Luxembourg is also represented in ISO, through the membership of the Institut Luxembourgeois de la Normalisation, de l'Accréditation, de la Sécurité (ILNAS).
318. Luxembourg's Space Strategy is articulated around four main priorities: (1) economic sustainability, (2) sustainability on Earth, (3) sustainability in Space, and (4) the sustainable use of space resources. LSA, STRATÉGE SPATIALE 2023–2027 (2022).

2.3 United Arab Emirates

On December 19, 2019, the United Arab Emirates (UAE) became the third country in the world—and first in the Arabic and Islamic world—to adopt a regulatory framework for space resource activities. The Federal Law "on the regulation of the space sector" of 2019[319] ("Emirati Law of 2019") distinguishes itself from its US and Luxembourgish equivalents by its broad scope. Indeed, it intends to regulate all activities of the UAE's space sector.[320] With its nine chapters and 54 articles, the law aims at "stimulating investment and encouraging private and academic sector participation in the Space Sector" and "to support the implementation of the necessary safety, security, and environmental measures to enhance the long-term stability and sustainability [of space activities]."[321] In comparison, US Title IV of the CSLCA and the 2017 Luxembourgish SRL both have a narrower scope, focusing solely on regulating space resource activities.

Beyond regulating a wide range of space activities, the Emirati Law of 2019 further discusses, *inter alia*, the role and competencies of the United Arab Emirates' Space Agency ("UAE Agency"),[322] the process to obtain a permit to carry out space activities, space debris mitigation, the liability and compensation regime for operators,[323] the registration of space objects[324] and meteorites[325] and sanctions.[326]

Accordingly, whereas subsection 2.3.1 focuses on the scope of the law, subsection 2.3.2 outlines the authorization process for space activities carried out under the Federal Law of 2019. Last, subsection 2.3.3 discusses the UAE's approach to sustainability in space.

319. Federal Law No. (12) of 2019, issued on 19/12/2019 on the regulation of the space sector (2019) (UAE), translation available online ["Emirati law of 2019"].
320. *See* Emirati law of 2019, *supra* 319, Art. 4 and especially 4§(2)(e).
321. *Id.*, Art. 2.
322. The Emirati Law of 2019 abrogates the Federal Decree-Law No. 1 of 2014 on the Establishment of the Emirates Space Agency and effectively replaces it with Chapter 2 of the new law. The Agency is a federal public authority which "enjoys an independent legal personality, a financial and administrative independence, and the legal capacity necessary [to achieve its goals and objectives]." In addition to authorizing and monitoring space activities under this law, the Agency oversees developing the State's space policies and strategies.
323. The Emirati Law of 2019 distinguishes between different situations in which liability issues may arise. Specifically, it makes a distinction between liability between contracting parties (Art. 20), liability "towards others" (Art. 21), liability in case of collision with another space object (Art. 22) and liability "in other cases" (Art. 23). These provisions clarify to which extent the operator and the State are liable for a damage resulting from the operator's activity. The law further recognizes the right of the United Arab Emirates to turn back to the operator for compensation in cases where the international liability of the State was engaged because of the authorized operator's activity (Art. 26).
324. Article 31 of the Emirati Law of 2019 implements in the national legal (federal) order of the United Arab Emirates the provisions of the UN Registration Convention.
325. The Emirati Law of 2019 discusses, in Art. 30, the establishment of a "special register" for meteorite. It also establishes that, depending on where a meteorite falls, it will belong either to the United Arab Emirates or a specific Emirate. Art. 30 further prohibits selling, buying, or transporting meteorites without proper authorization from governmental entities.
326. The administrative sanctions and penalties are stated in Chapter 8 of the Emirati Law of 2019. They include different periods of imprisonment and fines depending on the nature of the offense.

2.3.1 *Scope of the Law*

From the outset, the Emirati Law of 2019 appears to closely follow the emergence and development of new space ventures. In addition to applying to traditional space activities such as launches and satellite communications, the scope of the law also encompasses, *inter alia*, space mining, manned spaceflights, and high-altitude activities.[327] *In fine*, the Emirati Law of 2019 aims "to adhere to international treaties, and be clear, transparent, and flexible,"[328] notably by openly implementing its international obligations under the space treaties the United Arab Emirates has ratified.[329] Its flexibility is particularly reflected in Article 4 paragraphs 1 (o) and 2 (e) which provides that "[the law regulates] any other space activities" as well as "[a]ny other Space Sector-related activities" determined by a Cabinet decision, the "space sector" being "[t]he sector that includes all activities, projects and programs related to Outer Space."[330] These paragraphs supplement over 20[331] additional space-related activities listed in Article 4 and open the way for the Cabinet to apply the law to new activities as they emerge.

With regard to space resource activities specifically, the Law defines "space resources" as a "non-living resourc[e] present in outer space, including minerals and water."[332] Hence, the definition is in line with the one adopted in 2015 by the United States.[333] However, a novelty is a distinction made in the Emirati Law of 2019 between "Space Resources exploration or extraction activities" and "[a]ctivities for the exploitation and use of Space Resources for scientific, commercial or other purposes."[334] This distinction is based on the type of activity planned—exploration/extraction versus exploitation/utilization—rather than a, perhaps more expected, distinction based on the nature of the activity, i.e., scientific as opposed to commercial operations. The fact that Article 18 of the Law—which is titled "Exploration, Exploitation and Use of Space Resources"—does not retain this distinction when outlining the permit process for space mining activities is noteworthy.

Indeed, Article 18 expands on various aspects of carrying out space resource activities in paragraph 1, referring to the "exploration, exploitation and use of Space Resources, including their acquisition, purchase, sale, trade, transportation, storage

327. *Id.*, Art. 4.
328. Nour Salman, *UAE Space Law details announced to facilitate space sector development*, Emirates News Agency (2020), available online.
329. Emirati law of 2019, *supra* 319, Art. 2 (3). To date, the UAE is Party to the Outer Space Treaty, the Liability Convention, the Registration Convention and, more recently, the Rescue Agreement.
330. *Id.*, Art. 1.
331. Pursuant to Art. 4, the Emirati Law of 2019 applies, *inter alia*, to launch, reentry, removing or disposing of a space object from the orbit, operating the launch sites or reentry, satellite communication activities, space navigation, remote sensing, earth observation, space awareness activities, space resource exploration and exploitation activities, as well as space-supporting flights and high-altitude activities.
332. *Id.*, Art. 1 "space resource."
333. The CSLCA defines a space resource as "an abiotic resource *in situ* in outer space," "include-[ing] water and minerals." CSLCA, *supra* note 144, §51301.
334. Emirati law of 2019, *supra* 319, Art. 4 §§(1) (i) and (j).

and any Space Activities aimed at providing logistical services in this regard." In comparison to US Title IV, the Emirati Law of 2019 is not solely concerned with establishing the right to appropriate space resources. Where Title VI referred to "possess[ing], own[ing], transport[ing], use[ing], and sell[ing]" space resources, the UAE adopts a broader approach. This is because the State does not need to affirm that space resources can be appropriated; the United States and Luxembourg already did the legwork on that end. Thus, the State is more interested in integrating in its framework activities pertaining to space resource exploration, utilization, and exploitation.

More broadly, the Law of 2019 further applies to "space sector" related activities. Materially, it means that the law applies to activities "that target the Specified Area, including its discovery, making an impact thereon, using, or utilising it [...]" and to "activities, projects and programs related to Outer Space."

Interestingly, the law distinguishes the "specified area"—that is "any area above eighty kilometers or more than the average sea level" which refers to the lower estimation of the Karman line[335]—from "outer space," even though the Karman line is traditionally used to delimit outer space. According to Article 1, "outer space" means "[t]he area above the Earth's atmosphere." Why the distinction then? The term "specified area" is only used in Article 1 which defines terms of the law. Ultimately, it serves the qualification of various "space" activities. For instance, a "suborbital flight" involves a spaceflight which intends "to enter the Specified Area without the intention of completing an orbit around the Earth." High-altitude flights, however, refer to "activities that are above the range of air traffic control and lower than the Specified Area." In turn, this distinction between activities allows the UAE to implement different requirements during the licensing process.[336]

From a jurisdictional standpoint, the scope of the Emirati Law of 2019 is both territorial and personal. First, it applies to space activities carried out on the UAE's territory, be it on "lands, territorial sea, and airspace above it, including free zones or any areas of a special economic status."[337] The (quasi-)territorial scope of the law is further extended to "State's establishments outside [its] territory" and to activities carried out from State-registered "ships or aircraft [or] space object."[338]

The extensive definition in the law of what constitutes the "State's territory" directly contributes to the UAE's wish for transparency in the implementation of the UN Space Treaties' provision. Pursuant to Article VII of the Outer Space Treaty, the launching State is internationally liable for damage caused to another State Party. The term "launching State" includes the State "from whose territory or facility an object is

335. Originally, the Karman line—which theoretically delimits outer space from Earth—was determined at roughly 80 kilometers above sea levels. Nowadays, the "imaginary boundary" is set at a hundred kilometers from sea levels. Nadia Drake, *Where, Exactly, Is the Edge of Space? It Depends on Who You Ask*, National Geographic (2018), available online.

336. For instance, suborbital flights are regulated under the same provision as manned flights, whereas high-altitude flights under the same provision as space-supporting flights activities. Emirati Law of 2019, *supra* 319, Arts. 16 and 29.

337. *Id.*, Art. 1 definition of "State's Territory."

338. *Id.*, Art. 3 (1) and (2).

launched."[339] Therefore, by explicitly defining what carrying out space activities from its territory means, the UAE ensures it has legal control over activities that could engage its liability.

Second, the personal scope of the Emirati Law of 2019 extends to space activities carried out by "persons who hold the nationality of the State, or companies that have a headquarters in the State."[340] Similarly to US Title IV and the Luxembourgish SRL, the Emirati Law of 2019 allows foreign companies to operate under its regulatory regime under the condition that the legal entity has its headquarters in the United Arab Emirates.

2.3.2 Authorization Mechanism

Although not as detailed as the Luxembourgish SRL, the Emirati Law of 2019 implements in Article 14 a general obligation to obtain a "permit" from the UAE Agency in order to "own a Space Object, carry out or participate in Space Activities, or establish, use or possess related facilities or utilities."[341] The precise requirements to obtain a permit are not included in the law but left to a decision of the Council of Ministers or "whomever it delegates," whereas the Agency is in charge of reviewing the application and delivering the permit.[342]

However, the Emirati Law of 2019 sets up different permits for different activities. For instance, the law provides a different process to obtain permits to, *inter alia*, provide satellite communication services or manned spaceflight activities or even for the use of space nuclear energy sources.[343] In the case of manned spaceflight activities, the space operator must provide the UAE Agency with written approval from human participants proving that they have given their informed consent to take part in the activity. This requirement in Article 16 of the Emirati Law of 2019 shows the UAE's openness to NewSpace activities. Indeed, the request for informed consent—showing that the participant is fully conscious of the risks associated with the activity—is a clear sign that the provision does not solely apply to professional astronauts; it extends to so-called space tourists. This is further confirmed by the law requiring proof that the participant "has completed the necessary training, physical and health fitness to take the Spaceflight." If the provision only applied to professional astronauts, it could be presumed that they have received the appropriate training before being hired for the activity. Other than these requirements linked to the demonstration that participants to fly have received basic training to go to outer space, Article 16 leaves the details of additional conditions and requirements to the Board of Directors. These conditions could include, for instance, additional paperwork regarding the launching information, details about the spacecraft, its itinerary, etc.

339. Outer Space Treaty, Art. VII.
340. Emirati law of 2019, *supra* 319, Art. 3 (3).
341. *Id.*, Art. 14 (1).
342. *Id.*, Art. 14 (2).
343. *Id.*, Arts. 15 and 16.

The permit to use NPS takes a different approach. This is untestable since it is not directly linked to a space activity but rather to the utilization of dangerous radiological material. For this reason, the operator is prohibited—under Article 17—from using the energy sources without obtaining first a permit from the Agency. The high risk presented by its uses is reflected in the law by the involvement of several entities. Though the UAE Agency is in charge of delivering the permit, the "general conditions, controls and procedures" are determined by the Cabinet, whereas such decision was delegated to the Agency's Board of Governors for manned spaceflights. Furthermore, the operator is asked to justify the use of nuclear material in the application to obtain a permit. In a more general manner, Article 17 is concerned with ensuring that the legislations in force pertaining to "the peaceful use of nuclear energy" and "the use of space nuclear energy sources" are followed.

With regard to satellite communications, the defined process is an exception to the general framework to authorize space activities in the sense that the permit is not issued by the Agency. This is the prerogative of the Telecommunications Regulatory Authority (TRA). Nonetheless, the UAE Agency remains involved in the process as it must grant "prior no-objection" for the space operator to obtain its permit from TRA.[344]

Lastly, the authorization process for space resource activities per se follows the general process described in Article 14, i.e., conditions and control for the permit are determined by a decision of the Council of Ministers or its appointed delegate. A minor difference, however, is that the permit is granted by a decision of the Board of Directors "upon the proposal of the Director General,"[345] meaning the decision is taken by the highest authority in the UAE Agency.

In conclusion, the Emirati Law of 2019's approach to permitting space activities differs from its counterparts. With regard to space resource activities specifically, the United States is still debating over which authority should be competent, whereas Luxembourg provides a detailed procedure. Hence, the Emirati Law of 2019 stands in between the two: while it directly addresses the question of authorizing space resource activities and clearly identifies the competent authority, the details of the permit's requirements are relegated to pending implementing acts.

2.3.3 Environmental Component

In line with its objective to "[s]upport[t] the implementation of the necessary safety, security and environmental measures to enhance the long-term stability and sustainability of Space Activities and related activities,"[346] the Emirati Law of 2019 includes provisions pertaining to space debris mitigation. Moreover, though the law makes no direct to them, the UAE is further committed to COSPAR's PP policy.

344. *Id.*, Art. 15.
345. *Id.*, Art. 18 (2).
346. *Id.*, Art. 2 (2).

2.3.3.a Space Debris

According to Article 1, "space debris" is "[a] Space Object [i.e., a human-made object which is launched or aimed to be launched into or from outer space] that has no role or purpose, or the remains thereof, and the materials, waste, or fragments resulting therefrom, whether in Outer Space, including the Earth's orbit, or inside the Earth's atmosphere."[347]

This definition is broad from a spatial viewpoint. It refers to the "outer space" at large, not only Earth orbit or its atmosphere. It is interesting considering the international community's tendency to focus solely on Earth's near extraterrestrial environment, as illustrated by the IADC's definition which refers to "human-made objects [...] in *Earth orbit or re-entering the atmosphere*, that are non-functional" [italics added]."[348] With the explicit inclusion of "outer space" in the definition, the UAE prepares the ground for requiring necessary space debris mitigation measures for activities carried out beyond Earth orbit—or on celestial bodies, like space resource activities.

Furthermore, the Emirati Law of 2019 approaches the qualification of space debris by using general terms. This is appreciable because it allows for flexibility and transparency in the understanding of what constitutes space debris under the law. This is particularly useful for operators as they are required to take necessary measures and make plans to mitigate the risk, especially since there is, so far, no universally used definition of the term.[349] As such, "space debris" includes nonfunctional space objects and their remains as well as "the materials, waste, or fragments resulting therefrom."[350] Although the definition does not target specific elements like spacecraft or launch vehicles, the categorization seems to include any possible debris that could result from any activity making use of space objects. Then, a rover placed on the surface of the Moon, which is no longer functional, after having been used for, e.g., space resource activities could qualify as "space debris" under the Emirati Law of 2019.

Another interesting element in the Law is the placement, in its structure, of the provision pertaining to space debris mitigation. Indeed, Article 19 is placed right after the series of provisions regarding the process to obtain a permit to carry out a space activity. As it has already been observed, often, national space legislations incorporate space debris mitigation in their regulatory framework as a condition for licensing.[351] Here, similarly to the Finnish Space Act,[352] the two matters—licensing and space debris

347. *Id.*, Art. 1 "space object" and "space debris."
348. Mark Garcia, *Space Debris and Human Spacecraft*, NASA (2021) available online; UNCOPUOS, SDM Guidelines.
349. As stated previously, definitions vary from entity to entity. The European Space Agency, for instance, defines them as "all non-functional, artificial objects, including fragments and elements thereof, in Earth orbit or re-entering into Earth's atmosphere" and NASA as "artificial objects, including derelict spacecraft and spent launch vehicle orbital stages, left in orbit which no longer serve a useful purpose." ESA, *FAQ: Frequently asked questions*, available online.; NASA, Handbook for Limiting Orbital Debris, 21, NASA-HANDBOOK 8719.14 (2008).
350. Emirati law of 2019, *supra* 319, Art. 19.
351. *See, e.g.*, French Space Act, *supra* note 16, Art. 5; The Space Industry Regulations 2021 No. 792, section 2(2) (h) (UK); 2019 ACSFEA, *supra* note 200 (US); Austrian Outer Space Regulation, BGBl. II No. 36/2015, Art. 2 (4) (1) (AT).
352. *See* Finland, *supra* section 1.2.

mitigation measures—are not imbricated. Yet, they are not entirely disconnected either since an authorized operator must take such measures. If the title of Chapter 3—"Space Activities and Space Debris"—is any reflection, the two matters are put on the same level which makes space debris mitigation an important focus of the law.

In substance, every authorized operator must "take the necessary measures and plans to mitigate Space Debris and reduce the effects thereof, as determined by a decision issued by the Board of Directors."[353] They are also asked to notify the UAE Agency in any event pertaining to the creation of, or an encounter with, space debris. Specifically, Article 19 paragraph 2 demands immediate notification in cases where (a) space debris resulting from an authorized space object is created and (b) there is a high potential risk of the authorized space object losing control or colliding with another space object or debris. Furthermore, the operator must inform the UAE Agency of any measure or plan adopted to mitigate the risks outlined in (a) and (b), as well as any general adjustment made to the original plans to reduce the effect of space debris. Lastly, the operator is asked to report annually on "warnings or risks" related to any space activity using any space object in outer space.

2.3.3.b Planetary Protection

In addition to protecting the outer space environment from additional space debris, the UAE has also committed to COSPAR's PP policy. As noted *supra*, these guidelines are voluntary;[354] hence, their implementation is left to the discretion of States. Although the Emirati Law of 2019 makes no reference to COSPAR's policy or planetary protection in general, the UAE's continued correspondence with COSPAR during the planning of the *Emirates Mars Mission* (EMM) exhibits its willingness to comply.

The EMM is designed to observe Mars from orbit to study the Red Planet's atmosphere and climate.[355] In particular, the goal is to obtain a better picture of Mars' climate dynamics and global weather as well as to understand how the different layers of its atmosphere interact by having the *Hope probe* orbit the planet for a full Martian[356] year.[357] The probe was successfully launched in July 2020 and reached Mars' orbit in February 2021.

Since the EMM does not involve landing on the surface of Mars, it is classified as a Category III[358] mission under the COSPAR PP policy. Accordingly, the space operator is expected to provide documentation on the mission and to set up "some implementing

353. Emirati Law of 2019, *supra* note 319, Art. 19 (1).
354. *See* COSPAR, *supra* Chapter 3.
355. https://www.emiratesmarsmission.ae/mission/about-emm (last visited January 2024).
356. A Martian year lasts 687 days, i.e., about two Earth years long.
357. https://www.emiratesmarsmission.ae/ (last visited January 2024).
358. Category III of the COSPAR planetary protection policy corresponds to "certain types of missions (mostly flyby and orbiter) to a target body of chemical evolution and/or origin of life interest and for which scientific opinion provides a significant chance of contamination which could compromise future investigations" like Mars, Europa, and Enceladus. https://cosparhq.cnes.fr/assets/uploads/2021/07/PPPolicy_2021_3-June.pdf (last visited January 2024).

measures, including trajectory biasing, the use of cleanrooms during spacecraft assembly and testing, and possibly bioburden reduction."[359]

In this regard, the EMM Project manager sent, for instance, a pre-launch planetary protection report to COSPAR.[360] According to the reported words of the COSPAR PP Panel's Chair, the "activities described in EMM Planetary Protection Plan are in line with the requirements for Planetary Protection Category III mission to Mars described in COSPAR Planetary Protection Policy."[361] Furthermore, the EMM Project manager also stated during the UNCOPUOS LSC that the EMM would "continue engaging [the Chair] and COSPAR for feedback" and that the Mohammed Bin Rashid Space Centre—which is in charge of supervising the mission—"is committed to the Planetary Protection Policies and will apply them in all phases of Emirates Mars Mission."[362]

Thus, it can be concluded that the UAE's practice is to comply with COSPAR's PP policy, despite the Emirati Law of 2019 making no reference to planetary protection. However, the question remains of whether private operators will be held to the same standard and how so. A possibility would be to make compliance with COPSAR's PP policy, one of the conditions determined by the Council of Ministers.[363]

2.3.4 Conclusion

The Emirati Law of 2019 is a national space legislation of its time. It addresses topical subjects, such as NewSpace activities and the long-term sustainability of space activities. In this sense, the Law clearly includes within its scope emerging space activities and leaves the door open for future new space ventures. It further identifies the "long-term stability and sustainability" of space activities as an objective of the law.[364] To that end, the regulatory framework seeks the implementation of environmental measures, such as space debris mitigation and permits for the use of NPS.

Moreover, the Emirati Law of 2019 displays a very contemporary sense of adaptability as it aims for flexibility with different authorization—i.e., permit—requirements in place, based on the nature of the activity. As a result, the Law does not provide an elaborated authorization mechanism comparable to the one described in the Luxembourgish SRL. The Emirati law of 2019 does not even make any reference to an EIA obligation, though this may be part of the conditions that will be determined, in practice, by the Council of Ministers.

As a result, it is not possible to provide a substantial comparison between the UAE regulatory framework and a conceptual sustainability framework, which it

359. https://cosparhq.cnes.fr/assets/uploads/2021/07/PPPolicy_2021_3-June.pdf (last visited January 2024).
360. As reported in https://cosparhq.cnes.fr/assets/uploads/2021/02/PPP_Presentation-2021.1.pdf (last visited January 2024).
361. Omran Sharaf, *Planetary Protection in Emirates Mars Mission* (2017), https://www.unoosa.org/documents/pdf/copuos/lsc/2017/tech-03.pdf (last visited January 2024).
362. *Id.*
363. Emirati law of 2019, *supra* 319, Art. 14, §2.
364. *Id.*, Art. 2, §2.

proclaims to support. Too many details are left to the decision of an authorizing entity to have a precise overview of the actual conditions attached to a permit for space mining activities. Nonetheless, it can be noted that the Emirati law of 2019 refers to the long-term sustainability of space activities, which suggests the integration of a long-term perspective in mission design. Last, the provisions regarding the use of NPS, the implementation of space debris mitigation measures, and the State's open cooperation with COSPAR imply a desire to comply with international best practices.

2.4 Japan[365]

In 2021, Japan became the fourth State in the world to enact a law explicitly regulating space resource exploitation activities. The Japanese Space Resources Act (JSRA)—formally known as the *Act on Promotion of Business Activities Related to the Exploration and Development of Space Resources*[366]—entered into force in December of the same year. It applies to space resources-related activities carried out by private entities.[367] According to Article 2, the expression "space resource" refers to water, minerals, and other natural resources present in outer space, including on the Moon and other celestial bodies.[368]

Under the JSRA, private entities may seek authorization for three types of activities: (1) researching the presence of space resources for the purposes of mining and recovery; (2) mining, recovering, processing, and storing the resources which have been discovered; and (3) conducting other activities or actions "as prescribed by the Cabinet Office Order."[369] In addition, the Act explicitly excludes from its scope space resource activities carried out for scientific purposes only.[370]

From the outset, it should be noted that the JSRA does not operate as an independent instrument. Contrary to the Luxembourgish legislation,[371] the Japanese Act builds upon a pre-existing comprehensive regulatory framework for space activities.[372] As a result, space resource activities must comply with several domestic and international instruments. In particular, the planned activity must neither violate Japan's international obligations—including the ones resulting from the UN Space

365. Currently, no official translation of the Japanese law exists. Accordingly, unless provided otherwise, reference to the content of the law in this section is based on the work of Salmeri, *supra* note 277 at 161–165.
366. Act on Promotion of Business Activities Related to the Exploration and Development of Space Resources, Act No. 83 of 2021, *entered into force* Dec. 23, 2022, 141 Japan Official Gazette 4 (2022).
367. Salmeri, *supra* note 277 at 161.
368. For translation purposes, *see id.*; US Law Library of Congress, *Japan: Space Resources Act Enacted*, Library of Congress (2021) available online.
369. Japanese Space Resources Act, *supra* note 366, Art. 2; Salmeri, *supra* note 277 at 161.
370. *Id.*
371. Until 2017, the Luxembourgish regulatory framework for space activities was limited to activities related to electronic media. Loi du 27 juillet 1991 sur les médias électroniques, *supra* note 266.
372. Salmeri, *supra* note 277 at 161. For a comprehensive overview of the Japanese regulatory framework for space activities, *see* Hiroko Yotsumoto, Daiki Ishikawa & Tetsuji Odan, *The Space Law Review: Japan*, The Space Law Review (2021), available online.

Treaties ratified by the State—[373] nor basic principles laid down in the Japanese Basic Space Act.[374]

From an administrative standpoint, the entity is required to obtain an authorization from the Prime Minister in consultation with the Ministry of Economy, Trade, and Industry.[375] The specific conditions attached to the deliverance of the permit are laid down in Article 3 of the Act and supplement those already imposed in the 2016 Japanese Space Activities Act.[376] Accordingly, in addition to the conditions determined in the Act of 2016, the JSRA requires private entities to provide information on the purpose, duration, location, method, and content of the planned activity.[377] The Cabinet Office may also require the private entity to fulfill additional conditions. Moreover, the applicant is asked to provide a business plan. In order for the Prime Minister to deliver authorization, this business plan must conform to the basic principles of the Basic Space Act and should not impede the implementation of Japan's international obligations.[378] Additionally, the applicant must show they have the ability to carry out the proposed business plan.[379]

In another key provision, the JSRA further addresses the fundamental question of the ownership of acquired space resources. Pursuant to Article 5 of the Act, the licensed entity will acquire ownership over the resources provided that two conditions are met: (1) the space resource has been acquired through mining or recovery in respect of the provisions of the Act, and (2) the entity possesses it "with the intention to own."[380]

The JSRA further requires that the Government provides space operators "with technical advice, information and other assistance" in order to promote the development of commercial space resource utilization.[381] The Government is also responsible for monitoring "the application of the law, the progress of science and technology, the status of the regulatory efforts for the development of an international system as mandated under Article 7 (1)" in order to determine whether amendments are necessary.[382] This provision, in particular, reflects the adoption by Japan of the principle of adaptative governance.[383]

From an environmental perspective, Japan has aligned its practice with existing international standards. As showcased in the previous sections, States often use the licensing process as a means to implement environmental measures. However, in the absence of an official English translation of the relevant legislations, it is difficult to

373. Japan is Party to four of the five UN Space Treaties, namely the Outer Space Treaty, the Return and Rescue Agreement, the Liability Convention and the Registration Convention.
374. Japanese Space Resources Act, *supra* note 366, Art. 1.
375. *Id.*, Art. 3 §3.
376. Japan, Act on Launching of Spacecraft, etc. and Control of Spacecraft, Act No. 76 of Nov. 16, 2016.
377. Japanese Space Resources Act, Art. 3 §1; Japan, Basic Space Act, Act No. 43 of May 28, 2008.
378. *Id.*, Art. 3 §2; Yotsumoto, Ishikawa, and Odan, *supra* note 370.
379. *Id.*, Art. 3 §2.
380. The wording of the provision is based on Japan's domestic rules regarding the ownership of movable objects. Salmeri, *supra* note 277 at 164.
381. Japanese Space Resources Act, Art. 8.
382. *Id.*, Supplementary provisions, Art. 4; Salmeri, *supra* note 277 at 163.
383. According to Salmeri, this is the first time a national space legislation addressing space resource activities recognizes the importance of adaptive governance. *Id.*, at 164.

determine to which extent the Japanese regulatory framework implements international environmental standards. Consequently, rather than refer to the text of the law, the analysis of Japan's environmental framework for space activities is based on the State's report to the UNCOPUOS LSC regarding its implementation of nonlegally binding UN space instruments.[384] The reports note, for instance, that Japan has not had reasons to implement the provisions of the NPS Principles since it does not use NPS in outer space.[385]

With regard to the mitigation of space debris, Japan has incorporated the relevant measures in its 2016 Space Activities Act.[386] Similarly to other States, the space debris mitigation mechanism is integrated into the licensing requirements for the launching and control of a space object.[387] The detailed content of the measures and the procedures to follow are specified in documents prepared by the National Space Policy Secretariat of the Cabinet Office in 2017. Furthermore, the Japanese space agency—i.e., the Japan Aerospace Exploration Agency (JAXA)—has defined its own space debris mitigation standards, based on domestic law and the international nonlegally binding instruments developed by the IADC, the UNCOPUOS, and ISO. The current JAXA standard is consolidated in JAXA's *Management Requirements 003D* (JMR-003D) which provides "in-depth technical procedures for debris mitigation measures involving reentry and specifies detailed requirements."[388] This standard applies to all missions carried out by JAXA.

In a similar manner, JAXA has developed its own planetary protection standards based on COSPAR's PP Policy.[389] The Policy had historically been used by Japan for its spacecraft design requirements. However, with the evolution of space activities, notably on the Moon and Mars, JAXA felt it was necessary to develop additional planetary protection standards. As a result, the space agency adopted two new national mechanisms in 2019: an internal regulation and a unified standard, "the Planetary Protection Program Standards (JMR-014)." The internal regulation stipulates the "basic policy of JAXA's planetary protection measures," the assignment of the Agency's PPO, and delegates to the relevant internal entity the tasks of formulating and reviewing standards. As for the JMR-014 standards, it is "consistent with [COSPAR's] Policy."[390] It determines, *inter alia*, the administrative, technical, and procedural requirements for

384. To keep Member States appraised of the instruments and measures that have been implemented by States and international organizations, COPUOS LSC created a "compendium on mechanisms adopted in relation to non-legally binding United Nations instruments on outer space." The initial questionnaire was circulated during the 54th session of the LSC. Since then, several States have contributed updates to the compendium. Under these circumstance, Japan submitted answers in 2016, 2017, 2019 and 2022. *See, e.g.*, UNOOSA, *Compendium on non-legally binding UN space instruments* (2022) available online.
385. *Id.*
386. *Id.*, Japan, Act on Launching of Spacecraft, etc. and Control of Spacecraft, Act No. 76 of Nov. 16, 2016.
387. *Id.*
388. *Id.* Compendium.
389. Japan, Compendium on mechanisms adopted in relation to non-legally binding United Nations instruments on outer space, UNCOPUOS LSC, 58th Sess., 4, UN Doc. A/AC.105/C.2/2019/CRP.16 (2019).
390. *Id.*

planetary protection. The standard applies to any spaceflight mission involving JAXA's participation.

In the absence of an English translation of the JSRA, it is not possible to precisely evaluate the similarities between the law and the conceptual sustainability framework used in this research. However, it can be observed that Japan has adopted a licensing process for space activities that includes environmental requirements, at least with regard to space debris mitigation. Moreover, the NPS Principles were also considered by the State but ultimately left aside as Japan does not use NPS in outer space. It also appears that compliance with COSPAR's planetary protection requirements is a well-established practice, at least for space activities carried out by JAXA or in cooperation with the Agency. Given these elements, it is likely that the Japanese regulatory framework requires operators to comply with environmental standards—like COSPAR's and space debris mitigation measures—when carrying out space resource activities.

3 CONCLUSION

Although each domestic space legislation has its specifics, it remains possible to identify general trends. With the exception of the Luxembourgish SRL of 2017,[391] national space legislations either have a wide-ranging scope to apply to a variety of space activities—this is the case, for instance, of the revised Belgian Space Act and of the Emirati law of 2019—or they are tailored to a specific activity and part of a bigger regulatory framework. In this regard, it can be observed that, though the JSRA only applies to space resource activities, it does not operate as an independent instrument.[392] In a similar manner, Title IV of the CSLCA is supported by a strong legal framework, even though the State has yet to agree on the competent authorizing entity.

Another identifiable trend is the adoption of a licensing mechanism to authorize nongovernmental space activities. This is often done as a means to implement States' obligation under Article VI of the Outer Space Treaty. For the same reason, States often implement a supervising mechanism to monitor nongovernmental activities and ensure they are carried out in compliance with the requirements of the authorization. In practice, the obligation is enforced by States by requiring space operators to submit annual reports on their activity. This is notably the case with the laws of Belgium, Finland, and the UAE. It can also be noted that Luxembourg requires operators to have a "robust internal governance scheme" which allows for "monitor[ing] and report[ing] the risks it is or might be exposed to."[393] A particularity of the Finnish Space Act is worth mentioning here: the authorization and supervision procedures apply to all *civil* operators, hence including governmental activities which do not fall under the competence of the Ministry of Defense.

391. In the case of Luxembourg, the logic was reverse. The State first adopted a law with narrow objectives—the SRL—before establishing a general regulatory framework in 2020. Until then, other space activities were regulated by the 1991 Luxembourgish law on electronic media, thus excluding, *inter alia*, activities beyond Earth orbit.
392. The planned activity must comply with, *inter alia*, the Japanese Basic Space Act. *See* Japan *supra*.
393. SRL, Art. 7§2.

Lastly, the domestic space legislations analyzed in this chapter show that they tend to govern general scenarios. Accordingly, the domestic law does not provide every single detail about the rules governing space activities. In most cases, additional conditions may be imposed on the operator by the authorizing entity, as is the case in the Emirati Law of 2019, for instance.

With regard to the environmental component of the studied law, and more broadly of their capacity to promote sustainability of space activities, common trends can be identified regarding the implementation of the international nonbinding instruments discussed in Chapter 3 *supra*. In particular, it can be observed that all domestic space legislations—with the exception of Luxembourg—implement the normative content of the SDM Guidelines, though with varying degrees of detail. Similarly, several States have an established practice of complying with COSPAR's PP policy: if not by applying the standards directly, at least by adopting equivalent ones. Their implementation is mainly achieved through national or—in the case of European countries like Belgium—regional space agencies; they condition their cooperation to the respect of planetary protection measures. It can further be noted that States have considered in the past the implementation of the NPS Principles. Belgium, Finland, and the UAE all have provisions in their law regarding the use of NPS. As recently as 2022, the United States has reiterated its commitment to the Principles and encouraged other States to implement the NPS Safety Framework.[394] The NPS Principles were also considered by Japan, though the country eventually noted there was no need for it as it does not use NPS for its space missions.

This overall engagement is however limited by the fact that none of the laws addressed in this chapter integrate the precautionary approach discussed in Chapter 2 *supra*. However, some, meaning Belgium and Finland, have incorporated the EIA requirement within their domestic regulatory framework. This is particularly encouraging as it demonstrates that the international obligation, initially developed in the field of environmental law, can be transposed into space law without overburdening space operators. Altogether, it can be concluded that States are more likely to implement international (environmental) standards which are recognized as best practices and have been agreed upon at the highest international level, rather than unilaterally opt to incorporate environmental managing systems, like the EIA.

Therefore, national space legislations are a useful means to implement obligations contracted by States as a result of their adherence to a treaty. This is notably the case with the licensing process which is used at the national level to implement Article VI of the Outer Space Treaty. Moreover, these legislations can further be used to implement international nonlegally binding instruments—like the SDM Guidelines, thus, turning international "soft law" into "hard law" within the domestic legal order. They further allow for flexibility so that they can answer, as emphasized by the UNCOPUOS in its Recommendations on national legislations, States' "specific needs and practical considerations."[395] Additionally, the adoption of Title IV of the CSLCA by

394. NPS Safety Framework, *supra* Chapter 3.
395. UNCOPUOS' recommendations on national legislation, *supra* Chapter 3, at preamble.

the United States in 2015 shows that national space legislations can be used as a means to keep space law relevant by sparking discussions at the highest levels.

Notwithstanding these points, the limitations of domestic legislation must also be acknowledged. In particular, a national space legislation is only binding within its domestic legal order. A consequence of the limited scope of these legislations is that the enforcement of rights and obligations established in the instrument cannot be opposed to other States. Moreover, looking at the "bigger picture," unilaterally regulating space activities could result in a patchwork of national space legislations inconsistently interpreting international obligations.[396] As it has previously been mentioned, there is, for instance, no certitude that all States will agree on interpreting Article IX of the Outer Space Treaty broadly to include unforeseen environmental issues.

For this reason, national space legislations better operate under the umbrella of international—hard or soft—instruments. International space law provides uniformity and consistency, whereas national space legislations allow for necessary flexibility. Thus, it is not surprising that the Signatories of the *Artemis Accords* committed "to contribute to multilateral efforts to further develop international practices and rules applicable to the extraction and utilization of space resources, including through ongoing efforts at the COPUOS."[397] It will ensure overall consistency between States regarding the rules governing space resource activities.

396. Philip De Man, *State Practice, Domestic Legislation and The Interpretation of Fundamental Principles of International Space Law*, 42 SPACE POLICY 93 (2017) DOI: 10.1016/j.spacepol.2017.06.001.

397. Artemis Accords, *supra* note 160, section 10§4.

Conclusion

Sustainability in outer space is a constant and always changing problem, and, therefore, it would be inherently contradictory to pretend to have a definitive conclusion about legal developments pertaining to this issue. However, from the evolution of the legal field regarding space resource activities, some important takeaways must be underscored.

1 OVERVIEW OF THE MAIN FINDINGS

Curiously, despite a decade worth of intensive discussions on the importance of ensuring the long-term sustainability of space activities, there is very little literature pertaining to how sustainability is achieved in practice. There is no such thing as a manual that would provide step-by-step instructions on how to support the long-term sustainability of a space activity, especially if this activity is carried out beyond Earth orbits. This is the gap that this book has aimed to bridge.

The gap is not between ideas debated in legal fora and their translation into legal instruments but shows its fault lines within the instruments themselves. This is one of the main limits of the LTS Guidelines, for instance. Although the instrument defines space sustainability in an all-encompassing manner, its application is clearly aimed at activities in orbit. The fact that references to the protection of the outer space environment are, for the most, limited to the preamble of the LTS Guidelines rather than their commentary is telling. In comparison, there are about four times more references to space debris and Earth orbit. Moreover, it must be underscored that the LTS Guidelines do not explicitly delineate a detailed sustainability framework, especially from an environmental perspective. Rather, they provide insights of a general nature ranging from relevant elements for a regulatory framework to scientific and technical research and development.

A possible explanation is the absence of a clear understanding of what sustainability, and more broadly, sustainable development, means in practice. The "what" and "why" of sustainability are somewhat clear: they revolve around our ability to continue carrying out, in the long term, activities which benefit us. This is what we call the "sustainability equation": the codependent relation between socio-economic development and environmental protection. The "how," however, is a source of questions and debates. Authors appear to identify several elements that make up sustainable development, yet there is no common agreement. Likewise, when defined in the literature, space sustainability takes different forms depending on the type of activity considered: "how" these activities have to be carried out *in each case* entertains uncertainty about a global identification of "what" sustainability can be *in general.*

Altogether, a common agreement can be identified on the need for rules to support space sustainability because it will not occur spontaneously and therefore a *laissez-faire* attitude cannot be condoned. Yet, surprisingly, it seems that very few of the efforts are devoted to actually protecting the outer space environment from the consequences of our activities. Rather than being a priority—as it should be as one half of the sustainability equation—it is approached as something we must suffer through. Environmental considerations are burdensome and must be addressed because we *have* to rather than because we *want* to.

1.1 Design of a Conceptual Framework for the Environmental Sustainability of Space Resource Activities

Evidently, there are exceptions to this attitude of resignation. Progressively, we can see a shift in mentalities regarding sustainability. More and more initiatives refer to the "sustainable" and "rational" use of outer space. This is the case, for instance, in the 2020 *Artemis Accords* and in the *Building Blocks for the Development of an International Framework on Space Resource Activities* adopted in 2019 by the Hague International Space Resources Governance Working Group. Nonetheless, none of these instruments provide a clear path toward the *environmental* sustainability of space resource activities, even if the Building Blocks integrate environmental considerations. It is the object of the first chapter of this book to ponder several elements relevant to the matter. It establishes, from a mostly theoretical point of view, the necessity to adopt a (moderate) anthropocentric approach to environmental protection. The opposite ecocentric position would not allow any degree of contamination of the outer space environment, something that is, by definition, impossible when undertaking space activities in general.

The outcome is a conceptual framework based on key principles identified by legal scholars to operationalize sustainable development. We retain three specific principles: environmental integration, rational management of natural resources, and inter-generational equity. These principles are complemented by the elements of the second edition of the *Berlin Guidelines for mining and sustainable development*. They identify several elements which contribute to the environmental sustainability of terrestrial mining, such as the development of a licensing regime integrating environmental management systems—like a mandatory EIA—and compliance with best practices.

1.2 Contributions of Space Law and International Environmental Law to Environmentally Sustainable Space Resource Activities

Once a conceptual framework is established, the space law regime can be assessed on three levels: (1) international binding instruments; (2) nonlegally binding instruments, including international technical standards; and (3) domestic instruments. Moreover, the contribution of international environmental law has to be considered.

One outcome of a critical examination of space law in its entirety is the conclusion that this law provides a strong—though insufficient in many regards—basis to ensure the environmental sustainability of space (resources) activities. In particular, the Outer Space Treaty and the Moon Agreement both contain core principles that echo notions of intra- and inter-generational equity. This is, for instance, the case of the principle of "due regard" to the "corresponding interests" of other States Parties and of "present and future generations." Moreover, both treaties require States Parties to authorize and continuously supervise space activities carried out by nongovernmental entities. In practice, several States have implemented these obligations by adopting, at the domestic level, a regime for the delivery of authorizations to undertake space activities. In essence, these regimes are licensing regimes coupled with a series of requirements, such as respect of the State's international obligations. In most cases, these licensing regimes include environmental requirements, like the obligation to adopt space debris mitigation measures.

Furthermore, both the Outer Space Treaty and the Moon Agreement provide for an environmental regime that aims to avoid, *inter alia*, the forward contamination of outer space. Accordingly, Article IX of the Outer Space Treaty and Article 7 of the Moon Agreement require States to adopt measures to prevent the harmful contamination of outer space. States must take an active role by not only avoiding contaminating outer space but also by *preventing* it. The treaty also introduces the concept of an environmental "balance" on celestial bodies. In this regard, the environmental regime of the Moon Agreement is particularly advanced. However, due to its low rate of ratification, it does not establish a common regime for environmental protection of the outer space environment, which is, for the most, the one provided under the Outer Space Treaty.

This particular regime suffers from crippling definitional issues which are emphasized by the large degree of discretion left to States Parties in the implementation of their environmental obligations. There is no clear indication of what amounts to the "harmful contamination" of the outer space environment or how to objectively identify when it is "necessary" for States to adopt "appropriate" preventive measures. As a result, there exists a grey zone where activities carried out by space operators can be considered harmful to the environment but not to the extent that they are undeniably so. In this context, it is difficult to affirm that a State violated its environmental obligation under Article IX of the Outer Space Treaty.

Yet, not everything is lost. First, the treaty does integrate environmental considerations, though not to the extent of the Moon Agreement. Second, it provides for the adoption of preventive or mitigative measures when the situation calls for it. Third, we argue that the notion of "harmful contamination" can be interpreted as a form of "harmful interference," which would open the way to the consultation mechanism provided under Article IX of the Outer Space Treaty. Therefore, binding international space law already provides the groundwork for the implementation of several elements of the proposed sustainability framework.

Nonetheless, even this dynamic interpretation of the Outer Space Treaty does not fully balance out the legal gaps of the environmental regime of Article IX, at least, not if the goal is the establishment of a strong regime which truly integrates environmental considerations for the full life cycle of space activities. For this reason, we have to turn to other international instruments developed in the space sector, namely nonlegally binding instruments. These instruments are based on best practices in specific areas of space activities, such as the use of NPS, planetary protection, or the mitigation of space debris. They define recommendations to address a diversity of environmental issues raised by human activities in outer space. Ultimately, these instruments allow us to supplement the environmental regime of the UN Space Treaties, notably by being used as a basis to interpret environmental obligations under the Outer Space Treaty. They host general recommendations pertaining to specific aspects of space activities as well as precise technical standards, as is the case with the IADC's SDM Guidelines and COSPAR's planetary protection policy.

A definite advantage of nonlegally binding instruments is that they are more inclusive in their drafting process than treaties, in part because they are not necessarily the object of direct negotiations between States. COSPAR's policy, for instance, is defined by, *inter alia*, scientific experts. Likewise, the IADC's SDM Guidelines were drafted by space agencies. Even the drafting of the LTS Guidelines was established under the UNCOPUOS STC, before being adopted by the UNCOPUOS' Member States. Consequently, these instruments are often negotiated on the basis of the expertise of entities that are used to deal with the constraints of conducting activities in outer space.

A limitation to these instruments, however, is their voluntary character. Contrary to treaties, States are not under any obligation to comply with and enforce the normative content of these soft law instruments. This limitation, however, can partially be remedied by referring to another body of international law: environmental law. Specifically, the principle of due diligence—a principle of customary international law—requires States to implement their international obligation to the best of their ability. Accordingly, it is possible to draw a parallel between the due diligence obligation to fulfill international obligations to the best feasible extent and the existence of international instruments which formalize best practices in a specific area. Indeed, complying with best practices is a good start when having to prove an operator acted diligently, despite the occurrence of damage.

There is more to it: according to international jurisdictions, in an environmental context, the customary obligation of due diligence implies an obligation to undertake an EIA for the planned activity. Thus, we retrieve here another core element of the sustainability framework: the mandatory EIA. Under customary international law, States are obliged to undertake an EIA prior to the start of the activity. The timing of the application of the environmental mechanism is the only requirement. Other details pertaining to its implementation are left to the discretion of the States.

At this stage, it is possible to provide an answer regarding the extent to which international environmental law contributes to the sustainable development of space resource activities. On its own, this body of international law is not of great interest. The principle of due diligence is a broad one that needs to be operationalized, notably by the introduction of an EIA. However, as a complement to the international framework governing space resource activities, it has merits. In addition to bringing into the fray the obligation to undertake an EIA prior to the start of the planned activity, it further incentivizes States to comply with nonlegally binding instruments as a show of their (mandatory) diligent conduct.

Here, the recourse to international environmental law raises the question of its transposition to space activities. Reference to the Belgian and Finnish domestic regulatory framework for space activities indicates how—at least regarding EIAs—a transposition can operate. Both the Belgian Space Act and the Finnish Space Act include an obligation for space operators to undertake an EIA in order to obtain authorization to undertake space activities. A comparison of the two frameworks further establishes that EIA requirements do not have to be a burden on operators. If Belgium implements a very detailed EIA for space (resources) activities, Finland's approach is closer to the *laissez-faire* approach. It only requires operators to conduct an EIA; how they implement the obligation is left to their discretion. The rationale here is that the ones carrying out the activity are better placed to understand the impact of the planned activity on the environment and how to effectively mitigate those risks. Considering the importance of EIAs and how it is possible to keep large flexibility in their implementation, it is highly regrettable that none of the four space legislations explicitly regulating space resource activities have adopted a similar mechanism so far.

National space legislations are also a useful tool in implementing nonlegally binding instruments. Several domestic regulatory frameworks include requirements pertaining to the mitigation of space debris and the use of NPS in outer space. Often, compliance with these international technical standards conditions the obtention of authorization for space operators to carry out their activities. Overall, States show a tendency to adopt, in their domestic legal order, instruments which have been negotiated at the international level, like the SDM and LTS Guidelines. It would also explain why none of the selected national laws incorporate the valuable precautionary principle; its legal status under international remains uncertain.

Ultimately, space law at large is rather efficient in addressing environmental issues raised by space resource activities. It provides the legal basis on which environmental sustainability standards can be created. The results of the analysis carried out in Chapters 2 to 4 are summarized in Table 1. It highlights the capacity of space law instruments to implement the constitutive elements of the sustainability framework for space resource activities.

Table 1 Application of the Sustainability Framework to Space Resource Activities

Aim	*Action*	*Conclusions*
Environmental integration in policies	Incorporate rules on the protection of the outer space environment	- The UN Space Treaties provide for an environmental regime, but its operationalization is difficult. - International soft law instruments addressing specific environmental issues exist, but their implementation is voluntary. - National legislations often have an environmental component but varies in scope (i.e., space debris mitigation, to avoid "harmful contamination").
	Adopt a licensing process integrating environmental management processes	- The UN Space Treaties require States to "authorize" nongovernmental space activities. This is not a licensing regime per se, but States often interpret it as such (e.g., US, Luxembourg, Finland). - Authorization regimes enacted by States often include environmentally related procedural requirements (e.g., compliance with the SDM Guidelines, EIA).
	Require mandatory EIA	- Not a requirement in the UN Space Treaties. - None of the soft law instruments studied require an EIA per se, though some constituent elements can be identified as likewise (space debris mitigation plan pre-mission, NPS safety assessment). - EIA is a customary international obligation according to international jurisdictions. - Some national space legislations have included the obligation in their framework (e.g., Belgium and Finland).
	Monitor and audit activities	- The UN Space Treaties require States to "supervise" nongovernmental space activities, which is a form of monitoring. - National space legislations often include monitoring requirements, in the form of reporting on activities during and post-mission (e.g., Finland, Luxembourg). - Luxembourg also includes auditing requirements in its SRL framework.

Aim	*Action*	*Conclusions*
Rational management of natural resources	Manage space resources rationally	- The Moon Agreement explicitly includes the rational management of resources as one of the main purposes of the future legal framework. - LTS Guidelines promote the rational use of radio frequencies and Earth orbit, but no reference to mined space resources. - Belgian law specifically requires operators to adopt measures to ensure the sustainable and rational use of natural resources in space (i.e., orbits and *in situ* resources).
	Encourage reciprocal agreements to reduce pollution	- UN Space Treaties encourage cooperation among States in general. Otherwise, none of the selected instruments discuss the possibility of reciprocal agreements for mining purposes.
Inter-generational equity	Integrate a long-term perspective in mission design	- The Moon Agreement refers to "future generations" interests. - The LTS Guidelines are about the long-term sustainability of space activities, though their implementation is mainly focused on orbital space activities. - Some national space legislations refer to the sustainable use of outer space, which implies a long-term approach (e.g., Belgium, UAE, Finland).
	Adopt best environmental practices	- No obligation in the UN Space Treaties for States to comply with best practices. - Best practices are encompassed in individual international soft law instruments (e.g., SDM Guidelines). - Several States implement international standards at the national level (e.g., space debris mitigation measures, NPS requirements).
	Develop preventive and mitigative measures	- The UN Space Treaties require States to adopt measures to prevent the contamination of outer space. - Incorporated into international soft law instruments.

It is clear that the vast majority of the elements identified in the sustainability framework for space resource activities can already be found, to an extent, in norms applicable to such activities. Indeed, several provisions of the Outer Space Treaty provide a strong basis for the regime outlined in the framework we designed. This is notably the case with the international obligation—under Article VI of the treaty—to authorize and continuously supervise nongovernmental activities. In practice, States often implement these obligations in the form of a licensing regime and monitoring mechanisms for the planned activity.

One element that does not explicitly exist, in the instruments discussed in this work, is the one regarding the development of reciprocal agreements for the exploitation of space resources to limit the contamination of the outer space environment. The core idea is that, when possible, operators should be encouraged to work together on a mining site rather than working individually and, thus, opening several individual mines. In theory, this could be particularly beneficial for asteroid mining. These celestial bodies are made up of several precious mineral resources, not all of which are necessary of interest for a single operator. Thus, rather than exploiting several asteroids when one could provide resources of interest for several operators, an agreement could be struck between them. From a strategic standpoint, it would further reduce costs since each operator would not have to plan for the entire cycle of the mission, from technology design to landing and extracting resources to end-of-life measures.

2 OUTCOMES

The book questions whether the sustainable development of space resource activities compels us to create legal standards to regulate uncertain environmental consequences. The short answer is yes, for two reasons.

First, the current focus is on the sustainability of space activities in orbit. It is often considered the most pressing issue, and thus the one the majority of efforts are turned to. However, the current pollution of Earth orbits is, in part, the direct result of decades of space policies that did not include strong, explicit rules pertaining to the protection of the orbital environment. Therefore, deferring the establishment of environmental standards for space resource activities because they do not, presently, raise environmental issues is a sure path toward a similar disaster as the one resulting from space debris. The lack of scientific certainty regarding the environmental consequences of these activities cannot, rationally, be used as an excuse to postpone the adoption of environmental standards: our knowledge of outer space is limited; thus, we will never have a perfect understanding of our environmental impact. For this reason, it is better to adopt a precautionary approach to the matter by adopting measures from the outset rather than wait for the inevitable environmental issues space resource activities will raise.

Second, more fundamentally, the rules identified as implementing elements of the conceptual framework work because they are interpreted as such. There is no guarantee States will adopt a similar interpretation. For instance, how States Parties implement their obligation to authorize nongovernmental activities is left to their discretion. There is no obligation per se to adopt a licensing regime, though it is strongly encouraged by the international community. Furthermore, the analysis brings together rules and mechanisms which are otherwise scattered across several instruments and normative levels. They are the outcome of assembling together legally binding and nonlegally binding space international instruments, technical standards, national instruments, and customary norms of international (environmental) law.

Therefore, rather than creating standards as such, ensuring the environmental sustainability of space resource activities requires creating a *set of* standards coordinating largely existing elements.

2.1 Standards Supporting the Environmental Sustainability of Space Resource Activities

In essence, to support the long-term environmental sustainability of space resource activities, States should adopt instruments that incorporate the following environmental standards:

(1) *Environmental integration* in policies, notably by defining an environmental protection regime.
(2) Adoption of a *licensing regime* including environmental management systems, such as monitoring of the activities.
(3) *Mandatory EIA* prior to the start of the planned activity.
(4) Rational management of natural resources.
(5) Implementation of existing international technical standards and best practices.
(6) *Long-term perspective*, notably by taking into consideration the interests of both present and future generations.

2.2 Implementation of the Sustainability Standards

Ultimately, the goal is to bring together the standards of space (environmental) sustainability under one system. This brings back our initial question about which normative approach would have the most value for ensuring the environmental sustainability of space resource activities. A simple answer is that the implementation of these environmental standards requires a mixed approach that combines international and national instruments.

Space law is a multi-level regulatory regime: the combination of national and international instruments has been further emphasized by the adoption, in 2013, of General Assembly resolution 68/74, which endorses the UNCOPUOS' *Recommendations on National Legislation Relevant to the Peaceful Exploration and Use of Outer Space.*[1] Likewise, the ILA also adopted a resolution outlining a "Model Law" for States to implement their international obligations under the UN Space Treaties in their national legal order.[2] Obviously, the articulation of national and international instruments is not a random fact of international activities but, rather, the desired outcome of international efforts.

1. GA Res. 68/74, UNGAOR, 68th Sess., UN Doc. A/RES/68/74 (2013).
2. *Id.* Information on the activities of international intergovernmental and non-governmental organizations relating to space law, UNCOPUOS LSC, 52nd Sess., UN Doc. A/AC.105/C.2/2013/CRP.6 (2013).

These efforts delineate a coherent vision. Both legal orders, domestic and international, appear to have a precise role to play in the governance of space (resources) activities. The UN Space Treaties act as an umbrella which harmonizes and guides State's practice. They define what conduct is acceptable and not in outer space. As for national instruments, they are essential in implementing international obligations in the domestic legal order of States Parties, in a manner that is fitted to their specific needs and capacities. In time, however, this clear distinction between roles became somewhat muddled by the introduction of nonlegally binding international instruments.

Treaties—meaning binding international instruments—have a superior hierarchical legal value than national instruments.[3] They are the manifestation of States willingly consenting to limit the exercise of their sovereignty in some areas, here in the field of space law. As a direct result, they must regulate space activities at the national level within the constraints of the international limits they consented to. With international nonlegally binding instruments, however, there are no such constraints. Rather than defining what conduct is *acceptable*, they identify what conduct is *desirable*.

In this configuration, international soft law instruments continue to act as an umbrella which guides the actions of States. The key difference is that States are free to ignore the framework they provide. Furthermore, the normative content of these instruments only becomes enforceable through its implementation into the domestic legal order of States. Therefore, when considering which normative approach has the most value to support environmentally sustainable space resource activities, it is not sufficient to decide between international and national instruments. We also need to take into consideration the value of using binding and nonbinding instruments.

The incorporation of the environmental standards identified above, in a treaty, would mean that the international community is either willing to amend the Outer Space Treaty or to adopt a new treaty dedicated to the governance of space resource activities. The former is unlikely because of—in addition to having never been amended since its adoption—the considerable effort required and the new political environment needed. It probably makes it more efficient to aim for the negotiation of a new treaty, rather than for amending an old one.

A treaty would have the advantage of making the sustainability standards legally binding upon States. Yet, the adoption of a treaty does not guarantee its ratification by States, as we have seen with the Moon Agreement: although States reached a consensus on the text, the treaty was eventually ratified by only 18 States. Consequently, the binding character of the instrument adopted at the international level is not as relevant as it first appeared.

This is why the consideration of nonlegally binding instruments is crucial. As we have seen (Chapter 3), compared to treaties, these instruments have the advantage of being flexible; they can be more easily revised and adapted to new development in the

3. *See, e.g.*, VCLT, Art. 27 on the relationship between domestic law and the observance of treaties.

field. For instance, the IADC SDM Guidelines have been revised three times so far. Similarly, COSPAR's planetary protection policy was revised on several occasions. Most importantly, we have established that States are generally inclined to implement the content of soft instruments negotiated at the international level into their domestic legal order, or at the very least, to align their practice on these international technical standards.

Ultimately, binding or nonbinding, what remains essential is the adoption of a framing international instrument that incorporates in its core the standards identified above. It will show that a consensus regarding their necessity exists among States, and will thus provide an incentive—or an obligation—for States to truly integrate environmental considerations into the planning of their space resource activities.

Moreover, at the international level, the standards do not need to be precisely defined. The aim is to provide an incentive, not to scare away potential investors with burdensome environmental rules, something that is always a concern for the industry. States must also be able to adapt the standards to their needs. The expression "space resource activities" encompasses a diversity of activities, which in turn may result in very different environmental consequences. Therefore, it is sufficient to establish, for instance, that prior to the start of the activity, an EIA must be undertaken. There is no need—at the international level—to detail the constitutive elements which make an EIA.

Consequently, the international instrument should be complemented by national regulatory frameworks that will determine how operators must, in practice, implement the standards. Their implementation in the domestic legal order of States does not necessarily require enacting new national legislation. In many instances, States made provisions which allow the competent authority to subject the delivery of authorization to additional conditions. They could also be integrated into a licensing regime as standard requirements to obtain authorization to conduct space activities—as it is currently done under Belgian law—or as an independent obligation, as it is under the Finnish Space Act of 2018. We note, for instance, that several States already require their private operators to conduct an EIA and to include space debris mitigation measures.

Therefore, enhancing the environmental sustainability of space resource activities requires considering the standards in a multi-level matrix, one which combines international with national initiatives. The emergence of space resource activities, as a new activity, is an opportunity that must be seized to redefine how we approach the governance of space activities in general. Over the last decade, "sustainability" has progressively become a buzzword when discussing space activities. More and more, space actors cogitate on how to ensure the long-term sustainability of our activities in outer space. Although several means have been identified so far, they tend to be tailored to the need of orbital activities. Curiously, the protection of the outer space environment per se is rarely at the forefront of the discussion. Ultimately, the standards identified in this work aim to give, at last, the second part of the sustainability equation between socio-economic development and environmental protection its rightful place: not aside from economic development, but beside it.

3 FUTURE PERSPECTIVES

Because we focus in this book on sustainability, a variety of issues that will arise from space resource activities are left aside, such as the appropriation of space resources, rules governing mining rights, enforcement of the standards, and dispute settlement. All these elements, and more, will need to be taken into account to properly regulate the activity.

This is the case with domestic space legislation explicitly regulating space resource activities. They address several legal issues such as liability in case of damage resulting from the activity, the licensing regime's requirements, and sanctions in case of noncompliance. Sustainability is only one facet of governing space resource activities.

Moreover, the scope of the research is limited by our partial knowledge of the outer space environment and of how space mining activities will occur in practice. We made conjectures based on the environmental problems faced in the past. We know that the overuse of Earth orbits and the absence of end-of-life measures for satellites have impeded our activities in space. It seems logical to hypothesize that the absence of specific rules, combined with an increased presence in lunar orbit to control activities on the ground, will raise similar issues as the ones we currently face in LEO. By the same token, our concerns regarding the potential contamination of celestial bodies during flyby and landing missions will not disappear simply because we are undertaking a new activity. On the contrary, the means used to extract *in situ* resources from celestial bodies may create new forms of contamination that have not yet been considered. Only the future will tell once the technology has been developed and tested. One thing seems sure, however: we can assume from our experience on Earth that, without environmental management, the exploitation of natural resources will lead to overexploitation and scarcity of necessary resources in the long term.

Those, however, are only conjectures which cannot be confirmed or infirmed at this stage. Humanity will need to acquire more knowledge and experience to verify their accuracy. For this reason, it is important not to adopt—in the word of the US representative to the UNCOPUOS—"too rigid procedures."[4] Environmental integration must not be too constraining; otherwise, it may not only discourage operators from undertaking space resource activities but also render the framework rapidly obsolete. Accordingly, the environmental standards put forward in this work are general in nature so as to withstand time while effectively integrating the environmental dimension of sustainability.

In this spirit, though the purpose of the sustainability framework was initially designed to guide our reflection in the context of space resource activities, its listed standards can be applied more broadly to all space activities. Whatever the type of space activity humans undertake, it will indeed undeniably raise issues pertaining to their (environmental) sustainability. As we have learned it on Earth, and are learning it in space, our actions have an impact on surrounding areas. Activities in orbit already

4. *See* US' statement, *in* LSC Summary Records, UN GAOR, 5th Sess., at 7, UN Document. A/AC. 105/C.2/SR.68 (1966).

raise these issues. As we have emphasized over and over again, space resource activities will raise similar issues. It is a rational conjecture that other NewSpace activities—like human settlements and space tourism—will also raise these issues.

The environmental impact of our activities in space will vary depending on the type of activity, as it does on Earth. Fishing and mining do not raise the same issues after all. The consequences may not always be precisely identified. Nonetheless, it remains essential to integrate environmental considerations into the planning of current and future activities. This is where the standards for environmental sustainability identified above come into play.

The requirements of a licensing regime, monitoring, and development of an environmental regime are rooted in the design of the Outer Space Treaty, as is the idea of taking preventive environmental measures. Consequently, they are already designed—at the international level—for space activities in general. The rational management of natural resources applies indifferently, though in a different manner, to celestial bodies' *in situ* resources and orbits. Similarly, the obligation to conduct an EIA prior to the start of the planned activity can be implemented for all activities, as is the case already on Earth. Last but not least, one can only hope there exist best practices for each aspect of space activities such as space debris mitigation and planetary protection measures.

Ultimately, sustainability can *only* be achieved by balancing development *and* environmental protection. There is no path to long-term sustainability which does not include an environmental component; development alone only ensures activities will continue in the short term. It is undeniable that to rip the benefits of space resource activities in the long term, these activities will have to integrate the environmental component directly into their design. Consequently, the long-term sustainability of space resource activities does compel us to create new standards, even in the absence of full certainty regarding their environmental impact on outer space. This is largely dependent on the will of States. In the end, nothing makes up for the lack of a common vision.

APPENDIX

Berlin II Guidelines

Guidelines for mining and sustainable development

Fundamental Principles for the Mining Sector (Berlin Guidelines 1991, revised 2000)

Governments, mining companies and the minerals industries should as a minimum:

(1) Recognize environmental management as a high priority, notably during the licencing process and through the development and implementation of environmental management systems. These should include early and comprehensive environmental impact assessments, pollution control and other preventive and mitigative measures, monitoring and auditing activities, and emergency response procedures.
(2) Recognize the importance of socio-economic impact assessments and social planning in mining operations. Social-economic impacts should be taken into account at the earliest stages of project development. Gender issues should also be considered at a policy and project level.
(3) Establish environmental accountability in industry and government at the highest management and policy-making levels.
(4) Encourage employees at all levels to recognize their responsibility for environmental management and ensure that adequate resources, staff and requisite training are available to implement environmental plans.
(5) Ensure the participation of and dialogue with the affected community and other directly interested parties on the environmental and social aspects of all phases of mining activities and include the full participation of women and other marginalized groups.
(6) Adopt best practices to minimize environmental degradation, notably in the absence of specific environmental regulations.
(7) Adopt environmentally sound technologies in all phases of mining activities and increase the emphasis on the transfer of appropriate technologies

that mitigate environmental impacts, including those from small-scale mining operations.

(8) Seek to provide additional funds and innovative financial arrangements to improve environmental performance of existing mining operations.

(9) Adopt risk analysis and risk management in the development of regulation and in the design, operation, and decommissioning of mining activities, including the handling and disposal of hazardous mining and other wastes.

(10) Reinforce the infrastructure, information systems service, training and skills in environmental management in relation to mining activities.

(11) Avoid the use of such environmental regulations that act as unnecessary barriers to trade and investment.

(12) Recognize the linkages between ecology, socio-cultural conditions and human health and safety, the local community and the natural environment.

(13) Evaluate and adopt, wherever appropriate, economic and administrative instruments such as tax incentive policies to encourage the reduction of pollutant emissions and the introduction of innovative technology.

(14) Explore the feasibility of reciprocal agreements to reduce transboundary pollution.

(15) Encourage long-term mining investment by having clear environmental standards with stable and predictable environmental criteria and procedures.

Bibliography

(Unless provided otherwise, all websites were last accessed on January 2024)

Books

ARNOULD, JACQUES, ICARUS' SECOND CHANCE: THE BASIS AND PERSPECTIVES OF SPACE ETHICS (2011).

BADESCU, VIOREL, ASTEROIDS PROSPECTIVE ENERGY AND MATERIAL RESOURCES (2013).

BIRNIE, PATRICIA W., BOYLE, ALAN E. & REDGWELL, CATHERINE, INTERNATIONAL LAW AND THE ENVIRONMENT (3rd ed. 2009).

BODANSKY, DANIEL, BRUNNÉE, JUTTA & HEY, ELLEN (eds.), THE OXFORD HANDBOOK OF INTERNATIONAL ENVIRONMENTAL LAW (2007).

BOSSELMANN, KLAUS & GRINLINTON, DAVID P. (eds.), ENVIRONMENTAL LAW FOR A SUSTAINABLE SOCIETY, 1 (2nd ed. 2013).

BOSSELMANN, KLAUS, THE PRINCIPLE OF SUSTAINABILITY: TRANSFORMING LAW AND GOVERNANCE (2016).

Boyle, Alan E. & Freestone, David (eds.), INTERNATIONAL LAW AND SUSTAINABLE DEVELOPMENT: PAST ACHIEVEMENTS AND FUTURE CHALLENGES (2001).

BUGGE, HANS CHRISTIAN & VOIGT, CHRISTINA (eds.), SUSTAINABLE DEVELOPMENT IN INTERNATIONAL AND NATIONAL LAW (2008).

CASSELLA, SARAH (ed.), LE STANDARD DE DUE DILIGENCE ET LA RESPONSABILITÉ INTERNATIONALE (2018).

CORTEN, OLIVIER, MÉTHODOLOGIE DU DROIT INTERNATIONAL PUBLIC (2017).

CRAIK, NEIL, THE INTERNATIONAL LAW OF ENVIRONMENTAL IMPACT ASSESSMENT: PROCESS, SUBSTANCE AND INTEGRATION (2008).

DE MAN, PHILIP, EXCLUSIVE USE IN AN INCLUSIVE ENVIRONMENT (2016).

DE O. BITTENCOURT NETO, OLAVO ET AL. (eds.), BUILDING BLOCKS FOR THE DEVELOPMENT OF AN INTERNATIONAL FRAMEWORK FOR THE GOVERNANCE OF SPACE RESOURCES ACTIVITIES: A COMMENTARY (2020).

DUPUY, PIERRE-MARIE & KERBRAT, YANN, DROIT INTERNATIONAL PUBLIC (12 ed. 2014).

DUPUY, PIERRE-MARIE & VIÑUALES, JORGE E., INTERNATIONAL ENVIRONMENTAL LAW (2nd ed. 2018).

EKARDT, FELIX, SUSTAINABILITY TRANSFORMATION, GOVERNANCE, ETHICS, LAW (2020).

FIELD, TRACY-LYNN, STATE GOVERNANCE OF MINING, DEVELOPMENT AND SUSTAINABILITY (2019).

GOLD, JOSEPH, INTERPRETATION: THE IMF AND INTERNATIONAL LAW (1996).

HACKET, GEORGES, T., 2 SPACE DEBRIS AND THE CORPUS IURIS SPATIALIS (1994).

HOFMANN, MAHULENA ET AL., SPACE LEGISLATION OF LUXEMBOURG: A COMMENTARY (Mahulena Hofmann & P. J. Blount eds., 2022).

KALFAGIANNI, AGNI, FUCHS, DORIS & HAYDEN, ANDERS, ROUTLEDGE HANDBOOK OF GLOBAL SUSTAINABILITY GOVERNANCE (2019).

KRIGE, JOHN & RUSSO, ARTURO, 1 THE STORY OF ESRO AND ELDO, 1958-1973 (2000).

KULESZA, JOANNA, DUE DILIGENCE IN INTERNATIONAL LAW (Malgosia Fitzmaurice, Phoebe Okowa, & Sarah Singer eds., 2016).

LEWIS, JOHN S., ASTEROID MINING 101: WEALTH FOR THE NEW SPACE ECONOMY (David Gump ed., 2015).

LYALL, FRANCIS & LARSEN, PAUL B., SPACE LAW: A TREATISE (2nd ed. 2018).

MARBOE, IRMGARD (ed.), SOFT LAW IN OUTER SPACE: THE FUNCTION OF NON-BINDING NORMS IN INTERNATIONAL SPACE LAW (2012).

MEADOWS, DONELLA H. ET AL., THE LIMITS TO GROWTH: A REPORT FOR THE CLUB OF ROME'S PROJECT ON THE PREDICAMENT OF MANKIND (2nd ed. 1974).

MEADOWS, DONELLA, RANDERS, JORGEN & MEADOWS, DENNIS, LIMITS TO GROWTH: THE 30-YEAR UPDATE (2004).

NATIONAL ACADEMY OF SCIENCES (ed.) A REVIEW OF SPACE RESEARCH (1962) available online.

OLLINO, ALICE, DUE DILIGENCE OBLIGATIONS IN INTERNATIONAL LAW (2022).

PAIEMENT, PHILLIP, TRANSNATIONAL SUSTAINABILITY LAWS (2017).

ROMANO, CESARE, THE PEACEFUL SETTLEMENT OF INTERNATIONAL ENVIRONMENTAL DISPUTES: A PRAGMATIC APPROACH (2000).

SANDS, PHILIPPE & PEEL, JACQUELINE, PRINCIPLES OF INTERNATIONAL ENVIRONMENTAL LAW (3rd ed. ed. 2012).

SANDS, PHILIPPE, PRINCIPLES OF INTERNATIONAL ENVIRONMENTAL LAW (2nd ed. 2003).

SCHWARTZ, JAMES S. J. & MILLIGAN, TONY (eds.), THE ETHICS OF SPACE EXPLORATION, (2016).

SPACERESOURCES.LU, OPPORTUNITIES FOR SPACE RESOURCES UTILIZATION FUTURE MARKETS & VALUE CHAINS (2018).

TECHERA, ERIKA J. ET AL., ROUTLEDGE HANDBOOK OF INTERNATIONAL ENVIRONMENTAL LAW, (2nd ed. 2021).

TROUWBORST, ARIE, PRECAUTIONARY RIGHTS AND DUTIES OF STATES (2006).

VIIKARI, LOTTA, THE ENVIRONMENTAL ELEMENT IN SPACE LAW ASSESSING THE PRESENT AND CHARTING THE FUTURE (2008).

WESTRA, LAURA, BOSSELMANN, KLAUS & SOSKOLNE, COLIN, GLOBALISATION AND ECOLOGICAL INTEGRITY IN SCIENCE AND INTERNATIONAL LAW (2011).

Book Chapters & Works in Collection

Adger, W. Neil & Jordan, Andrew, *Sustainability: Exploring the Processes and Outcomes of Governance, in* GOVERNING SUSTAINABILITY 3–31 (Andrew Jordan & W. Neil Adger eds., 2009).

Aoki, Setsuko, The Standard of Due Diligence in Operating a Space Object, 55 in IISL Proceedings 392–405 (2012).

Aust, Helmut Philipp & Feihle, Prisca, *Due Diligence in the History of the Codification of the Law of State Responsibility, in* Due Diligence in the International Legal Order 42–58 (Heike Krieger, Anne Peters, & Leonhard Kreuzer eds., 2020).

Bartolini, Giulio, *The Historical Roots of the Due Diligence Standard, in* Due Diligence in the International Legal Order 23–41 (Heike Krieger, Anne Peters, & Leonhard Kreuzer eds., First edition ed. 2020).

Bastida, Elizabeth, *Integrating Sustainability into Mining Law: The Experience of Some Latin American Countries*, 51 *in* International Law and Sustainable Development: Principles and Practice 575–605 (2004).

Bergamasco, Federico, Space Mining and The Protection of Extra-Terrestrial Environment in The Light of Article IX of The Outer Space Treaty, 60 in IISL Proceedings 1–8 (2017).

Beyerlin, Ulrich & Grote Stoutenburg, Jenny, *Environment, International Protection*, Max Planck Encyclopedias of International Law (Rüdiger Wolfrum ed., Oxford University Press ed. 2013).

Blomeyer-Bartenstein, Horst, *Due Diligence*, 10 Encyclopedia of public international law 138–143 (Rudolf Bernhardt ed., 1987).

Blount, P. J., *Article 2 Definitions, in* Space Legislation of Luxembourg: A Commentary 97–103 (2022).

Blowers, Andrew & Glasbergen, Pieter, *7 The Search for Sustainable Development*, 1 *in* Environmental Policy in an International Context 163–183 (Pieter Glasbergen & Andrew Blowers eds., 1995).

Bodansky, Daniel, *Deconstructing the Precautionary Principle, in* Bringing New Law to Ocean Waters 381–392 (David D. Caron & Harry N. Scheiber eds., 2004).

Bohlmann, Ulrike M. & Summerer, Leopold, *The STSC/IAEA Safety Framework for Space Nuclear Power Source Applications—Influence of Non-Binding, in* Soft Law in Outer Space: The Function of Non-Binding Norms in International Space Law 233–265 (2012).

Bosselmann, Klaus, *Sustainable Development Law, in* Routledge Handbook of International Environmental Law 30–42 (Erika J. Techera et al. eds., 2020).

Boyle, Alan E., *Soft Law in International Law-Making, in* International Law 119–137 (Malcom Evans ed., 5th ed. 2018).

Brunnée, Jutta, *The Stockholm Declaration and The Structure And Processes Of International Environmental Law, in* The Future of Ocean Regime-Building 39–62 (Susan Rolston, Theodore McDorman, & Aldo Chircop eds., 2009).

Bugge, Hans Christian, *1987–2007: "Our Common Future" Revisited, in* Sustainable Development in International and National Law 2–83 (Hans Christian Bugge & Christina Voigt eds., 2008).

Campbell, C. Lee & Heck, Walter W., *An Ecological Perspective on Sustainable Development, in* Principles of Sustainable Development 47–67 (1 ed. 1997).

Carpanelli, Elena & Cohen, Brendan, Interpreting "Damage Caused by Space Objects" under the 1972 Liability Convention, 56 in IISL Proceedings 29–45 (2013).

Chung, Gordon, Emergence of Environmental Protection Clauses in Outer Space Treaty: A Lesson from the Rio Principles, in A FRESH VIEW ON THE OUTER SPACE TREATY 1–13 (Annette Froehlich ed., 2018).

Committee to Review the Planetary Protection Policy Development Processes et al., *Chapter 2. Historical Origins of Planetary Protection Policies, in* THE GOALS, RATIONALES, AND DEFINITION OF PLANETARY PROTECTION: INTERIM REPORT (2017).

Cordonier Segger, Marie-Claire, *Sustainable Development in International Law, in* SUSTAINABLE DEVELOPMENT IN INTERNATIONAL AND NATIONAL LAW 86–199 (Hans Christian Bugge & Christina Voigt eds., 2008).

de O. Bittencourt Neto, Olavo, Preserving the Outer Space Environment: The "Precautionary Principle" Approach to Space Debris, in IISL PROCEEDINGS 341–351 (2013).

de Sadeleer, Nicolas, *The Precautionary Principle, in* ENVIRONMENTAL PRINCIPLES: FROM POLITICAL SLOGANS TO LEGAL RULES 135–361 (2nd ed. 2020).

Deléage, Jean-Paul, *Environnement—Un enjeu planétaire,* ENCYCLOPÆDIA UNIVERSALIS (1991).

Di Pippo, Simonetta, *Foreword: International Space Law and the United Nations Office for Outer Space Affairs, in* INTERNATIONAL SPACE LAW: UNITED NATIONS INSTRUMENTS iii–iv (United Nations ed., 2017).

Dupuy, Pierre-Marie & Barral, Virginie, *Principle 4: Sustainable Development through Integration, in* THE RIO DECLARATION ON ENVIRONMENT AND DEVELOPMENT: A COMMENTARY 157–180 (Jorge E. Viñuales ed., 2015).

Foster, Caroline E., *Due Regard and Due Diligence, in* Global Regulatory Standards in Environmental and Health Disputes: Regulatory Coherence, Due Regard, and Due Diligence 89–131 (2021).

Freeland, Steven, *Article 7 of the Moon Agreement,* II *in* COLOGNE COMMENTARY ON SPACE LAW 372–377 (Stephan Hobe, Bernhard Schmidt-Tedd, & Kai-Uwe Schrogl eds., 2013).

Freeland, Steven, *The Role of 'Soft Law' in Public International Law and Its Relevance to the International Legal Regulation of Outer Space, in* SOFT LAW IN OUTER SPACE: THE FUNCTION OF NON-BINDING NORMS IN INTERNATIONAL SPACE LAW 9–30 (Irmgard Marboe ed., 2012).

Gaja, Giorgio, *General Principles of Law,* MAX PLANCK ENCYCLOPEDIAS OF INTERNATIONAL LAW (Rüdiger Wolfrum ed., 2020).

Gautier, Philippe, *Non-Binding Agreements,* MAX PLANCK ENCYCLOPEDIAS OF INTERNATIONAL LAW (Rüdiger Wolfrum ed., 2006).

Gerhard, Michael, *Article VI,* 1 *in* COLOGNE COMMENTARY ON SPACE LAW 103–125 (Stephan Hobe, Bernhard Schmidt-Tedd, & Kai-Uwe Schrogl eds., 2009).

Goh Escolar, Gérardine & Reynders, Martin, *NPS Principles: Historical Background and Context,* 3 *in* COLOGNE COMMENTARY ON SPACE LAW 698 (Stephan Hobe, Bernhard Schmidt-Tedd, & Kai-Uwe Schrogl eds., 2015).

Grote Stoutenburg, Jenny & Beyerlin, Ulrich, *Environment, International Protection,* OXFORD PUBLIC INTERNATIONAL LAW (2013).

Haley, Andrew G., *Space Medical Jurisprudence,* 1 *in* SPACE LAW AND GOVERNMENT 274–297 (1963).

Hall, Loretta, *The History of Space Debris, in* ROADMAP TO THE STARS (2014).

Hartmann, William K., *Space Exploration and Environmental Issues, in* BEYOND SPACESHIP EARTH: ENVIRONMENTAL ETHICS AND THE SOLAR SYSTEM 119–139 (1986).

Hens, Luc, *The Rio Declaration on Environment and Development*, II *in* AREA STUDIES: REGIONAL SUSTAINABLE DEVELOPMENT: AFRICA 162–186 (Emmanuel Kwesi Boon ed., 2002).

Hobe, Stephan, Stubbe, Peter & Tronchetti, Fabio, *Historical Background and Context of the Moon Agreement*, II *in* COLOGNE COMMENTARY ON SPACE LAW 336–347 (Stephan Hobe, Bernhard Schmidt-Tedd, & Kai-Uwe Schrogl eds., Carl Heymanns Verlag ed. 2013).

Hofmann, Mahulena, *COSPAR Recommendations in a New Context? Environmental Aspects of Space Mining, in* PROCEEDINGS OF THE INTERNATIONAL INSTITUTE OF SPACE LAW 2016 (P.J. Blount et al. eds., 2017).

Hofmann, Mahulena, *The Role of COSPAR Guidelines in Interpreting Article IX OST*, 54 *in* INTERNATIONAL INSTITUTE OF SPACE LAW 311-317 (2011).

Horneck, Gerda & Cockell, Charles S., *Planetary Parks: Suggestion for a Targeted Planetary Protection Approach*, 38 *in* THE IAA COSMIC STUDY ON PROTECTING THE ENVIRONMENT OF CELESTIAL BODIES 45–49 (Mahulena Hofmann, Petra Rettberg, & Mark Williamson eds., 2010).

Jaeckel, Aline L., *The Precautionary Principle in International Law, in* The International Seabed Authority and the Precautionary Principle: Balancing Deep Seabed Mineral Mining and Marine Environmental Protection 27–69 (2017).

Jakhu, Ram S. & Freeland, Steven, The Relationship Between the Outer Space Treaty and Customary International Law, in IISL PROCEEDINGS (2016).

Koivurova, Timo, *Due Diligence*, MAX PLANCK ENCYCLOPEDIAS OF INTERNATIONAL LAW (Rüdiger Wolfrum ed., 2010).

Leister, Valnora & Kovudhikulrungsri, Lalin, *Outer Space: Of the People, by the People and for the People*, 52 *in* IISL PROCEEDINGS (2009).

Leterre, Gabrielle, *Article 4 Liability for Damage, in* SPACE LEGISLATION OF LUXEMBOURG: A COMMENTARY 109–111 (2022).

Leterre, Gabrielle, Space Mining and Environmental Protection: Recycling International Agreements into New Legal Practices, 62 in IISL PROCEEDINGS 83–94 (2020).

Lowe, Vaughan, *Sustainable Development and Unsustainable Arguments, in* INTERNATIONAL LAW AND SUSTAINABLE DEVELOPMENT: PAST ACHIEVEMENTS AND FUTURE CHALLENGES (Alan Boyle & David Freestone eds., 1999).

Lyall, Francis, *Planetary Protection from a Legal Perspective: General Issues*, 38 *in* THE IAA COSMIC STUDY ON PROTECTING THE ENVIRONMENT OF CELESTIAL BODIES 55–62 (Mahulena Hofmann, Petra Rettberg, & Mark Williamson eds., 2010).

Marboe, Irmgard, *The Importance of Guidelines and Codes of Conduct for Liability of States and Private Actors, in* SOFT LAW IN OUTER SPACE: THE FUNCTION OF NON-BINDING NORMS IN INTERNATIONAL SPACE LAW 119–144 (Irmgard Marboe ed., 2012).

Martinez, Peter, *Space Sustainability, in* HANDBOOK OF SPACE SECURITY: POLICIES, APPLICATIONS AND PROGRAMS 257–272 (Kai-Uwe Schrogl et al. eds., 2015).

Mathews, Freya, *Environmental Philosophy, in* HISTORY OF PHILOSOPHY IN AUSTRALIA AND NEW ZEALAND 543–591 (Graham Oppy & N.N. Trakakis eds., 2014).

Mayence, Jean-François, Article IX of the Outer Space Treaty and the Concept of Planetary Protection: Toward a Space Environment Law?, 53 in IISL PROCEEDINGS (2010).

McMahon, Mary, *Environmental degradation, in* GEMET (n.d.) available online.

Millbrooke, Anne, *History of the Space Age, in* HANDBOOK OF SPACE ENGINEERING, ARCHAEOLOGY, AND HERITAGE 195–207 (Ann Darrin & Beth L. O'Leary eds., 2009).

Neger, Thomas & Walter, Edith, *Space Law—an Independent Branch of the Legal System*, 7 *in* OUTER SPACE IN SOCIETY, POLITICS AND LAW 234–245 (Christian Brünner & Alexander Soucek eds., 2011).

Oduntan, Gbenga, *The Never-Ending Dispute: Legal Theories on the Spatial Demarcation Boundary Plane between Airspace and Outer Space.*, *in* SOVEREIGNTY AND JURISDICTION IN THE AIRSPACE AND OUTER SPACE: LEGAL CRITERIA FOR SPATIAL DELIMITATION (2012).

Omes, Elisabeth, *PSA-PSF: convergences et divergences, in* Les professionnels du secteur des assurances au Luxembourg. Les apports de la loi du 12 juillet 2013 117–152 (2014).

Perek, Luboš, *Outer Space as Natural Resource, in* THE SETTLEMENT OF DISPUTES ON THE NEW NATURAL RESOURCES 217–225 (René-Jean Dupuy ed., 1983).

Porras, Daniel A., The United Nations Principles Relevant to the Use of Nuclear Power Sources in Outer Space: The Significance of a Soft Law Instrument after Nearly 20 Years in Force, in SOFT LAW IN OUTER SPACE: THE FUNCTION OF NON-BINDING NORMS IN INTERNATIONAL SPACE LAW 205–232 (Irmgard Marboe ed., 2012).

Raulin, Francois, *Prevention from Chemical and Radioactive Contamination—A Significant Element of Planetary Protection*, 38 *in* THE IAA COSMIC STUDY ON PROTECTING THE ENVIRONMENT OF CELESTIAL BODIES 40–44 (Mahulena Hofmann, Petra Rettberg, & Mark Williamson eds., 2010).

Ribbelink, Olivier, *Article III*, 1 *in* COLOGNE COMMENTARY ON SPACE LAW 65–69 (Stephan Hobe, Bernhard Schmidt-Tedd, & Kai-Uwe Schrogl eds., 2009).

Rolston, III Holmes, *The Preservation of Natural Value in the Solar System, in* BEYOND SPACESHIP EARTH: ENVIRONMENTAL ETHICS AND THE SOLAR SYSTEM 140–182 (1986).

Sadeleer, Nicolas de, *The Principle of Prevention, in* ENVIRONMENTAL PRINCIPLES: FROM POLITICAL SLOGANS TO LEGAL RULES 61–90 (2002).

Sergio Marchisio, *Article IX*, I *in* COLOGNE COMMENTARY ON SPACE LAW 169–182 (Stephan Hobe, Bernhard Schmidt-Tedd, & Kai-Uwe Schrogl eds., 2009).

Shelton, Dinah, *Soft Law, in* ROUTLEDGE HANDBOOK OF INTERNATIONAL LAW 68–80 (David Armstrong ed., 2009).

Shelton, Dinah, *Stockholm Declaration (1972) and Rio Declaration (1992)*, MAX PLANCK ENCYCLOPEDIAS OF INTERNATIONAL LAW (2008).

Smith, Lesley Jane, *Legal Aspects of Satellite Navigation, in* HANDBOOK OF SPACE LAW (Frans von der Dunk & Fabio Tronchetti eds., 2015).

Soucek, Alexander & Tapio, Jenni, Normative References to Non-Legally Binding Instruments in National Space Laws: A Risk-Benefit Analysis in the Context of Domestic and Public International Law, 2018 in IISL PROCEEDINGS 553–580 (2018).

Tennen, Leslie I., *The Role of COSPAR for Space Security and Planetary Protection, in* HANDBOOK OF SPACE SECURITY 1559–1580 (Kai-Uwe Schrogl ed., 2020).

Thürer, Daniel, *Soft Law*, MAX PLANCK ENCYCLOPEDIAS OF INTERNATIONAL LAW (Rüdiger Wolfrum ed., 2009).

Toulemon, Robert, Prieur, Michel & Loyer, François, *Environnement*, 8 ENCYCLOPÆDIA UNIVERSALIS 1055 (1990).

Viikari, Lotta, *Environmental Impact Assessment in the Space Sector*, *in* THEORY AND PRACTICE OF TRANSBOUNDARY ENVIRONMENTAL IMPACT ASSESSMENT 265–288 (C. J. Bastmeijer & Timo Koivurova eds., 2007).

von der Dunk, Frans et al., Scoping National Space Law: The True Meaning of "National Activities in Outer Space" of Article VI of the Outer Space Treaty IISL PROCEEDINGS 227–237 (2020).

von der Dunk, Frans, *International Space Law*, *in* HANDBOOK OF SPACE LAW 29–126 (Frans G. von der Dunk & Fabio Tronchetti eds., 2015).

Vondrak, Richard R., *Lunar Base Activities and the Lunar Environment*, *in* LUNAR BASES AND SPACE ACTIVITIES OF THE 21ST CENTURY 337 (Wendell W. Mendell et al. eds., 1992).

Walter, Edith et al., *"Hot" Issues and Their Handling*, *in* OUTER SPACE IN SOCIETY, POLITICS AND LAW 491–725 (Christian Brünner & Alexander Soucek eds., 2011).

Williamson, Mark, *Scope and Methodology*, 38 *in* THE IAA COSMIC STUDY ON PROTECTING THE ENVIRONMENT OF CELESTIAL BODIES 7–15 (Mahulena Hofmann, Petra Rettberg, & Mark Williamson eds., 2010).

Wolfrum, Rüdiger, *Sources of International Law*, MAX PLANCK ENCYCLOPEDIAS OF INTERNATIONAL LAW (Rüdiger Wolfrum ed., 2011).

Journal Articles

Abeyratne, R., *The Use of Nuclear Power Sources in Outer Space and Its Effect on Environmental Protection*, 25 J. SPACE L. 17–28 (1997).

Aganaba-Jeanty, Timiebi, *Space Sustainability and the Freedom of Outer Space*, 14 ASTROPOLITICS 1–19 (2016).

Arnould, Jacques, *Chapitre 1. Espace, Éthique et Imagination*, 30 J. INT. BIOETHIQUE ETHIQUE SCI. 15–26 (2019).

Arnould, Jacques, *Quelle ethique pour l'espace?*, 43 MURS 27–38 (2004).

Audouze, Jean, *Chapitre 2. La COMEST et l'éthique de l'Espace*, 30 J. INT. BIOETHIQUE ETHIQUE SCI. 27–34 (2019).

Baker, Howard A, *Protection of The Outer Space Environment: History and Analysis of Article IX of The Outer Space Treaty*, 12 ANN. AIR & SPACE. L. 143–173 (1987).

Barnidge, Robert P. Jr., *The Due Diligence Principle under International Law*, 8 Int. Community Law Rev. 81–122 (2006).

Barnidge, Robert P., *States' Due Diligence Obligations with Regard to International Non-State Terrorist Organisations Post-11 September 2001: The Heavy Burden That States Must Bear*, 16 Ir. Stud. Int. Aff. 103–125 (2005).

Bastida Virgili, B. et al., *Risk to Space Sustainability from Large Constellations of Satellites*, 126 ACTA ASTRONAUTICA 154–162 (2016).

Beard, Jack, *Soft Law's Failure on the Horizon: The International Code of Conduct for Outer Space Activities*, 38 Univ. Pa. J. Int. 335–424 (2016).

Benko, Marietta, Gruber, Gerhard & Schrogl, Kai Uwe, *UN Committee on the Peaceful Uses of Outer Space: Adoption of Principles Relevant to the Use of Nuclear Power Sources in Outer Space and Other Recent Developments*, 42 ZLW 35–64 (1993).

Bergstresser, John, *To Boldly Go: An Analysis of Luxembourg Space Resources Law in Light of the EU Treaty*, Bus. Law Rev. 143–151 (2021).

Bird, Robert C., *Procedural Challenges to Environmental Regulation of Space Debris*, 40 ABJL 635–685 (2003).

Block, Walter E. & Huebert, J. H., *Space Environmentalism, Property Rights, and the Law*, 37 U. Mem. L. Rev. 281–309 (2007).

Blount, Percy J., *Renovating Space: The Future of International Space Law*, 40 Denv. J. Intl'l L. & Pol'y 515–532 (2011).

Boas, Ingrid, Biermann, Frank & Kanie, Norichika, *Cross-Sectoral Strategies in Global Sustainability Governance: Towards a Nexus Approach*, 16 Int. Environ. Agreem.: Politics Law Econ. 449–464 (2016).

Bourély, Michel G., *La protection de l'environnement dans l'espace extra-atmosphérique*, 10 Ann. Air & Space. L. 277–295 (1985).

Brachet, Gérard, *Les enjeux d'un développement durable des activités spatiales*, n° 61 Geoeconomie 95–106 (2012).

Brachet, Gérard, *The Origins of the "Long-Term Sustainability of Outer Space Activities" Initiative at UN COPUOS*, 28 Space Policy 161–165 (2012).

Broniatowski, David A. & Weigel, Annalisa L., *The Political Sustainability of Space Exploration*, 24 Space Policy 148–157 (2008).

Cameron, James & Abouchar, Juli, *The Precautionary Principle: A Fundamental Principle of Law and Policy for the Protection of the Global Environment*, 14 B. C. Int'l & Comp. L. Rev. 1–27 (1991).

Carrio, Luis et al., *Understanding Sustainability in the Human Exploration Campaign*, *in 2022* IEEE 1–19 (2022).

Chang, I-Shih, *Overview of World Space Launches*, 16 J. Propuls. Power 853–866 (2000).

Charvolin, Florian, *1970: L'année clef pour la définition de l'environnement en France*, Rev. Hist. CNRS (2001).

Cheney, Thomas et al., *Planetary Protection in the New Space Era: Science and Governance*, Front. Astron. Space Sci. 1–8 (2020).

Cheng, Bin, *The Legal Status of Outer Space and Relevant Issues: Delimitation of Outer Space and Definition of Peaceful Use*, 11 J. Space L. 89–105 (1983).

Christensen, Ian et al., *New Policies Needed to Advance Space Mining*, 35 Issues Sci Technol 26–30 (2019).

Christol, Carl Q., *International Liability for Damage Caused by Space Objects*, 74 AJIL 346–371 (1980).

Christol, Carl Q., *Protection of Space from Environmental Harms*, 4 Ann. Air & Space. L. 433–458 (1979).

Cinelli, Claudia & Pogorzelska, Katarzyna, *The Current International Legal Setting for the Protection of the Outer Space Environment: The Precautionary Principle Avant La Lettre*, 22 Rev. Eur. Comp. Int. 186–201 (2013).

Cockell, Charles S & Horneck, Gerda, *Planetary Parks—Formulating a Wilderness Policy for Planetary Bodies*, 22 Space Policy 256–261 (2006).

COSPAR, *COSPAR Policy on Planetary Protection*, 211 Space Research Today 12–25 (2021).

Coulomb, Jean-Louis, *L'Année Géophysique Internationale (1957–1958)*, 70 L'Astronomie 1 (1956).

Couston, Mireille, *Chapitre 3. Le Statut de l'espace et Des Corps Célestes*, 30 J. Int. Bioethique Ethique Sci. 35–60 (2019).

Dahl, Carol, Gilbert, Ben & Lange, Ian, *Mineral Scarcity on Earth: Are Asteroids the Answer*, 33 Miner Econ 29–41 (2020).

Daly, Herman E., *Sustainable Development: From Concept and Theory to Operational Principles*, 16 Popul. Dev. Rev. 25–43 (1990).

Davidian, Ken, *Definition of NewSpace*, 8 New Space 53–55 (2020).

De Lucia, Vito, *Beyond Anthropocentrism and Ecocentrism: A Biopolitical Reading of Environmental Law*, 8 J. Hum. Rts. & Env't. 181–202 (2017).

De Man, Philip, *State Practice, Domestic Legislation and the Interpretation of Fundamental Principles of International Space Law*, 42 Space Policy 92–102 (2017).

Debus, A., *Estimation and Assessment of Mars Contamination*, 35 Adv. Space Res. 1648–1653 (2005).

Dembling, P.G, *Cosmos 954 and the Space Treaties*, 6 J. Space L. 129–136 (1978).

Dembling, Paul G. & Arons, Daniel M., *The Evolution of the Outer Space Treaty*, 33 J. Air L. & Com. 419–456 (1967).

Dempsey, Paul Stephen & Manoli, Maria, *Suborbital Flights and the Delimitation of Air Space Vis-à-Vis Outer Space: Functionalism, Spatialism and State Sovereignty*, XLII Ann. Air & Space L. 209–252 (2017).

Di Pippo, Simonetta, *The Contribution of Space for a More Sustainable Earth: Leveraging Space to Achieve the Sustainable Development Goals*, 2 Global Sustainability e3 (2019).

Du, Rong, *China's Approach to Space Sustainability: Legal and Policy Analysis*, 42 Space Policy 8–16 (2017).

Durrieu, Sylvie & Nelson, Ross F., *Earth Observation from Space—The Issue of Environmental Sustainability*, 29 Space Policy 238–250 (2013).

Eritja, Mar Campins, *L'appréhension jurisprudentielle du principe de précaution par le Tribunal international du droit de la mer*, 46 RJE 83–103 (2021).

Flournoy, Alyson, *In Search of an Environmental Ethic*, 28 Colum. J. Envtl. L. 63–118 (2003).

Fon, Vincy & Parisi, Francesco, *Stability and Change In International Customary Law*, 17 SCER 279–309 (2009).

Freeland, Steven, *Common Heritage, Not Common Law: How International Law Will Regulate Proposals to Exploit Space Resources*, 35 QIL (2017).

Freestone, David, *The Road from Rio: International Environmental Law After the Earth Summit*, 6 J. Environ. Law 193–218 (1994).

Gagnon Thompson, Suzanne C. & Barton, Michelle A., *Ecocentric and Anthropocentric Attitudes toward the Environment*, 14 J. Environ. Psychol. 149–157 (1994).

Gilbert, Alexander & Vidaurri, Monica, *Major Federal Actions Significantly Affecting the Quality of the Space Environment: Applying NEPA to Federal and Federally Authorized Outer Space Activities*, 44 Environ 233–272 (2021).

Gisler, Monika & Sornette, Didier, *Exuberant Innovations: The Apollo Program*, 46 Soc 55–68 (2009).

Glavin, D.P. et al., *Biological Contamination Studies of Lunar Landing Sites: Implications for Future Planetary Protection and Life Detection on the Moon and Mars*, 3 Int. J. Astrobiology 265–271 (2004).

Goodland, Robert, *The Concept of Environmental Sustainability*, 26 Annu. Rev. Ecol. Evol. Syst. 1–24 (1995).

Gorove, S., *Pollution and Outer Space: A Legal Analysis and Appraisal*, 5 NYU J. Int'l L. & Pol. 53–65 (1972).

Gorove, Stephen, *Cosmos 954: Issues of Law and Policy*, 6 J. Space L. 137–146 (1978).

Gupta, Vishakha, *Critique of the International Law on Protection of the Outer Space Environment*, 14 Astropolitics 20–43 (2016).

Haanappel, P.P.C., *Some Observations on the Crash of Cosmos 954*, 6 J. Space L. 147–149 (1978).

Hall, R., *Comments on Traffic Control of Space Vehicles*, 31 J. Air L. & Com. 327 (1965).

Handmer, Annie & Freeland, Steven, *The Use of Law to Address Space Debris Mitigation and Remediation: Looking Through a Science and Technology Lens*, 87 J. Air L. & Com. 375 (2022).

Hanlon, Michelle, *"Due Regard" for Commercial Space Must Start with Historic Preservation*, 28 Global Bus. L. Rev. 130–156 (2021).

Henderson, Paul G. W., *Fiscal Incentives for Environmental Protection: The Way Forward*, 2 SAJELP 151–168 (1995).

Higuera, Gerardo Inzunza, *What Got Us Here, Won't Get Us There: Why U.S. Commercial Space Policy Must Lie in an Independent Regulatory Agency*, 73 Hastings Law J. 105–128 (2022).

Hofmann, Mahulena & Bergamasco, *Federico, Space Resources Activities from the Perspective of Sustainability: Legal Aspects*, 3 Global Sustainability (2020).

Hofmann, Mahulena, *Entered into Force: The 2020 Space Law of Luxembourg*, 46 Air and Space Law (2021).

Iliopoulos, Nikolaos & Esteban, *Miguel, Sustainable Space Exploration and Its Relevance to the Privatization of Space Ventures*, 167 Acta Astronautica 85–92 (2020).

Jakhu, Ram S., Freeland, Steven & Chen, Kuan-Wei, *The Sources of International Space Law: Revisited Space Law*, 67 ZLW 606–667 (2018).

Jasentuliyana, Nandasiri, *Space Debris and International Law*, 26 J. Space L. 139–162 (1998).

Jollivet, Marcel & Pavé, Alain, *L'environnement: un champ de recherche en formation*, 1 Nat. Sci. Soc. 6–20 (1993).

Kaiser, Stefan A., *Legal Protection Against Contamination from Space Resource Mining Space Law*, 66 ZLW 282–289 (2017).

Keeble, Brian R., *The Brundtland Report: "Our Common Future"*, 4 Medicine and War 17–25 (1988).

Kfir, Sagi & Perry, Ian, *Title IV of the U.S. Commercial Space Launch Competitiveness Act of 2015: A Critical Step Forward in Facilitating the Development of a Viable Space Infrastructure*, 5 NEW SPACE 163–169 (2017).

Klick, Karen, *Extraterritorial Reach of NEPA's EIS Requirement after Environmental Defense Fund v. Massey*, 44 AM. U. L. REV. (1994).

Kminek, Gerhard et al., *The International Planetary Protection Handbook*, 205 SPACE RESEARCH TODAY e1–e120 (2019).

Kopal, Vladimir, *The Use of Nuclear Power Sources in Outer Space: A Net Set of United Nations Principles*, 19 J. SPACE L. 103 (1991).

Koskina, Anthi & Angelopoulou, Konstantina, *Space Sustainability in the Context of Global Space Governance*, 2 ATHENA 29–72 (2022).

Kovar, Jeffrey D., *A Short Guide to the Rio Declaration United Nations Conference on Environment and Development (UNCED)*, 4 COLO. J. INT'L ENVTL. L. & POL'Y 119–140 (1993).

Lampert, Adam, *Over-Exploitation of Natural Resources Is Followed by Inevitable Declines in Economic Growth and Discount Rate*, 10 NATURE COMMUNICATIONS 1419 (2019).

Langhelle, Oluf, *Sustainable Development: Exploring the Ethics of Our Common Future*, 20 INT. POLITICAL SCI. REV. 129–149 (1999).

Larsen, Paul, *Application of the Precautionary Principle to the Moon*, 71 J. AIR L. & COM. 295–306 (2006).

Larsson, Marie-Louise, *Legal Definitions of the Environment and of Environmental Damage*, 38 SCANDINAVIAN STUDIES IN LAW SCANDINAVIAN STUDIES IN LAW 155–176 (1999).

Lichtenstein, Cynthia Crawford, *Hard Law v. Soft Law: Unnecessary Dichotomy?*, 35 INT. LAWYER 1433–1441 (2001).

Liu, Hao & Tronchetti, Fabio, *The American Space Commerce Free Enterprise Act of 2017: The Latest Step in Regulating the Space Resources Utilization Industry or Something More?*, 47 SPACE POLICY 1–6 (2019).

MacAvoy, Joseph, *Nuclear Space and the Earth Environment: The Benefits, Dangers, and Legality of Nuclear Power and Propulsion in Outer Space*, 29 WM. & MARY ENVTL. L. & POL'Y REV 191 (2004).

MacWhorter, Kevin, *Sustainable Mining: Incentivizing Asteroid Mining in the Name of Environmentalism*, 40 WM. & MARY ENVTL. L. & POL'Y REV. 645–676 (2016).

Marchisio, Sergio, *The Evolutionary Stages of the Legal Subcommittee of the United Nations Committee on the Peaceful Uses of Outer Space*, 31 J. SPACE L. 219–242 (2005).

Martinez, Larry F., *Legal Regime Sustainability in Outer Space: Theory and Practice*, 2 GLOBAL SUSTAINABILITY e26 (2019).

Martinez, Peter, *Development of an International Compendium of Guidelines for the Long-Term Sustainability of Outer Space Activities*, 43 SPACE POLICY 13–17 (2018).

Matte, Nicolas M., *Environmental Implications and Responsibilities in the Use of Outer Space*, 14 ANN. AIR & SPACE L. 419–447 (1989).

Meeker, Leonard C., *The First Decade of Law in Space*, 3 INT. LAWYER 193–203 (1969).

Miller, Ryder W., *Astroenvironmentalism: The Case for Space Exploration as an Environmental Issue*, 1 Electronic Green Journal (2001).

Mineiro, Michael C., *FY-1C and USA-193 ASAT Intercepts: An Assessment of Legal Obligations under Article IX of the Outer Space Treaty*, 34 J. Space L. 321 (2008).

Miraux, Loïs, *Environmental Limits to the Space Sector's Growth*, 806 Science of The Total Environment 150862 (2022).

Miraux, Loïs, Wilson, Andrew Ross & Dominguez Calabuig, Guillermo J., *Environmental Sustainability of Future Proposed Space Activities*, 200 Acta Astronautica 329–346 (2022).

Mirmina, Steven A., *Reducing the Proliferation of Orbital Debris: Alternatives to a Legally Binding Instrument*, 99 AJIL 649–662 (2005).

Morelli, John, *Environmental Sustainability: A Definition for Environmental Professionals*, 1 J. Environ. Sustain. (2013).

Newman, Christopher J. & Williamson, Mark, *Space Sustainability: Reframing the Debate*, 46 Space Policy 30–37 (2018).

Newman, Christopher J., *Seeking Tranquillity: Embedding Sustainability in Lunar Exploration Policy*, 33 Space Policy 29–37 (2015).

Nicolet, Marcel, *Les tenants et les aboutissants de l'Année Géophysique Internationale*, 69 Bulletins de l'Académie Royale de Belgique 168–181 (1983).

O'Grady, John P., *How Sustainable Is the Idea of Sustainability?*, 10 ISLE 1–10 (2003).

Oduntan, Gbenga, *The Never-Ending Dispute: Legal Theories on the Spatial Demarcation Boundary Plane Between Airspace and Outer Space*, 1 Hertfordshire Law Journal 64–84 (2003).

Okowa, P. N., *Procedural Obligations in International Environmental Agreements*, 67 Br. Yearb. Int. Law 275–336 (1997).

Ouedraogo, Awalou, *La Due Diligence En Droit International: De La Regle de La Neutralite Au Principe General*, 42 Rev. Gen. 641–684 (2012).

Palmroth, M. et al., *Toward Sustainable Use of Space: Economic, Technological, and Legal Perspectives*, 57 Space Policy 101428 (2021).

Pattberg, Philipp & Widerberg, Oscar, *Global Sustainability Governance: fragmented, orchestrated or polycentric?*, N° 45 Civitas Europa 373–392 (2020).

Peeters, Walter, *Evolution of the Space Economy: Government Space to Commercial Space and New Space*, 19 Astropolitics 206–222 (2021).

Perek, Lubos, *Scientific Criteria for the Delimitation of Outer Space*, 5 J. Space L. 111 (1977).

Phillips, Charles R., *The Planetary Quarantine Program: Origin and Achievements*, NASA General Technical Series 58 (1974).

Pisillo-Mazzeschi, Riccardo, *The Due Diligence Rule and the Nature of the International Responsibility of States*, 35 Ger. Yearb. Int. Law 9–51 (1992).

Popova, Rada & Schaus, Volker, *The Legal Framework for Space Debris Remediation as a Tool for Sustainability in Outer Space*, 5 Aerospace 55 (2018).

Qizhi, He, *Environmental Impact of Space Activities and Measures for International Protection*, 16 J. Space L. 117–128 (1988).

Qizhi, He, *The Outer Space Treaty in Perspective*, 25 J. Space L. 93–100 (1997).

Qizhi, He, *The Problem of Definition and Delimitation of Outer Space*, 10 J. SPACE L. 157–163 (1982).

Reiman, Saara, *Is Space an Environment?*, 25 SPACE POLICY 81–87 (2009).

Rex, Dietrich, *Will Space Run out of Space? The Orbital Debris Problem and Its Mitigation*, 14 SPACE POLICY 95–105 (1998).

Roberts, Lawrence D., *Ensuring the Best of All Possible Worlds: Environmental Regulation of the Solar System*, 6 NYU. ENVTL. L. J. 126–160 (1997).

Robinson, George S., *Interplanetary Contamination: The Ultimate Challenge for Environmental and Constitutional Lawyers*, 31 J. SPACE L. 117–164 (2005).

Rolland, Sonia E., *The Precautionary Principle: Development of an International Standard*, 23 Mich. J. Int. Law 429–469 (2002).

Rosen, Marc A., Issues, Concepts and Applications for Sustainability, GLOCALISM (2018).

Ruggerio, Carlos Alberto, *Sustainability and Sustainable Development: A Review of Principles and Definitions*, 786 SCI. TOTAL ENVIRON. 1–11 (2021).

Rummel, J. D. et al., *COSPAR's Planetary Protection Policy: A Consolidated Draft*, 30 ADV. SPACE RES. 1567–1571 (2002).

Rummel, J. D., Race, M. S. & Horneck, G., *Ethical Considerations for Planetary Protection in Space Exploration: A Workshop*, 12 ASTROBIOLOGY 1017–1023 (2012).

Rummel, John D., *Planetary Exploration in the Time of Astrobiology: Protecting against Biological Contamination*, 98 PNAS 2128–2131 (2001).

Sadeh, Eligar, *Space and the Extraterrestrial Environment, in* SPACE 2002 AND ROBOTICS 2002 571–579 (2002).

Schwartz, James S. J., *On the Moral Permissibility of Terraforming*, 18 ENVIRON 1–31 (2013).

Scott, Henry T., *Improving the Shield: Mitigating the Danger of Space Debris by Enforcing and Developing Already Existing Space Law Section II: Space Law: Part A: Leading Articles*, 34 ANN. AIR & SPACE. L. 713–774 (2009).

Soroye, Peter, Newbold, Tim & Kerr, Jeremy, *Climate Change Contributes to Widespread Declines among Bumble Bees across Continents*, 367 SCIENCE 685–688 (2020).

Steffen, Olaf, *Explore to Exploit: A Data-Centred Approach to Space Mining Regulation*, 59 SPACE POLICY 1–11 (2022).

Stirling, Andrew, *The Appraisal of Sustainability: Some Problems and Possible Responses*, 4 LOCAL ENVIRONMENT 111–135 (1999).

Stokes, H. et al., *Evolution of ISO's Space Debris Mitigation Standards*, 7 J. SPACE SAF. ENG. 325–331 (2020).

Sundahl, Mark J., *Regulating Non-Traditional Space Activities in the United States in the Wake of the Commercial Space Launch Competitiveness Act*, 42 AIR AND SPACE LAW (2017).

Tan, David, *Towards a New Regime for the Protection of Outer Space as the Province of All Mankind*, 25 YALE J. INT'L L. 145–194 (2000).

Tapio, Jenni, *The Finnish Space Act: En Route to Promoting Sustainable Private Activities in Outer Space*, 43 AIR AND SPACE LAW (2018).

Tennen, Leslie I., *Evolution of the Planetary Protection Policy: Conflict of Science and Jurisprudence?*, 34 ADV. SPACE RES. 2354–2362 (2004).

Tennen, Leslie I., *Towards a New Regime for Exploitation of Outer Space Mineral Resources*, 88 Neb. L. Rev. 794–831 (2009).

Toussaint, Camille & Dumez, Hervé, *Gérer un méta-problème: le cas des débris spatiaux*, 141 ANNALES DES MINES 3–12 (2020).

Tronchetti, Fabio, *Private Property Rights on Asteroid Resources: Assessing the Legality of the ASTEROIDS Act*, 30 SPACE POLICY 193–196 (2014).

Trouwborst, Arie, *Prevention, Precaution, Logic and Law: The Relationship between the Precautionary Principle and the Preventative Principle in International Law and Associated Questions*, 2 ERASMUS LAW REVIEW 23 (2009).

Trur, Aurélie, *Governance Aspects of Space Sustainability: The Role of Epistemic Actors as Enablers of Progress*, 180 ACTA ASTRONAUTICA 451–459 (2021).

UNEP, *Report of the Working Group of Experts on Liability and Compensation for Environmental Damage Arising from Military Activities*, 27 ENVIRON 134 (1996).

Vecchio, Valentina, *Customary International Law in the Outer Space Treaty: Space Law as Laboratory for the Evolution of Public International Law*, 66 ZLW 491–502 (2017).

Viikari, Lotta E., *Environmental Impact Assessment and Space Activities*, 34 ADV. SPACE RES. 2363–2367 (2003).

Wälde, Thomas, *Environmental Policies Towards Mining in Developing Countries*, 10 J. ENERGY NAT. RESOUR. LAW 327–357 (1992).

Werber, Morton, *Objectives and Models of the Planetary Quarantine Program*, NASA GENERAL TECHNICAL SERIES 140 (1975).

Wessel, Brian, *The Rule of Law in Outer Space: The Effects of Treaties and Nonbinding Agreements on International Space Law*, 35 HASTINGS INT'L & COMP L REV. 289–322 (2012).

Wilkins, Hugh, *The Integration of the Pillars of Sustainable Development: A Work in Progress*, 4 MCGILL INT'L J. SUST. DEV. L. & POL'Y 163–188 (2008).

Wilkins, Hugh, *The Need for Subjectivity in EIA: Discourse as a Tool for Sustainable Development*, 23 ENVIRON. IMPACT ASSESS. REV. 401–414 (2003).

Williamson, Mark, *Lunar Exploration and Development—A Sustainable Model*, 57 ACTA ASTRONAUTICA 161–166 (2005).

Williamson, Mark, *Planetary Spacecraft Debris: The Case for Protecting the Space Environment*, 42 ACTA ASTRONAUTICA 445–455 (2000).

Williamson, Mark, *Protection of the Space Environment: The First Small Steps*, 34 ADV. SPACE RES. 2338–2343 (2004).

Williamson, Mark, *Space Ethics and Protection of the Space Environment*, 19 SPACE POLICY 47–52 (2003).

Williamson, Ray A., *Assuring the Sustainability of Space Activities*, 28 SPACE POLICY 154–160 (2012).

Xu, Fengna, *Environmental Protection in the Exploitation and Use of Space Resources*, 565 IOP CONF. SER.: EARTH ENVIRON. SCI. 1–6 (2020).

Miscellaneous

Other documents

Artemis Accords: Principles for Cooperation in the Civil Exploration and Use of the Moon, Mars, Comets, and Asteroids for Peaceful Purposes (2020) available online.
Canada: Claim Against the Union of Soviet Socialist Republics for Damage Caused by Soviet Cosmos 954, 18 ILM 899–930 (1979).
COSPAR Charter (1998), available online.
Council Directive 85/337/EEC of 27 June 1985 on the assessment of the effects of certain public and private projects on the environment OJ L 175, 5.7.1985.
IADC, IADC Space Debris Mitigation Guidelines, IADC Steering Group and Working Group 4, IADC-02-01 Rev. 3 (2021).
ILA Res. 6/2012 (2012).
ILA, Resolution 3/2002 on sustainable development (2002).
ILA, Study Group on Due Diligence in International Law, First Report (2014) available online.
ILA, Study Group on Due Diligence in International Law, Second Report (2016) available online.
ILC Draft Articles on Prevention of Transboundary Harm from Hazardous Activities, with commentaries, 2001 ILC Yearbook II/2.
ISO Membership Manual, 6 (2015) available online.
ISO Statutes, available online.
UNEP, Goals and Principles of Environmental Impact Assessment (1987) available online.
United Nations, Berlin II: Guidelines for Mining and Sustainable Development (2002).

Reports, Studies & Theses

Bouillon, Christophe & Havard, Michel, Rapport d'information par la commission du développement durable et de l'aménagement du territoire, en conclusion des travaux d'une mission d'information sur la gestion durable des matières premières minérales, Assemblée nationale, 26 octobre 2011 (FR).
Campbell, Michael D. et al., *The Role of Nuclear Power in Space Exploration and the Associated Environmental Issues: An Overview*. A Report by the Uranium Committee of the Energy Minerals Division (AAPG ed., 2009).
Chassot, Laurent et al., Droit spatial national—Etude portant sur l'analyse de différentes législations spatiales nationales, en vue d'une réflexion de lege ferenda (gbf Avocats SA ed., 2021) available online.
CRNS & Ifremer (eds.), Impacts environnementaux de l'exploitation des ressources minérales marines profondes. Expertise scientifique collective (2014) available online.
IPCC, Climate Change 2014: Synthesis Report. Contribution of Working Groups I, II and III to the Fifth Assessment Report of the Intergovernmental Panel on Climate Change (2014) available online.

Jóhannsdóttir, Aðalheiður, The Significance of the Default: A Study in Environmental Law Methodology with Emphasis on Ecological Sustainability and International Biodiversity Law (Uppsala University, 2009).

Leterre, Gabrielle, Providing a legal framework for sustainable space mining activities (University of Luxembourg, 2017).

Michael B. Duke, Wendell W. Mendell & Paul W. Keaton, *Report of The Lunar Base Working Group*, Laboratory Publication (1984) available online.

Mudge, Adam, *Incentivizing "Active Debris Removal" Following the Failure of Mitigation Measures to Solve the Space Debris Problem: Current Challenges and Future Strategies* (McGill University, 2020).

Pompidou, Alain, *The Ethics of Space Policy* (UNESCO ed., 2000) available online.

Pring, Georges W., *International Law and Mineral Resources*, *in* Mining, Environment and Development: A Series of Papers Prepared for the United Nations Conference on Trade and Development (1999).

Rettberg, Petra, Hofmann, Mahulena & Williamson, Mark (eds.), *The IAA Cosmic Study "Protecting the Environment of Celestial Bodies"* (2010).

Salmeri, Antonino, The Multi-Level System of Space Mining: Regulatory Aspects and Enforcement Options (University of Luxembourg, 2022).

Space Security Index, Condition and Knowledge of the Space Environment (2020) available online.

UN Environment, Assessing Environmental Impacts—A Global Review of Legislation (UNEP ed., 2018) available online.

Press Releases, Hearings, Speeches & Statements

IISL Board of Directors, *IISL Position Paper on Space Resource Mining*, International Institute of Space Law (2015) available online.

IISL Directorate of Studies, Background Paper on the topic: Does International Space Law Either Permit or Prohibit the Taking of Resources in Outer Space and on Celestial Bodies, And How Is This Relevant for National Actors? What Is the Context, And What Are the Contours and Limits of This Permission or Prohibition? (2016) available online.

IISL Statement by the Board of Directors of the IISL on Claims to Property Rights Regarding the Moon and Other Celestial Bodies (2004), available online.

Sadek, Saly, New Satellite Market Forecast Anticipates 1,700 Satellites to Be Launched on Average per Year By 2030 as New Entrants and Incumbents Increase Their Investment in Space, Euroconsult (2021) available online.

US Department of State, Russia Conducts Destructive Anti-Satellite Missile Test (2021) available online.

US Department of State, *The Next Fifty Years of the Outer Space Trea*ty (2016) available online.

US Executive Office of the President, *Protecting & Preserving Apollo Program Lunar Landing Sites & Artifacts* (Office of Science and Technology Policy ed., 2018) available online.

US House of Representatives' Subcommittee on Space, Regulating Space: Innovation, Liberty and International Obligations (2017).

US Mission UNVIE, *2022 COPUOS STSC–US on Space Debris* (2022) available online.

US Mission UNVIE, 2022 COPUOS STSC–US on the Use of Nuclear Power Sources in Outer Space (2022) available online.

US Senate Committee on Commerce, Science, & Transportation, Space Situational Awareness, Space Traffic Management, and Orbital Debris: Examining Solutions for Emerging Threats (2021) available online.

US Senate Subcommittee on Space, Science, and Competitiveness, Reopening the American Frontier: Exploring How the Outer Space Treaty Will Impact American Commerce and Settlement in Space (2017).

US White House, Vice President Harris Advances National Security Norms in Space: New U.S. Commitment on Destructive Direct-Ascent Anti-Satellite Missile Testing (2022) available online.

Newspaper Articles, Blogs & Radio Broadcast

Ambert, Valentine, Des déchets au-dessus de nos têtes? La problématique des débris spatiaux, YOUMATTER (2020) available online.

ARTE, *Est-on en train de nous voler l'espace?* LA RÉPONSE À PRESQUE TOUT (2022) available online.

Bartels, Meghan, Why NASA's Mars rover Perseverance will use nuclear power to keep itself warm, SPACE.COM (2020) available online.

BBC News, What does Trump actually believe on climate change? (2020) available online.

Beclard, Julien, Vers une écologie spatiale: les défis d'une politique spatiale responsable et durable, ETOPIA (2019) available online.

Benadia, Frédéric, "On a besoin d'aller dans l'espace pour mieux vivre sur Terre," Jacques Arnould, chargé des missions éthiques au CNES, JOURNAL DE L'AVIATION (2021) available online.

Bianchi, Frédéric & Kupferman, Pierre, *Obama a donné le top départ de la ruée vers l'or spatial*, BFM BUSINESS (2015) available online.

Boccardo, Gustavo, UPDATE: Planetary Protection Obligations of States Pursuant to the Space Treaties and with Special Emphasis on National Legislations Provisions, GLOBALEX (2018) available online.

Brachet, Gérard, *Protecting our space interests*, 10 ROOM (2016) available online.

Degeorges, Marion, Les Etats-Unis peuvent-ils s'emparer des matières premières de l'espace?, LES ECHOS (2015) available online.

Erwin, Sandra, U.S. declares ban on anti-satellite missile tests, calls for other nations to join, SPACENEWS (2022) available online.

France Info, La Station spatiale internationale a dû manœuvrer pour éviter une possible collision avec un débris (2020) available online.

Gilbert, Alex, *Mining in Space Is Coming*, MILKEN INSTITUTE REVIEW (2021) available online.

Griffin, Andrew, *It's now legal to own and mine asteroids*, THE INDEPENDENT (2015) available online.

Grush, Loren, House bill would regulate bold commercial space missions—but not very closely, THE VERGE (2018) available online.

GTS Editorial, *Space Agencies Around the World*, GOING TO SPACE (2022) available online.

Holmes, Ruth, UK "space junk" project highlights threat to missions, PHYS.ORG (2016) available online.

Kyle, Ed, *Space Launch Report: Orbital Launch Summary by Decade*, SPACELAUNCHREPORT.COM (2021) available online.

Latham & Watkins Aerospace, Defense & Government Services Industry Group, *House Passes Space Commerce Free Enterprise Bill to Increase US Support for Commercial Spaceflight, in* CLIENT ALERT COMMENTARY (2018) available online.

Mayence, Jean-François, La Belgique se dote d'une législation sur les activités spatiales. Pourquoi?, DROIT & TECHNOLOGIES (2008) available online.

O'Toole, Thomas, *Man-Made Junk Jams Space*, WASHINGTON POST (1985) available online.

Oosterveld, Valerie & Campbell, Anne, Space Resource Discussions in the UN Committee on the Peaceful Uses of Outer Space, OPINIO JURIS (2021) available online.

Parachini, Alexandra, Schneider: "Le Luxembourg prend plus de place dans l'espace que sur Terre" LE QUOTIDIEN (2016) available online.

Pultarova-Senior, Tereza, Air pollution from reentering megaconstellation satellites could cause ozone hole 2.0, SPACE.COM (2021) available online.

Raimi, Daniel, Space Resources: Exploring the Final Frontier with Alex Gilbert, RESOURCES RADIO (2020) available online.

Smith, Marcia, Draft Bill Would Give Commerce, Not FAA, "Mission Authorization" Function, SPACEPOLICYONLINE (2017) available online.

Speck, Emilee, NASA's Apollo moon program wasn't sustainable, but with commercial space, Artemis can be, CLICKORLANDO.COM (2021) available online.

Stotler, Charles, The Space Review: The ASTEROIDS Act and hearing: some observations on international obligations, THE SPACE REVIEW (2014) available online.

Sturcke, James, *Astronaut loses tools during spacewalk*, THE GUARDIAN (2008) available online.

Teitel, Amy Shira, How JFK, LBJ and Nixon All Put Their Stamp on the Apollo 11 Moon Landing, HISTORY (2019) available online.

Yotsumoto, Hiroko, Ishikawa, Daiki & Odan, Tetsuji, *The Space Law Review: Japan*, THE SPACE LAW REVIEW (2021) available online.

World Population Review, *Countries with Space Programs 2022* (2022) available online.

Electronic Resources of National, Regional, and International Organizations & Institutes

BELSPO, Directory of authorizations delivered in application of the law of 17/09/2005 (2022) available online.

BELSPO, *List of space objects* (2022) available online.

BELSPO, *The Belgian Space Law* (2022) available online.

Chambre du Commerce du Luxembourg, *A la conquête de l'espace* (2019) available online (last accessed January 2024).

COSPAR Communications, COSPAR updates its Planetary Protection Policy for missions to the Moon's surface, PRESS RELEASE (2021) available online.

COSPAR, COSPAR Policy on Planetary Protection (2021) available online.

ESA, How much do space activities pollute? (2018) available online.

ESA, *Planetary protection,* ESA INT. (2022) available online.

ESA, *Planetary Protection,* TEC (n.d.) available online.

ESA, *Space debris by the numbers* (2022) available online.

Garcia, Mark, *Space Debris and Human Spacecraft,* NASA (2021) available online.

Hofmann, Mahulena, *Sustainability Aspects in the UN Space Treaties and the LTS Guidelines, in* ENSURING THE SUSTAINABILITY OF OUTER SPACE: THE ROLE OF SPACE LAW AND POLICY (NPOC Space Law Austria, 2022), online.

ispace, Inc., *Case Studies,* UNOOSA (2021) available online.

LSA, *Stratége Spatiale* 2023–2027 (2022) available online.

Mayence, Jean-François, *Experiences with Implementing the LTS Guidelines from the Belgian Perspective, in* ENSURING THE SUSTAINABILITY OF OUTER SPACE: THE ROLE OF SPACE LAW AND POLICY (NPOC Space Law Austria, 2022) available online.

NASA, Artemis I—Flight Day 26: Orion splashes down, concluding historic Artemis I mission—Artemis (2022) available online.

Pinto-Bazurco, Jose Felix, *The Precautionary Principle,* INTERNATIONAL INSTITUTE FOR SUSTAINABLE DEVELOPMENT (2020) available online.

Salman, Nour, UAE Space Law details announced to facilitate space sector development, EMIRATES NEWS AGENCY (2020) available online.

Sanz Fernández de Córdoba, S., *100km Altitude Boundary for Astronautics,* FAI, available online.

Schiltz, Jean-Louis, *Preserving Space Environment—Law & Regulations, in* SPACE RESOURCES WEEK 2022 (ESRIC, 2022) available online.

Sommariva, Andrea, The Evolution of Space Economy: The Role of the Private Sector and the Challenges for Europe, ISPI (2020) available online.

SpaceResources Initiative, Etienne Schneider about the legal and regulatory framework of the SpaceResources.lu initiative, YOUTUBE (2017) available online.

SSERVI, NASA Looking to Mine Water on the Moon and Mars (n.d.) available online.

SWF, Planetary Protection and Lunar Activities (2020) available online.

SWF, Space Sustainability: A Practical Guide (2018) available online.

Tabor, Abigail, What is LCROSS, the Lunar Crater Observation and Sensing Satellite?, NASA (2019) available online.

UNOOSA, *Benefits of space* (n.d.) available online.

UNOOSA, *Case Studies,* SPACESUSTAINABILITY.UNOOSA.ORG (2021) available online.

UNOOSA, Compendium on non-legally binding UN space instruments (2022) available online.

UNOOSA, European Global Navigation Satellite System and Copernicus: Supporting the Sustainable Development Goals (United Nations ed., 2018) available online.

UNOOSA, Space Law: National Space Law Database (n.d.) available online.

UNOOSA, Space4SDGs: How space can be used in support of the 2030 Agenda for Sustainable Development (n.d.) available online.

US Law Library of Congress, *Japan: Space Resources Act Enacted,* LIBRARY OF CONGRESS (2021) available online.

Table of Treaties and International Agreements

Table of International Law Cases

ICJ

Arbitration

ITLOS

Other jurisdictions

Table of United Nations Documents

UN General Assembly Resolutions

Reports of the UN Committee on the Peaceful Uses of Outer Space

Other UN documents

Table of National Instruments and Cases

Luxembourg

United Arab Emirates

United States

Others

Index

U

AEROSPACE LAW AND POLICY SERIES

1. Erwin von den Steinen, *National Interest and International Aviation*, 2006 (ISBN 90-411-2455-1).
2. Ludwig Weber, *International Civil Aviation Organisation: An Introduction*, 2007 (ISBN 978-90-411-2622-1).
3. Niels van Antwerpen, *Cross-Border Provision of Air Navigation Services with Specific Reference to Europe: Safeguarding Transparent Lines of Responsibility and Liability*, 2008 (ISBN 978-90-411-2688-7).
4. Brian F. Havel, *Beyond Open Skies: A New Regime for International Aviation*, 2009 (ISBN 978-90-411-2389-3).
5. Jiefang Huang, *Aviation Safety through the Rule of Law: ICAO's Mechanisms and Practices*, 2009 (ISBN 978-90-411-3115-7).
6. Marian Hoeks, *Multimodal Transport Law: The Law Applicable to the Multimodal Contract for the Carriage of Goods*, 2010 (ISBN 978-90-411-3246-8).
7. George N. Tompkins, Jr., *Liability Rules Applicable to International Air Transportation as Developed by the Courts in the United States: From Warsaw 1929 to Montreal 1999*, 2010 (ISBN 978-90-411-2646-7).
8. Daniel Calleja Crespo and Pablo Mendes de Leon (eds), *Achieving the Single European Sky: Goals and Challenges*, 2011 (ISBN 978-90-411-3730-2).
9. Donal Patrick Hanley, *Aircraft Operating Leasing: A Legal and Practical Analysis in the Context of Public and Private International Air Law, Third Edition*, 2022 (ISBN 978-94-035-4030-6).
10. Mikołaj Ratajczyk, *Regional Aviation Safety Organisations: Enhancing Air Transport Safety through Regional Cooperation*, 2015 (ISBN 978-90-411-5861-1).
11. Benjamyn I. Scott (ed.), *The Law of Unmanned Aircraft Systems, Second Edition*, 2022 (ISBN 978-94-035-4573-8).
12. Stamatis Varsamos, *Airport Competition Regulation in Europe*, 2016 (ISBN 978-90-411-6831-3).
13. Katarzyna Malinowska, *Space Insurance: International Legal Aspects*, 2017 (ISBN 978-90-411-6784-2).
14. John Milligan, *European Union Competition Law in the Airline Industry*, 2017 (ISBN 978-90-411-6618-0).

15. Dejian Kong, *Civil Liability for Damage Caused by Global Navigation Satellite System*, 2019 (ISBN 978-94-035-1171-9).
16. Pablo Mendes de Leon and Niall Buissing (eds), *Behind and Beyond the Chicago Convention: The Evolution of Aerial Sovereignty*, 2019 (ISBN 978-94-035-1131-3).
17. Neta Palkovitz, *Regulating a Revolution: Small Satellites and the Law of Outer Space*, 2019 (ISBN 978-94-035-1762-9).
18. Federico Bergamasco, Roberto Cassar, Rada Popova & Benjamyn I. Scott, *Cybersecurity: Key Legal Considerations for the Aviation and Space Sectors*, 2020 (ISBN 978-94-035-0110-9).
19. Luis Fernando Fiallos Pazmiño, *The International Civil Operations of Unmanned Aircraft Systems under Air Law*, 2021 (ISBN 978-94-035-2854-0).
20. Merinda E. Stewart, *Freedom of Overflight: A Study of Coastal State Jurisdiction in International Airspace*, 2021 (ISBN 978-94-035-3804-4).
21. Cyril-Igor Grigorieff, *Uniformity and Fragmentation of the 1999 Montreal Convention on International Air Carrier Liability*, 2022 (ISBN 978-94-035-3732-0).
22. Mahulena Hofmann, P.J. Blount, Gabrielle Leterre, Antonino Salmeri & Laetitia Zarkan, *Space Legislation of Luxembourg: A Commentary*, 2022 (ISBN 978-94-035-4381-9).
23. Jacomo Restellini, *Labour Relations in Aviation*, 2022 (ISBN 978-94-035-4561-5).
24. Antonino Salmeri, *The Multi-level Governance of Space Mining*, 2023 (ISBN 978-94-035-1856-5).
25. Gabrielle Leterre, *Protecting the Last Frontier: Space Mining and Environmental Sustainability*, 2024 (ISBN 978-94-035-3317-9).

www.ingramcontent.com/pod-product-compliance
Lightning Source LLC
Chambersburg PA
CBHW071330230926
51849CB00002B/355

* 9 7 8 9 4 0 3 5 3 3 1 7 9 *